ENGLISH LITERATURE AND THE WIDER WORLD

General Editor: Michael Cotsell

Volume 3
1830–1876

Creditable Warriors

"St. George and the Dragon," Venetian fifteenth-century *bas-relief*, now in the Victoria and Albert Museum, reproduced from Ruskin's *St. Mark's Rest*

ENGLISH LITERATURE AND THE WIDER WORLD

General Editor: Michael Cotsell

Volume 3

1830–1876

Creditable Warriors

edited by

MICHAEL COTSELL

The Ashfield Press

London – Atlantic Highlands, NJ

First Published in 1990 by The Ashfield Press Ltd.,
17 Pemberton Gardens, London N19 and
171 First Avenue, Atlantic Highlands, NJ 07716

Library of Congress Cataloging-in-Publication Data
(Revised for vol. 1)

English literature and the wider world.

Includes bibliographies and indexes.
Contents: v. 1. All before them / edited by John McVeagh—v. 3.
Creditable warriors, 1830–1876 / edited by Michael Cotsell.
1. English literature—Foreign influences. 2. Travel in literature. 3.
Exoticism in literature. 3. Authors, English—Journeys. I. Cotsell,
Michael. II. McVeagh, John. PR125.E54 1990 820'.9'008 88–7489
ISBN 0–948660–08–2 (v. 1)
ISBN 0–948660–10–4 (v. 3)

British Library Cataloguing in Publication Data

English literature and the wider world.
Vol. 3 : Creditable warriors 1830–1877.
1. English literature, 1660–1918 –
Critical studies. Essays
I. Cotsell, Michael
820.9

ISBN 0–948660–10–4

Printed in the United States of America

But, it may be said, as a rule, that every Englishman in the Duke of Wellington's army paid his way. The remembrance of such a fact surely becomes a nation of shopkeepers. It was a blessing for a commerce-loving country to be overrun by such an army of customers; and to have such creditable warriors to feed.

Thackeray, *Vanity Fair*, Chapter 28.

CONTENTS

CONTENTS

LIST OF ILLUSTRATIONS

GENERAL EDITOR'S PREFACE

The expansion of Europe is arguably the most momentous development of modern history. Britain has played a major role in that expansion. As tourists, travelers, and explorers; as traders and colonists; as warriors and imperialists, the British have been an expanding people. The idea has been familiar for three hundred years and is a recognized thematic for the historian. But in literary studies the overall significance of British expansion for the understanding of what is called English literature has not been fully addressed. Recent critics and scholars—Martin Green, Edward Said, Gayatri Spivak—have begun to point to this fact and to speculate about what is a surprising, even disturbing omission.

Literary history, it seems, has been developed to reinforce an ethos of homogeneous and high-minded nationhood. We may think that two things have been concealed in the traditional account: the relation of the imagination to power and the demand of the national imagination for something more than the national life has provided. Comparative literature has indeed studied analogous developments in cultures and traced influences of ideas and forms, but has not explored the manner in which English literature has been shaped by the undeniable experience of what we are here calling "expansion," and the extent to which it has sought to supplement the domestic experience.

The series *English Literature and the Wider World* seeks to rectify these omissions. The four volumes of the series, dealing with the period 1660–1918, demonstrate that the response to the geography and peoples of the non-English world has always been a major part of the story of the British literary imagination. They show that few literary genres or writers of significance can be properly understood without consideration of this perspective.

Each volume contains a substantial editor's introduction, which discusses the political events of the period, conditions of travel, the literary response to the wider world, and the response to the particular regions of the world. The introductions provide the context for a dozen or so essays by contributing scholars which read the important authors in each period whose work draws significantly on the non-English world; this turns out to be the majority of important English writers. A guide to authors' travels and to further reading completes each volume.

The essays represent a variety of critical approaches, and it is hoped that they will provide stimulus to further interpretations. Of necessity, the essays concentrate on major figures. The unwished-for effect is that minor writers and travel writers of great interest go relatively neglected outside of their treatment in the introductions. But the series will encourage further studies of relations between the canon and writers on its geographical and other margins.

The series looks at how the British have imagined the world. It is in a sense an account of both an experience and an illusion—that of British centrality—and it thus runs the risk of duplicating anglocentrism. We can only hope that we have proceeded with some awareness of this limitation. The term "English literature" has been retained, though it refers also to Scots and Welsh literature: we have tried to recognize that the British margins may well experience different relations with the world beyond Britain. Ireland has been treated as part of the wider world, although for the period covered by these volumes it was, in one way or another, politically attached to Britain. The reader who is unhappy with this choice might like to consider the alternative. British interrelations with Ireland have been and are complex: the inclusion of writers of Irish birth or residence in this volume is not an attempt to appropriate them for a British tradition.

The series has been supported by a generous subvention from the University of Delaware, and in this connexion I would like to thank Provost Leon Campbell, Dean Helen Gouldner, and Professor Jay Halio.

The series is gratefully dedicated to Mario Pazzaglini.

MICHAEL COTSELL
University of Delaware

ACKNOWLEDGMENTS

I am grateful to the City Museum and Art Gallery, Birmingham, for permission to reproduce Ford Madox Brown's *The Last of England*; to the Tate Gallery for permission to reproduce Arthur Hughes's *"That Was a Piedmontese . . ."*; and to the British Museum for permission to reproduce David Roberts's *Mount Tabor, from the Plain of Esdraelon* and John Ruskin's *Fribourg*.

For help with identifying potential contributors and other assistance I am grateful to Professor K.J. Fielding, Professor George Levine, Professor J.R. Watson, Professor Robert L. Patten, Professor Percy Adams, Professor Michael Timko, and Professor George Ford.

I am indebted to Deirdre David, Simon Gatrell, Elizabeth Helsinger, Park Honan, Jacob Korg, Deborah Phelps, and Daniel Schwarz for providing material used in the *Guide to Authors* section, and to Professor Hans-Peter Breuer for material on Samuel Butler.

John McVeagh, Simon Gatrell, and Kevin Kerrane read versions of the introduction. Professor K.J. Fielding read the Carlyle essay. I thank them for their many useful suggestions.

I am especially grateful to my research assistant Patience Phillips for collecting material for the *Guide to Authors* and for assisting in much other research, and at every stage of the editing: the volume and indeed the series owe a great deal to her meticulous and thoughtful work. I also thank Donald Brown for his help in gathering material.

The Department of English at the University of Delaware provided financial assistance toward the preparation of the typescript. Finally, my thanks go to Suzanne Potts who typed the work in many revisions; her help has been invaluable throughout.

INTRODUCTION

1. Political Developments

By the 1830s peace in Europe seemed secure. France, the traditional enemy, was (with occasional scares) less and less seen as a threat: addressing Prince Talleyrand, the French ambassador (1830–34), in his *England and the English* (1833), Edward Bulwer-Lytton observed: "I think your Excellency must have perceived, since your first visit to England [1792–94], there has been a great change from what formerly was a strong national characteristic;—*We no longer hate the French*" (ch. 3). Spain and Portugal seemed moribund; Germany, with the exception of Prussia, and Italy existed only as disunified petty states; the more remote Austrian Empire did not pose a threat. Since 1815 Europe had lain open to trade and travel. There were revolutions, but no European wars, until the struggles for German and Italian unification in the late 1850s and 1860s, and, in the period covered by this volume, no war in Europe at all in which Britain was involved. Russia, illiberal and with rival imperial ambitions, was perceived to be the greatest threat, and the war with Russia in the remote Crimea, 1854–56, is the military event of the period.

Britain's military and naval strength reflected a greater strength. Britain was the richest nation in the world, and the only industrialized one. In 1834, the Colonial Reformer Edward Gibbon Wakefield imagined the amazement of an American visitor, who, having toured Europe, came to England. London, of course, "abounds with proof of its enormous wealth," and the great provincial towns exceed in wealth those of every other country; each rank of life is wealthier than its European counterpart (*England and America*, 1833, "The Wealth of England"). Thus if a prejudice against foreigners remained, Bulwer-Lytton remarked, it had changed its character: "We do not think them, as we once did, *inherently*, but *unfortunately*, guilty!—in a word, we suspect them of being *poor*. They strike us with the unprepossessing air of the shabby genteel" (ch. 3).

Britain was not only the "workshop of the world," she was also the trader, shipper, engineer, and banker of the world. At the heart of this achievement was technology, in which Britain far outstripped its rivals for the first half of the century. In *Eothen* (1844), the best-selling account of travels in the Middle East, Alexander Kinglake parodied the typical conversation between the English traveler and the Ottoman Pascha:

Traveller.   [to his translator] . . . say that the English really have carried machinery to great perfection. . . .

Pascha.   —I know it—I know all—the particulars have been faithfully related to me, and my mind comprehends locomotives. . . . whirr! whirr! all by wheels! whiz! whiz! all by steam! (ch. 1)

It was a widely shared feeling that it was the destiny of Britain to expand and to widen its trade and influence: the "Extension of Britain" (Wakefield, *A Letter from Sydney*, 1829); *Greater Britain* (Dilke, 1868); *The Expansion of England* (Seeley, 1883). The Napoleonic Wars had left Britain not only dominant in Europe, but with a new "Empire," ample recompense for the loss of the American colonies. British territories stretched from Canada and the West Indies to the great base of power in the east, India, and beyond to Australia. The piecemeal process of gathering an Empire continued throughout this period. In distant places there was not a year of Victoria's reign when there was not some "little war" in progress, among them the wars on the northwest frontier of India; the so-called "Kaffir Wars" in the eastern Cape Province of South Africa; the wars with the Maoris in New Zealand; the "Opium Wars" with China; the enforcement of trade on Japan. With the exception of famous setbacks, they were fought without great loss of European life, and, at such distances, the throb of the war drum sounded only like the pulse of the expanding national life. Safely and comfortably at peace in Europe, Britain was horizoned by scenes of potential adventure, heroism, and glory.

The colorful Lord Palmerston, Foreign Secretary or Prime Minister for much of the period until 1860, perfectly embodied a representative view. The popularity of Palmerston—sturdily independent, cautiously progressive in support of liberal and national causes in Europe, bellicose and interventionist beyond Europe, a Russophobe and supreme publicist—indicates the English satisfaction at robustly cutting a figure in the world. He was the chief presider over the loosely conceived policy that in modern times has been called "the imperialism of free trade,"[1] an informal cooperation of emigration; colonization; and diplomatic, and, if necessary, naval and military intervention, in the interests of commerce. It remains true that for much of this period the emphasis was rather on free trade than on imperialism. Such was the confidence in Britain's trading position that the appropriation and direct rule of territory was not a formal priority. "The mere extent of Empire," Thomas Babington Macaulay told the House of Commons in 1833, "is not necessarily an advantage. . . . It would be, on the most selfish view of the case, far better for us that the people of India . . . were ruled by their own kings, but wearing our broadcloth, and working with our cutlery"

2

("Government of India"). Actual rule could, therefore, assume an altruism, and even its ultimate passing away could, for the time being, be contemplated with a degree of equanimity.

The acceleration of English reform at the beginning of this period was influenced by events in Ireland and Europe. The agitations of Daniel O'Connell in Ireland brought about the Catholic Emancipation Act of 1829. The July Revolution of 1830 in France sparked off risings throughout Europe and accelerated the passage of the Reform Act of 1832. Yet insofar as reform was a child of foreign influences, it was an ungrateful one. Its very success in England led, in the following years, to a diminishment of sympathy with foreign radical nationalism, though fear of further democracy was equally a factor. The unwritten British constitution had again proved itself to be the triumph of the race. To satirize it, as Charles Dickens or Matthew Arnold were to do, was to risk being judged "not English." Thus Thackeray, writing in 1839, was scornful of French celebrations of the July Revolution: "Why should men be so mighty proud of having, on a certain day, cut a certain number of their fellow-countrymen's throats?" (*The Paris Sketch Book*, 1840, "The Fêtes of July"). Where the revolutions of 1830 had failed, liberal and nationalist politics turned to conspiracy: Mazzini spent much of his exile in England, published essays on Italy in English periodicals, and was a friend of Thomas and Jane Carlyle, but there was limited sympathy for his politics. There was also a waning of enthusiasm for countries that had attained independence. For the author of *The Crescent and the Cross* (1845), Eliot Warburton, there was "an annoying—almost a painful—sense of incongruity" between Greece ancient and modern: "a Bavarian king and an alien people" playing "their game" in "Athena's sacred precincts" (ch. 19). Anthony Trollope, in 1859, relayed the anecdote of the Frenchman who told the dying Simon Bolivar he had come to South America for freedom: "For freedom!" said Bolivar. "Then let me tell you have missed your mark altogether; you could hardly have turned in a worse direction" (*The West Indies and the Spanish Main* ch. 16).

The new ideologies brought to prominence by the passage of the Reform Act also tended to narrow attitudes and restrict sympathies. Evangelicalism tended to heighten the traditional English mistrust of continental immorality and dislike of Catholicism. Tolerance for the religions of the East also waned: they were simply idolatry, the worship of various devils. Utilitarianism was also narrow in its sympathies. In the first chapter of his influential *The History of British India* (1817), James Mill had written that, "When we look at the particulars of those pretended reigns of mighty kings, the universal lords of India, under whom science flourished, and civilisation rose to the greatest height, we meet with nothing but fable . . . wild, and inconsistent, and hyperbolical." The Utilitarian incomprehension of poetic modes of expression reveals itself in such a passage.

This is not to say that these ideologies did not have projects for abroad. Evangelicalism promoted much increased missionary activity, with large consequences in India, the Cape Colony, New Zealand and elsewhere, where philanthropic interest in native peoples often provoked the hostility of settlers. The Anti-Slavery Society had been founded in 1823, and one of the earliest acts of the reformed Parliament was the emancipation of slaves in British colonies (1833). British cruisers continued to harass slavers off the West Africa coast (in 1850 there were two dozen at work), and the impetus of the emancipation movement, actively propagated in the 1830s and 1840s by the African Civilization Society of Thomas, later Sir Thomas, Fowell Buxton, was sufficient to attain active government support, for instance for the ill-fated Niger Expedition of 1841 (satirized by Dickens in *Bleak House*).

In India, a new class of officials, influenced by evangelicalism, directed its energies both against "suttee, Thugeee, human sacrifices, Ghaut murder, religious suicides, and other excrescences of Hinduism," as Charles Trevelyan (later the brother-in-law of Macaulay) called them, and against "Orientalists," an older generation of officials indulgent of eastern ways (*The Education of the People in India*, 1838, ch. 3); Trevelyan attained notoriety by denouncing a superior for peculation. India was a favorite realm of the reformers, among them the Utilitarians: both James and John Stuart Mill worked at the India Office. But reform was accompanied by an unassailable sense of superiority. John Stuart Mill excepted India from the arguments for personal and social freedom in his *On Liberty* (1859) and *Representative Government* (1861). Macaulay, whose intervention was decisive in establishing an English, rather than Indian, system of education, declared "a single shelf of a good European library was worth the whole native literature of India" ("Minute on Indian Education," 1835).

Another major consequence of reform was a new emphasis on the "colonies of settlement." A group called the Colonial Reformers set out to satirize what it regarded as the indifference of officialdom and to promote a positive attitude to the colonies. They had two main proposals. One was that the colonies of settlement should attain to representative parliamentary government, though not universal suffrage, with the minimum necessary number of powers reserved to the Mother Country. This idea got its opportunity with a rebellion in Lower Canada in 1837. When Lord Durham, a member of the Colonial Society, went out as governor, he took with him two of the leading Reformers, Charles Buller and Edward Gibbon Wakefield. The result was *The Durham Report* of 1839, which in the 1840s was to form the basis of government in Canada, the Australian colonies, the

4

Cape Province and New Zealand. This peaceful transition was doubtless one of the political achievements of the age.

The other proposal of the Reformers was to regulate emigration through the sale of Crown Lands—"waste lands" as they were called. They sought the emigration overseas of all the best elements of hierarchical English society on the model of the ancient Athenian colonies. Wakefield argued that the colonies would thus not be "new societies, strictly speaking" but "so many *extensions* of an old society" (*Letter from Sydney*, "Extension of Britain"). Particular schemes of the reformers met only mixed success— there was initial failure in South Australia, for instance—and it must be added that the great bulk of emigration in the period continued to be to the United States and that much subsequent emigration to Australia and New Zealand was the consequence of the rush for gold. Emigration, the product of powerful and complex forces, could not be wholly regulated.

America exerted a great influence on these thinkers. They wished to avoid the loss of further colonies. They wanted British colonies to rival the United States as a destination for emigrants. And, though they were sympathetic to American society—as many of their fellow countrymen were not—they wanted the British colonies to avoid some of the developments of American democracy. Their attitude points to an important element in the westward looking (and future looking) of the English in this period: they could not wholly like America, and knew its interests were not theirs. As well, there were recurrent buffetings between Britain and the expanding and bellicose United States over Canada and Central and South America.

Differences between the active proponents of expansion and the leading free-traders have been exaggerated, but nevertheless existed. The leading representatives of the "Manchester School," Richard Cobden and John Bright, were at the height of their influence in the late 1840s, with the repeal of the Corn Laws (1846) and subsequently of the Navigation Acts. Cobden and Bright believed that free trade would lead to universal peace. They thought colonies were costly and represented a military risk (for instance along the long border between Canada and the United States). They sought peaceful cooperation between nations, rather than projects of colonization or aggrandizement, and they were frequently critical of Palmerston's bravura style.

While Britain was celebrating free trade, Europe was experiencing revolution and reaction: 1848 was a year of revolution throughout Europe. Unlike in 1830, when revolutions abroad expedited reform at home, the predominant sense now was of the contrast between the conditions at home and abroad.[2] Only in Ireland were events more pressing. The famine of 1845–50 devastated the country (it was a contributory cause of the repeal of the Corn

5

Laws). In 1840, the radical nationalist Young Ireland movement was formed, and in 1848 there was a rising, though it was easily suppressed. Irish agitation throughout this period continuously provoked English reflection and legislation, but both were fundamentally limited by a basic assumption that Union was necessary and was best for Ireland, a view which drew on the almost uniform characterization of the Irish peasantry as racially and religiously inferior.

Liberal politicians and writers could be excited by the prospect of European revolutions, but a more widespread response came to their subsequent suppression. Popular feeling ran high against the parts played by the Russians and Austrians in Poland and Hungary and by Austria and France in Italy. The coup d'état of Louis Napoleon in France (1851) led to fears of French aggression, the first real sign of national insecurity for over thirty years. It was with respect to Napoleon III's Second Empire that the term "imperialism" came into English political usage, referring to a politics that employed demagogy, the *prestige* of foreign adventure, and financial speculation.[3]

Russia, however, was the main focus of indignation. Popular Russophobia had been growing from the 1820s. It was encouraged by Palmerston, and, more heatedly, by a group of propagandists of whom the most notable was David Urquhart. Liberal opinion pointed to the crushing of Polish risings; conservatives thought that Russia posed a threat in the middle east and on the northwest frontier of India.[4] The Crimean War of 1854–56, a purely strategic conflict in which the British played their traditional role of supporting the "sick man of Europe," Turkey, assumed an intense ideological coloring. It was widely urged that the war would be a war against freedom's enemy and that it would redeem Britain from its Mammon-worship (the sentiments are expressed in Tennyson's *Maud*, 1855), as though by fighting Britain were somehow both contributing to progress abroad and making up for economic conditions at home.[5] The war was necessarily a disappointment then; its mismanagement produced the most severe domestic crisis of the period (reflected in Dickens's *Little Dorrit*, 1855–57); and the reports of the war correspondent W.H. Russell gave events a terrible immediacy. Nevertheless, under Palmerston it was pursued to a kind of victory, and from this time, the emergence of a more jingoistic ideology can be discerned. Cobden and Bright, identified with pacifism, lost their seats in the election of 1857.

An event later in the same year was to confirm the new militarist note: the Indian Mutiny of 1857–58. Reform in India had been accompanied by conquest and expansion, often pursued with a large degree of independence from the government at home. A disastrous incursion into Afghanistan, in which all but one member of the British force were killed in the retreat through the Khyber Pass (1842), was followed by the subjection of Sind

"Miss Wheeler Defending Herself Against the Sepoys at Cowporne," from Charles Ball, *The History of the Indian Mutiny* (1858–59)

(1843–45) and the Punjab (1845–46, 1848–49). An extraordinarily high-handed style of rule, a mixture of the ideology of the public school, Carlylean power relationships, and muscular Christianity, was adopted in these areas. When the Mutiny came, the atrocities committed by some Sepoys, and in particular the massacre of English women and children at Cawnpore, produced a brutal reaction from the British forces in India, and an equally unpleasant hysteria at home.[6] Macaulay wrote in a letter of August 10, 1857:

> The cruelties of the Sepoys, and, above all, the indignities which English ladies have undergone, have inflamed the nation to a degree unprecedented within my memory. All the philanthropic cant of Peace Societies, and Aborigine's Protection Societies, and Societies for the Reformation of Criminals, is silenced. There is one terrible cry for revenge.[7]

The Mutiny made heroes of its suppressors and served to further glorify militarism. It focused racism against non-European peoples, and, as Macaulay remarked, discredited philanthropy at home.

Italy, as a country at once artistic and scenic, had long attracted a degree of liberal and anti-Catholic sympathy. It now assumed a growing importance as an alternative ideological focus to Empire. English support for the Italian struggle was an election issue between conservatives and liberals in 1859.[8] Despite French involvement, the moderation of Cavour had made Italian nationalism respectable. Its ideological appeal is clear from its role in the development of Gladstone's liberalism. He had a long-standing interest in Italy, and particularly Dante, and his early visits there moved him from a Bible-based evangelicalism to a greater appreciation of the function of the church, which in turn fed his deep-rooted constitutionalism. A subsequent visit to Naples led to an impassioned denunciation of Neapolitan domestic tyranny (*Letters to the Earl of Aberdeen*, 1851). Gladstone came to see Cavour's pursuit of Italian unity as the pattern of a progress that was necessary if revolution was to be avoided. In his view, Italian unification was "a marvel," and "one of the great events of the century." On the other hand, he mistrusted Garibaldi and cut short his 1864 visit to England.[9] Appreciation of other European nations was now generally greater than it had been earlier in the period, though there was some waning of enthusiasm for Italy after unification was achieved in 1870. Napoleon III was not widely admired, and his adventurism was mistrusted, but the society of the Second Empire was fascinating. Features of the organization of the emerging German state also found many English admirers. "Culture" had, with Matthew Arnold, entered into the political arena, and Europe, not Empire, was the scene of culture.

8

Nevertheless, by the 1860s the confidence of the early mid-century was cooling. Ireland was again unsettled. Read in another way, the emergence of Italy was itself the sign of new competitive forces. The American Civil War (1861–65) was another disturbing factor. The motives of the North were viewed skeptically (see *Punch* cartoons in the period)[10]; the gentlemen of England openly sympathized with the gentlemen of the South, and hoped for the division of a rival power; and the Manchester cotton trade was adversely affected by the blockade of southern ports. On the other hand, liberals (and the term now begins to be appropriate) like Cobden and Bright supported the North: John Stuart Mill thought a Confederate victory would be "a victory of the powers of evil which would give courage to the enemies of progress" (*Autobiography* ch. 7). Relations between Britain and the North were repeatedly badly strained: "If the Americans don't embroil us in a war before long, it will not be their fault," Dickens wrote in a letter in 1865.[11] No less important was the fact that Prussia emerged in the 1860s as a new power in successive wars against Denmark (1864), Austria (1866) and France (1870), which led to a united Germany. Britain threatened Prussia over Denmark in 1864 and then backed down: it was a year of humiliation. In 1870, Russia took advantage of the confusion to repudiate the Crimea settlement. In Dickens's *Our Mutual Friend* (1864–65), the chauvinistic Mr. Podsnap "talks Britain, and talks as if he were a sort of Private Watchman employed, in the British interests, against the rest of the world. 'We know what Russia means, sir,' says Podsnap; 'we know what France wants; we see what America is up to; but we know what England is. That's enough for us'" (bk. 4, "The Last"). All the same it is not the confidence of Mr. Dombey in *Dombey and Son* (1847–48) who believed that "the world was made for Dombey and Son to trade in" (ch. 1). Arnold, in his essay "My Countrymen" (1866), characterized the mood of the period as a mixture of weakness and bluster. There was a new degree of apprehensiveness. In an important essay of 1870, James Anthony Froude remarked that if "a hostile power could by any means obtain twenty-four hours' command of the channel, London would inevitably be taken" ("The Colonies Once More," rpt. *Short Studies on Great Subjects*, Second Series). In 1871, there was excited discussion of a fictional account of the invasion of Britain by Germany.[12]

It was against this background that in the 1860s and 1870s a new emphasis on Empire was made. Froude, who was to become a major advocate of Empire, argued that the emergence and the growing strength of the economies of Britain's rivals made possession of the colonies essential. Disraeli had begun to out-Palmerston Palmerston, and in 1872, he made two keynote speeches, laying down the "national" character of conservatism, against the "cosmopolitan" character of liberalism. He now began to move the focus to the glamorous East. There was the bold gesture of the purchase of the Suez canal with the aid of the wealth of Rothschild (1875). Then, in 1876, despite opposition, Disraeli passed the Royal Titles Act. The Queen of England was now also the Empress of India, a signal instance of the advent of what a modern historian has called "flamboyant imperialism."[13] Indeed, it was in these years that Disraeli's opponents began to employ the term "imperialism."[14]

It would be easy to exaggerate the change of mood. It would also be easy to exaggerate the degree of polarization emerging between the imperialists and their opponents, though the sharp lines of division over the case of Governor Eyre, who brutally and illegally suppressed a rebellion in Jamaica in 1865, indicate that it was growing. Yet a deep change was in preparation. The outbreaks of racism and bellicosity in the 1850s and after demonstrate a loss of confidence in general and inclusive progress. If, because of British exploration, the world seemed smaller than previously at the beginning of this period, by its end it seemed smaller in a more threatening and constraining way: it became a finite field of resources to be competed for. It could be put this way: at the beginning of this period, the British saw themselves as *the* world people; by its end, they were beginning to acknowledge a world of other peoples, all henceforth, as a result of the technological transformation and expansion in which the British were leaders, in uneasy relation. Though the grand theme of Empire lay ahead, it was not wholly the expression of confidence.

2. Travel and Travel Writing

The great influence on mid-Victorian travel was the advent of steam, which served to render more places more accessible to more people. The traveler to Europe could take the steamer to Calais or Bologne or Dieppe, and, after 1843, having traveled by road to Rouen, the train to Paris. By the 1860s he could reach Turin in thirty-three hours for the cost of £7.8s.[15] The world beyond Europe was similarly more accessible. Thackeray, who went by Peninsular and Oriental steamer to Cairo, imagined writing to his family that "they were not to expect him at dinner on Saturday fortnight, as he would be at Jerusalem that day" (*Cornhill to Grand Cairo* [1846], "Preface"). The steamers of the P & O and the Overland Route across Egypt established by Thomas Waghorn in 1830 brought India closer to home, changing the whole feeling of being posted there (compare Thackeray's account of Dobbin's agonized feelings during the long voyage around the Cape in *Vanity Fair*, ch. 43), and, to some extent, relations between the Indian administration and that at home.

Nevertheless, early and mid-Victorian travel remained challenging, as even later Victorians appreciated ("Early Victorian Travelling," *Blackwood's* 162 [1897]: 181–93). Channel crossings by paddle steamer were by no means always smooth. Before the advent of rail, even the "grand bus route" through France to Italy and "the little bus route" along the Rhine[16] required travel by diligence or a vehicle such as the "English travelling carriage of considerable proportions, fresh from the shady halls of the Pantechnicon," requiring four horses and a postilion in "immense jack boots" that the Dickens family took to Italy (*Pictures from Italy*, 1844, ch. 1). Off those routes, travel again reverted to the conditions of an earlier age. Dickens describes the Dorrit party crossing the Alps at Great Saint Bernard: "A craggy track, up which mules in single file scrambled and turned from block to block, as though they were ascending the broken staircase of a gigantic ruin" (*Little Dorrit* bk. 2, ch. 1). In Spain or the remoter regions of Italy travel was by horseback or in the most dilapidated of horse-drawn vehicles, with delays caused by bad roads, flooded rivers, and so on. Inns were usually uncomfortable, rarely clean, and served bad food. Beyond Europe, the traveler equipped his party in a manner not very different from the explorer: Francis Galton's *The Art of Travel: or, Shifts and Contrivances Available in Wild Countries* (1855) provides information on the preparation of medicine chests, carriages, clothing, bedding, food, water for drinking, and guns: his frontispiece shows a man fording a river by holding his horse's tail. As well, the traveler had to cope with guides (the courier in France became the *vetturino* in Italy and the dragoman in the East) and other aides-de-camp. In the East it was often best to hire a friendly sheikh and his followers to protect one from the attentions of other such groups. The robust quality of the age is caught in Harriet Martineau's remark: "A woman who can walk far and easily, and bear the thirst which is the chief drawback in walking in the Desert, may set out for Mount Sinai without fear" (*Eastern Life* pt. 2, ch. 1). Nor were long journeys by sea comfortable by modern standards: the art historian Lord Lindsay complained of being cooped up in a steamer for a month on the way east. Dickens's account of a rough Atlantic passage in steerage in *Martin Chuzzlewit* (1843–44, ch. 15) is well-known: many emigrants could testify to the same order of experience, or worse.

But more and more people were traveling. Mass tourism now became a reality, opening up the world beyond England first to the wealthy middle classes (say, the Ruskins), then the comfortable middle classes (say, the Meagleses of Dickens's *Little Dorrit*), then to the less well-off. The advent of Cook's Tours is the distinctive sign of this: the first tour to Paris was in 1855, to Switzerland in 1863. Middle-class tourism produced a little literature, generally satirical. Thackeray is one of its founders (*The Book of Snobs*,

1847; *The Kickleburys on the Rhine*, 1850). Later there are Charles Lever's *The Dodd Family Abroad* (1853–54); Richard Doyle's *The Foreign Tour of Messrs. Brown, Jones and Robinson* (1855); and Anthony Trollope's *Travelling Sketches* (1866), among others. Indeed, after the mid-century, the tourist becomes a representative figure in major literature. One consequence of mass tourism was to drive those who sought to escape the crowd into irritation (as Ruskin fulminated at the idea of arriving at Venice by train) or further afield: to the tops of the Alps, for instance, where Leslie Stephen and the Alpine Club clambered for the benefits of raw experience (see below p. 29). Pedestrianism, brought in by Wordsworth and Coleridge, and popularized by George Borrow and alpinists like Alfred Wills, was one protest against the age, but, as Trollope suggested, the process was endless: "There will soon be no peak not explored, no summit in Europe that is not accessible, no natural fortress that has not been taken. The Alpine club will have used up Switzerland" ("The Alpine Club Man," *Travelling Sketches*).

Another type likely to resent the mere casual tourist was the inhabitant of one of the multitude of little English "colonies" in the attractive cities and towns of Europe, self-contained mini-societies such as flourished at Boulogne and Dieppe. Some of these have significance for literary history, notably the colony at Florence, the members of which included Robert and Elizabeth Barrett Browning, Frances and Thomas Trollope, and Walter Savage Landor. The tendency was to be self-contained or to assume a proprietary interest in the host country or region. There was very insignificant contact with local populations, or at least with social equals: indeed for many middle-class English abroad only the aristocracy or senior military officers appeared as equals. The attraction of Europe, both Ruskin and Browning admit, is lack of contact. As businessmen or pleasure seekers, the mid-Victorians were everywhere in Europe, but, if we except a few intellectuals, they formed no part of a cosmopolitan society.

The mid-Victorian tourist was not complete without a guide book. John Murray's famous "Hand-Books," the first of which was Murray's own *A Hand-Book for Travellers in Switzerland* (1837), are immense and detailed compendiums of how-to-do-it, history, information about the best sights, and assimilated cultural response. The traveler with a Murray had the means to know more about a country than most of its inhabitants. The best of them, Richard Ford's *Handbook for Travellers in Spain* (1845) or the Reverend John Mason Neale's *Hand-Book for Travellers in Portugal* (1855), are minor works of literature in their own right. One effect of the guide books was to drive subsequent travel writers away from the over-described great sights and works of art and more toward personal impression and ordinary people. Dickens's *Pictures from Italy* expressly dissents from routinely admiring masterpieces, offering instead "faint reflections—mere shadows in the water—of places to which the imaginations of most people are attracted in greater or lesser degree" (ch. 1). The guide books were also perceived to enshrine the taste of earlier generations, the Classical, as in the Reverend John Chetwood Eustace's *A Tour through Italy* (1815), which Dickens criticized in *Little Dorrit*, or the Romantic: at Athens, Thackeray complained that "The Great Public admires Greece and Byron: the public knows best. Murray's 'Guide-book' calls the latter 'our native bard' . . . *Mon Dieu!*" (*Cornhill to Grand Cairo* ch. 5).

Writing about the wider world was voluminous. Travel books were a staple of the publishing trade, the most successful of them bestsellers by any standard: Kinglake's *Eothen*, for instance. Many travelers wrote; indeed, the traveler's journal became something of a joke. It was not so for Harriet Martineau, who, in *How to Observe* (1838), put the whole thing on a systematic basis. She was as good as her word, as her *Eastern Life, Past and Present* (1848) suggests: "On the Nile, it was easy to keep a full journal, and not wholly disagreeable. In the Desert it required strong resolution" (pt. 2, ch. 2). Hers is the spirit of the age. Article 8 of the Wesleyan-Methodist "Instructions to Missionaries" reads, "It is preemptorily required of every Missionary in our Connexion to keep a Journal, and to send home frequently . . . copious extracts."[17] This material was relayed to the public through religious journals. Merchants, colonial administrators, military men and war correspondents were among others involved in the vast business of information gathering.

Notable are the scientific travelers, whose activities were now encouraged by the British Association for the Advancement of Science (1831), which promoted expeditions, conferences, and the processing and publication of data. Science and expansion marched hand in hand. The controversial sciences of the day, geology and the natural sciences, were also the great traveling sciences: Lyell, Tyndall, Brown, Darwin, Hooker, Bates, and Wallace all furthered their researches abroad. Remote or tropical regions of the world entered the English consciousness of the day primarily in scientific travel writing: the South American jungles, for instance, in the work of Wallace and Bates (*Travels on the Amazon and Rio Negro*, 1853, etc.). The genre combines factual observation, scientific reflection, and adventure: mountaineering, as in Tyndall's *The Glaciers of the Alps* (1860), or hunting as in Wallace's *The Malay Archipelago: the Land of the Orang-utan, and The Bird of Paradise, a Narrative of Travel, with Studies of Man and Nature* (1869).

The vast flow of information from abroad penetrated every level of journalism, the reviews, the magazines, and popular papers. Information and anecdotes from abroad perfectly fitted Dickens's demand for facts presented with fancy: *Household Words* would not treat "of the hopes, the enterprises,

13

triumphs, joys, and sorrows, of this country only, but, in some degree, of those of every nation upon earth. For nothing can be a source of real interest in one of them, without concerning all the rest" ("A Preliminary Word," 1 [1850]: 1). As well, exhibitions (preeminent, of course, the Great Exhibition of 1851), panoramas, and the work of traveling artists served to bring the wider world home. In turn, expansion opened up new markets (and questions about copyright). North America was one: hence the number of authors' reading and lecturing tours. Murray launched the "Colonial and Home Library" in 1843 with George Borrow's *The Bible in Spain*: the advertisement for the series declared that it would "furnish the settler in the backwoods of America, and the occupant of the remotest cantonments of our Indian dominions, with the resources of recreation and instruction." It would be a "'Library for Empire.'"

It is difficult to generalize about travel writing as a literary form in the period. It was widely practiced by major writers; indeed, in no earlier period did major writers travel as often and as far. The form is not approached with the conscious aesthetic sense of the late nineteenth or twentieth centuries, but it is a mistake to see it as being merely lively and interested: a vein of self-exploration runs through many works. A successful travel book could be the passport to the intellectual societies and clubs of the day, even to a career. Certain writers made a specialty of abroad or of a region (the East is a favorite); for others it was a major part of a career, as it was for Harriet Martineau, whose work points to the fact that travel writing was a form through which women could speak not only about action and adventure but authoritatively about the great issues of the day: a marginal sagedom.

Writing about distant regions and empire produced an emphasis on observation and action: the external. Such an orientation demanded the overcoming of the subjective. The writings of Tom Arnold about New Zealand begin with the agonized reflections of the "'Equator Letters'" (see below p. 44). Arnold sought a more robust and natural life, but his one attempt at exploration induced in him a panic, which is related in a letter to his mother: "A sort of horror fell upon me, the might of Nature, seemed to rise up, irresistible,—all pervading, and to press down upon my single life."[18] It is thus revealing to see him adopting the persona and language of the adventurous factual observer in a later essay ("Reminiscences of New Zealand," *Frazer's* 64 [1861]: 246–56). The movement from the subjective toward the objective world of expansion can be perceived in a number of literary careers: in Froude's or Charles Kingsley's, for instance.

Finally, if tourism was satirizable, emigration was not. There were few writers, just as there must have been few British (or Irish) families, who went unaffected: Carlyle's brother Alexander emigrated to Canada; Trollope's son Frederick to Australia; Browning's friend Alfred Dommett and Charlotte Brontë's Mary Taylor to New Zealand; Arthur Clough in Mazzini's Rome writes to Tom Arnold in New Zealand; Matthew Arnold is at Paris when his brother William dies at Gibraltar on the way home from India. Large-scale emigration was a great expression of British energy and a promise of new hope, but it was also a condemnation of society at home. It opened up the poignancies of partings and reunions, relatives and friends amidst the alien corn, the mood caught by Browning in "The Guardian-Angel":

> My love is here. Where are you, dear old friend?
> How rolls the Wairoa at your world's far end?
> This is Ancona, yonder is the sea. (ll. 54–56)

3. The Literary Response

The traditional justification of expansion—commerce bringing civilization and Christianity—was a commonplace in the age of Palmerston. It would be mistaken, however, to underestimate the idealism of the period. The evangelical impulse gave a new seriousness to the idea of expansion as a mission or quest; reform brought an earnestness to the prospect; even the free-trade dream of universal peace partakes of this same high-minded idealism, though in Carlyle, Thackeray,[19] and Tennyson it is imagined that there will be some final war of trade barriers before

> the war-drum throbbed no longer, and the battle flags were furled
> In the Parliament of Man, the Federation of the world (*Locksley Hall*, 1842, ll. 127–28)

That mid-century symbol of free trade, the Great Exhibition, was criticized by Barrett Browning (*Casa Guidi Windows*, 1851) and by Tennyson (*Maud*, 1855) not because of its implicit claim for British centrality, but because it seemed to stand for a preference for prosperous peace over active involvement in making good the British promise for the world. The difference that develops is between those who wish Britain to further causes of popular and national freedom and those who wish to emphasize the extension of British rule.

Early and mid-Victorian expansion was supported by a loose racial myth, of which Carlyle and Charles Kingsley (*The Roman and the Teuton*, 1864) were two popularizers. The British were *the* Germanic, Teutonic, Nordic race, as opposed to inferior Latin, Celtic, and Semitic peoples. The myth is of a hardy, northern people destined to expand. In Kingsley's "Ode to the North-East Wind," the "black North-easter," the "wind of God," "Drives

15

our English hearts of oak/Seaward round the world" (ll. 57, 66, 68–69). The northeaster, of course, blows westward ho! To challenge these racial evaluations as Matthew Arnold did (*On the Study of Celtic Literature*, 1867) was to run against the current of the age, and, in Arnold's case, against the example of his father, "that Teuton of Teutons, the Celt-hating Dr. Arnold."[20] In terms of English history, expansion was celebrated as the expression of the Anglo-Saxon as opposed to Norman character (see, for instance, Dickens, *A Child's History of England* ch. 3), which was to associate it with middle-class values of law, industry, and domestic sentiment; it was also associated with Elizabethan expansion (Froude, "England's Forgotten Worthies," 1852, *Short Studies*, First Series; Kingsley, *Westward Ho!*, 1855), which allowed for values of adventure. The stirring "Preface" to Dilke's *Greater Britain* (1868) is a representative instance of the combination of these two values, though there is some shift in the period from the former to the latter.

In fact, writers in this period can usefully be divided into two main groups (though no writer exclusively inhabits one group). There are those who are imaginatively drawn to expansion, and those, generally more critical of British society, who look to the culture of Europe. The former group further divides into those who look to steady domestic expansion (Trollope, for instance) and those who emphasize adventure and rule (the Kingsley brothers, Charles and Henry). Amongst the Europeanists, an emphasis on Germany may point to a westward view (as with Carlyle), though it does not necessarily do so (George Eliot). The high value placed on Italy and, later, on France points to some feeling for Celtic and Latin cultures and scenes, though it is misleading to speak of a cult of the South in this period.[21] The East belongs to empire and adventure but to a lesser degree is also read as the place of a spiritual alternative to western values. The movement from one orientation to another may be a major feature of a writing career: Dickens, for instance, checked in his enthusiasm for America, moves imaginatively eastward towards France, Italy, and even the Orient; Thackeray, on the other hand, moves from the satiric use of Celtic and European settings and characters towards a somewhat vapid celebration of fraternal Anglo-American relations.

Not everyone could share the terms of Macaulay's fulsome panegyric to an expanding people in the *History of England* (1849–55) or of Carlyle's celebration of the English in *Past and Present* (1843):

> Thy Epic, unsung in words, is written in huge characters on the face of this Planet,—sea-moles, cotton-trades, railways, fleets and cities, Indian Empires, Americas, New Hollands; legible throughout the Solar System! (pt. 3, ch. 5)

16

It is true that no writer totally or permanently abandons allegiance to the great prospect of the expansion of English values. Even its satirists, like Arnold or Samuel Butler, travel in its footsteps, and though Thackeray or Dickens may laugh at the middle-class Englishman abroad with his hands in his pockets, they know his centrality and worth: he is a creditable warrior indeed. On the other hand, there is much in the literature, particularly after the mid-century, that criticizes expansion by reference to higher cultural values; that questions whether it does not betray its own ideals and descend into mere power; that saps and undercuts its confidences; and that registers a weariness and melancholy beneath the busy assumption of world-responsibility. It is striking that women writers are most ready to champion foreign causes or life in exile abroad as a fulfillment for favored characters (Barrett Browning, Eliot, and Charlotte Brontë).

The developed sense of social responsibility of the early to mid-Victorians characterizes much of their response to the wider world. This is expressed not only in the allegiance to the expansion of English domestic values, but also in the concern for the betterment of foreign peoples, and in the use of images drawn from the European cultural tradition to instruct or enlarge English society.

This social sense can be seen in the period's revision of earlier imaginative employments of the wider world. For instance, the imagination of the period does not characteristically suggest the relativity of cultural forms and points of observation as the eighteenth century did. Carlyle and Arnold employ fictional foreign spokesmen in their social criticism—Teufelsdröckh, Arminius, and others—in the eighteenth-century tradition, but, as a reviewer of Arnold put it, "The citizen of the world is nowhere a very popular character."[22]

The writing of the period also tends to modify the Romantic cult of abroad—if it can be called that—even reject it, particularly as it was represented by Byron. Thackeray, for instance, complained that "Lord Byron wrote more cant . . . than any poet I know of. Think of 'the peasant girls with dark-blue eyes' of the Rhine—the brown-faced, flat-nosed, thick-lipped, dirty wenches! . . . That man *never* wrote from his heart" (*Cornhill to Grand Cairo* ch. 5). In a similar vein, Leslie Stephen (who had climbed it) reflected on the fascination that Mont Blanc had for Byron: "Byron's misanthropy, real or affected, might identify love of nature with hatred of mankind: and a savage, shapeless and lifeless idol was a fitting centre for his enthusiasm." (*The Playground of Europe*, 1871, ch. 4).

The passages from Thackeray and Stephen can be taken as pointers to the reevaluation in this period of two aesthetic categories of importance in relation to abroad, the sublime and the picturesque. With respect to the sublime, the early and mid-Victorians were, on the whole, repulsed by hostile landscapes, "all that expands the spirit, yet appalls" as Byron had put it in *Childe Harold* (3. 62). It has been observed that the novelists of the period avoid the heights ("the Heights are where society is not"[23]) and even Ruskin modified the appreciation of mountains in this direction. Nor was the imagination of the period drawn to Arctic wastelands.[24] Of barren landscapes, the desert had most appeal, but if Landseer's painting *Man Proposes, God Disposes* (1864) has been said to epitomize the horror of the Arctic waste, then Holman Hunt's *The Scapegoat* (1854), painted at the Dead Sea, suggests an analogous dread of desert isolations.

The response to the picturesque took a similar turn. Carlyle was repeatedly critical; Ruskin, in the fourth volume of *Modern Painters*, straight-forwardly characterized love of the picturesque as "indifference to misery." Famous ruins remained on the travelers' itinerary, of course, but mostly there was an attempt to enjoy the exploration, respond to the beauty, and escape the message. In Browning's poem "Love Among the Ruins," which can be read against the Byronic poetry of Italian ruin, the human interest is what emerges most strongly: "All the causeys, bridges, aqueducts,—and then, All the men!" (65–66).

Similarly, if the Gothic interest in the arbitrary exercise of power, in dungeons and executions, and in the fate of political prisoners continued (in Browning's poems about the Italian Renaissance or *A Tale of Two Cities*, for instance), it was modified by a new concern for ordinary peoples and their lives. On the other hand, if this social sense was checked—as it almost always was in encounters with non-European peoples—then a note of hostility and fear entered in. The early to mid-Victorians had a less global sense of humanity than either their Enlightenment or Romantic predecessors, partly because they had a larger global presence.

Each of the major literary forms of the period—the novel, poetry, and nonfiction prose—draws on the wider world, as does drama. As the essays that follow suggest, it is difficult to think adequately about the work of most of the novelists of this period without taking the wider world into account. There is some continuation of the picaresque novel of travel (Thackeray's *Barry Lyndon*, for instance) and of Romantic voyagings and fascinations with colorful and exotic settings (in the novels of Disraeli, Bulwer-Lytton and others), and the novel of imperial adventure has its origins in the work of Frederick Marryat and, later, the Kingsleys. More significantly, the novel form is developed in the work of major writers to incorporate complex meditations on Britain's place in world history: among major novels with this international dimension are Thackeray's *Vanity Fair*, Dickens's *Little Dorrit*, Trollope's *The Way We Live Now*, and Eliot's *Daniel Deronda*. The period also sees the founding of national (the Australian) and sub-national (the Anglo-Indian and Anglo-Irish) fictions.

In poetry, not even the Romantic period draws so much on other countries: we have only to think of the work of Arnold, Clough, Robert and Elizabeth Barrett Browning. If the laureate, Tennyson, seems an exception, it is because he is not so much drawn to Europe, as, appropriately, he is a poet of empire. It was once a widely accepted argument that Victorian poetry withdrew from the age, and certainly the poets—most memorably, Matthew Arnold—remark on the unpoetic qualities of the English life of their time. Where they went, however, was not on the whole some cloistered fairyland, but abroad. There they found natural beauty and ancient culture, and explored tensions of distance and displacement, a more suggestive European sense of history and modernity, wider but subtly emptied prospects.

Similarly, a major common characteristic of the prose writers, those who came to be called "sages" and their fellows, is their rhetorical employment of the wider world to challenge British society; what is obvious of Ruskin and Arnold is also true of Carlyle and Newman. In the drama in the first half of the century there is a general movement from Romantic and Gothic subjects (including the Eastern) to the nautical and domestic, but the drama of the mid-century encompasses both the sensational use of foreign settings (Bouccicault's *The Corsican Brothers*, 1848) and more realistic contemporary material (Tom Taylor, *Our American Cousin*, 1861).[25]

The victories of the Napoleonic Wars stood as founding memories, representing the capacity of the national life for the heroic and self-sacrificing. This feeling is reflected in popular song and drama; in the novels of the naval school of the 1830s and 1840s, of which Marryat is the leading figure; in the positive images of military-style society in the work of Carlyle and others; and in the patriotic poetry of Tennyson. Travelers abroad encountered the very scenes of British valor: in Browning's "Home-Thoughts, from the Sea," the sight of Cape St. Vincent, Trafalgar and Gibraltar leads to the question: "'Here and there did England help me: how can I help England?'" The little wars were to add their effect.

In the late 1820s and 1830s a romantic taste for abroad was continued in minor poetry, and in the literature of the annuals and keepsakes. Byron's influence was strong on Ruskin; on the early novels of Disraeli; and on the fiction of Bulwer-Lytton, who set interminable novels in France, Italy, Germany, and Spain, drawing on many of the stock romantic characterizations of those countries. But, as we have seen, a reaction set in: Thackeray was the principal spoiler, tracking Byron everywhere; Carlyle and Dickens also contributed.

The greatness of England was itself becoming one of the wonders of the world, as in the famous passage in Disraeli's *Coningsby* (1844):

19

"Ah! but the Mediterranean!" exclaimed Coningsby.
"What would I not give to see Athens!"
"I have seen it," said the stranger, slightly
shrugging his shoulders; "and more wonderful things.
Phantoms and spectres! The Age of Ruins is past. Have
you seen Manchester?" (bk. 3, ch. 1).

The traffic of the passage is toward Manchester, which becomes romantic.
As the pace of political and social change accelerated at home in the 1830s
and 1840s, the imagining of a wider world was increasingly bent toward the
dynamic center, seeking to enlarge it or convert it in some way. Carlyle's
Sartor Resartus (1833–34) is an early example of this tendency, and John
Henry Newman's account in the *Apologia* (1864, ch. 1) of his return to
England in 1833, to the beginning of the Oxford Movement, suggests how
travel could both develop a sense of alternative and a new urgent commitment. On the other hand, expansion and emigration seemed to offer a
solution to the "Condition of England" problem: this is a theme in Carlyle's
Chartism (1839) and *Past and Present* (1843), for instance. Later, as the
process at home seem unaffected, the non-English world could be used to
image a neglected alternative or possibility, as Newman contrasted the great
world of the Catholic Church with that of Oxford in his *An Essay on the
Development of Christian Doctrine* (1845), or Ruskin, having urged the
value of European Gothic in *The Seven Lamps of Architecture* (1849), then
pointed to the dark meaning of *The Stones of Venice* (1851–53).

Even when only marginally present, Britain's relations with the wider
world play an important part of the great mid-century novel (consider the
avoidance of tragedy in the emigrations in Dickens's *David Copperfield*). In
a number of the greatest novels they are a major and explicit theme. In
Dickens's *Dombey and Son*, the self-centered world of Dombey's trade
(extending from India to the West Indies where Walter is exiled) is brought
to a crisis in France where a succession of rapid journeys communicates a
new and disturbing sense of previously unimagined experience. Elizabeth
Gaskell's powerful historical novel, *Sylvia's Lovers* (1863–66), points to the
tensions of the period after the mid-1850s. Gaskell sets up a contrast through its
two heroes between brave, if shallow, adventurism (associated with Arctic
whaling and Nelson's navy) and a decent commercial spirit that, having
betrayed its values, must make expiation in battle in the Holy Land.

The rejection of the free trade ethos of peace and prosperity, and the more
aggressive imperialist note introduced by the Crimean War, are evident in
Tennyson's *Maud* (1855) and in the development of the fiction of the
Kingsley brothers. Charles Kingsley's earliest novels, *Yeast* (1848) and *Alton*

20

Locke (1850), are radical denunciations of poverty in England. In 1855, Kingsley published *Westward Ho!*, a celebration of the adventurism and expansion of the Elizabethan era. In the meantime, Henry had gone out to dig for gold in Australia (1853–58), where, unsuccessful in his own eyes, he did not keep contact with home. Charles's next novel, *Two Years Ago* (1857), has as its hero a boyish-manly adventurer who goes to the goldfields, and finds its solution to the "Condition of England" problem in the sacrifice of the Crimean War effort. Henry Kingsley then returned home and himself began to write novels in the vein of public schoolboy imperial adventure, drawing in the Crimea, the Indian Mutiny, and Australia, the deepest theme of which is the vigor of English gentry stock; these works repeatedly repudiate radicals and philanthropists, who are always shown to be of unsound lower-middle-class origin. Trollope shared some of these views and expansion becomes a major theme in his work, but in him it is pursued with growing doubts about its meaning and consequences.

Poetry in the early 1850s turns to Europe, utilizing travel to develop a note of what might be called intensified displacement, audible in Arnold, in Clough's use of the tourist, and, above all, in Browning's subtle explorations of historical and geographical disconnection. As well, the figure of the English tourist or traveler abroad is, after the 1850s, repeatedly employed to suggest a busy insensibility. One example is Dickens's practical Mr. Meagles in *Little Dorrit*, another work influenced by the Crimean conflict. Arnold, contemplating the death of his colonial administrator brother and his wife, is moved as much to asperity as to pity:

> We who pursue
> Our business with unslackening stride,
> Traverse in troops, with care-filled breast,
> The soft Mediterranean side,
> The Nile, the East,
>
> And see all sights from pole to pole,
> And glance, and nod, and bustle by,
> And never once possess our soul
> Before we die. ("A Southern Night" 65–72)

In the 1860s and '70s, the European and liberal perspective is represented in the positive response to Italian unification in the poetry of Barrett Browning and Swinburne, and in the novels of George Meredith; in the social criticism of Arnold, whose prose mounts a great campaign against the philistinism of Greater Britain (including the United States); in the aesthe-

21

ticism of Swinburne and Walter Pater; and in the enlarged cultural meditations of George Eliot. Eliot and Trollope are the main developers of the
provincial novel in the period, but in both writers the form is drawn towards
deep and troubling awareness of international themes. In *Adam Bede* (1859),
for instance (which she worked on during her first European journey), Eliot
introduces this powerful reflection at the discovery of Hetty's unwanted
pregnancy:

> What a glad world this looks like, as one drives or rides along the valleys
> and over the hills! I have often thought so when, in foreign countries,
> where the field and woods have looked to me like our English Loam-
> shire . . . I have come on something by the roadside which has reminded me
> that I am not in Loamshire: an image of a great agony—the agony of the
> Cross. (ch. 35).

The passage accuses the English of insularity and complacency, as does the
well-known account of Dorothea in Rome in *Middlemarch* (discussed below
pp. 270–71). Eliot was always moving toward the break with the values of
the English gentry and the search for a higher national cause that she portrays
in *Daniel Deronda* (1874–76).

The English set out to fill and flourish in the so-called "waste lands," but
where was the expansion leading? There is Browning's Childe Roland,
riding out into the wilderness: "Now for a better country" ("'Childe
Roland to the Dark Tower Came'", 128). Or Clough's remark that Carlyle
"has led us out into the desert, and he has left us there."[26] Or Arnold's
"Rugby Chapel," published in the year of the Indian Mutiny, a tribute to
the father who contributed so much to the ethos of empire, the conclusion of
which, uniting the idea of the chosen people with that of an imperial
expedition, is sapped by doubts:

> Ye fill up the gaps in our files,
> Strengthen the wavering line,
> Stablish, continue our march,
> On, to the bound of the waste,
> On, to the City of God. (204–8)

Even the poet of empire, Tennyson, seems to end with this question: the last
"dim, weird battle of the west" of the reign of the Christian King Arthur, by
which "the whole Round Table is dissolved," is fought "on the waste sand
by the waste sea" ("The Passing of Arthur," first version 1842, revised 1869,
94, 402, 92).

22

In addition, the message of the waste lands in the work of the scientific travelers, geologists, and evolutionists was assimilated into literature before the publication of the *Origin of Species* in 1859. Sir Charles Lyell's *Principles of Geology* (1830–33), for instance, makes repeated use of descriptions of waste lands and ruin. In this work Lyell also cites the allegory of the traveler in the Arabian tale who visited a "very ancient and wonderfully populous city" and then returned five centuries later: *"I found the sea in the same place"* (ch. 3). It is well-known that such passages influenced Tennyson's *In Memoriam* (1850):

> There rolls the deep where grew the tree.
> O earth, what changes hast thou seen!
> There where the long street roars hath been
> The stillness of the central sea. (123.1–4)

Thus expansion could be returned upon the center, rendering it a dream.

4. The Literary Response Region by Region

France "France has been so betravelled and beridden and betrodden by all manner of vulgar people," Carlyle complained in 1824, "that any romance connected with it is entirely gone off ten years ago."[27] The more sensitive and leisurely came to appreciate a way of life that was less disturbed by industrialism. In *Praeterita* (1885–89), Ruskin called Rouen one of the "three centre's of my life's thought," a sign of the growing English appreciation of French cathedral towns (Roman France now attracted less interest). He also defined the attraction of provincial Abbeville: "Here I saw that art (of its local kind), religion, and present human life, were yet in perfect harmony" (35.156).[28] Both tourism and the "colonies" in France find their way into literature. From the mid-1840s Dickens regularly traveled to France (see his essay "A Flight," *Reprinted Pieces*). In three of his major mid-century novels, *Dombey and Son*, *Bleak House*, and *Little Dorrit*, he made a motif of a hurried journey across France. Thackeray created a little literature out of the disreputable life of the English colonies at Boulogne and Paris; such scenes enabled him to tell some of his nastiest tales (*The Paris Sketch Book* and *The Yellowplush Papers*, 1837).

The fall of the Bastille marked the beginning of modern European history, and the response to France was largely determined by how seriously the revolutionary tradition was taken. The great monument to the revolution, was, of course, Carlyle's epic *The French Revolution* (1837). Dickens's use of the prison symbol (which had an intense personal significance for him) suggests the development of one reaction to the revolutionary tradition. *Little Dorrit*, written after the failure of the revolutions of 1848, begins in a prison at Marseilles, and allusion is made to the revolutionary song that originated there. Though the action of the novel traverses much of Europe, society in it remains imprisonned. *A Tale of Two Cities* (1859) is set in revolutionary times and depends heavily on Carlyle's work, yet in it the revolution becomes only a horrific backdrop to an intense evocation of private imprisonment.

Dislike of French morals, literature, and politics predominates in the early part of the period. In Thackeray's view, there was in France "a rich store of calm internal *debauch*, which does not, let us hope and pray, exist in England"; he asked "Why, ye gods, do Frenchmen marry at all?" He was scornful of revolutionary politics: though he admired Carlyle's work, he suggested the Revolution should be treated as a comedy, "handed over to Dickens or Theodore Hook." He was also among those who reported on the "horrors" of Dumas and Balzac, and he devoted a contemptuous chapter of *The Paris Sketch Book* to George Sand ("On Some French Fashionable Novels," "The Fêtes of July," "Madame Sand and the New Apocalypse"). Carlyle also attacked Sand in *Latter-Day Pamphlets* (1850). The French had been the national enemy ("They hate us," Thackeray explained), but after an exchange of royal visits in the 1840s such a view became increasingly unreal.

The most developed criticism of France in the literature of the period is to be found in the novels of Bulwer-Lytton: indeed, in *Zanoni* (1842), *Lucretia* (1846), and *The Caxtons* (1849), Bulwer defines an English ideal by contrast to France. On the other hand, there were those who looked to France for a lead. Dr. Arnold, Carlyle, and John Stuart Mill were among those stimulated by the Revolution of 1830. Others were influenced by French literature, notably by George Sand. France was beginning to again stand for ideas. There were thus many among the literati who were excited by the Revolution of 1848. Carlyle wrote to Emerson that it was "long years since I have felt such deep-seated pious satisfaction at a public event."[29] Clough was in Paris for five weeks in 1848: "The great impression," he wrote Tom Arnold, "being that one was rid of all vain pretences and saw visibly the real nation." He thought, however, that "France's prospects are dubious and dismal enough," and, in the event, the doubt seemed justified: "Something I think we rash young men," Clough wrote again, "may learn from the failure and discomfiture of our friends in the new Republic. The millennium, as Matt [Matthew Arnold] says, won't come this bout."[30]

The coup d' état of Napoleon III (1851) brought the Second Republic to an end. Browning was in Paris at the time, and dated his "Essay on Shelley" from there, a gesture of sympathy, but one which well suggests the distance of English writers from revolutionary commitment. Elizabeth Barrett

24

Browning was to become an enthusiast for Napoleon III, believing that he was a true champion of Italian liberty. Browning could not share her enthusiasm, and his complex monologue, "Prince Hohenstiel-Schwangau, Saviour of Society" (1871), written after his wife's death and a year after the fall of the Emperor, presents Napoleon as self-justifying and lacking convincing ideals. Walter Bagehot also happened to be in Paris during the coup d'état. His keenly paradoxical defense of Napoleon argued that the French were too intelligent for liberty; they lacked the stupid British adherence to forms and conventions which guaranteed parliamentary government.[31]

Politics aside, the society of the Second Empire proved increasingly attractive. As Arnold declared in 1865, "For show, pleasure, and luxury this place is, and every day more and more, the capital of Europe."[32] Arnold was the leading spokesman for French culture and ideas in the 1850s and 1860s. French thought, notably that of Renan, Taine, and the positivism of August Comte, was now widely influential in England. Aestheticism also looked to France. Dante Gabriel Rossetti's visit to the 1855 Art Exposition confirmed his allegiance to *l'art pour l'art*. Swinburne, an enthusiast for the French avant-garde and the republicanism of Victor Hugo, visited Paris in 1861 and 1862. In a series of essays and in his own poetry (*Poems and Ballads*, 1866), he made a sustained and at times lurid case for French criticism and poetry. In a more restrained fashion, Walter Pater was developing a view of the continuity of French culture.[33]

Finally, though there was some feeling that they had invited disaster, sympathy for the French increased after the defeat in the Franco-Prussian war (1870); it is significant that the events of the Paris Commune produced less interest than those of either 1830 or 1848, though Ruskin and others deplored what Bagehot called "The Destruction in Paris of What the World Goes to See at Paris."[34] Nevertheless, French politics retained a dangerous socialist tinge; French literary influence was mistrusted by critics of the "sensation novel" in the 1860s and of the decadent aesthetes in the 1870s; and even Arnold remarked on French lubricity. For all the growing appreciation, there is a discernible tendency, even in the language of its advocates, to characterize France as an asocial society, one where passion, art, and intellect go unchecked by the affections and conscience that cement the social bond.

Holland and Belgium Turning to the Lowlands, there is a notable lack of imaginative response to Holland in this period. It is Belgium, rather than Holland, that attracts attention. There, of course, was much-visited Waterloo. "Let an Englishman go and see that field, and he *never forgets it*," Thackeray wrote in 1840 (*Little Travels and Road-Side Sketches*, 1844–45, ch. 3), though a member of a younger generation, Dante Gabriel Rossetti, was skeptical: "Between you and me, William, Waterloo is simply a bore."[35]

Less predictable attractions were the ancient towns of Ghent and Bruges. The young Disraeli on his first tour abroad in 1824 thought Bruges "the city of cities";[36] Thackeray found Bruges "the quaintest and prettiest of all the quaint and pretty towns I have seen" (*Little Travels* ch. 2). Carlyle's reaction is described below (pp. 86–88). Rossetti, too, was impressed by Bruges ("This is a most stunning place") and the paintings of Memling and Van Eyck he saw there and at Ghent had a significant influence on his art.[37] Belgium had won its independence in 1830 and was quick to develop on the English model. Charlotte Brontë's work is much influenced by her time as a teacher in Brussels (1842-44). Her employer, M. Heger, with whom she fell in love, was a distinguished and progressive educationalist. As for Carlyle, for Brontë it was the combination of the progressive and modern with the Catholic and traditional that allowed the significant impact.

Germany The sites and legends of the Rhine, like other Romantic enthusiasms, came to be regarded as a little commonplace and risible, too much the property of tourists. Thackeray's 1850 Christmas book, *The Kickleburys on the Rhine*, gives a satiric account of the typical tourist journey: "And so we pass by tower and town, and float up the Rhine. We don't describe the river. Who does not know of it? It is as familiar to numbers of people as Greenwich." The spa and gambling towns of south Germany, notably Baden-Baden, also attracted large numbers of visitors, and make a notable appearance in the opening chapters of George Eliot's *Daniel Deronda* (1874–76).

Nevertheless literary enthusiasm for German scenery and people continued, for instance in Bulwer-Lytton's pastiche, *The Pilgrims of the Rhine* (1832). Meredith attended the famous Moravian school at Neuwied on the Rhine between 1842 and 1844. He returned to the Rhineland on his honeymoon, and included six sonnets entitled "Pictures of the Rhine" in his *Poems* (1851). German scenes and peoples enter deeply into three of his novels written in this period: *Farina: A Legend of Cologne* (1857), which takes the form of a German legend or fairy tale; *The Ordeal of Richard Feverel* (1859); and *Harry Richmond* (1871). (Meredith's work as a whole is discussed in Volume 4 of this series.)

In the 1820s and 1830s Carlyle took over the role of Coleridge as the great interpreter of "deep thinking" Germany. Germany was, however, to him "a country of the mind" at that time: he made his first journey there in the 1850s. G.H. Lewes was the next leading interpreter of Germany (*Life of Goethe*, 1855). Another great Germanist, Marian Evans (George Eliot), the translator of Strauss and Feuerbach, traveled there with Lewes for the first time in 1858. At Nuremburg she found the mass at the Frauenkirche more congenial than the service in Protestant St. Sebald's:

I loved the good people about me, even to the soldier who stood with his back to us, giving us a full view of his close cropped head. . . . There was a little baby, in a close-fitting cap on his little round head, looking round with bright black eyes as it sucked its bit of bread. . . . Nothing could be more wretched as art than the painted Saint Veronica opposite me, holding out the sad face on her miraculous handkerchief. Yet it touched me deeply, and the thought of the Man of Sorrows seemed a very close thing—not a faint hearsay.[38]

The intellectual who had rendered the Christian story a myth (Strauss) found a moving spiritual breadth and continuity in popular European Catholicism.

Aspects of the Prussian state, notably its system of education, impressed English intellectuals, but the rise of a unified and militaristic Germany inevitably altered the picture of a scenic and intellectual land. The Prussian militarism of an earlier age had been regarded with distaste by the early Victorians: Macaulay dismissed Frederick in a notable review of Thomas Campbell's edition of Shoberl's *Frederick the Great and his Times* (1842), and Thackeray presented Frederick's Prussia as the cruelest of nations in *Barry Lyndon* (1844). Carlyle is thus the exception to the general view, his mammoth *History of Frederick the Great* (1858–65) a last attempt to persuade the British of the merits of strong leadership. Arnold nicely pointed to the significance of 1870 in some English eyes, when in *Friendship's Garland* (1871) he has his sympathetic spokesman for Prussian culture, Arminius, conscripted into the Prussian army and shot during the occupation of Paris.

Eastern Europe Eliot and Lewes continued their 1858 journey into the Austro-Hungarian Empire, visiting ancient walled Vienna and Prague. Numbers of Victorians, of course, traveled into Austro-Hungary, notably Trollope, whose *Nina Balatka* (1867) is an important response to the Jewish community of Prague. Eliot became aware of the breadth and depth of European culture. Both Vienna and Prague appear in her strange short story "The Lifted Veil" and in *Daniel Deronda*. Particularly, a visit to the Alter Friedhof and the Old Synagogue at Prague were to prove important.[39] Subsequent visits to Germany (in the 1860s and 1870s) led to familiarity with Jewish artists and intellectuals. It is clear from *Daniel Deronda* that part of the attraction of the Jews for her was their ideal of a national spiritual quest, but, through the presentation of the Princess and Deronda himself, the novel also portrays the European Jew as the conscious bearer of a European cultural tradition at once painfully complex and immensely rich. Arnold presents a comparable view in his sonnets about the great tragedienne, Rachel:

Germany, France, Christ, Moses, Athens, Rome.
The strife, the mixture in her soul, are ours. ("Rachel III" 12–13)

Indignation and sympathy about Russian oppression is the dominant theme in the minor literature that deals with Poland in the period. Russia itself was traveled and reported on, but the prevailing idea was also formed by that tyranny. Tennyson's attack on Russia in *Maud* (1855), at the time of the Crimean war, is echoed in much strident popular verse.

Scandinavia, Iceland, and the Arctic There was no great response to the modern society of the Scandinavian countries, though they were much-traveled by sportsmen. The mythology and early history of the Norse peoples were of interest, however. In 1856, Lord Dufferin made the voyage to Iceland and the Arctic circle in his yacht, *Foam*. He gives a memorable expression of the attraction of a northern mythology for a northern Briton: "In that iron clime, amid such awful associations, the conflict going on was too terrible—the contending powers too visibly in presence of each other, for the practical, conscientious Norse Mind to be content with the puny Godships of a Roman Olympus" (*Letters from High Latitudes*, 1857, Letter 8). Richard Burton's and William Morris's reactions to Iceland are described in the next volume of this series.

Further north, on the whaling coasts of Spitzberg, Dufferin's party came across a coffined skeleton on the beach: "A poor scarecrow, gibbeted for ages on this bare rock, like a dead Prometheus" (Letter 11). The scene may serve to epitomize another mid-Victorian response to the frozen north. Arctic expeditions had attracted considerable interest, in particular the expeditions of Sir John Franklin. But Franklin's third expedition (1845) failed to return. Public sympathy, which focused on the brave figure of Lady Franklin at home, was shocked by reports from Eskimoes that the party had been driven to cannibalism. Dickens's *Household Words* was particularly attentive to the Franklin story. Wilkie Collins's play, *The Frozen Deep* (1857), in which Dickens and Collins acted, tells of a noble self-sacrifice in such regions: a repudiation of the message of the Franklin expedition.[40] Of major writers, only Charlotte Brontë and Elizabeth Gaskell (*Sylvia's Lovers*) maintain a taste for the "arctic sublime."

Switzerland As a nation, the Swiss were admired for their tradition of liberty, though closer acquaintance often produced surprisingly disparaging accounts of the Swiss character; many contrasted the conditions in Catholic and Protestant cantons. It was impossible not to think of Byron or Shelley or Coleridge in the Alps, but the great age of mountain poetry was past. Wordsworth, in a letter to the *Morning Post* in 1844, argued that it was the very improvements in communication that had destroyed the sense of the sublime.[41] The cause probably lay deeper. Tennyson's idyll in *The Princess* (1847), "Come down, O maid, from yonder mountain height," which was written in Switzerland, urges her descent,

> for Love is of the valley, come,
> For Love is of the valley, come thou down (7.183–84)

"I was satisfied with the size of the crags," he remarked, "but mountains, great mountains, disappointed me."[42]

Painting of the mountains continued longer, in the work of John Martin, Francis Danby, and, above all, J.M.W. Turner. The great literary tribute to the Alps of the period, the fourth volume of Ruskin's *Modern Painters* (1856), is also the great tribute to Turner's genius. Ruskin's ability to evoke the mountain glory in his poetic prose is undeniable, but so are his differences from Turner. There is something characteristic and touching about his desire, late in life, to buy a mountain, with the intention that proper irrigation be established to protect the peasantry from destructive inundations. Only then could the mountain glory be wholly enjoyed.

Ruskin, like the Romantic poets before him, praised the Alps from the valleys, passes, and glaciers. A new generation of Englishmen was climbing them. The Alpine Club was formed in 1857. Made up mainly of university men, often lawyers and scholars, it included among its members scientists like the geologist John Tyndall (*Glaciers in the Alps*, 1860; *Hours of Exercise in the Alps*, 1871) and distinguished agnostics like Frederic Harrison and Leslie Stephen.[43] The Alpine Club placed an emphasis on vigor, and through vigor on moral health. Their critics tended to suggest that they were more likely to cry "Hurrah!" than "Ah!" at the top of a mountain peak. The ethos of the period is best expressed in Alfred Wills's lively *Wanderings among the High Alps* (1856) and in Leslie Stephen's *The Playground of Europe* (1871), which includes an influential history of the taste for mountain scenery and Stephens's own criticisms of the Romantics.

Italy It must be rare for one country to have exercised such a power over the imagination of another as Italy did over the British imagination in the mid-nineteenth century. Of course, the traditional appreciation of the warmth, color, beauty, and sensuousness of Italy was heightened by the contrast with the increasing respectability of British life and the growing ugliness of the urban and industrial scene. This is the point of Ruskin's famous contrast in *The Stones of Venice* between St. Mark's and its piazza and an English cathedral close (10.78-84). Nevertheless, the enthusiasm for *la dolce vita* is characteristically restrained, and perhaps deepened, by concerns and values that distinguish the period. It is significant that no literary work considers sexual adventure in Italy until Clough's *Dipsychus*

(1865; unpublished during his life): as its title suggests, its hero is undecided about the idea. But the response to Naples acts as a better illustration. Here is the notorious Lady Blessington, writing in 1823 (though her work, *The Idler in Italy*, was not published until 1839):

> The gaiety of the streets of Naples at night is unparalleled. . . . All are gay and animated; from the occupants of the coronetted carriage down to the *lazzaroni*, who, in the enjoyment of the actual present, are reckless of the future. . . . Above this scene of life and gaiety, this motley assemblage of the beautiful and grotesque, was spread a sky of deep azure thickly studded with stars.

Here, ten years later, is John Henry Newman:

> It is a frivolous dissipated place—this is Carnival-time and all sorts of silly public Saturnalia between King and people are going on and religion is turned into a mere medium of gaeity and worldly festivity.[44]

This evangelical response is extreme, of course, and it is not as though Victorians did not come to Naples in large numbers, scramble up and slide down Vesuvius, and visit the excavations at Pompeii and Herculaneum. Nevertheless, Newman was not the only writer in the period to find the city godless. Naples is the scene of Clough's poem, "Easter Day. Naples, 1849," with its jarring refrain "Christ is not risen!" (5). English awareness of political oppression also affected appreciation of the Kingdom of the Two Sicilies.

Classical Italy was not the focus it had been for the Grand Tourist. The Victorian traveler was more likely to see Italy through the medium of Shakespeare and the Romantics, particularly Byron. Samuel Rogers's *Italy* (1822–28), a series of poetic tales and reflections, including many scenes from Renaissance and modern Italian life, was, with its vignettes by Turner (so important for young Ruskin), the perfect medium for further popularizing Italy. Rogers also showed some concern for Italian liberty, and English and Italian historians (notably Sismondi) were creating an awareness of the political potential of the Italian past.

A new response to Italy was centered in Christian feeling, starved for images of spirituality, personal and civic, of a compelling beauty and integrity. Its expression is the taste for *trecento* and *quattrocento* art, which is associated with the art historians Charles and Lady Eastlake, Lord Lindsay, and Anna Jameson, and with the Arundel Society (1848–97), set up to record and preserve early fresco cycles. The greatest representative of this taste was Ruskin, and it continues into the poetry and paintings of the Pre-Raphaelite Brotherhood, notably the work of Dante Gabriel Rossetti (who, though of Italian origin, never visited Italy).

Such a taste found itself in centers other than Rome (which the young Ruskin found uninteresting) or Naples. Ruskin, in fact, came upon the realization of what was to be a great part of his life's work at Lucca and Pisa. At Pisa, Leigh Hunt had been struck by how "Antiquity refuses to look ancient in Italy" (*Autobiography*, 1850, ch. 19). The perfect buildings of the two small cities offered Ruskin the image of spiritual community that could transcend time and ruin: before seeing Lucca, he said, "All architecture, except fairy-finished Milan, had depended with me for its delight on being partly in decay." And then there was Pisa, and particularly the Campo Santa where Ruskin thought he saw "the entire doctrine of Christianity, painted so that a child could understand it" (35.350, 346-47, 351).

It was thus the Florence of Giotto, Dante, and the Republic rather than that of Michelangelo and the Medicis that attracted. Browning took two poems from Vasari's celebration of the Florentine Renaissance (*Lives of the Artists*), but characteristically chose a painter working before the event ("Fra Lippo Lippi") and one working in a silvery melancholy after its height ("Andrea del Sarto"). George Eliot's carefully researched novel of the Florentine Renaissance, *Romola* (1862–63), the product of visits to the city in 1860 and 1861, is sympathetic to its greatest critic, Savonarola. Indeed, the Renaissance as a whole was resisted. Ruskin thought that Browning's "The Bishop Orders His Tomb at Saint Praxed's Church" (1845) said all that he himself wished to say about the Renaissance, "its worldliness, inconsistently, pride, hypocrisy, ignorance of itself, love of art, of luxury, and of good Latin" (6.449). The revaluation of the Renaissance in the work of Pater and John Addington Symonds is the subject of an essay in the next volume of this series.

Ruskin's greatest Italian work, *The Stones of Venice* (1851–53), traces a Venice founded in almost Protestant purity of purpose at Torcello; flowering in the Gothic (which gave the Victorians a master text in the chapter "The Nature of Gothic"); and declining in the worldliness of the Renaissance: a message for another great maritime power. But there is a counter movement in his response, a celebration of color and sensuousness, the evocation of purple and sunset glories (such as Turner evoked). Venice, soaked in associations of Shakespeare, Byron, and Turner, stood for the glory of life, even for the imagination itself: the mood of the Venetian passages in Disraeli's *Contarini Fleming* (1832) and of Dickens's "A Dream" in *Pictures from Italy* (1846).

The Victorians often compared themselves to the ancient Romans, but to an age for which the classical world often seemed only cruel and the

Renaissance a glut of power and flesh, Rome had lost some of its appeal; to this was added the British distaste for Catholic ritual and for the squalid conditions of the city. Rome confused. The young Newman found it "a cruel place" though, of course, he changed his view: indeed, his disturbed reflections are at the beginning of the process.[45] Clough's Claude, in *Amours de Voyage* (1850), is cooler but the perception is not dissimilar to young Newman's; the reaction of George Eliot's Dorothea to the city's "stupendous fragmentariness" is described elsewhere (pp. 270–71).

There were a number of ways in which the Victorians shaped the rich and troubling experience of Italy. One, the way of Newman and other Catholic converts, was to embrace its mystery: the coexistence of spirit and glorious corrupt world locked in unending struggle. That this was felt as an enlargement of insular Protestant imaginings is testified to by the color and vigor of Newman's Catholic works. Even among nonconverts, hostile reaction to continental Catholicism was increasingly mixed with the recognition of an attraction and value.

Another response was to turn away from the hackneyed themes of the cultural heritage and attend more to the contemporary life of the Italian people, as Dickens did in *Pictures from Italy* or Browning did throughout his work; even Ruskin came to reject his habitual contrast between contemporary Italy and the ideal world represented by its art: "But all this I have felt and learned, like so much else, too late.... My mind was not yet catholic enough to feel the Campo Santa belonged to its own people more than to me" (*Works*, 35.357–58).[46]

Italian liberation also allowed writers to develop a heroic vein: Clough's "Say not the struggle naught availeth" was written while he was in Rome in the last brave days of Mazzini's Roman Republic. Mazzini figures significantly in the English literature of the 1850s and 1860s, praised by Elizabeth Barrett Browning and Meredith (*Sandra Belloni*, 1864; *Vittoria*, 1866) and lauded to the skies by Swinburne, whose adoption of the most extreme of republican views in *A Song of Italy* (1867) and *Songs before Sunrise* (1871) enabled him to denounce Christianity as a whole by denouncing Catholicism.

Spain The literary response to Spain is, at center, a tale of two men. Richard Ford's residence in Spain from 1830 to 1834 led to his *Handbook for Travellers in Spain* (1845), one of Murray's series. It was Ford who recommended that Murray publish George Borrow's *The Zincali; or, An Account of the Gypsies of Spain* (1841), which was followed by *The Bible in Spain* (1843), two of the most personable and vivid travel books of the period, which for long enjoyed a wide readership. The idea of George Eliot's narrative poem, *The Spanish Gypsy* (1868), came from a Titian painting she

"Arch from the Façade of the Church of San Michele at Lucca," from
John Ruskin, *The Seven Lamps of Architecture* (1849)

saw in Venice in 1864, though she was unable to finish the work until she had visited Spain in 1867. Her theme of a gypsy woman sacrificing her love to lead her people to the promised land of North Africa points to her growing interest in the idea of a new spiritual nationality in the East.

The Mediterranean The possession of India was the fundamental determinant of British experience of the Middle East in this period, and even of the Mediterranean south of Naples. A line of British possessions lay along the sea route from London to Cairo and from the Red Sea to Bombay. The scenes of past British naval and military glory and the evidence of present power pointed to a still larger role in the region: in Eliot Warburton's words, "as every traveller will bear witness: *England is expected in the East*" (*The Crescent and the Cross*, vol. 1, ch. 32). Sir Stratford Canning, British Ambassador at Constantinople (1842–58), exercised an extraordinary influence. Layard and Robert Curzon both served under Canning. The involvement of a number of travel writers in the Crimean War points to the relations of writing and power in the region: Layard visited the scene of conflict and led the parliamentary opposition to the conduct of the war; Burton volunteered as a military aide; Kinglake's *The Invasion of the Crimea* (1863–87) is the great history of the war.

The early Victorian traveler to the Mediterranean and the Levant (the "Levant" is defined by Warburton as the term "applied not only to the shores but to the seas, over which the sun *rises* to the morningward of Malta," and as synonymous with the "'East,'" [*The Crescent and the Cross* vol. 2, ch. 1]) was reminded of childhood and adolescent reading in Greek and Roman literature; in the *Arabian Nights* and European imitations such as Ridley's *Tales of the Genii*; in Gibbon and earlier historians of the ancient world (Josephus, Rollin); in Byron; and, of course in the Bible. Travel to the East could thus evoke the earliest imaginative wakening. Sailing past Ithaca, Newman wrote to his mother, "I could not have believed that the view of these parts would have so enchanted me . . . . My feelings . . . were not caused by any classical associations, but by the thought that I now saw before me was in real shape those places which had been the earliest vision of my childhood."[47] Not surprisingly, for imaginations so prepared, the experience of the Mediterranean and its shores was profound.

The succession of coasts and ports along the route southwards and eastwards was stunning. Ports of call along the Iberian coast might be the traveler's only experience of Portugal and Spain. From Gibraltar, Disraeli made the excursion to Granada, was delighted by the "Saracenic" architecture, and pretended to be a Moor: the East began in Spain.[48] It began, too, at Gibraltar, where Thackeray saw "swarthy Moors, in white or crimson robes; dark Spanish smugglers in tufted hats, with gay silk handkerchiefs round their heads . . . porters, Galician or Genoese" (*Cornhill to Grand Cairo* ch. 4), the picturesque and confusing mixture of costumes and peoples in the ports and great cities of the region on which all travelers remark, and which Dickens was to make a major motif in the first chapter of *Little Dorrit*:

> Hindoos, Russians, Chinese, Spaniards, Portuguese, Englishmen, Frenchmen, Genoese, Neapolitans, Venetians, Greeks, Turks, descendants from all the builders of Babel, come to trade at Marseilles.

Then there was the fascination of the African coast, Morocco, Algiers ("Thrilling name!" thought Lord Lindsay), and, inland of Cape Bon, the site of ancient Carthage. Malta was a frequent place of quarantine.

Greece Disraeli made his first foray into Greece from Corfu (the Ionian Islands were in British hands until 1864), choosing to follow Byron's footsteps to the oriental fiefdom of Iannina. Robert Curzon took the same route from Corfu to Iannina and then across northern Greece to Mount Athos. Kinglake missed Greece altogether, taking the overland route from Vienna through what is now Bulgaria to Constantinople. Layard, wishing to "journey through countries rarely visited by English travellers," took a similar route. At Scutari he had his

> first glimpse of Eastern life, and the scene as we passed through the bazaars crowded with men and women—Turks, Albanians, and Greeks of various tribes and races in their varied and gay costumes—was to me singularly novel and interesting. (*Autobiography and Letters* ch. 3)

The Greeks are part of the East, and it is the East that produces the travel writing of distinction in the period.

The Greek idea stood high, of course, but it is arguable that the literary imagination of the period responds more readily to the Eastern than to the purely Greek: even the Homeric poem *par excellence* of the great spokesman for the Homeric ideal in poetry, Matthew Arnold's "Sohrab and Rustum" (1853), is, in fact, set in Persia, the scene culled from Arnold's youthful reading in Alexander Burnes's *Travels into Bokhara* (1834). There is a similar reaction away from the Greek toward a "Levantine" style in art and architecture. To Ruskin, Byzantine architecture showed that

> those builders had truer sympathy with what God made majestic, than the self-contemplating and self-contented Greek. I know that they are barbaric in comparison; but there is power in their barbarism . . . which

could not rest in the expression or seizure of finite form. It could not bury itself in acanthus leaves. (*Works* 8.120–21)

The contrast is analogous to that Ruskin was to make between the Venetian Gothic—which is, of course, "Byzantine" in style—and the Renaissance architecture of Venice. Robert Curzon, touring in search of illuminated manuscripts, described the artistic style of the monasteries of Mount Athos as "a sort of Byzantine, of which St. Mark's in Venice is the finest specimen in Europe" (*Visits to Monasteries in the Levant* ch. 24). Thackeray made the same connection, remarking of Islam that, "Never did a creed possess temples more elegant; as elegant as the Cathedral at Rouen, or the Bapistery at Pisa" (*Cornhill to Grand Cairo* ch. 15). "Levantism" for the early and mid-Victorian imagination rivals the English Gothic (proposed by Pugin and others) as the style to oppose to both Classicism and modernity. Further, the geographical Levant included the classic scene, providing a blending of cultures and sights that blurred the categories of conscious discourse as it evoked the rich field of childhood imagining.

The Middle East Life on horse- or camel-back in the East excited the sense of adventure. The East was an enlargement, an opportunity to act the master, to explore the power and the freedom of the self, and to escape the sentimentality, repression, and moralized discourse of home. Byron's influence was strong. In *The Crescent and the Cross* (1845), Eliot Warburton summed up his feelings there by quoting the lines from Byron's "The Dream" that begin:

> in the wilds
> Of fiery clime he made himself a home,
> And his soul drank their sunbeams. He was girt
> With strange and dusky aspects: he was not
> Himself like what he had been. (106–10)

English travelers come nearer to celebrating non-European life in their accounts of the bravery, simplicity, and authenticity of the life of the desert Arabs than they do in discussing any other part of the globe in this period. The Turks, too, were admired for their bravery.

The period produces a number of eccentric and independent Orientalists who are not unwilling to shock values at home. Edward Lane, for instance, author of *Manners and Customs of the Ancient Egyptians* (1836), dwells at length on the erotic and the disturbing. Kinglake's *Eothen* (1844), the great travel book of the period, is a celebration of almost existential daring and authenticity. Kinglake's was the first of a number of fine travel books about the East published in the 1840s: his friend Eliot Warburton published *The Crescent and the Cross* in 1845; Robert Curzon followed with his *Visits to Monasteries in the Levant* in 1849; Layard's *Nineveh and its Remains* appeared in 1849. Perhaps the most striking of Mideastern travelers is the prolific Richard Francis Burton, who also made a major contribution to travel writing about India and Africa. Disguised as a Pathan doctor or *hakim*, Burton traveled in pilgrimage to the holy cities of Medina and Mecca (*Personal Narrative of a Pilgrimage to El-Medinah and Meccah*, 1855), his remarkable acting abilities and knowledge of eastern languages and society concealing his identity from his fellow pilgrims. In his writings about the East and his translation of the *Arabian Nights* (1885–88), Burton always sought to challenge English proprieties.

The Levant was also the biblical scene: "In a word, it is the Holy Land that occupies my thought, and I propose to make a pilgrimage to the sepulchre of my Saviour," Disraeli's Tancred declares (*Tancred*, 1847, bk. 2, ch. 1). By his time there was a steady stream of travelers there. Evangelicals went to the Holy Land to confirm biblical prophecies of destruction, "the literal accomplishment of prophecy, as displayed in the actual condition of Egypt, Edom and Syria," as Lord Lindsay wrote (*Letters on Egypt, Edom and the Holy Land*, 1838, "Preface"). Layard's excavations at Nineveh also seemed to confirm biblical prophecy. The interest in his work led to the founding of the Palestine Exploration Fund (1864) which undertook the excavation of Jerusalem between 1867 and 1870.[49]

Yet many Victorians could not be content with a view of accursed civilizations and regions. Like Tancred, they sought evidences of a continuing spirituality in a place, and they preferred to see progress in history. Harriet Martineau was one who (to adapt George Eliot's words about Rome) attempted to trace the soul in its growing shape across the East. In her view, each stage of her journey from Egypt, through Sinai, to the Holy Land, represented a stage of spiritual development (respectively, monotheism, the moral law, and personal holiness). In Egypt and Sinai contemporary life seemed to confirm her view, the "pure piety of the Arab tribes" for instance persuading her that Moses was right to lead his people into the desert (*Eastern Life, Past and Present* pt. 2, ch. 2).

But Jerusalem, the goal of her journey, was a great disappointment, as it was for other travelers. The city was a hellhole of religious controversy, "A Babel of worshippers," Kinglake called it (*Eothen* ch. 16), its population, according to Warburton, made up of "professors of various creeds, each hating and fearing the other as alien and stranger" (*The Crescent and the Cross* vol. 2, ch. 7). Martineau reflected that "in Italy I found the Christian mythology and superstitious observances very distressing to witness; but I could have had no idea how much more painful the spectacle is in Palestine."

Her recourse was to escape the city to Gethsemane, "the most sacred shrine of sorrow," a lonely identification with a divinity that the surrounding world seemed to ignore (*Eastern Life* pt. 3, ch. 3).

Jerusalem was not the end of Martineau's journey. The logic of her chronological design demanded that she go on to consider "Syria and its Faith." There appears almost a relief in this; as for Kinglake at Jerusalem, for Martineau only the indifferent Turks behave decently in the hectic mass of rival believers. Jerusalem was Babel—as the cities of the East were from Gibraltar on—and it was better to be released from the pressure of the search for the ultimate place to the spirited enjoyment of the scenes and peoples of the region. The quest of Disraeli's Tancred is similarly dispersed into adventure.

Nineveh, too, had an ambiguous message. Layard recognized that he had discovered a new and more disturbing image of ruin:

> The graceful column . . . the richly carved cornice or capital half-hidden by the luxuriant herbage; are replaced by the stern shapeless mound rising like a hill from the scorched plain. . . . A feeling of awe succeeds to wonder; for there is nothing to relieve the mind, to lead to hope, or to tell of what has gone by. (*Nineveh and Its Remains* ch. 1)

The huge statuary he excavated and sent to the British Museum elicited the most notable ruin poem of the period, Dante Gabriel Rossetti's "The Burden of Nineveh" (1850).

India The best travel writing about India in the period derives from the excitement of the expansion of British India into the northwest. Alexander Burnes, author of *Travels into Bokhara* (1834), was employed by the East India Company, and traveled, sometimes in disguise, deep into the Asian hinterland. Burton was employed as a government agent to go in disguise to investigate the danger of the homosexual brothels of the Sind.

British India of the eighteenth century was given glamorous definition by Macaulay in his two essays, "Clive" (1839) and "Warren Hastings" (1841), but the new image of Anglo-India is more evident in the work of Thackeray (see below, pp. 100–101). The spirit of reform is well-represented in Sir Philip Meadows Taylor's account of the suppression of Thugee, *Confessions of a Thug* (1839), and in one of the most interesting minor novels of the period, *Oakfield; or, Fellowship in the East* (1854), by William Delafield Arnold, the fourth son of Arnold of Rugby. Oakfield is ostracized by his fellow officers through his earnest religious attempts to reform their language and manners and his refusal to fight a duel. The novel only succeeds in resolving the crisis of his alienation by making him a hero of adventure in the Sikh wars.

With the Indian Mutiny, Arnold produced a series of engaged articles in *Frazer's Magazine* (1857–58) which abandon the scrupulosities of *Oakfield*: he believed that "the Civilization of 50 Years perished in 50 hours."[50] The Mutiny had an immense impact in England; over 500 books of all kinds appeared on the subject between 1857 and 1862. The anonymous author of an 1897 article in *Blackwood's*, "The Indian Mutiny in Fiction," remarked that, "Of all the great events of this century, as they are reflected in fiction, the Indian Mutiny has taken the firmest hold on the popular imagination." Its fiction is, predictably, largely adventure writing of the most brutal kind, tales of "valour and heroism, cruelty and treachery, sharp agony and long endurance, satiated vengeance and bloodthirsty hatred" (161: 218–19).

It is a sign of a developing division that the era of such popular fiction was also an era of great Indian scholarship, notably the work on Sanskrit writings of Friederich Max Muller who settled at Oxford in 1848. One of those influenced by Sanskrit literature was Matthew Arnold. His sonnet, "East and West" (1867), describes the present relations of the two cultures:

> In conquering sunshine bright
> The man of the bold West now comes arrayed;
> He of the mystic East is touched with night. (12–14)

Among the conquerors had been his younger brother, William. William's wife, Frances, died in the Punjab in 1858, and William himself died at Gibraltar, on the voyage home in 1859. Matthew's two night-touched elegies, "Stanzas from Carnac" and "A Southern Night" (1859), dissent from the whole imperial project.

There is imagery in many writings of the mid-century of the civilizations of the East as at once barbaric and ancient: a combination that excludes progress. For instance, Kingsley's Chartist novel, *Alton Locke* (1850), ends with an evolutionary-expansionary dream passage, an important point in the author's transition from radical to imperialist. *Prior to the beginning* of the evolutionary process, the hero finds himself in Hindustan, attempting to climb up from "among monstrous shapes of gods and fiends, that mouthed and writhed and mocked at me" (ch. 36). Those on the spot were coming to the same conclusion. In his *Ceylon* (1859), Sir James Emerson Tennent concluded that Buddhism could not be effective against the long tradition of demon worship because it lacked the higher appeal of Christianity. He was nevertheless forced to conclude that Christianity itself had made little headway. Thus in post-Mutiny India a new emphasis was made on the rituals of power.[51]

The Far East The penetration of the Far East increased the number of hostile stereotypes. The image of the opium-smoking Chinese is particularly cruel, of course, since the British had forced the opium trade onto China (the Opium Wars, 1839–42, 1856–60). But gone were the days of Oliver Goldsmith's citizen of the world, Lien Chi Altangi; "Better fifty years of Europe," Tennyson concluded in *Locksley Hall* (1842), "than a cycle of Cathay" (184). Dickens visited a Chinese junk, the *Keying*, moored at Blackwall in London, in 1848: "Here at any rate, is the doctrine of finality beautifully worked out. . . . Thousands of years have passed since the first Chinese junk was constructed on this model; and the last Chinese junk that was ever launched was none the better for that waste and desert of time" ("The Chinese Junk," *Miscellaneous Papers*). Nevertheless, in certain leading examples of the "sensation novel" of the 1860s, notably Wilkie Collins's *The Moonstone* (1868) and Dickens's *The Mystery of Edwin Drood* (1870), elements of eastern barbarism are introduced into the English scene to suggest an uncomfortable complicity.

The Pacific Japan, surprisingly, retained an Arcadian image.[52] The Pacific islands, on the other hand, fared no better than China. Dickens's reflection on "the Pacific Ocean, with its lovely islands, where the savage girls plait flowers, and the savage boys carve cocoa-nut shells, and the grim blind idols muse in their shady groves to exactly the same purpose as the priests and chiefs," is representative. It leads him to the conclusion that "the noble savage is a wearisome impostor wherever he is" (*The Uncommercial Traveller*, 1861, "Bound for the Great Salt Lake").

The West Indies Anti-slavery feeling continued throughout the period. Ruskin, in a well-known passage in *Modern Painters*, pronounced Turner's painting *The Slave Ship* "the noblest . . . ever painted by man," but, outside of the fiction of Harriet Martineau ("Demerara"; *The Hour and the Man*, 1841, about Toussaint L'Ouverture) and Barrett Browning's poetry, the anti-slavery movement does not excite a significant literature. The popular imagination was skeptical of the emotion expended on blacks. In Marryat's *Peter Simple* (1834), two sailors ask why slaves do not run away:

"Run away! poor creatures," said the black gentleman. "Why, if they did, they would be flogged."
"Flogged-heh; well, and if we ran away, we are to be hanged. They nigger's better off nor we: ar'n't he, Tom?" (ch. 16)

Like Carlyle's infamous "The Nigger Question" (1849), Dickens's criticism of the Niger expedition of 1841–42 and satire on the "telescopic philanthropy" of Mrs. Jellyby and her Borrioboola-Gha project in *Bleak House*

(1852–53) derive from the feeling that the suffering of the English poor was being neglected because of the gullible idealizing of black peoples. But the extent of the contribution that West Indian slavery had made to the British economy; the moral insistence of the anti-slavery agitation; the fate of the white owners when blacks refused to work plantations after emancipation; the consequent decline of the sugar trade (expedited by the implementation of free trade in the 1840s) had by the mid-century created a complex nexus of guilt and hostility, which was intensified by the British association of dark peoples with repressed and feared aspects of themselves.

Africa At the beginning of Queen Victoria's reign, Africa was still largely the dark continent. Exploration had slowed: there was a steady, if declining, stream of books about Africa in the 1840s, but by the 1850s the reviews were carrying less and less African material. Richard Burton contrasted the diminished taste of the 1850s for African material with that of the 1820s in his two-part essay "Zanzibar; and, Two Months in East Africa" (*Blackwood's* 83 [1858]: 200–24, 276–90). But the great age of African exploration was about to begin, and with it a renewal of public interest. Burton's first African book, *First Footsteps in East Africa; or, An Exploration of Harar*, appeared in 1856. His "Preface" criticizes the philanthropist and "Free-trade bosh," points to French and Russian expansion, and calls for aggressive territorial aggrandizement.[53] Burton and Speke then explored the Great Lakes region of East Africa (1857–58). Public interest was enlivened by a fierce contest between them as to who had discovered the source of the Nile. The work of the greatest explorer of the age was different in tone, however. David Livingstone's *Missionary Travels and Researches in South Africa* (1857) and *Narrative of an Expedition to the Zambesi and its Tributaries* (1865), which announced the "discovery" of the Victoria Falls, were popular successes, and the romance of his story was confirmed by Stanley's famous dicovery of Livingstone himself (*How I Found Livingstone . . . in Central Africa*, 1872). Livingstone represents a late expression of high-minded philanthropy, although his works repeatedly report a disillusionment with African peoples.

South America Britain recognized the independence of the South American countries in the 1820s and enjoyed a considerable trade with South America, but there was little literary response to the new republics. The great scientific journey to South America was, of course, Darwin's, described in *The Voyage of the Beagle* (1844). Darwin took with him the first volume of Sir Charles Lyell's *Principles of Geology*, and ordered the second from Buenos Aires. In South America, Darwin found confirmation of Lyell's claim for the age of the earth. Hearing the pebbles rolling in the streams of the Cordillera, he reflected that "the sound spoke eloquently to the geologist. . . . It was like thinking on time" (ch. 15). The second element in Darwin's theory of natural selection, pressure of population, originates from a study of man, Thomas Malthus's *An Essay on the Principle of Population* (1798). Again Darwin found confirmation, in the wars of extermination of the Spanish settlers against the Indian peoples of the Argentine, and in the annihilation of the native Tasmanian population, that "wherever the European has trod, death seems to pursue the aboriginal. . . . The varieties of man seem to act on each other in the same way as different species of animals—the stronger always extirpating the weaker" (ch. 19). Colonialism proved the point, but so also did savagery: in winter, the Indians of Tierra Del Fuego ate their old women before their dogs: " 'Doggies catch otters, old women no.' " (ch. 10). It needed only the natural laboratory of the Galapagos to clinch the argument.

We have seen that racist feeling was on the increase in the 1850s. So were racial theories (a significant example is Robert Knox's *The Races of Man*, 1850).[54] Theories of competition between species provided further justification of expansion. For instance, in *Greater Britain*, Charles Dilke includes in his account of New Zealand a chapter entitled "The Two Flies," which alludes to a Maori song:

> As the Pakeha fly has driven out the Maori fly . . .
> So will the Pakeha destroy the Maori.

Dilke admired the Maoris, but as he explained, "natural selection is being conducted by nature in New Zealand on a grander scale than any we have contemplated, for the object of it here is man" (pt. 2, ch. 6).

Canada Of the three major areas of settlement colonies, Canada, Australia, and New Zealand, Canada attracted least literary attention. Those who disliked America, like Marryat or Dickens, might say a few positive words (*American Notes* ch. 15), but the judgment of Charles Dilke is more characteristic: "The pulse-beat of the Continent finds no echo here" (*Greater Britain* pt. 1, ch. 6). Trollope agreed: "I must confess that in going from the States into Canada, an Englishman is struck by the feeling that he is going from a richer country into one that is poorer, and from a greater country into one that is less" (*North America* ch. 4). All travelers admired the Niagara Falls, however.

New Zealand New Zealand excited a special feeling among those who were interested in settlement overseas. In the writings of the Colonial Reformers the argument that colonies should be extensions of England by no means

42

"Fuegians Going to Trade in Xapallos with the Patagonians," from Captain
Robert Fitzroy, *Narrative of the Surveying Voyages of His Majesty's Ships
"Adventure" and "Beagle"* (1839)

obscured the strong feeling that they should be better societies. New Zealand seemed a country where such a better society had its best hopes. Both Carlyle and Dr. Arnold—two potent influences—were excited by the idea of emigration there. Dr. Arnold bought two hundred acres in the original Wakefield settlement, and thought of emigrating "if there was any prospect of rearing any hopeful form of society."[55]

In the 1840s, Clough and Froude, both troubled by religious doubt and distressed by social conditions at home, considered going. For Tom Arnold the idea of "New Zealand and the Life of a Colonist" became an obsession. His reasoning is described in his semi-fictionalized "'Equator Letters'" (1847), which was circulated in manuscript among his friends. After describing his difficulties with orthodox belief, Arnold turns to the subject of a wealthy and uncaring society: "I am one of this rich class. . . . The life I lead is an outrage and a wrong to humanity." Since he could not "herd amongst . . . suffering wretches" at home, he would emigrate. Clough's narrative poem, *The Bothie of Tober Na-Vuolich* (1848), which has been called "a small epic . . . of colonialization,"[56] was influenced by Tom's choice but the restless model for its hero could not make a life in New Zealand, and went on to Tasmania to marry and to convert to Catholicism—the beginnings of the unsettled career described in Arnold's *Passages in a Wandering Life* (1900).

Another young man attracted to New Zealand was Samuel Butler, who, having given up the idea of taking holy orders, went out in 1859, and within five years made enough as a sheep breeder to return to England with a comfortable income. Butler gives a lucid and attractive account of passage and life on a sheep farm in his *A First Year in Canterbury Settlement* (1863). He was both a better farmer and a better explorer than Tom Arnold, and his ventures into the interior, which reminded him of northern Italy and the Alps, provide the opening scenes of his satiric masterpiece, *Erewhon* (1872). *Erewhon* relates to New Zealand in other ways than its setting: its disturbingly rational account of a society based on an ethic of physical vigor, rather than on conventional moral concerns, is partly a sly look at the idealization of the physical life in writings about settler life in the Antipodes. It also subtly suggests a bathos in the idea of the extension of England: Butler's hero crosses a great mountain range at the far end of the world and discovers a society which, despite its topsy-turvy qualities, is only prim, hypocritical and respectable England all over again.

Australia The image of the Australian colonies passed through a number of phases. It is first of the horrors and brutalities of transportation; then, of an idyllic home for settlers or a transplanted gentry; finally, the discovery

44

of gold at Ballarat in 1851 and the subsequent gold rush bring the diggings to the foreground. Australia entered into the literature of the period before the diggings, but the gold rush made it a prominent theme in the fiction of the late 1850s. This is in keeping with a broader movement to the novel of adventure in this period, but the novels about Australia are particularly a reaction to a rough and uncontrolled society of English, operating outside normal English social constraints. This is underlined by the fact that a number of these novels hark back to the times of transportation.

Bulwer-Lytton's *The Caxtons* (1849), which includes some poorly sketched Australian scenes, has been seen as the first novel of colonial settlement. It enabled Bulwer to discuss his colonial theories; he was to be briefly Colonial Minister (1858–59) in Disraeli's government. Other writers were also responding positively to the prospect of emigration, as Dickens did in his journalism and in *David Copperfield*. Browning's Gigadibs, disgusted with the sophisms of Bishop Bloughram, takes his family out:

> bought, not cabin-furniture
> But settler's implements (enough for three)
> And started for Australia ("Bishop Bloughram," 1010–12)

Charles Reade's melodrama *Gold* (1853) signals the beginnings of his interest in Australia. It was followed by the novel *It is Never Too Late to Mend* (1856), a powerful if simplistic denunciation of transportation and of prison policies at home, which includes vividly imagined Australian scenes. Charles Kingsley, who thought *The Caxtons* "absolutely the best novel extant in the English language," introduced scenes at the diggings into *Two Years Ago* (1857). His brother Henry's novels of adventure in the Australian bush make the most extended imaginative engagement with the region in the period. The convict scenes in Dickens's *Great Expectations* (1860–61), which is set in the days of transportation, owe something to both Reade and Henry Kingsley. Magwitch's return from Australia allowed Dickens to give expression to class resentments: "'I've come to the old country for to see my gentleman spend his money like a gentleman,'" the reformed convict says (ch. 40). Magwitch does not succeed as he wishes, but in these novels all the respectable characters (if we except the Micawbers) are restored to England and to wealth, and, above all, to land.[57] In *John Caldigate* (1879), Trollope wondered whether the respectability survived the experience.

America At the height of Mr. Pickwick's problems in Dickens's *The Pickwick Papers*, old Tony Weller suggests he go to America: "'Let the gov'ner stop there . . . and then let him come back and write a book about the 'Merrikins as'll pay all his expenses and more, if he blows 'em up enough'" (ch. 45). Dickens doubtless had in mind the fury in America over criticisms made in Captain Basil Hall's *Travels in North America in the Years 1827 and 1828* (1829) and in Frances Trollope's *Domestic Manners of the Americans* (1832). Very soon, other British travelers had upset their hosts: Harriet Martineau (*Society in America*, 1837; *Retrospect of Western Travel*, 1838), even though she was largely sympathetic to the American experiment, and Captain Marryat (*A Diary in America*, 1839), who thought American democracy a mistake. With his *American Notes* (1842) and *Martin Chuzzlewit* (1842–44), Dickens himself was to prove the greatest offender; the great progressive writer of the age could not appreciate the great progressive country. It is a symptomatic response.

One reason for the reaction was overly high or unrealistic expectations. A reviewer of Mrs. Trollope's work remarked that she was "led to take a harsher view in consequence of having set out on her crusade with inflamed notions of republican perfection."[58] Martineau also set out an enthusiast ("America was meant to be everything") and found that the country did not meet her standard: the ideals of the Founding Fathers![59] Dickens may have had a shrewder idea, but nevertheless, his whole rhetoric is cast in terms of great expectations unfulfilled. Travel to America thus functioned to disabuse the English of any lingering allegiance to the language of the age of revolutions.

This happened the more readily because the Americans themselves employed such a language, and, unable to see its actual political and social usages, the English concluded it was hyperbole or hypocrisy. But this was only part of the problem with American discourse. English travelers went to America to observe and to write about what they saw (Harriet Martineau's *How to Observe* derives from her American journey). They found themselves in turn observed, immensely talked to and at, and, if already famous, talked and written about. It is these powers of observation and expression that produce the greatest resentment: Americans talking up their own society or, worse, criticizing England; Americans holding meetings and speechifying; above all, American newspapers. America was unique in this possession of a voice: the settlement colonies were too underdeveloped to be anything but spoken for; the traveler in Europe was protected by his selective use of language, moving in the encapsulated space of tourist or *milord*. By virtue of a common language the English traveler came closer to America than to any other culture. It was as though his or her lines had been stolen.

It has been rightly observed that the English found America institutionalized: what else was there to see?[60] The traveler was forced into the narrow and rather exhausting business of assessing and comparing workhouses, prisons, model factories, schools. The result is an understandable restiveness. The other point of comparison was manners, as Mrs. Trollope's title suggests. There were aspects of manners, such as Mrs. Trollope encountered in Cincinnati, that simply belong to frontier life; others, like the spitting Dickens makes so much of, that were unquestionably uncouth. But it is unlikely that they would have offended so greatly without the accompanying speech. It is not the man lounging on the porch that offends, but that the man has a point of view, and feels entitled to it.

The greatest failures of the travelers seem to be their inability to enjoy nature in America (if we except Niagara) and their inability to respond to the excitement of American society. They found nature scruffy, unformed (as of course it was), depressing, even drear, as both Mrs. Trollope and Dickens found the Mississippi. They also found Americans "sharp" and avaricious and pleased to be: this is part of the play of Dickens's title *American Notes for General Circulation*. British emigrants poured into America, choosing it as a destination over the settlement colonies by a ratio of about three to one. Dickens, in particular, seems unable to accept this choice. The Micawbers will be happy and succeed in Australia, but the poor immigrants to Cairo are wickedly exploited dupes (*Martin Chuzzlewit* chs. 23, 33).

The steady flow of travel writing in the 1840s and 1850s inevitably produced an increasingly detailed and more complex picture of American life. Feelings became intense again at the time of the Civil War. Walter Bagehot, for instance, influential as the editor of *The Economist*, argued that American expansion had gone so unchecked that "the national sense and the national morality had both suffered in the process": defeat of the Union would thus be a good thing ("English Feeling Towards America," 1861).[61] On the other side, there were those like Martineau who wrote in support of a war against slavery. So shaken were relations between the two countries that some British writers were at pains to try and restore them, notably Anthony Trollope (*North America*, 1862), whose fiction also makes an extended examination of Anglo-American relations.

Trollope's work shows his desire to include America in the greater English family. This is the theme of Charles Dilke's *Greater Britain*. On the other hand, Arnold, reviving the argument that America lacked culture and an aristocracy, made an ironic application of this view in his discussions of "the condition of the English race in the United States": "I supposed that the American Philistine was a livelier sort of Philistine than ours" ("A Word More about America," 1885). Between them, Arnold and Dilke represent the new terms of response in the later part of this period: the view from culture, which always turns America back toward the standard of English society (as Henry James's novels do), and the positive response to westward expansion. Dilke remarks that "New England is not America" (pt. 1, ch. 5), and celebrates adventure on the frontier, the railroads, and the California gold-rush; he is even interested in the Mormons (as Richard Burton was), who for Arnold were the epitome of culturelessness doing what it liked.

Ireland We can conclude with the oldest colony. Throughout the period, Ireland was a major source of violence and political upheaval in English politics. Just as it was in an unusual political relation to Britain, so its cultural relations are close and complex: we do not here discuss the Protestant Anglo-Irish writers who are an important part of the British literary scene (some of whom—Charles Lever, for instance—made important contributions to the literature of adventure and tourism). The representation of Ireland in specifically English fiction is discussed in the essays on Thackeray and Trollope below.

Ireland was also woven into the religious movements of the day. The suppression of the Irish bishoprics and Catholic Emancipation were among the causes of the Oxford Movement. James Anthony Froude, having fallen under Newman's influence at Oxford, spent some time with an Anglo-Irish family: "There were murders now and then in the mountains, and I was startled at the calmness with which they were spoken of. We were in the midst of the traditions of 1798." Young Froude was impressed: "Modern history resumed its traditionary English aspect" ("The Oxford Counter-Reformation," 1881, *Short Studies*, Fourth Series). Thus was born the author of *The English in Ireland in the Eighteenth-Century* (1872–74) and the advocate of empire. Newman's conversion to Catholicism was to subsequently take him to Ireland (where he was followed by Tom Arnold, Aubrey de Vere, Gerard Manley Hopkins, and others). To develop interest in his proposed Catholic University, he delivered a series of lectures in Dublin that were to become *The Idea of a University* (1859; under this title, 1873): his project is a sympathetic instance of an attempt to transport the English idea, its failure a sign of the inevitable resistances.

NOTES

1. John Gallagher and Ronald Robinson, "The Imperialism of Free Trade," *The Economic History Review*, 2nd ser. 6 (1953): 1–15; also the same authors' *Africa and the Victorians: The Official Mind of Imperialism* (London: 1965) ch. 15 "Nationalism and Imperialism."
2. Élie Halévy, "English Public Opinion and the French Revolutions of the Nineteenth Century," *Studies in Anglo-French History*, ed. Alfred Coville and Harold Temperley (London: 1935) 51–60.
3. Richard Koebner and Helmut Dan Schmidt, *Imperialism: The Story and Significance of a Political Word* (Cambridge: 1965) 1–2.

4. John Howes Gleason, *The Genesis of Russophobia in Great Britain* (Cambridge, MA: 1950).
5. Olive Anderson, *A Liberal State at War: English Politics and Economics During the Crimean War* (London: 1967).
6. It was widely, though mistakenly, believed that English women were raped. Thus an unidentified writer in *Frazer's* magazine remarked that "the transformation of Lord Angelo from the chaste judge to the pernicious caitiff-deputy, was less sudden" (56 [1857]: 627). Charles Kingsley's letters about the Mutiny verge on hysteria.
7. *The Letters of Thomas Babington Macaulay*, ed. Thomas Pinney (Cambridge: 1981) 6.103.
8. Derek Beale, *England and Italy, 1859–60* (London: 1961).
9. D.M. Schreuder, "Gladstone and Italian Unification, 1848–70: The Making of a Liberal?" *EHR* 85 (1970): 475–501.
10. Oscar Maurer, "'Punch' on Slavery and Civil War in America 1841–1865," *Victorian Studies* (1957): 5–28.
11. *The Letters of Charles Dickens*, ed. Walter Dexter, Nonesuch Edition (London: 1938) 3.445.
12. Sir George Tankyns Chesney, "The Battle of Dorking: Reminiscences of a Volunteer," *Blackwood's* 109 (1871): 539–72. See also I.F. Clarke, "The Battle of Dorking: 1871–1914," *Victorian Studies* 8 (1965): 309–28.
13. Richard Shannon, *The Crisis of Imperialism 1865–1915* (London: 1974) 52–53. The phrase "flamboyant imperialism" comes from R. Muir, *A Short History of the British Commonwealth* 2.602.
14. Koebner and Schmidt 107–9. The year 1876 also saw the publication of W.M. Thornburn's *The "Great Game"*.
15. Mona Wilson, "Holidays and Travel," *Early Victorian England 1830–65*, ed. G.M. Young (London: 1934) 2.303.
16. Ibid.
17. Qtd. by Philip D. Curtin, *The Image of Africa: British Ideas and Action* (London: 1965) 324.
18. *Letters of Thomas Arnold the Younger 1850–1900*, ed. James Bertram (Dunedin, NZ: 1980) 8–9.
19. Carlyle, *Past and Present* bk. 4, ch. 3; Thackeray, *From Cornhill to Grand Cairo* ch. 4.
20. Qtd. by Frederic E. Faverty, *Matthew Arnold the Ethnologist* (Evanston, IL: 1951) 76.
21. See, for instance, how the traditional enthusiasm for Italy is modified to characteristic mid-Victorian religious and social concerns. Pater and Symonds signal the return of a cult of the South. When George Eliot wishes to bring Grandcourt and Gwendolen to the nadir of their high life, she takes them to the French Riviera (*Daniel Deronda*). I am disagreeing with some of the emphasis of John Pemble's excellent study, *The Mediterranean Passion: Victorians and Edwardians in the South* (Oxford: 1987).
22. "Pagan Patriotism," *Saturday Review* 20 (1865): 324. Qtd. by Faverty 5.
23. George Levine, "High and Low: Ruskin and the Novelists," *Nature and the*

49

Victorian Imagination, ed. U.C. Knoepflmacher and G.B. Tennyson (Berkeley, Los Angeles, and London: 1977) 137.
24. Chauncey H. Loomis, "The Arctic Sublime," *Nature and the Victorian Imagination* 95–113.
25. Michael Booth, *Prefaces to Nineteenth-Century Theatre* (Manchester: 1980) 1–54.
26. *The Letters of Matthew Arnold to Arthur Hugh Clough*, ed. Howard Foster Lowry (London and New York: 1932) 47.
27. *The Collected Letters of Thomas and Jane Welsh Carlyle*, Duke-Edinburgh Edition, ed. C.R. Sanders, K.J. Fielding, Clyde Ryals, et al. (Durham, NC: 1970) 3.179.
28. Quotations from Ruskin are from *The Complete Works of John Ruskin*, Library Edition, ed. E.T. Cook and Alexander Wedderburn, 39 vols. (London: 1903–12).
29. Qtd. by Michael Goldberg, "Carlyle, Dickens and the Revolution of 1848," *Dickens Studies Annual* 12 (1983): 225.
30. *The Correspondence of Arthur Hugh Clough*, ed. Frederick L. Mulhauser (Oxford: 1957) 1.180–81, 243.
31. *The Collected Works of Walter Bagehot*, ed. Norman St. John-Stevas (London: 1965–74) 4.15–84.
32. *The Letters of Matthew Arnold 1848–1888*, ed. George W.E. Russell (New York: 1900) 296.
33. Enid Starkie, *From Gautier to Eliot: The Influence of France on British Literature 1851–1939* (London: 1960).
34. *The Collected Works of Walter Bagehot* 8.197.
35. *The Letters of Dante Gabriel Rossetti*, ed. Oswald Doughty and John Robert Wahl (Oxford: 1965) 1.81.
36. Qtd. by William Flavelle Monypenny, *The Life of Benjamin Disraeli Earl of Beaconsfield* (London: 1910) 1.43.
37. *Letters of Rossetti* 1.84.
38. Qtd. by Gordon S. Haight, *George Eliot: A Biography* (Oxford: 1968) 256.
39. Haight, *George Eliot* 263.
40. Chauncey H. Loomis, "The Arctic Sublime"; *Under the Management of Mr. Charles Dickens: His Production of "The Frozen Deep,"* ed. Robert Louis Brannan (Ithaca, NY: 1966).
41. *The Prose Works of William Wordsworth*, ed. W.J.B. Owen and Jane Worthington Smyser (Oxford: 1974) 3.353–54. Wordsworth also gives a brief account of the history of the taste for mountain scenery.
42. *The Letters of Alfred Lord Tennyson*, ed. Cecil Y. Lang and Edgar F. Shannon, Jr. (Cambridge, MA: 1981) 1.264.
43. David Robertson, "Mid-Victorians among the Alps," *Nature and the Victorian Imagination* 113–36.
44. *The Letters and Diaries of John Henry Newman*, ed. Ian Ker and Thomas Gornall, S.J. (Oxford: 1979) 3.216.
45. John Pemble remarks on "the emotional impact that the idea of Catholicity acquired in Rome. . . . It became an accusation that made the heart sick; an

experience with a power to modify attitude" (*The Mediterranean Passion* 227).

46. As Pemble observes, the common Italian people did not appear as vulgar as the masses at home, and there was the opportunity of relief from the attitude of social responsibility (*The Mediterranean Passion* 128).
47. *Letters of Newman* 3.172.
48. Monypenny, *Life of Disraeli* 1.147–49.
49. Dr. John Pemble, "The Owls of Babylon," BBC Radio Talk, 31 May 1986. Script kindly provided to me by Dr. Pemble. See also *The Mediterranean Passion* 185 ff.
50. Qtd. by Frances J. Woodward, *The Doctor's Disciples* (London: 1954) 214.
51. Bernard S. Cohen, "Representing Authority in Victorian India," *The Invention of Tradition*, ed. Eric Hobsbawm and Terence Ranger (Cambridge: 1983) 179–85.
52. Toshio Yokoyama, *Japan in the Victorian Mind* (London: 1987).
53. Philip D. Curtin, *The Image of Africa*, to which this paragraph is indebted.
54. For Knox and other mid-century racial theorists, see Philip D. Curtin, *Imperialism* (New York: 1971).
55. Arthur Stanley, *The Life of Dr. Arnold* (1844) 2.164.
56. James Bertram, ed. *New Zealand Letters of Thomas Arnold* (London and Wellington, N.Z.: 1966) xxviii. This volume includes the text of the "'Equator Letters,'" 207–19.
57. Coral Lansbury, *Arcady in Australia: The Evocation of Australia in Nineteenth-Century English Literature* (Melbourne: 1970).
58. *Literary Gazette* 24 March 1832, qtd. by Joseph Jay Jones, "British Literary Men's Opinions About America, 1750–1832," diss. Stanford U, 1934.
59. Marghanita Laski, "Harriet Martineau," *Travelers to the New Nation 1776–1914*, ed. Marc Pacther (Washington, D.C.: 1976) 38–46.
60. Peter Conrad, *Imagining America* (New York: 1980) 3–60, to which this discussion is indebted.
61. *Collected Works of Walter Bagehot* 4.327.

DISRAELI ABROAD: THE MAKING OF A "CONTINENTAL MIND"

Daniel Schwarz, Cornell University

An 1833 entry in Benjamin Disraeli's diary shows that his novels compensate for his failure to excel even as they protest against accepted English conventions and manners:

> The world calls me "conceited"—The world is in error. I trace all the blunders of my life to sacrificing my own opinion to that of others. When I was considered very conceited *indeed*, I was nervous, and had self-confidence only by fits. I intend in future to act entirely from my own impulse. I have an unerring instinct. I can read characters at a glance; few men can deceive me. My mind is a continental mind. It is a revolutionary mind. I am truly great in action. If ever I am placed in a truly eminent position I shall prove this. I could rule the House of Commons, although there would be a great prejudice against me at first. It is the most jealous assembly in the world. The fine character of our English society, the consequences of our aristocratic institutions renders a *career* difficult.[1]

Here is the myth of a strong, confident, gifted "continental" personality functioning in a larger world than the English one that Disraeli felt stifled his creativity and ignored his genius. Disraeli used his travels to define the heroic and spiritual self he believed that he needed to discover to make himself the political visionary he sought to be.

Disraeli's career as artist and politician should be seen in the context of the Romantic movement. His imaginative use of travel followed in the footsteps of the Romantics, especially Byron, who regarded the continent, and in particular Italy and Greece, as exotic, passionate, impulsive, and liberated from repressed sexual restraints. For example, Disraeli's *Contarini Fleming* (1832) is built upon the premise that is voiced to Contarini by the oracular figure, Winter: "Never apologize for showing feeling . . . when you do so you apologize for truth" (52; bk. 1, ch. 13). Disraeli may have set the novel in Europe to place it in the tradition of European novels (including Goethe's *Sorrows of Young Werther* and *Wilhelm Meister* and the works of Chateaubriand and Senancour) where feeling has epistemological value as the avenue to truth. Indeed he may have tentatively modeled himself on Goethe, who had recognized Disraeli's genius. Disraeli implies that each man has the capacity to discover his own truth by means of experience, if he is aided by an active imagination. Speaking through Contarini, Disraeli reaffirms the Romantic view that our major source of knowledge is an individual's experience; truth is not in the world outside, but within the self.

Disraeli first left England with his father in summer 1824 for a tour of Belgium and the Rhine valley. The heir to the Romantic cult of abroad and its hyperbolic response to European beauty, according to biographer Robert Blake, Disraeli recalled that it was "when descending those magical waters of [the Rhine]" that he decided not to be a lawyer.[2] Disraeli's letters show how he revels in the variety of foods and wine, and how his imagination and iconoclasm enable him to stand aside and observe (or rather recreate) what he saw—but we must remember that his optics are hardly a photographic eye; his travels are catalysts for discovering aspects of the self as much as experiences that teach him about other cultures. In 1826 Disraeli toured Europe with his friends the Austens: he visited Geneva, Paris, and many of the major cities of Italy. In his imagination, he was following the path of Byron whose genius, boldness, worldliness, and iconoclasm fascinated him: Byron was a model of the man who had written the text of his life. Disraeli actually met Byron's boatman in Geneva and later employed his gondolier as a servant.

Books 6 through 8 of his first novel, *Vivian Grey* (1826–27), are exaggerated versions of what he experienced on the Rhine. For the picaro Vivian, travel provides less a moral education than a panorama of human foibles. Once Vivian reforms and begins his travels, Disraeli uses his perspective to support the narrator's satire of various vices. Book 5 deals with gambling as a form of dissipation; Book 6, Chapter 1 addresses excessive and pointless drinking; Book 6, Chapter 2 satirizes another kind of vanity, that of the world of fashion where the silliest garb and the foolish character Von Aslingen, who has the audacity to wear it, are honored; Book 7, Chapter 3 exposes the intellectual pretensions of philosophers and literary critics; Book 7, Chapter 8 mocks the pretensions of military men; and Book 7, Chapter 9 satirizes the pretensions and wasted energy of fancy dress balls.

Beckendorff, the major figure in Books 6 and 8 of *Vivian Grey*, is a Byronic figure who has a philosophy that Disraeli himself might have articulated at most stages of his career:

A man's fate is his own temper; and according to that will be his opinion as to the particular manner in which the course of events is regulated. A consistent man believes in Destiny, a capricious man in Chance. . . . Man is not the creature of circumstances. Circumstances are the creatures of men. We are free agents, and man is more powerful than matter. I recognize no intervening influence between that of the established course of nature and my own mind. (368–69; bk. 6, ch. 7)

That Beckendorff believes a man may shape his own destiny by the sheer force of his will and personality reflects Disraeli's own view. Indeed, Beckendorff is the successful version of the egoistic alternative that Vivian, but not his creator, had put behind him. For Disraeli, Beckendorff is the mythic European figure, the forceful continental man, who can shape events to the demands of his ego, but who will use power for glorious and inspiring ends.

In 1830 Disraeli visited the Middle East on a journey with William Meredith that lasted almost fifteen months. He visited Gibraltar, Malta, Corfu, Constantinople, Cairo, Alexandria, and Jerusalem, a city which was to be vital to his defining his spiritual identity as a Jewish hero with particular spiritual insight. At his several stops, his behavior and dress were flamboyant. He was learning to impress his various hosts with his energy, wit, and confidence—a lesson for his later political career, for as Blake puts it, "the world will take a man at his own valuation."[3] In Greece he thought of himself as an heir to Odysseus: "Five years of my life have been already wasted and sometimes I think my pilgrimage may be as long as that of Ulysses."[4] His tone also reveals a kind of Romantic listlessness that sometimes interrupts the hyperactive mood of his letters from his Grand Tour.

The trip to the East was a catalyst for *The Wondrous Tale of Alroy* (1833) and provides material for *Contarini Fleming* (1832) and *Tancred* (1847), the last novel of the Young England trilogy. His high-spirited letters on this trip show how Disraeli was able to shape situations to meet his own desires; how his mind darted from one subject to another, and how he saw all external reality in terms of his own experience, as when he described his first view of Jerusalem. "I" is the pronoun that dominates: "I was thunderstruck. I saw before me apparently a gorgeous city. Nothing can be conceived more wild, and terrible, and barren than the surrounding scenery, dark, stony, and severe. . . . Except Athens I never saw anything more essentially striking; no

55

city except that, whose site was so pre-eminently impressive."[5] The journey ended with the blow of Meredith's death due to smallpox; the blow was doubly severe to Disraeli because Meredith was to marry his sister Sarah to whom he was very close.

Disraeli's third novel, *Contarini Fleming*, published in 1832, when he was only twenty-seven, mimes his poetic and psychological development, its external events—particularly those of travel abroad—a correlative to Contarini's state of mind. For Disraeli the Romantic is most concerned with creating a myth of abroad that reflects his own inner feelings. Contarini may nominally have an independent existence but he is inseparable from the complex Disraeli, representing an early version of the political identity Disraeli had envisaged: that of the bold, passionate, imaginative, and original man of action. The plot dramatizes, to quote from Contarini's concluding homily, that, "Circumstances are beyond the control of man; but his conduct is in his own power" (373; bk. 7, ch. 2).

But Disraeli really believed that circumstances could be significantly influenced by character. The novel's last paragraphs make clear that creativity is not necessarily limited to poetry and may include unspecified activities relating to "the political regeneration of the country to which I am devoted" (372; bk. 7, ch. 2). For Contarini that is Italy, but within the novel Disraeli uses Italy as a metaphor for England. Disraeli's prophetic tone is an outgrowth of the strain of moral seriousness that we have noted before. Nor must we forget that the 1830s were the period when Carlyle and others were appointing themselves legislators to a changing world. Disraeli understood that the Reform Act of 1832, which extended the franchise to the middle class, was opening the door to people of ability and energy like himself.

One aspect of Contarini's travels requires further discussion. Contarini, whose father is a Saxon, expresses a characteristic Disraeli theme when he speaks disparagingly of the Franks. He stresses their comparatively recent history as a civilized people and depicts them as visitors to the lands in which they are not the majority. Disraeli's protagonists, from Contarini to Tancred to Lothair, are always more at home in the East than are other Europeans and find there a spiritual equilibrium that they miss in their own culture. Disraeli took great pride in his Jewish heritage. He empathized with those who had a non-European heritage and resented the pretensions of those who thought that the Europeans were the fathers of civilization. This reflected, no doubt, his own frustration at being patronized by Anglo-Saxons whom he regarded as only a few centuries removed from barbarism in contrast to the Semitic people's substantial contribution to Western civilization. At this stage of his career, the glorification of the Arabs was Disraeli's metaphor for illustrating the importance of the Jewish race. We must recall that in the 1830s Arab and Jew more or less peacefully coexisted in the Middle East.

Since Disraeli regarded the Arabs as brothers of the Jews, his glorification of them disguised similar claims for the Jews. The Bedouins, he wrote in *Contarini Fleming*, "combined primitive simplicity of habits with the refined feelings of civilization, and . . . in a great degree, appeared to me to offer an evidence of that community of property and that equality of condition, which have hitherto proved the despair of European sages, and fed only the visions of their fanciful Utopias" (350; bk. 6, ch. 3). Yet, because Disraeli does not build on this concept it does not become part of the novel's imaginative world. Contarini's principles have no relation to the simple nomad precepts of the Bedouins.

Alroy (1833) is Disraeli's ultimate heroic fantasy. He uses the figure of the twelfth-century Jewish prince, David Alroy, as the basis for a tale of Jewish conquest and empire. The historic Alroy was a self-appointed messiah in Kurdistan during a period of severe tribulation and unusual suffering for the Jews, but Disraeli extends Alroy's power and prowess and introduces supernatural machinery and ersatz cabalistic lore and ritual. Undoubtedly the tale of a Jew becoming the most powerful man in an alien land appealed to Disraeli, who at the age of twenty-eight had not yet made his political or artistic reputation. Imagining the vast geographical scope of the East opened his mind to romance and visionary experience.

In *Alroy* Disraeli creates a context where the marvelous is possible. Moreover, he wishes to present himself as an original artist and to flout conventional expectations as to what a work of prose fiction should be. In the original "Preface" to *Alroy*, Disraeli stressed the genius of his own achievement, particularly the prose poetry: the work is written in a prophetic tone and biblical rhythms as if Disraeli were proposing this as his contribution to Jewish lore. The apparently fastidious notes are in the tradition of Talmudic learning that addresses texts as sacred and values scholarship as homage to God. Although the author takes himself as seriously as he ever does in any of his prose fictions, Disraeli's propensity for elaborate description, which provided so much of the fun of the first novels, finds an outlet in the wonders of life in Baghdad, as in the following passage:

> The Princess accepted a spoon made of a single pearl, the long, thin golden handle of which was studded with rubies, and condescended to partake of some saffron soup, of which she was fond. Afterwards she regaled herself with the breast of a cygnet stuffed with almonds, and stewed with violets and cream. . . . Her attention was then engaged with a dish of those delicate ortolans that feed upon the vine-leaves of Schiraz, and with which the Governor of Nishabur took especial care that she should be well provided. Tearing the delicate birds to pieces with her still more delicate

57

fingers, she insisted upon feeding Alroy, who of course yielded to her solicitations. (177; bk. 9, ch. 2)

As Disraeli's letter from the Eastern trip makes clear, the catalyst for such a passage was his travels, but, as always, his imagination embroidered reality.

Disraeli wanted to establish the authenticity of his wondrous tale. For that reason he created as an editor a Jewish historian and scholar. He must have known that very few readers would discover that he had taken liberties with the Alroy legend and really knew only scattered bits and snips of the Cabala tradition. One wonders whether the notes are in part an elaborate joke at the expense of readers who would take the editor and themselves too seriously and accept what is often mumbo jumbo. Is there not a note of deadpan humor in the following from the 1845 preface: "With regard to the super-natural machinery of this romance, it is Cabalistical and correct"?

Interweaving personal recollections of the East with abstruse knowledge of Jewish lore, the fictional editor's notes mediate between the text and the audience. *Alroy* fuses the myths of the Chosen People, of return to the homeland, and of the long-awaited Messiah. As is appropriate in Judaic tradition, Alroy turns out to be a heroic man, but not without human limitations. His demise may be Disraeli's unconscious affirmation of the Jewish belief that the Messiah has not yet come to redeem mankind. When Jabaster rebukes him for not following his mission ("you may be King of Bagdad, but you cannot, at the same time, be a Jew"), a spirit shrieks "MENE, MENE, TEKEL, UPHARSIN," the words upon the wall that Daniel interprets to mean that God had weighed Belshazzar and his king-dom and found them wanting (156–7; bk. 8, ch. 6). Significantly, Alroy regains the Jewish title, Prince of Captivity, after he is overthrown as Caliph. In his final suffering and humility, he has achieved the stature that the Jewish exiled prince, Disraeli's metaphor for himself, deserves.

The Wondrous Tale of Alroy indicates Disraeli's commitment to his Jewish heritage. His surrogate, the narrator, glories in the Jewish victories and in the triumph of the Prince of Captivity over his oppressors and regrets his fall due to pride and worldliness. Disraeli found the medieval world in which Alroy lived an apt model for some of his own values: he saw in that world an emphasis on imagination, emotion, and tradition; respect for political and social hierarchies; and a vital spiritual life. *The Wondrous Tale of Alroy* anticipates Disraeli's attraction to the Middle Ages held up by the Young England movement. Writing of the flowering of medieval Jewry under Alroy enabled him to express his opposition to rationalism and Utilitarianism.

Doubtless Disraeli's journey to Jerusalem stimulated his fantasies of revived Jewish hegemony. Moreover, he believed that the Jews are not only an especially gifted race but the most aristocratic of races. He also believed that the Jewish race is the source of all that is spiritual in European civilization, most notably Christianity. *Alroy*, his only historical romance other than *The Rise of Iskander* (1833), resulted from Disraeli's desire to depict Jews on a heroic scale. But it also derived from the discrepancy between his aspirations and his position in the early 1830s. In *Alroy*'s hyperbolic self-dramatization we detect the thinly disguised voice of the young frustrated Disraeli who has not yet begun to fulfill the "ideal ambition" of which he wrote in his diary. Yet with typical Disraelian emotional resilience, *Alroy*'s early self-pity and ennui give way to the vision of a transformation of his condition: "I linger in this shadowy life, and feed on silent images which no eye but mine can gaze upon, till at length they are invested with all the terrible circumstance of life, and breathe, and act, and form a stirring world of fate and beauty, time, and death, and glory" (8; bk. 1, ch. 1).

Disraeli's work often draws upon the tradition of the imaginary voyage. In this tradition, *The Voyage of Captain Popanilla* (1828) is certainly indebted to Swift's *Gulliver's Travels* and *The Tale of a Tub*, and probably to Samuel Johnson's *Rasselas* and Voltaire's *Zadig* and *Candide* as well. It was in this short work that Disraeli first discovered that he could use fiction to express his political and philosophic views. This prepared him for writing the Young England trilogy of the 1840s, in which ideas and principles are paramount.

In *The Voyage of Captain Popanilla*, Disraeli voices his suspicion of all systems and dogma and mocks exclusive reliance on reason. The novel begins by satirizing Utilitarianism, but soon moves on to include many of the fundamental assumptions on which early nineteenth-century British economic and political life were based. Although Disraeli was later to become an advocate of some of the particular institutions that he ridicules in *The Voyage of Captain Popanilla*, such as the Corn Laws and the colonial system, this early novella foreshadows many of Young England's values, especially its dislike of materialism and expediency. The Young England trilogy develops Popanilla's disdain for a culture that reduces man to a machine and that glorifies reason and logic at the expense of mystery and imagination. Prior to discovering the books of Useful Knowledge, Popanilla seemed to be in a paradise, but man's zeal to improve himself is his curse. After he is captivated by his own wisdom and becomes something of a nuisance, he is sent away by the king. He journeys to Vraibleusia—Disraeli's ironic version of England—where he has a series of adventures which reveal the limitations of some English social and political assumptions.

For Disraeli, Young England was a political program that provided not only an alternative to Utilitarianism and Chartism, but also a practical way of advancing his position. With its advent, for the first time since the beginning of his parliamentary career in 1837, he returned to fiction. He understood the potential of presenting his ideas in an imaginative framework. *Coningsby* (1844) reflects the mixture of idealism, fantasy, and escapism that informed Disraeli's dream that a youthful coterie would revive England. In *Sybil* (1845) he comes to grips with the economic deprivation experienced by the rural and urban poor and appears ambivalent about the notion that one heroic man can make a substantive difference. Finally, in *Tancred* (1847), his mind turns to the East as a fanciful alternative.

One function of the trilogy is to establish the importance of Judaism to Western civilization. He created Sidonia—in the line of the earlier larger-than-life figures from his imaginative, mythic abroad, such as Contarini and Alroy—as a mouthpiece to argue in *Coningsby* and in the first two books of *Tancred* for the historical significance of the Jewish people. Tancred's pilgrimage to Jerusalem in search of Semitic spirituality—a pilgrimage undertaken at the urging of Sidonia—and his discovery of the Hebraic basis of Christianity dramatize Disraeli's intense personal need to reconcile his Jewish origins with the Christian religion. He believed that Christianity was completed Judaism, although he may have unconsciously taken this position because of his need to justify his own conversion. He argued in *Lord George Bentinck* (1852) that the Jew converted to Christianity professes the "whole Jewish religion and believes in Calvary as well as Sinai" (324). In his study of Disraeli's Jewish aspect, Cecil Roth writes:

> But it seems as though the Christianity which he professed, quite sincerely, in his own mind was not that of the established Church, but a Judaic ethical monotheism, of which the Jew Jesus was the last and greatest exponent. As he put it, Christianity was developed Judaism and Judaism a preparation for Christianity. Jesus was the ideal scion of the Jewish people . . . in whose teachings the Mosaic faith received its culmination, the New Testament being the perfection, and climax, of the Old.[6]

Disraeli's self-confidence in part depended upon his belief that the Jews deserved esteem as an especially gifted *race*. Often, and with considerable justification, Disraeli is accused of political expedience and intellectual legerdemain. But the defense of Jews was an article of faith. Disraeli risked his chances for leadership when he insisted in 1847 that his friend Baron Lionel de Rothschild be allowed to take his seat in Parliament without taking the Parliamentary oath "on the true faith of a Christian."[7] On that occasion, he invoked arguments similar to those that appeared in both

Tancred and later in *Lord George Bentinck* to support the Baron's position.

The comprehensive political consciousness of the narrator of the Young England trilogy is the intellectual and moral position toward which the hero of each volume develops. The narrator traces the quest of each hero— Egremont, Coningsby, and Tancred—to discover the appropriate values by which each can order his own life and fulfill the prominent public role that he feels himself obliged to play. Each of the protagonists overcomes doubt and anxiety, because he convinces himself that he possesses the unique intellectual and moral potential to shape not merely his own life but the very historical process. Each protagonist's quest is conceived as a heroic attempt to discover the values essential for a new breed of political leaders who will recognize both the supremacy of the monarchy and the importance of serving the common people. Coningsby's ambition and self-confidence; Egremont's compassion and consciousness of the miseries of others, and Tancred's spiritual faith and willingness to act on behalf of his beliefs are the ideals to which others (Disraeli's aristocratic audience and hence political leaders) must strive.

In *Tancred*, the concluding novel of the political trilogy, Disraeli uses travel to Jerusalem to address the spiritual problems in England. Declining to enter Parliament when he comes of age, Tancred, the only son of the Duke and Duchess of Bellamont, undertakes a journey to Palestine. There he has a vision of the angel of Arabia who urges him to "announce the sublime and solacing doctrine of theoretic equality" (291; bk. 4, ch. 7). In part, Disraeli is engaged in defending his own Jewish heritage. As Blake has written:

> His theological ideas were, in reality, the realization of his own peculiar psychological dilemma. It suited him to blur as far as possible the differences between the Jewish and Christian faiths. He almost seemed at times to regard Christ's Jewishness as more important than His divinity. To him the Jew is a proto-Christian, and Christianity is completed Judaism.[8]

Tancred is in some ways a retelling of *Alroy*, for fantasies of conquering the world oscillate with loving a Jewish woman named Eva.

That the angel's revelation is not tested as a viable system is a failure of *Tancred* which severely affects the argument of the entire trilogy. The novel does not explore the meaning of the angel's message as a plausible alternative to political intrigue in Asia or to the decline of the monarchy and the church in England. Disraeli's dramatization of Tancred's communion with the angel reflects the compelling urge to experience the presence of a higher being which permeated the Victorian period. While for some readers the ending is comic, Tancred's quest is not as bizarre as it seems. As Élie Halévy notes, when writing about religious questions in the 1840s:

> The belief was beginning to spread in British Protestant circles that the Second Advent of Jesus to judge the living and the dead must be preceded by a return of the Jews to Jerusalem, and the rebuilding of Solomon's Temple that on the very spot where the Saviour had been crucified they might be confuted, converted and pardoned.[9]

Disraeli's readers would have thought it was particularly appropriate that Tancred discovers the Jewish origins of Christianity in Jerusalem. But the shibboleth of theocratic equality does not justify the angel's appearance, and the angel's words are vague, if not bathetic:

> The equality of man can only be accomplished by the sovereignty of God. The longing for fraternity can never be satisfied but under the sway of a common father. The relations between Jehovah and his creatures can be neither too numerous nor too near. In the increased distance between God and man have grown up all those developments that have made life mournful. Cease, then, to seek in a vain philosophy the solution of a social problem that perplexes you. Announce the sublime and solacing doctrine of theocratic equality. (*Tancred* 291; bk. 4, ch. 7)

Tancred becomes a ludicrous parody of, rather than—as Disraeli intended—an heir to, those biblical heroes to whom God and his angels spoke. Does not the book's ending imply Disraeli's failure to integrate a spiritual vision into his political ideology as well as a dwindling away or at least a deflection from his imaginative goals?

Despite some continuity with its predecessors, *Tancred* does not fulfill its function as the climactic volume of the political trilogy. Originally conceived as a novel about reviving the sacred position of the Anglican church by rediscovering its spiritual principles, *Tancred* becomes, whether Disraeli intended it or not, a kind of clumsy metaphor for the discovery of the divine within oneself. *Tancred* reflects Disraeli's continuing admiration for romance plots. Like Byron's heroes Childe Harold and Don Juan, or Sir Walter Scott's heroes in his historical romances, Tancred inhabits an imagined world where day-to-day details rarely intrude into his quest. As an imaginary voyage, *Tancred* is loosely held together by the hero's journey, which introduces him to incredible people and fantastic places. The novel begins in the present in England, but Tancred's crusade is virtually a journey backward in time; he discovers remote cultures with religious beliefs and political customs that are now regarded condescendingly by Christian England: Judaism, the pagan worship of the Greek gods, and feudalism.

Tancred does develop some of the social and political themes begun in *Coningsby* and *Sybil*, however. Tancred journeys to Jerusalem after convincing himself of the superficiality of contemporary English civilization and the futility of its politics. Disraeli frequently uses foreign scenes in his novels as a metaphor for English issues, as a kind of political parable. In other words, imaginary versions of "abroad" are tropes to crystallize issues on which he wished to speak. The political world of the Mideast parodies the intrigues of English politics; the major difference is that weapons rather than votes are the method of settling political disagreements. Syria's history parodies England's—a civil war follows the deposition of a strong monarch and, when the feudal (or territorial) system is endangered, monarchist sentiments revive. In the Lebanese mountains Tancred discovers the mirror of Young England's dreams: "a proud, feudal aristocracy; a conventual establishment . . . a free and armed peasantry . . . [and] bishops worthy of the Apostles" (338: bk. 4, ch. 12). Predictably, the Young Syria Movement appeared in 1844 to "profess nationality as their object" and to plead for the restoration of a strong monarchy (214; bk. 5, ch. 1).

Despite the 1870 "General Preface" that sees the Young England trilogy as a unified political vision, we should not forget the intensely personal tone of Disraeli's later letters. The following comment is quite typical: "My books are the history of my life—I don't mean a vulgar photograph of incidents, but the psychological development of my character." Like other Victorians, Disraeli sought for absolutes in a world of moral turmoil. That Disraeli's narrators and major characters speak *ex cathedra* in generalizations and abstractions may derive from the author's desire to emulate in the fabric of his fiction the scope and seriousness of Victorian philosophical and religious tracts. But behind the dramatization of the education of Tancred, Coningsby, and Egremont lies Disraeli's quest for the principles with which he could structure his public life.

Disraeli wrote his late novel *Lothair* (1870) to examine the implications of a variety of nineteenth-century political, social, and religious systems. In these later years, he had come to see England as a middle ground between the political extremes active in Europe. The title character of *Lothair* again travels abroad to increase his experience. He discovers a Europe dominated by a military struggle between the democratic forces of revolution and those of conservative but manipulative Roman Catholicism. By contrast, Palestine represents the ideal of spiritual wisdom.

Lothair is an orphan who succeeds to a huge inheritance at his twenty-first birthday. His father had appointed as his guardians his Scottish Presbyterian uncle, Lord Cullodan, and Cardinal Grandison, who wishes to convert Lothair to Catholicism. The book opens at Brentham, where Lothair is captivated by the gracious, if somewhat idle, life of the Duke and his family; he is also enchanted with the Duke's daughter, Lady Corisande, to whom he would have proposed had the Duchess permitted it. The Duke and his family are Anglicans. The Cardinal introduces Lothair to the St. Jerome family, including the beautiful Clare Arundel (who, like Sybil, plans on becoming a nun), because he knows that the intense spiritual life of Vauxe will be more appealing if accompanied by sexual attraction. At Vauxe, Lothair is exposed to the ritual and ceremony of Catholicism as well as to the subtle arguments of the priests.

But Lothair also becomes acquainted with Theodora, who is not only indifferent to religion but has been the inspiration for the revolutionary Mary Anne societies and is active in revolutionary movements throughout Europe. Lothair is physically attracted to Theodora. With his loyalties divided among three women and three distinct sets of values, he celebrates his coming of age with a lavish party at his Muriel estate, where Corisande helps foil the plot to convert him to Catholicism. But Theodora wins his loyalty, and he vows to devote his life to her. He goes to Italy and enlists in battle beside Theodora and her colleague, General Bruges, in opposition to the forces sponsored by the Pope. In the fight, she is killed and Lothair is seriously wounded. He is nursed to health by Roman Catholics in Rome at the St. Jerome Palace under the direction of Clare Arundel. He agrees to take part in a Catholic service at which she gives thanks for his restored health, but he discovers that this service is part of a scheme to win him to the church.

He eventually reaches Syria, where he meets Paraclete, another of Disraeli's wisdom figures, who, after espousing Disraeli's view that God shapes history by assigning genius to particular races, assures him that despite what the Catholics imply, there is more than one true faith: "In my Father's house are many mansions" (411–12; ch. 77). Eventually Lothair returns to England, marries Corisande, and embraces the Anglican church. But the very circularity of form in which Lothair returns to his starting point, Brentham, to claim his original beloved, Corisande, undercuts the idea that he has progressed. No one, including Lothair, appears ready to give the ship of state real direction.

Disraeli means to serve up more than an intellectual smorgasbord in which the reader is exposed to various positions: *Lothair* discriminates the wheat from the chaff within each doctrine. Although the novel goes to great length to expose Catholic guile, Disraeli still admires the religious intensity of Catholic ceremonies and rituals. While the Anglican church seems more moderate in its religious commitment and more concerned with this world than the next, it is a national church which has united and may continue to unite England. It may be a virtue that it does not overwhelm the lives of its devotees and seems to make rather gentle demands upon them. It allows even its most devoted followers to love passionately. If Theodora and the Mary Anne societies ask that one give one's life to their cause, they nevertheless offer solace—no different from that offered by traditional religion—to people to whom the wealthy and powerful, and perhaps the organized churches, do not give their full attention. Yet although Lothair is too submissive and too emotionally captivated to withstand Theodora's influence, he intellectually understands the problem of apotheosizing one's conscience: "Your conscience may be divine . . . and I believe it is; but the consciences of other persons are not divine, and what is to guide them, and what is to prevent or to mitigate the evil they would perpetuate?" (163; ch. 31).

By 1870, Disraeli was far more a relativist than in the Young England novels. He was tolerant of different value systems but critical of duplicity and self-indulgence. While not unsympathetic to Theodora's view that a man's conscience is his church, a view that reflects his own youthful attitude, Disraeli now makes clear the necessity of a national church not only as a political institution, but as the representation of a controlling deity to which a people is morally responsible. The Disraeli of the 1870s knew the danger of each man's acting according to his own conscience.

Lothair's popularity can be attributed not only to Disraeli's status as a former prime minister but to its anti-Catholicism. Contemporary readers would have recognized his references to the conversion of the Marquess of Bute, which intensified the pervasive anxiety that the Anglican church would be rent by an exodus to Catholicism. Disraeli feared that one of the pillars of the English social and political system was variously threatened by Catholicism, popular political movements, and atheism. He had convinced himself that Irish disestablishment was a threat to England's national church. It was not the dogma of the Anglican church with which he was concerned, but the substantial contribution that a national church with allegiance only to the crown and to the people made to England's political health. That the England depicted by Disraeli in *Lothair* is torn by religious dissension and lacks political direction reflects some bitterness over his last tumultuous months as prime minister in 1868. He had lost office in the 1868 election because Gladstone had come out clearly for the disestablishment of the Church of England in Ireland and was supported in that position by Disraeli's ally, Archbishop Manning, who abandoned Disraeli as soon as he saw that the liberals under Gladstone would do better for the Catholics. Disraeli's disillusionment with Roman Catholicism had been intensified in 1868 because he not only felt that he had been betrayed by Manning (the model for Cardinal Grandison), whose support he had for a Catholic university subsidy before Gladstone won the Archbishop's favor by sponsoring Irish disestablishment, but he also probably resented the Catholics for causing the difficulties in Ireland which led to his downfall.

But in 1874 the Tories won a clear victory, and Disraeli began his second term as Prime Minister. He became the advocate of Empire, purchased the Suez Canal, and in 1876 made Victoria Empress of India. In the same year Queen Victoria raised him to the peerage as the first (and only) Earl of Beaconsfield, and he moved over to the House of Lords. In 1878 he played a leading part at the Congress of Berlin in the renewed system of European power brokerage. It was as if he had really fulfilled not only his heroic fantasies of power—fantasies bred in the East, dramatized in *Alroy* and *Tancred*, and now operative in the East—but also his boldest views of himself as a sophisticated "continental" figure: a Beckendorff and, more importantly, a Sidonia.

NOTES

Page references throughout the text refer to the readily accessible Hughenden Edition (London: 1881). The source for the original edition of *Vivian Grey* is the less accessible but authoritative Centenary Edition, ed. Lucian Wolf (London: 1904–5). Unfortunately only two volumes ever appeared in this edition.

1. "Multilated Diary," Hughenden Papers, A/III.C.
2. Robert Blake, *Disraeli* (London: 1966) 22.
3. Blake 61.
4. Qtd. in Blake 65.
5. *Home Letters, Written in 1830 and 1831*, ed. Ralph Disraeli (London: 1885) 118–19.
6. Cecil Roth, *Benjamin Disraeli* (New York: 1952) 79.
7. See Blake 258–61.
8. Bclake 204.
9. Élie Halévy, *Victorian Years 1841–1895*, trans. E.I. Watkin (New York: 1951) 62.

NEWMAN AND THE MEDITERRANEAN

Ian Ker, College of St. Thomas

John Henry Newman's voyage to the Mediterranean in 1832–33 was one of the most important events of his life. Not only did it have a significant influence on the development of his religious views, as well as on the beginning of the Oxford Movement, but it elicited from Newman some of his most fascinating and vivid writings. The many lengthy letters he wrote home, together with the autobiographical account he subsequently wrote of his traumatic illness in Sicily, apart from being documents of the highest literary interest, surely deserve a special place in the literature of travel.

At the beginning of September 1832 Newman was invited by his friend Hurrell Froude to join him and his father on a Mediterranean cruise. Tempting as the invitation was, it "quite unsettled" him. There were several obvious objections to being away for so long a period of time, and he was also nervous about his health after a recent minor breakdown he had suffered. On the other hand, the prospect of traveling abroad for the first time was irresistible. He was "suspicious of becoming narrow-minded," and wanted at least "to experience the feeling and the trial of expansiveness of views, if it were but to be able to *say* I had, and to know how to meet it in the case of others."[1] This was especially important for a thinker who always stressed the importance of having a "view" of a subject, while consistently condemning all kinds of what he called "viewiness" (*The Idea of a University* 12). In the end, the chance "to enlarge one's ideas . . . and to have the name of a travelled man" proved decisive (99).

On Monday, 3 December 1832, Newman left Oxford for Falmouth. From Whitchurch he wrote to his mother that he was beginning "one of the few recreations, which I can hope, nay or desire, to have in this world." But he did not intend the forthcoming holiday to be "any thing else than a preparation and strengthening-time for future toil—rather, I should rejoice to think that I was in this way steeling myself in soul and body for it" (123). As he was waiting for the mail coach to take him to Falmouth, he wrote the poem "Angelic Guidance," which speaks of "'the vision' which haunted

"Mount Tabor, from the Plain of Esdraelon," from David Roberts RA, *The Holy Land* (1842)

me"; leaving Oxford "for foreign countries and an unknown future," he "naturally was led to think that some inward changes, as well as some larger course of action, were coming upon me" (*Apologia* 41). The two predictions turned out to be remarkably prophetic.

On 8 December they set sail from Falmouth on board the packet *Hermes*. Three days later they caught sight of the Spanish mountains—"the first foreign land I ever saw," Newman wrote home excitedly (129). A few days after they came in view of the coast of Portugal—"in that indescribable peculiarity of foreign scenery which paintings attempt." He did not know if the cause was the "clearness of the air," but it was "as different from England as possible." The sight of "the first foreign soil I have come near" was "like a vision," he exclaimed. It seemed incredible that "scenes so unlike home should be so near home"; they were after all still in Europe (138). They had a brief "wonderful" visit to Gibraltar, but Newman was strangely disconcerted by the sights, as he explained uneasily to his sister Harriet:

> I no longer wonder at younger persons being carried away with travelling, and corrupted—for certainly the illusions of the world's magic can hardly be fancied while one remains at home. I never felt any pleasure or danger from the common routine of pleasures, which most persons desire and suffer from—balls, or pleasure parties, or sights—but I think it does require strength of mind to keep the thoughts [where] they should be while the varieties of strange sights, political moral and physical, are passed before the eyes. (146)

He was soon to come to the conclusion that foreign travel was "indefinitely more delightful in retrospect even than in actual performance" (266), on the ground that "the gratification of travelling" consisted "chiefly in the retrospect—there is far too great hurry and excitement at the time to leave room for much actual enjoyment—but afterwards, the memory of every moment and of every little incident from without, awakens strange feelings of regret and almost tenderness." Not only was it impossible to "realize such things at the moment," but there was also the unreality of seeing sights without a proper perspective, for "we cannot recollect all the associations with which the place is really connected in our minds." The difficulty of deciding the merits of traveling had, in a way characteristic of Newman, turned into a problem of reality: if sightseeing was inevitably unreal at the time, it could become real by recollection after the event. He compared the "pure trouble" of traveling "while it lasts" with the "anxiety" he experienced when writing: it was something one wanted "to have got thro'" and which "has its enjoyment" in the end result (253–55).

To his mother he wrote that, "however interested" he had been in what he had seen, he did not think that he would "ever for an instant" not have "preferred . . . to find myself suddenly back again in the midst of those employments and pleasures which befall me in the course of ordinary duty." He had "good hope" that he would not be "unsettled" by his "present wanderings." Resolutely, he dismissed the temptation of "all these strange sights" as "but vanities, which bring no sensible good, and scarcely affect the imagination." His protestation of indifference is partly belied by the reflection that immediately follows:

What has inspired me with all sort of strange reflections . . . is the thought that I am on the Mediterranean—for how much is implied in that one circumstance! Consider how the Mediterranean has been in one sense the seat of the most celebrated Empires and events, which have had their day upon its coasts—think of the variety of men, famous in every way in history to whom the sea has been known—Here the Romans engaged the Carthaginians—here the Phoenicians traded—here Jonah was in the storm—here St Paul was shipwrecked—here the great Athanasius voyaged to Rome and to Constantinople.

The thought of the great Greek Father of the Church further prompted him to offer his mother some verses which begin with the prayer for an Anglican Athanasius:

When shall our northern Church her champion see,
    Raised by high heaven's decree,
To shield the ancient faith at his own harm? (155–56)

When reading the Fathers in Oxford, he had been unable to help comparing unfavorably the "divided and threatened" Church of England with "that fresh vigorous Power" of the first centuries. The heroism of the early Church had both "exalted and abashed" him:

I felt affection for my own Church, but not tenderness; I felt dismay at her prospects, anger and scorn at her do-nothing perplexity. I thought that if Liberalism once got a footing within her, it was sure of the victory in the event. I saw that Reformation principles were powerless to rescue her. As to leaving her, the thought never crossed my imagination; still I ever kept before me that there was something greater than the Established Church, and that was the Church Catholic and Apostolic, set up from the beginning, of which she was but the local presence and organ.

70

He had already decided before leaving England that there was "need of a second reformation" (*Apologia* 40). If he was to have any hand in the work himself, he could not deny that the scenes in which he now found himself, however distracting from the point of view of spiritual composure and concentration, were full of imagination and stimulus for the battles and conflicts that lay ahead.

After spending a wretched Christmas anchored off Malta (they could not go ashore because of the cholera epidemic), they set sail for Corfu. Now he was "full of joy to overflowing—for I am in the Greek sea, the scene of old Homer's song and of the histories of Thucydides" (167). Finding himself close to Ithaca, the home of Odysseus, he had difficulty expressing his feelings: "They were not caused by any classical association, but by the thought that I now saw before me in real shape those places which had been the earliest vision of my childhood" (172). The *Odyssey* was the first book (in Pope's translation) which he had "ever learned from, as a child" (193). When they reached Corfu, he was "astonished" to realize how little Greek authors like Homer and Thucydides had said about the magnificent scenery.

While he was in Corfu he tried to find out about the Greek Orthodox Church. He heard the priests were ignorant but "moral in their lives." He suspected that "outward ceremonies are the substitute for holiness, as among the Jews," but in one country church he visited he found "little objectionable . . . and much that was very good" in the devotional books he looked at (181). While the strict fasts of the Orthodox impressed him—they seemed to him to be "the distinguishing feature of the Greek communion as Masses etc is of the Latin"—nevertheless he considered that "they both answer the same purpose, and are a substitute apparently for moral obedience, and an opiate to the conscience" (239).

They returned to Malta on 10 January 1833, when they had to go into quarantine. Newman felt "much more comfortable now than on that restless element which is the type of human life, and much less wearied in this prison than when seeing sights" (187). Shut up in his Maltese prison, he felt at peace and certainly "not cut out for a great politician, or as any instrument of change little or great in the Church, for it makes me wretched to be in motion." Such a disclaimer was often to come to his lips in the course of his life, but the reality was as often the reverse, as the admission which follows suggests: "Yet I suppose in these times we must all of us more or less expect to find our duty lie in agitation and tumult." Indeed, his own trials on board ship, "as I lay tossed in my luxurious berth in the steam-packet," had made him "realize somewhat of the cross of that blessed Apostle who was in watchfulness and weariness so often." St Paul's voyage to Rome had become real in all its arduous actuality for the first time. In the same way, actually seeing Greece had "thrown a new light upon the whole of its history"; the country was so mountainous he could not conceive how communication had been possible, "how they ever could make war—how they ever extended the march of intellect." He also now saw a value in the new realism which travel had given him: "I think travelling a good thing for a secluded man, not so much as showing him the world, as in realizing to him the limited sphere of his own powers." He could not think of "one fact or impression about mankind" which he had gained as a result of his experiences, but he had "deepened" his "conviction of the intellectual weakness which attaches to a mere reading man—his inability to grasp and understand and appropriate things which befall him in life" (193–94). A conviction of the unreality of deriving a religion from books was always to be an important element in Newman's thinking. Some of the doctrines he had first imbibed from reading Evangelical authors had received their concrete refutation several years before in the form of the real people he had encountered when working for the first time on a parish after ordination. Now also he was in a position to compare the early Church, which he had read about in the Fathers, with the actual "unreformed" Churches of the East and West, which traced their origins to that early, undivided Church, and particularly, of course, with the Roman Church, which his reading as an Evangelical had convinced him was anti-Christian. An important part of this last conviction was to dissolve under the experience of seeing what sort of people real Roman Catholics actually were.

A letter written to his mother from Malta shows how ambivalent his feelings were becoming about these great "unreformed" Churches. "Every thing" in the Roman Catholic cathedral he found "admirable, if it did not go quite so far—it is a beautiful flower run to seed." He insisted he had not changed his views, for although he could not but admire what he saw, "it is fearful to have before one's eyes the perversion of all the best, the holiest, the most exalted feelings of human nature." More interesting was the impact of experiencing the Orthodox Church for the first time; he wondered uneasily, "what answer do Protestants make to the *fact* of the Greek Church invoking Saints, overhonoring the Virgin, and substituting ceremonies for a reasonable service, which they say are the *prophetic* marks of Antichrist?" The next day, however, was Sunday and the nostalgic thought of an English Sunday steadied his feelings: "We do not know how great our privileges are—all the quiet and calmness connected with our services etc is so beautiful in the memory and so soothing after the sight of that most excited religion which is around me—statues of Madonnas and Saints in the Streets, etc etc. A more poetical but not less jading stimulant than the pouring-forth in a Baptist Chapel" (198–99). The attraction of Anglican sobriety and decorum had reasserted itself.

They left Malta on 7 February. After a visit to Sicily, which "filled"

Newman "with inexpressible rapture" and to which he felt "drawn as by a loadstone" (213), they reached Naples on the 14th. Visits to Catholic churches led him to think that the Latin Mass was "less reverend than the Greek, being far more public—there is no skreen—the high altar is in sight" (214). As a city, Naples did not particularly impress its English visitors: it was a *"watering place"* and, as such, Newman remarked with puritanical feeling, was "a place for *animal* gratification" (226).

Rome, which they reached on 2 March, was very different—"a wonderful place" and the "first city" to impress Newman (227). Indeed, it was "of all cities the first" and all the cities he had seen were "but as dust, even dear Oxford inclusive, compared with its majesty and glory." But his feelings were again very mixed. After all, Rome bore an "awful" aspect as "the great Enemy of God"; its "immense . . . ruins, the thought of the purposes to which they were dedicated, the sight of the very arena where [St.] Ignatius [of Antioch] suffered, the columns of heathen pride with the inscriptions still legible . . . brand it as the vile tool of God's wrath and again Satan's malice." From the religious point of view, too, "pain and pleasure" were "mixed": it was "strange to be standing in the city of the apostles, and among the tombs of martyrs and saints." With a glance at the situation at home, Newman thought he detected the "timidity, indolence, and that secular spirit which creeps on established religion every where" (232). He tried to explain his curious "mixture of feelings, partly such as those with which one would approach a corpse, and partly those which would be excited by the sight of the spirit which had left it": he had not seen much of the city, "but the effect of every part is so vast and overpowering—there is such an air of greatness and repose cast over the whole, and . . . there are such traces of long sorrow and humiliation, suffering, punishment and decay" (233–34).

Again and again in his letters to England, he spoke of his "mingled feelings" about Rome, a conflict which induced a kind of emotional and intellectual paralysis:

You are in the place of martyrdom and burial of Apostles and Saints — you have about you the buildings and sights they saw — and you are in the city to which England owes the blessing of the gospel — But then on the other hand the superstitions;—or rather, what is far worse, the solemn reception of them as an essential part of Christianity—but then again the extreme beauty and costliness of the Churches—and then on the contrary the knowledge that the most famous was built (in part) by the sale of indulgences—Really this is a cruel place.—There is more and more to be seen and thought of, daily—it is a mine of all sorts of excellences, but the very highest.

He continued to analyze his feelings about foreign travel. He felt that he had "learned thus much by travelling, to think all places about the same, which I had no notion of before—I never could believe that horses, dogs, men and houses were the same in other countries as at home—not that I exactly doubted it, but my imagination could not embrace the notion." The wonder of sightseeing was strangely self-destructive: "It is astonishing how little it seems to have been at places when one *has* been at them." Walking round Corfu and Rome "and having the same thoughts, feelings, and bodily sensations as at home" made it hard to believe that one was actually in a foreign country. In a way, therefore, travel had an anti-romantic effect, for it "in a measure destroyed the romance which I threw around every thing I had not myself witnessed. . . ." The romance that there was necessarily short-lived: Newman did not, for example, want to see Egesta again if possible, a place which had moved him more than any other except Ithaca, "lest I should get familiar with it—as it is I have something for memory to dwell upon—the first impression of things is the poetical one." He also maintained that he had "experienced none of that largeness and expansion of mind" which he had been told he would "get from travelling" (240–42, 45). But the claim was misleading: his religious vision had certainly been dramatically widened, and there is no question that his imagination, if not his mind, had been powerfully affected by witnessing at first hand that Church which his early Evangelical formation had convinced him was the Church of the Antichrist, a view which in a more modified and less extreme version he still held. Nevertheless, he could not disabuse himself of the deeply ingrained belief that the city of Rome itself was "one of the 4 beasts" (249). As to Roman Catholicism, on the other hand, he carefully assured one of his sisters that while there were "great appearances . . . of piety in the Churches," there was no denying that "as a system," it was a "corrupt religion" (265).

On the feast of the Annunciation, Newman went to High Mass in the Church of Santa Maria Sopra Minerva. The Pope and his "court" were present. Newman was scandalized by the "unedifying dumbshow," and he could not "endure the Pope's foot being kissed, considering how much is said in Scripture about the necessity of him that is greatest being as the least, nor do I even tolerate him being carried in on high." But while he knew that, as "one of the 4 monsters of Daniel's vision," Rome was "a doomed city," and he began "to think that it was a sin, as such, in the Church's uniting itself with that enemy of God, who from the beginning sat on the 7 hills, with an enchantress's cup, as the representative and instrument of the Evil Principle":

> yet as I looked on, and saw all Christian acts performing the Holy Sacrament offered up, and the blessing given, and recollected I was in

church, I could only say in very perplexity my own words, "How shall I name thee, Light of the wide west, or heinous error-seat?"—and felt the force of the parable of the tares—who can separate the light from the darkness but the Creator Word who prophesied their union? And so I am forced to leave the matter, not at all seeing my way out of it.—How shall I name thee? (267–68)

He was to ponder that question for a long time to come, but there is no doubt that the image of the "Antichrist" had at least been dented. Recognizing both the revulsion and the attraction in him, he tried to distinguish between "the Roman C. system" which he had "ever detested" and "the *Catholic* system" to which he was "more attached than ever." He was impressed by the clerical students he saw ("so innocent and bright, poor boys") and, while he feared that "there are very grave and farspreading scandals among the Italian priesthood, and there is mummery in abundance—yet there is a deep substratum of true Christianity" (273–74).

He was sorry to leave Rome at the beginning of April. In leaving Rome, "not as a city, but as a scene of sacred history," he felt he had left behind "a part" of his heart. Sadly he sighed to his sister:

Oh that Rome were not Rome; but I seem to see as clear as day that a union with her is *impossible*. She is the cruel Church—asking of us impossibilities, excommunicating us for disobedience, and now watching and exulting over our approaching overthrow. (282, 284)

He had, however, now come to the conclusion that there was an important distinction between Rome as a place and Rome as a church: it did not follow from the fact that there was "really a sort of Genius Loci which enthralls the Church which happens to be there" that the church itself was the "new form of the old evil" of ancient Rome. Not unnaturally, he was perplexed: "how a distinction is to be drawn between two powers, spiritual and devilish, which are so strongly united, is as much beyond our imagination, as it was beyond the power of the servants in the parable to pull up the tares from the wheat." Indeed, the parable struck him as an astonishing prophecy of the scandals of the Papacy—a point he would one day decide proved the opposite of what he now thought it proved. As he was to explain in the *Apologia*, his "imagination" had been "impressed" and his "heart was touched also" by what he had seen of Roman Catholicism, but in spite of his "tender feelings," his "reason" had not been "affected at all"—"My judgment was against her, when viewed as an institution, as truly as it ever had been." The Roman Church seemed quite clearly to be a continuation of the old Rome—it even used the same language as "its bond of union *as* an Empire."

Its "policy" was "crafty, relentless, inflexible," it sacrificed "the good of its members" to its own "splendour and strength" as in enforcing celibacy on its clergy, and it upheld a "polytheistic, degrading, idolatrous" religion. The obvious goodness, on the other hand, of so much that he had seen merely proved that it was the "slave" of the evil spirit which still ruled Rome. He was confident that the day would come "when the captive will be set free"; in the meantime it was all very distressing and puzzling (288–89; *Apologia* 58–59).

He had decided to make a return trip to Sicily—"Think what Spring is! and in Sicily! it is the nearest approach to Paradise, of which sinful man is capable" (266). He felt

> drawn by an irresistible attraction to the fair levels and richly verdured heights of Sicily. What a country it is! a shadow of Eden, so as at once to enrapture and to make me melancholy. It will be a vision for my whole life; and, though I should not choose, I am not sorry to go alone, in order, as Wordsworth would say, to commune with high nature. (277)

The Froudes left for Marseilles, while Newman set off for Naples. He was now by himself for the first time in a foreign country. He wrote to his sister Jemima that for a moment he half-repented his decision: "I was going among strangers into a wild country, to live a wild life, to travel in solitudes and to sleep in dens of the earth; and all for what? for the gratification of an imagination . . . drawn by a strange love of Sicily to gaze upon its cities and mountains" (282). One interesting reason he had for going by himself to Sicily was that he thought it was no "bad thing to be cast upon oneself as a discipline—for no one can tell what may happen in time to come" (245). But although it would be a valuable "privation" to be without companions, he could not deny that he was "drawn back by an irresistible love of Sicily, of which I have seen just so much as to wish to see more." The special attraction of the island was not just its ancient history, but its peculiar symbolic value as a monument to paganism: "it is so beautiful and so miserable that it is an emblem of its own past history, i.e. the history of heathen countries, being a most noble record stone over the grave of high hopes and aims, pride, sin, and disappointment" (247–48). He was looking forward excitedly to seeing the island again:

> Its history begins with the earliest times and lasts thro' both Greek and Roman annals, down to the eras of the Saracen invasions and Norman chivalry. In it I read the history of all that is great and romantic in human

nature, and the man in all his strength and weakness, with high aims and manifold talents corrupted by sin and humbled by continual failure.

Apart from Rome, he had not been particularly interested in seeing Italy, "but Greece has ever made my heart beat, and Sicily is Greece in a way." Its ancient Doric settlements seemed "so wonderful" and the remains were better preserved than those of mainland Greece; there was "something mysterious about them—their power is prior to the time of history." Observing that "the simplicity of their architecture seems to imply a corresponding simplicity in their religion," he wondered "whether holy ones did not walk the rounds of the primitive temples, till the pride of science and literature extinguished the rays which had been providentially left among them." Then there was the sheer beauty of the island, which was "really a strange incentive" to revisit it, particularly at that time of year: "Spring has been to me the most elevating and instructive time of the year—somehow it whispers of the good which is to come, when our bodies are to rise—and it throws the thoughts back upon Eden we have lost, and makes the heart contrite by the contrast between what is and what might be." He hastened to add that he despised "sentimentality" and was "up in arms against the Shelleyism of the day, which resolves religion into feeling, and makes it possible for bad men to have holy thoughts. Doubtless no religious emotion is worth a straw, or rather it is pernicious, if it does not lead to *practice*." But rejection of a religion of feeling (whether the result of Romantic sensibility or Evangelical emotionalism) did not mean that psychological factors were irrelevant to action. And this, interestingly enough, was Newman's final justification for his return to Sicily by himself, an adventure about which he not unnaturally had misgivings, particularly in view of his reservations about the value of travel in general:

Good thoughts are only good so far as they are taken as means to an exact *obedience* or at least this is the chief part of their goodness. Do not think me to be carried away with the mere poetical pleasure of an indulged imagination. . . . In truth I find nothing is supporting in trouble and anxiety as bright seasons which remain in the memory and are recalled at pleasure. Why was St Paul caught into the third heaven but that he might have a vision to soothe him amid the dust of the world? and when it is put into our power to see scenes, which speak more of God than any thing which is not miraculous, surely we may innocently take them and use them with thankfulness. Thus I have reasoned with myself, and I think justly, when the time and expenses of my expedition seemed at first to shake me as devoted to a mere selfish gratification. But it is not so. Evil is before us. Clouds seem to gather round the Church. No one can tell what his lot will be. Certainly a Clergyman's office will be no pleasant one. Another holiday I shall never have. (291–92)

The wild primeval landscapes of Sicily might seem to have little to do with the Whig reformers at home, but they were to recreate and reinvigorate him for the battles in defense of the Church of England that lay ahead.

On 19 April the wind at last blew fair and Newman embarked on an English sailing brig bound for Messina. The day after arriving he set off by foot toward the south of the island. He "felt amused and almost ashamed" to be "the chief of a cavalcade" consisting of a servant called Gennaro from Naples and a muleteer with mules for the baggage. It seemed a somewhat "princely retinue," and the sight of his unclerical shadow, clad as he was in "a straw hat and a flannel jacket," only added to his discomfiture (302). When they reached Taormina, the view from the ancient theater was "a nearer approach to seeing Eden, than anything [he] . . . had conceived possible." The magnificent scenery even had a spiritual effect on him: "I felt for the first time in my life with my eyes open that I must be better and more religious, if I lived there." Words practically failed him as he attempted vainly to describe the astonishing panorama: "It realized all one had read of in books of the perfection of scenery—a deep valley—brawling streams—beautiful trees—but description is nothing—the sea was heard in the distance." It was a "superb view, the most wonderful I can ever hope to see." They travelled on to the foot of Mt Etna ("magnificent beyond description" [303–4]), but the snow still lay thick on it, so that he gave up the idea of attempting to climb it. Not only was his leg strained and his feet covered in blisters from walking, but he was tired out after sleepless nights in cheap, flea-infested inns.

They spent a night at Catania, where Newman cleaned up and rested, before taking the boat to Syracuse, where the sirocco which had been threatening for several days finally came down in heavy rain. He decided to return immediately the next day to Catania while the wind was still blowing in the right direction. However, they were blown off course and had to spend the night in a cove only a few miles from Syracuse.

On 1 May they set off inland from Catania in a northwesterly direction. Newman was already feeling under the weather with feverish symptoms, which was not very surprising after sleeping out of doors on a chilly night. The scenery again seemed to him "like the Garden of Eden most exquisitely beautiful." He began to be in great pain and he "fell to tears" thinking of his youngest sister Mary (who had died at the age of nineteen), as he "looked at the beautiful prospect" (*Autobiographical Writings* 123. The quotations that follow are from this account). They managed to reach Leonforte, but unfortunately the best inn was already occupied by a Sicilian duke. Next morning Newman felt very ill but managed eventually to make his way to the better inn, which had been vacated. As he lay in bed, he felt he was being punished for self-will (his last sermon before leaving Oxford had been on the sin of wilfulness) in leaving the Froudes and coming on his own: he remembered too that it was almost exactly three years since the row over the Oriel tutorship, and he began to wonder if he had not been over-hasty and whether he had not borne resentment against Dr. Hawkins, the Provost. Still, nobody had actually advised him against coming to Sicily, and he "kept saying" to himself "I have not sinned against light." Next day the feelings of self-reproach returned and he began to think his religious principles were hollow and shallow. To stop his "mind from thinking of itself," he "kept counting the number of stars, flowers, etc., in the pattern of the paper on the walls." Some beggars started whining outside in the street, a "low feeble monotonous cry" which seemed interminable. There was no doctor available nor any medicine, apart from the camomile tea his servant made. It was obvious to Gennaro that his employer was seriously ill with fever (there was an epidemic) and that he might well die, so he hinted Newman might leave him the baggage. Newman gave him Froude's address in the event of his death, but emphatically discounted the possibility—"God has still work for me to do." Refusing to accept that he was seriously ill, he insisted in his somewhat delirious state on setting out again on the road. But they had hardly gone half a mile before he started to feel very hungry and then very thirsty. He "began sucking some most delicious oranges which were on the way side" and "kept thinking" what he would be able to tell his mother and sisters "about the fineness of these oranges—not sweet or tart, but a fine aromatic bitter" (125–28).

After collapsing, he was taken to the nearby town of Castro Giovanni, where there was a doctor. It seemed that he had fallen victim to an epidemic of gastric or typhoid fever, from which numbers of people were dying and which was often accompanied by cholera. The fever did not reach its crisis until 13 May, running a few days longer than its usual course. Apart from a fair that took place outside his window, the most aggravating noise, ironically, was the church bell that rang for Mass every day: "I used quite to writhe about and put my head under the bed clothes—and asked Gennaro if it could not be stopped." No doubt, he later reflected, his Sicilian attendants attributed his irritation to "a heretic's misery under a holy bell." After about a week he got up and took his first walk outside: "As I sat in the chair, I could not command myself, but cried profusely, the sight of the sky was so piercing" (132–33).

At last, on Saturday, 25 May they left Castro Giovanni. Newman was yet again overwhelmed by the beauty of the countryside—"Spring in its greatest luxuriance." He overcame his scruples about traveling on a Sunday, and on the Monday they reached Palermo. When he got up in the morning, he "sat some time by the bed side, crying bitterly and all I could say was, that I was sure God had some work for me to do in England" (136). Needless to say, his Neapolitan servant had no idea what he was talking about. When he came to write his marvellously vivid account of his illness over a year later, Newman thought that the Devil had seized the opportunity of his "unlooked for" return to Sicily to destroy him before he could be "a means of usefulness" (121–22). Many years later he looked back on the episode as the third of the "three great illnesses" in his life, which had led to such decisive developments in his religious life (268). As for the actual trip to Sicily, he had returned for two reasons: first, to see its antiquities, which he had failed to do, and second, to see the countryside, about which he could "only say that I did not know before nature could be so beautiful"—it was indeed "like the garden of Eden" and had surpassed all his expectations (315).

Day after day for nearly three weeks he waited in Palermo for a sailing, feeling very homesick and longing to return to England. His "impatience" was "calmed" by visits to churches; but the "still retreats" which their coolness offered from "the city's sultry streets" (*Apologia* 43) inspired the deeply ambivalent poem which begins:

> Oh that thy creed were sound!
> For thou dost soothe the heart, Thou Church of Rome,
> By thy unwearied watch and varied round
> Of service, in thy Saviour's holy home. ("The Good Samaritan")

Finally, on 13 June he was able to embark on an orange boat bound for Marseilles. They were "becalmed a whole week in the Straits of Bonifacio" (*Apologia* 43) but eventually reached Marseilles on 27 June. The next day Newman set off for Lyons. Again he was held up, "as tho' some unseen power, good or bad, was resisting my return." For weeks now the tears had come into his eyes whenever he thought of home—but he was sure the "severe lesson of patience" was God's will. The distance from Marseilles was only two hundred miles, a journey of forty-eight hours, but on arrival he found his ankles so swollen that he was forced to rest a day in "a miserably dirty inn." The "only anticipation" he now had "of the future" was that "thwarting awaits me at every step" (310–11).

At last, on Monday, 8 July 1833, he crossed the Channel from Dieppe and reached London the same night. He arrived in Oxford the next evening.

The following Sunday, July 14th, Mr. Keble preached the Assize Sermon in the University Pulpit. It was published under the title of "National

Apostasy." I have ever considered and kept the day, as the start of the religious movement of 1833.

The "movement," of course, was the Oxford or Tractarian Movement, into which Newman immediately threw himself with immense enthusiasm and vigor. When he looked back on his own part in its first beginnings, he was struck by how "officious" an agitator he had been. It was "uncongenial to my natural temper, to the genius of the Movement, and to the historical mode of its success." He could only attribute it to

> that exuberant and joyous energy with which I had returned from abroad, and which I never had before or since. I had the exultation of health restored, and home regained. . . . And my health and strength come back to me with such a rebound, that some friends at Oxford, on seeing me, did not well know that it was I, and hesitated before they spoke to me. And I had the consciousness that I was employed in that work which I had been dreaming about, and which I felt to be so momentous and inspiring.

But "perhaps," he reflected, "those first vehement feelings which carried me on, were necessary for the beginning of the Movement" (*Apologia* 43, 49–50, 44).

The expedition to the Mediterranean, then, has a special significance for the Movement of 1833, of which Newman very soon assumed the leadership. The letters which record it not only contain vivid descriptions of high literary quality, but they are also of intellectual interest for their subtle reflections on the value of travel in general. And as biographical documents, they are of great importance for revealing the effect that first-hand experience of the reality of Roman Catholicism had on an imagination "stained" early in life by reading Protestant polemic that "the Pope was the Antichrist" (*Apologia* 20).

NOTES

Quotations from Newman's works are from the following editions: *Apologia pro Vita Sua*, ed. Martin J. Svaglic (Oxford: 1967); *Autobiographical Writings*, ed. Henry Tristram (New York: 1957); *The Idea of a University*, ed. I.T. Ker (Oxford: 1976); and *Verses on Various Occasions* (London: 1880).

1. *The Letters and Diaries of John Henry Newman*, Vol. 3, ed. Ian Ker and Thomas Gornall, S.J. (Oxford: 1979), 93. All subsequent quotations from the letters are from this volume.

CARLYLE, TRAVEL, AND THE ENLARGEMENTS OF HISTORY

Michael Cotsell, University of Delaware

It is indeed an "extensive Volume", of boundless, almost formless contents, a very Sea of Thought; neither calm nor clear, if you will; yet wherein the toughest pearl-diver may dive to his utmost depth, and return not only with sea-wreck but with true orients. (*Sartor Resartus* 10; bk. 1, ch. 2)

Sartor Resartus (1833–34) humorously enacts Thomas Carlyle's imaginative relation to England: an incomprehensible and fragmentary German philosophy and life delivered, by "the kindness of a Scottish Hamburg Merchant, whose name, known to the whole mercantile world, he must not mention" (74; bk. 1, ch. 22), to a confused English editor who has the task of getting the thing into some sort of order for the English reader. Carlyle, of course, had not traveled to Germany, preferring at the time to keep it a "country of the mind." Travel, though, is a major part of Teufelsdröckh's experience. His sorrows become his travels, "a perambulation and circumambulation of the terraqueous Globe" (47; bk. 2, ch. 6), beginning with an evocation of mountain grandeur, though, typically, Carlyle disabuses his hero of a taste for the picturesque, that "epidemic, now endemical, of View-hunting" (151; bk. 2, ch. 6). Teufelsdröckh becomes a wanderer seeking to escape from his own shadow, and in that Byronic, but his wanderings provide the dimension of his experience:

My breakfast of tea has been cooked by a Tartar woman, with water of the Amur, who wiped her earthen kettle with a horse-tail. I have roasted wild-eggs in the sand of Sahara; I have awakened in Paris *Estrapades* and Vienna *Malzleins*, with no prospect of breakfast beyond elemental liquid. (155–56; bk. 2, ch. 6)

The "bewildered Wanderer," interrogating the world for meaning, traverses it to its Mediterranean origins: the "Sybil-cave of Destiny," a "grim Desert" with "no Pillar of Cloud by day, and no Pillar of Fire by Night" (161; bk. 2, ch. 7). After his experience in the Rue Saint-Thomas de l'Enfer, Teufelsdröckh continues his "Pilgrimings" in a different spirit, open to the world, rather than demanding of it. He now concerns himself with the varieties of human activity that travel reveals, the building of cities, battlefields, "great Scenes"—the "Palm-trees of Tadmor," the "ruins of Babylon," the "great Wall of China"—and "Great Events"—"the World well won, and the World well lost," and the "birth-pangs of Democracy." He attends Schiller and Goethe at Jena, meets Napoleon and compares him to an American backwoodsman, and encounters a Russian smuggler at midnight in "Arctic latitudes" (176–77; bk. 2, ch. 8). At the work's end he is inspired by the July Revolution of 1830 in Paris—"*Es ghet an*" (It is beginning) (296; bk. 3, ch. 12)—though he may be in London. Travel is an essential of the narrative mode of *Sartor Resartus*. It also informs the work's thought: the philosophy of clothes depends on the estrangement of the traveler's eye, and the vision of "Natural Supernaturalism" is filled with the wonderous reports of scientific travelers: "The Ocean Tides and periodic currents, the Trade winds, and Monsoons"; "the *infernal* boiling-up of the Nether Chaotic Deep"; "the Giddy Alpine heights of Science" (258, 266; bk. 3, ch. 8).[1]

The form of *Sartor Resartus* suggests something about the relations of Carlyle's imagination to the England he wished to influence. He sought to defamiliarize English society, to reveal its spiritual lineaments, and to expand and mobilize its thought and energies. He also strove to present history to the English as though contemporary England was poised at a crisis, and contemporary England refused to be that. His imagination was filled with images of men of great faith wrestling with societies in the making, with fierce militarists and violent revolution—with, in fact, history that is not English. Even the great undeniable fact of poverty did not stir the English system as it stirred him. English history never quite rises to the scenario Carlyle demands. In the end this gap, which gradually widened through his career, produced in him a fury and, as regards England, a corresponding unreality.

It is as though England could never fulfill the imaginative demand of this intensely earnest Scot, and, correspondingly, as though Carlyle could never finally *imagine England* as he wished. Perhaps the most significant instance of this is his failure to activate his project of a major work on Cromwell, to tell the heroic English story that, in his view, most closely matched the great events of modern European times. It was partly a matter of historical distance, partly also a sense of the tedium of tracing complicated constitutional issues. At any rate, it is Cromwell abroad, terrorizing Ireland, who most comes to life in Carlyle's imagination. Indeed, Carlyle may be said to imaginatively circle English history, seeking to inspire it to a sense of crisis and potential grandeur. His imaginative bearing is very often from abroad. He is the great interpreter of Germany, the historian of the French Revolution. His home in Chelsea was habituated by European dissidents of one order or another—Mazzini and his followers, Alexis de Rio, Cavaignac, Duffy and other Young Irelanders—whatever he thought of them. In 1849, at the time of the Irish famine, he wrote:

> Ireland really *is* my problem; the breaking point of the huge suppuration which all British and all European society now is. Set down in Ireland, one might at least feel, *"Here* is thy problem: In God's name what wilt thou do with it?"[2]

No English writer of the period felt like that about Ireland. Even Carlyle's linking of "all British and all European society" in a common problem is uncharacteristic of English political thought.

It is not surprising, then, either that Carlyle traveled, or that his travels had important consequences for his writings. Admittedly, he was a reluctant and unhappy traveler and he mistrusted the cult of tourism—seeking after the picturesque, dawdling around art galleries. Nor was he, by Victorian standards, a great traveler, though he thought of going further than he went; he did not see the Alps or visit Italy (and then he only crossed the border) until very late in life. But, after the early and brief visit to Paris made in 1824, Carlyle wrote extended accounts of four of the seven further visits he was to make abroad (the exceptions are his first brief visit to Ireland in 1846, his similarly brief trip to Germany in 1852, and the Italian trip, which are reported in letters). Composed directly on his return with an evident imaginative fluency, each of these accounts has a distinct mood and theme, and three of them inform to an important degree a subsequent major work.

Carlyle's vivid impressionistic mode of seeing is evident in his letters from Paris in 1824. He seeks for images of a state of society; he eliminates causation other than in moral terms. The result is an impression at once perceptive and prejudiced, penetrating and idiosyncratic; a sharp confrontation between the will to significance and the immediate facts. This gives the travel writings their literary quality; if they are insufficient as historical analysis, they become history: testaments of a man alive in his times. In Paris, Carlyle juxtaposes details of the life of the city so as to provide a moral commentary on the state of society:

> Their shops and houses are like toyboxes; every apartment is tricked out with mirrors and expanded into infinitude by their illusion. . . . The people's character seems like their shops and faces; gilding and rouge without; hollowness and rottenness within. . . . Oh the hateful contrast between physical perfection and moral nothingness! Between this extreme of luxury and the extreme of wretchedness unrelieved by hope or principle! Yesterday I walked along the *Pont Neuf*; jugglers and quacks and cooks and barbers and dandies and gulls and sharpers were racketting away with a deafening hum at their manifold pursuits; I turned aside into a small mansion with the name of *Morgue* upon it; there lay the naked body of an old grey-headed artisan whom misery had driven to drown himself in the river! His face wore the grim fixed scowl of despair; his lean horny hands with their long ragged nails were lying by his sides; his patched and soiled apparel with his apron and *sabots* were hanging at his head; and there lay fixed in his iron slumber, heedless of the vain din that rolled around him on every side, was this poor outcast stretched in silence and darkness forever.[3]

Although it would be exaggerated to read this as the germ of the early chapters of *The French Revolution* (1837), it would seem equally unlikely that this personal experience failed to provide some stimulus to Carlyle's subsequent studies.

A more substantial claim can be made for the first of his extended travel writings, his "Notes of a Three-Days' Tour to the Netherlands" of 1842. Again, it is a sense of a society that Carlyle establishes, though a very different society. All travelers, of course, remark on the societies they encounter, and contrast them with their own. But certain Victorian writers, acutely conscious of their own society as a precarious organization, in a way that previous generations were not, sought for and found in foreign scenes images of a society that had a quality of life and spirituality absent from contemporary England.

Carlyle's "Three-Days' Tour" is a concentrated and unified piece, which, from the moment of parting company with the motley assemblage of English travelers on the down-river steamer and the dubious vivacities of the ballroom at Margate, continuously celebrates images of right society, right ways of life: the neat little cutter, the *Vigilant*, a "model; clean all as a lady's work box" (498); the admirable crew and "little Captain" (501); clean, orderly, and Protestant Ostend. At the center of the experience, though, are the cities of Bruges and Ghent, which for Carlyle provide images of the continuity of civic order and efficiency:

> This city of the "Bridges", with its winding streets, its broad market-places, its fantastic edifices secular and religious very strange to a modern eye. Honour to the long-forgotten generations; they have done *something* in their time: this city, nay this country is a work of theirs. Sand downs and stagnating marshes, producing nothing but heath, but sedges, docks, marsh-mallows, and miasmata: so it lay by nature; but the industry of man, the assiduous, unwearied motion of how many spades, pickaxes, hammers, wheelbarrows, mason-trowels, and ten-thousandfold industrial tools have made it—this! A thing that will grow corn, potherbs, ware-houses, Rubens Pictures, churches and cathedrals. Long before Caesar's time of swords, the era of *spades* had ushered itself in, and was busy. "Tools and the man!" "Arms and the man" is but a small song in comparison. (506)

It is the churches that at once draw and challenge Carlyle, not only because of their architectural grandeur, but because they represent both the civic spirit and a traditional Catholicism alive in the present day:

> few things that I have seen were more impressive. Enormous high arched roofs (I suppose not higher than Westminster Abbey, but far more striking to me, for they are actually in *use* here), soaring to a height that dwarfed all else; great high altar-pieces with sculpture, wooden-carvings hanging in mid-air; pillars, balustrades of white marble, edged with black marble . . . above all, actual human creatures bent in devotion there . . . it struck me dumb.(509–10)

The sight of the past and present of Catholic devotion produces in Carlyle a painful oscillation. "You could not say," he believes, that the worshippers "were without devotion," but he feels for their "fat priests" a "kind of hatred." Yet this reaction is checked: "Things are long-lived, and God above appoints their term"; and checked again by the reflection that, "At bottom, one cannot *wish* these men kicked into the canals; for what would follow were they gone? Atheistic Benthamism, French editorial 'Rights of man' and *grande nation*, that is a far worse thing, a far *untruer* thing." (510).

Proceeding to Ghent, Carlyle again develops the sense of living order:

> a good leaden gutter ran round the eaves, our window-rabbets were of

white polished stone, all was right and tight, and, in its exotic shape and arrangement, yet perfection of result, a kind of pleasure to contemplate. (629)

Missing his rendezvous with his companions, he is freed to his own response: "I wandered at my own sweet will" (631). It is an unusually open and happy moment in Carlyle's writing. Once again it is a Catholic church that impresses most. Carlyle is led to appreciate that civic values and religious devotion were linked for the church builders; modern times, by comparison, seem devoid of adequate belief. It is a moment which is self-confessedly significant for him:

> An ancient pious burgherhood, looking ever into Eternity out of their busy Time-element, has left here a touching proof of its wealth, devoutness, generous liberality, and *taste*. . . . Good merchant burghers of Ghent—ah me, what a brutal heathenism are our Railway Terminuses, Pantechnicons, Show-bazaars in comparison: *good* so far as they go; yes,—but going no farther than the *beaver* principle in man will carry him; as if man had no *soul* at all, but only a work-faculty. . . . Such thoughts crowded on me in all these places; and their architectural twirls and fantasticalities, steeples like giant pepperboxes, like slated unicorns' horns, three hundred feet in height,—like slated Mandarins, with slate umbrellas, like what slate and stone absurdity you will, were full of beauty and meaning to me.—(632–33)

The playfully fantastic imagery at the conclusion of this passage recognizes that the imagination has been provoked to activity.

There are points of criticism and discontent in what follows, but the concluding paragraph of the piece emphasizes its nature as a vision of social alternative:

> Thus had kind destiny projected us rocket-wise for a little space into the clear blue of Heaven and Freedom: thus again were we swiftly reabsorbed into the great smoky simmering crater, and London's soot volcano had recovered us. (640)

The pitch is forward and hopeful, and the phrase "Heaven and Freedom" suggests the clear vision of a potential modern spirituality.

The place of the "Three-Days' Tour" in the compositional history of Carlyle's works at this time is indicated by Jane Carlyle's first unenthusiastic response to it: "Is it not a mere *evading of your destiny* to write Tours just now! with that unlaid and unlayable ghost of Cromwell beckoning you on!" The Cromwell was faltering. In midsummer of 1842 Carlyle had indeed been thinking of abandoning the task. He traveled to the Netherlands early in August and wrote up the "Three Days' Tour" between 12 and 16 August. By August 20 he was again "writing, writing"; according to his recent biographer, Fred Kaplan, it may have been the Cromwell or the beginning of something on the "'condition of England.'"[4] Then in the first week of September, he took horse and made a brief Cromwellian tour, which is doubtless the source of the tourist-like opening of *Past and Present*. By November he had begun writing *Past and Present*. It is thus likely that the tour to the Lowlands played some part in freeing and engaging Carlyle's imagination in a way that the Cromwell project was failing to do. It helped him toward a vision of a Catholic past that was not mere superstition, but which expressed a combination of human enterprise and devoutness that might presage what a future could be. Ghent and Bruges challenged him to look at Europe's past through other than narrow Protestant or even puritan eyes; and to see that the spirit he sought to activate might have inhabited medieval and Catholic Europe. As well, the two cities provided an image of that past alive in the present; the geographical coexistence of that world with modern Britain parallels Carlyle's dramatic juxtaposition of past and present in his great work. It may be that this journey enabled Carlyle's imagination to make this leap. Through travel, he learned to overcome both the distance and the determinations of history. Travel restored his imagination and enabled him to envisage a form in which the imagination restores history.

Carlyle did not travel abroad again until his brief trip to Ireland in 1846, which was connected with the Cromwell project. He had become acquainted with Gavan Duffy and others of the Young Irelanders, and though he could not share their political views, he was, in a measure, sympathetic to the spirit of their enterprise. It was through this connection that he came to visit Ireland again, for a longer visit, in 1849, and to write his longest travel work, *Reminiscences of My Irish Journey in 1849*.

Carlyle's *Irish Journey* is almost totally opposed in spirit to the "Three-Days' Tour": it is a work of hopelessness and anger, envisioning not the promise of society but its complete and desperate failure. The difference between the two works is evident even in a comparison of the two accounts of passage. Instead of the bright images of human capability of the passage to Ostend, the passage in the *Irish Journey* is a kind of horror of desolation. There is an upright ex-sergeant on board, and a "good old Captain," but far more striking is the "lean, angry misguided, entirely worthless looking creature" (15) who quarrels with his captain, gets drunk, and then is lost overboard: "I was struck in general with the air of faculty *misbred*, and gone to waste" (17). Two Irish women, genteel poor, "*mis*venturous," have given up their plan to emigrate to Australia and are "cowering back to Ennis in Clare" (21). There is a sick and paralyzed man on deck.

If the human spirit seems lonely, weak, and defeated, the seascape emphasizes the hopelessness. The coastline provides a desolate geology lesson. "After Wight, Needles &c. (terribly worn, almost dilapidated and ruinously looking)" (14); the rocks at the Lizzard have "a haggard skeleton character, worn haggard by the wild sea" (28); "sheer and black. . . . angry skeleton rocks in these ever-vexed waters" (29); "like the ruins of a Cathedral" (28); "no motion that was not of the *chaotic* powers" (32). The coast speaks the hostility of nature and the failure of the human dream.

Ireland appears to lowered spirits flat, "rather *bleared*," "feeblish," "out of repair" (35); a "state of ineffectuality," the "afternoon sinking lower," the "genius of vacancy alone possessing it" (36–37). Carlyle is set down in Dublin "in wind and dust, myself a mass of dust and inflamatory ruin" (38). Then, as the account of Ireland proceeds, Carlyle develops the notion of the country's malformation, ill-condition, even idiocy. Kilkenny is an "idle old city; can't well think how they live" (85), Youghal a "dingy town," the houses "dim, half dilapidated," the population "dingy semi-savage" (110–11). Of the countryside around Killarney he remarks:

Ragged wet hedges, weedy ditches; nasty ragged, spongy-looking flat country hereabouts;—like a *drunk* country fallen down to sleep amid the mud. (135)

There is a sense of Irish life as moronic, deceitful, slovenly.

The Irish landscape, far from being romantically beautiful or stirring, is similarly lowering. A day's outing at Killarney is devoted to the "picturesque," but "*something* of dilapidation, beggary, human fatuity in one or other form, is painfully visible in nearly all" (139). The best that can be said is that there is "a wild beauty looking thro' the squalor of one's thoughts" (140). Carlyle finds nothing attractive about the Irish boglands: "all this region, by nature, execrable, drowned bog" (177). The best efforts Carlyle comes across, those of the benevolent landlord Lord George Hamilton, are insufficient: "'improvements' all are swallowed in the chaos, chaos remains chaotic still" (240). Faced with a "*continent* of haggard crag-and-heather desolation" (241), Carlyle expresses a crisis in confident Victorian improvement.

The Irish landscape bespeaks the failure of man's works and also of his faith. In marked contrast to his experience of Bruges and Ghent, Carlyle now finds the ruins of religious buildings: it is as though the idea of *Past and Present* is cancelled out. At Howth, there is the "big old Abbey over-grown with thistles, nettles, burdocks and the extremity of squalor" (65); at

him and presented him with images of intermixed natural beauty and relaxed historical continuity. One of the most striking images he offers is a description of a country house so homely and functional that it reminds him of ancient ways of life:

> Aspect of the House and Establishment was curiously *medieval* to me, brought Ulysees and *his* to mind: mongrel between palace and farmhouse; irregularity, dust and neglect combining with a look of sufficiency and even opulence. (23)

Suggestions of the heroic and medieval ages are combined within a picturesque present that charms by its diversity and by the sense of a mixture of labor and calmness. Things all come together right in such an image: the mind is relieved from the burdens of concern, the demands of history, and expands into a more curious and relaxed appreciation.

This is not without a sense of loss, but the sense of loss is somehow uninsistent and poses no crisis. Carlyle's own imaginative task on this journey can be compared to that of the raiser of monuments, architectures which challenge the complacency of the present, but which can rapidly become mundane. Two such images, which recall the experiences of the 1852 journey, presage this fate. At Prag:

> In a Barber's shop, corner of the *Markt* and big street near hand to our right, are two Blocks with elaborate shining wigs on them, newest fashion: one is an ideal Block of the usual fashion; the other is, recognisably at once,—the Head of Goethe! Such a form of "fame" I had never fallen in with before. (85)

Similarly, a curious comparison to the advocate of Goethe and the author of *Frederick* can be developed from his account of the "monument" of the pamphleteer Fuchs:

> poor old Fuchs he had set his heart on a monument to Mollwitz Battle, and could not get the people to subscribe freely; wrote that distracted Pamphlet, still little subscribing; quarried and hewed and carted hither, at his own expense, from Strehlen Quarries, a big granite Obelisk with proper inscription, built a stone and mortar basis for it and small artificial height; had not cash for the requisite *pulley*—machinery;—assembled all the people to "inaugurate," and bring Obelisk and basis together; discoursed with unction, eloquent rigmarole, amid a crowd of people (perhaps twenty or 30 years ago); and there the Obelisk still lies; cattle have

93

scratched away the masonry a good deal, anu poor old Fuchs is dead, leaving a grin of mockery in his fellow-creatures. (64)

A similar feeling is developed in the accounts of the difficulty of finding people who can identify or recognize the features of the scenes of Frederick's battles. Often the locals are vague or useless. People would like to be helpful but are not; views, usually attempted from church steeples, are obtained with difficulty. It is, Carlyle observes, a "rare case" when he ends up seeing what another points out; only a "young gentleman" (63) at Mollwitz and an "intelligent" village schoolmaster (99), who yet cannot read the Latin epitaph on the monument to Marshall Keith, are helpful. He learns that the bones of seven hundred men killed in the churchyard of the latter's village were only discovered "in founding a new cattle-house for our Schoolmaster" (98). Such passages communicate a sense of human relationship neither spiritually and socially integrated, as was imagined in the "Three Days' Tour," nor tragically and miserably separate as in the *Irish Journal*. There is much friendliness and cooperation, but also distance, forgetfulness, indifference, and incomprehension.

It is not so much as heroic scenes, but as theaters of earnest futility, that Frederick's battlefields appear, though even that description is too poignant, for the landscape, at once banal and beautiful, repeatedly distracts the eye from the contemplation of the past. The scenes are pleasantly unevocative: Zorndoff is "a littery but substantial clay village," the "'impassable bogs'" of the battle "hard meadow now" (150); another site is "a wide nearly level region, growing lupins, potatoes, scraggy grass, much fir-wood round it" (57); at another, the "'six hills'" of the battle are "trifling swells in the ground" (75). At the beginning of the work, Carlyle complains about being dragged about sightseeing, "the Picturesque all to do" (32). But, despite his complaints, he is genuinely struck by the view at the Stubbenkammer: "a sheer white precipice, sharp-edged [,] hard [,] plunges down 400 feet or so,—awful to look upon;—and lifting your head there is nothing but the shipless immensity of Baltic lying eastward" (38). This distraction from history to the peaceful meaninglessness of the wide natural world is a repeated movement in the work. Germany shows a breadth and continuity of human and natural life that brings a curious quiescence to the urgencies of Carlyle's vision. *Frederick the Great* (1858–65), of course, continued his heroic project, but it is not unaffected by the sense of irony and distraction that the *Journey* displays.

The travel works enable us to reflect on Carlyle as an advocate of expansion and empire. His favorite scenarios of strong men wrestling with undeveloped nature and peoples (see the essay "Dr Francia," 1843) were very adaptable to imperial purposes, and his influence on advocates of imperialism like Froude and the Kingsleys was as strong as it was on the "socialist" tradition in which Ruskin and Morris figure. An imagery of expansion runs through his works, even when it is not the primary subject as it is in parts of "Chartism" (1839) and *Past and Present* (1843). The project of *Sartor Resartus* is characterized in this way:

> How often have we seen some such adventurous . . . wanderer light on some out-lying, neglected, yet vitally-momentous province . . . thereby, in these his seemingly so aimless rambles, planting new standards, finding new habitable colonies. (7; bk. 1, ch. 1)

The frustrated later works can be emphatically imperial, for instance, "Shooting Niagara" (1867); in this last attack on the progress toward democracy in Britain he rather ludicrously recommends that the younger sons of the aristocracy each be given a sugar island to bring into order. But Carlyle's sense of the world, as it reveals itself in his travel and other writings, is too large to be accommodated within the single vision of imperial rule. There is an attractive moment in *Past and Present* when, having applauded the epic of British expansion, Carlyle breaks in with a passage beginning, "Or let us give a glance at China." What follows is an urbane and relaxed account of the lucid reasonableness of Chinese religion and society, which concludes with the reflection that:

> These three hundred millions actually make porcelain, souchong tea, with innumerable other things; and fight, under Heaven's flag, against Necessity;—and have fewer Seven-Years Wars, Thirty-Years Wars, French-Revolution Wars, and infernal fightings with each other, than certain millions elsewhere have! (232–33; bk. 3, ch. 15)

A far cry from "Better fifty years of Europe than a cycle of Cathay" (Tennyson, *Locksley Hall*, 1842, 184). Carlyle exceeds his own heroic vision of history, which is to say that he was larger than his will.

NOTES

Quotations from the works of Carlyle are from the following editions: *Sartor Resartus*, ed. Charles Frederick Harrold (New York: 1937); *Past and Present* ed. Richard D. Altick (New York: 1977); "The Nigger Question," *Critical and Miscellaneous Essays* Vol. 4, *The Works of Thomas Carlyle*, Centenary Edition, 30 vols (London: 1899); "Notes of a Three-Day's Tour to the Netherlands," ed. Alexander Carlyle, *Cornhill Magazine* 53 (1922): 493–512, 626–40; *Reminiscences of My Irish*

Journey in 1849, ed. James Anthony Froude (London: 1882); "Excursion (Futile Enough) to Paris; Autumn 1851: Thrown on Paper, Pen Galloping, From Saturday to Tuesday, October 4–7, 1851," *Last Words* (1892; London: 1971) 149–91; *Journey to Germany Autumn 1858*, ed. R.A.E. Brooks (New Haven: 1940).

1. As K.J. Fielding has remarked in his "Unpublished Manuscripts I: Carlyle Among the Cannibals" (*Carlyle Newsletter* 1 [1979]: 22–28), "Carlyle was drawn to travel books just because they brought a new revelation about Creation." (23).
2. Quoted from Carlyle's Journal by Froude, *Irish Journey* v.
3. *The Collected Letters of Thomas and Jane Welsh Carlyle*, Duke-Edinburgh Edition, ed. C.R. Sanders, K.J. Fielding, Clyde Ryals, et al (Durham, NC: 1970–) 3.178–83.
4. See Fred Kaplan, *Thomas Carlyle: A Biography* (Ithaca, NY: 1983) 293; and *Collected Letters* 15.32.

THACKERAY: FROM EUROPE TO EMPIRE

Robin Gilmour,
University of Aberdeen

An exploration of William Makepeace Thackeray and the wider world might well begin with the opening of Chapter 7 of *From Cornhill to Cairo* (1846), the account of his first sight of Constantinople from the sea. After the disappointment of Athens, Thackeray was delighted with Constantinople, and he went straight to a favorite stock of imagery for an appropriate comparison:

> When we rose at sunrise to see the famous entry to Constantinople, we found, in the place of the city and the sun, a bright white fog, which hid both from sight, and which only disappeared as the vessel advanced towards the Golden Horn. There the fog cleared off as it were by flakes; and as you see gauze curtains lifted away, one by one, before a great fairy scene at the theatre, this will give idea enough of the fog; the difficulty is to describe the scene afterwards, which was in truth the great fairy scene, than which it is impossible to conceive anything more brilliant and magnificent. I can't go to any more romantic place than Drury Lane to draw my similes from—Drury Lane, such as we used to see it in our youth, when, to our sight, the grand last picture of the melodrama or pantomime were as magnificent as any objects of nature we have seen with maturer eyes. Well, the view of Constantinople is as fine as any of Stanfield's best theatrical pictures, seen at the best period of youth, when fancy had all the bloom on her—when all the heroines who danced before the scene appeared as ravishing beauties . . . and the sound of the bugles and the fiddles, and the cheerful clang of the cymbals, as the scene unrolled, and the gorgeous procession meandered triumphantly through it—caused a thrill of pleasure, and awakened an innocent fullness of sensual enjoyment that is only given to boys. (139)

It is characteristic of Thackeray that what begins as a rather tired, semi-epic simile should be invigorated as it descends to the homely realities of Drury Lane, pantomime, and childhood memory. The effect is anti-Romantic, but only partly so. To compare the sight of Constantinople with Clarkson Stanfield's theatrical scenery is of course to flout the whole premise of the Sublime, which requires an answering solemnity in the face of the vast and the historic. But the comparison is not entirely flippant; it has its own emotional honesty and psychological exactness. The enchantment of the moment is caught, the sheer excitement of encountering a place that is both new and familiar; for by invoking the clichéd representation of a Stanfield diorama, with its "glorious accompaniment of music, spangled houris, warriors, and winding processions" (139), Thackeray reminds us just how much our images of abroad, and our expectations in going there, have been formed by the cultural stereotypes acquired in impressionable years. (Similarly Alexander Kinglake recorded in *Eothen* his disappointment on discovering that a visit to the site of Troy failed to live up to the expectations formed by his childhood reading of Homer.)

Moreover, the Drury Lane analogy, while hostile to the Romantic sublime, is ultimately hospitable to the ordinary Victorian traveler: it makes a link between the exotic and the mundane, and suggests—as travel writing too seldom does—that the response to abroad need not require abandoning the framework of values and associations which sustain life at home. So *Cornhill to Cairo* is continually involved with other travel writing, and aware of the burdens it imposed. To go to the Mediterranean in the 1840s was to carry with one not only the associations of a classical education, but the knowledge that Chateaubriand, Byron, Shelley, Kinglake, and the ubiquitous John Murray had been there before; and Thackeray, the great Victorian master of intertextuality, foregrounds this awareness in his writing, exposing the degree to which classical legend and Romantic rapture had by that date fused into a stultifying decorum. It is this sense of a great weight of respectable assumption being thrown off that makes his famous response to Athens, for example, so tremendously liberating in its directness and honesty.

"Before tourism there was travel," Paul Fussell observes, "and before travel there was exploration."[1] If the dawn of the age of tourism can be dated to the day in July 1841 when Thomas Cook chartered a special train for a temperance meeting in Loughborough, and if, more specifically, continental tourism can be traced to his successful excursions to the Paris Exhibition of 1855, then Thackeray belongs to the threshold of the age of tourism, the time when the leisurely bourgeois traveler was about to give way to the hectic bourgeois tourist. He was quick to exploit the tourist in his writing, both as a fictional subject—Fitz-Boodle abroad, the Kickleburys on the Rhine—and as a narrative persona, in the shape of Titmarsh the traveling cockney. He perceived early that while the traveler and the tourist are ostensibly engaged in a similar enterprise, they are in the last analysis mortal enemies. The traveler is a romantic who seeks an authentic individual encounter with other civilizations, someone who values the otherness of those civilizations, is informed about their culture and history, and deplores (usually) the encroachment of modernity upon them. The tourist, on the other hand, is a citizen of the modern world who knows that modernity, in the shape of the annual holiday and the railway timetable, has made his journey possible. Lacking the leisure of the traveler, he is aware that the stay abroad must necessarily be brief, and is consequently a prey to the anxieties which this breeds, in particular the pressure to cram with information beforehand, and the fear of missing anything when there, which made the Victorian tourists so conspicuous in their "Murrayolatry"—forever consulting their red-backed Murray's *Handbooks*, which to foreign observers looked like prayer books.[2]

Thackeray is marvelously alive to the tourist's view of things. He shares their preoccupation with the creature comforts. He will spend more time on a description of the Turkish bath at Constantinople than on St. Sophia's, more on the design of the mosquito tent than on the architecture of the Parthenon. (Such reversals of expectation bring abroad to life, since the grander sights had been done to death, as Thackeray points out.) He is sensitive to the burden of expectation the tourist carries, and of what he calls the "fatigue of sublimity" (131)—the combined weight of the classics at school, the raptures of famous travelers, and the exhausting detail of the guidebooks. Far from being philistine and insular, his anti-Romanticism clears the ground for an authentic response, whether he is disagreeing with Byron about the attractions of Greek wine and women, or refusing to go into conventional raptures about the Pyramids. Along with this absence of humbug goes a refusal to deplore modernity or elevate the chivalric past at the expense of the steamboat present. At Rhodes he notes the "double decay" of the Knights of St. John and of the Turks who conquered them. The stately, picturesque buildings are now inhabited by shabby merchants and retired officers: "The lords of the world have run to seed. The powerless old sword frightens nobody now." And then, in words that look forward to his own "Novel Without a Hero," he takes Scott to task for glamorizing the crusades: "When shall we have a real account of those times and heroes—no good-humoured pageant, like those of the Scott romances—but a real authentic story to instruct and frighten honest people of the present day, and make them thankful that the grocer governs the world now in place of the baron?" (166).

Honesty, and in particular honesty about the ambivalence of his own response, is the striking quality of Thackeray's travel writings. It makes them restless, unsettling, fragmentary works, memorable in detail but inconclusive in development. Their influence is to be seen in other works of the Victorian imagination, such as Arthur Clough's *Amours de Voyage*. When Claude in that tourist-poem opens his account of Italy with

> Rome disappoints me much; I hardly as yet understand, but
> *Rubbishy* seems the word that most exactly would suit it

it is hard to think that Clough had not been influenced by reading *Cornhill to Cairo*. Beguiling as Thackeray's irreverence is, however, one should not forget that it rests upon a knowledge of the wider world more direct and extensive than that of any other major Victorian novelist other than Trollope. It takes a certain confidence, after all, to describe Rome as rubbishy, or to say of the ruins at Athens, as Thackeray did in a letter, that "they are magnificent & mouldy and of the colour of rotten Stilton cheese"[3]—an irreverent comparison which a Murrayolater would never risk, for fear of seeming ignorant and philistine. Just as Thackeray could mock the snob because he had a certain confidence in his own status as a gentleman, so his ability to demystify the traveler's sublime, to put himself in the shoes of the Victorian tourist abroad, came from the assurance of a traveled mind. In what follows I want to explore the wide geographical reach of his imagination, tracing his use of India, continental Europe, and Ireland in his early writing up to *Vanity Fair* (1847–48), and then going on to consider his later use of America, in *The Virginians* (1857–59), and the part it plays in his attempt to mythologize an English-speaking commonwealth as a counterweight to the ills of the Old World.

In the background was India. Thackeray's father and grandfather worked for the East India Company, and both his stepfather, Major Carmichael-Smyth, and his wife's father had given distinguished military service there. He spent the first five years of his life in Calcutta, and after his return to England grew up in a closely knit group of Anglo-Indians. India, physical India, did not burn itself into Thackeray's imagination as it did into Kipling's; it was potent more as a family memory, suffused with what he calls in *The Newcomes* (1853–55) the "strange pathos" accompanying "all our Indian story" (66), the melancholy of a social group forced to endure many separations and never entirely at home, perhaps, in either society. It is the India of the wealthy "Collector" and the army officer, rather than that of the ordinary soldiers and stoical administrators celebrated by Kipling. Thackeray's imaginative use of the subcontinent has little of Kipling's force and directness. In the early writings it figures as a brilliantly manipulated stereotype, a compound of elephants, tigers, tiffin, sieges, and boastful

Anglo-Indians like Major Gahagan and Jos Sedley. But in *Vanity Fair* it deepens to become the hinterland of Empire, and in *The Newcomes*, with its many partings and returns, India is central to the definition of Colonel Newcome's quixotic virtue.

It seems fitting that when Thackeray set sail from India in 1816 he should have traveled on a ship called the *Prince Regent*, and that when it stopped at St. Helena he should have been taken for a glimpse of Napoleon Bonaparte. The Regency was to be the setting of *Vanity Fair*, his most famous novel, and the defeat of Napoleon at Waterloo its central historical event; and in its heroine, Becky Sharp, he created a character whose cultural ambidexterousness in relation to England and France reflected Thackeray's own. France, and more specifically Paris, was the place abroad that he knew best, visited most frequently, and felt most at home in. First and foremost, Paris was always a place of escape for him. "I . . . never landed on Calais pier," he wrote in *The Paris Sketch Book* (1840), "without feeling that a load of sorrows was left on the other side of the water" (28). Paris offered the young Thackeray escape from the restrictions of his home and his mother's evangelical earnestness; it was the center of what he later called "the Incontinent." On his first visit there, in the summer of 1829, he fell under the spell of gambling; on his second, the following spring, he met Mlle. Pauline, a 35-year-old *grisette* who had been a governess in an English family: she may have become his mistress, and certainly played a part in the genesis of Becky Sharp. He also discovered the delights of Parisian ballet, then being revolutionized by Taglioni, which, as John Carey has shown, always had a strongly sensual appeal for Thackeray.[4]

Paris never ceased to hold its undergraduate promise of thrilling freedoms and dangerous pleasures, but Thackeray's residence there in the 1830s made him thoroughly familiar with the more respectable aspects of Parisian culture: its literature, theaters, politics, restaurants. He also got to know the various enclaves of the British abroad, ranging from the demimonde of bankrupts, cardsharpers, con men and con women, through the artists with whom he studied, to the genteel exiles eking out a respectable life in Paris on incomes and pensions too small to sustain a genteel life at home. It was among the latter, the "Trojans" as he called them in *Philip* (1861–62), that Thackeray found his wife, Isabella Shawe, and the fact that her family had come from India was one of several threads linking Europe and Empire in his experience (another was the decamping of the Carmichael-Smyths to Paris in 1838, and their residence there until 1859). This phase of his life is represented in *The Paris Sketch Book*, a scrappy mixture of travel essays, stories, art and literary criticism, and in the Paris chapters of the *Yellowplush Papers* (1837–38). What is notable about these works is the creative freedom Thackeray seems to have found in the French setting, enabling him to present disturbing material in an astringent and unmoralizing way. In "A Gambler's Death," the suicide of Jack Attwood, old Charterhouse chum and down-at-heels gambler, is set plainly in its sordid context of debt, despair, and uncaring friends; the "MORAL" at the end tells how his friends, having attended Jack's funeral half-drunk, "were very happy to get home to a warm and comfortable breakfast, and finished the day royally at Frascati's" (125). A similarly bleak recognition of human selfishness and indifference, and one clearly aimed at the ethical optimism of Dickens's *Pickwick Papers*, is the un-Weller-like moment in *Yellowplush Papers* when the footman Charles Yellowplush accepts the Earl of Crabs's bribe to desert his master, Deuceace. Predator and prey are more sharply defined in the climate of expectation the traveler moves through, and Romantic sentiment—what Yellowplush calls "flumry"—is either a hypocrisy or a dangerous illusion. Deuceace switches the direction of his courtship rhetoric instantly when he discovers the ugly Matilda, and not Lady Griffin, is the heiress, and Matilda's transports are seen to be factitious, nourished by her reading in "The Sorrows of MacWhirter" and other Romantic literature. So, too, the commercial traveler in "A Caution to Travellers," Sam Pogson, is led to the fleecing by Baroness Florval-Derval "because he was given to understand, by Lord Byron's *Don Juan*, that making love was a very correct, natty thing" (*Paris Sketch Book*, 27). In these works Paris provides the meeting-point for two of Thackeray's strongest impulses, his anti-Romanticism and his fascination with roguery, giving him the opportunity to develop themes, characters, and perspectives which would bear fruit in *Vanity Fair*.

The familiarity with French culture established at this period was to serve his later work in other ways too, contributing to the distinctive poise and urbanity of his mature narrative style, and helping to give authority to his imagination of upper-class manners. When he started to demolish the fashionable novel in *Vanity Fair* and *Pendennis*, the simpering Francophilia of its practitioners was an easy target for him, while at the same time he was able to avoid the charge of provincialism in his satire because of his mastery of the Parisian cosmopolitanism on which the aristocracy—or at least its more sophisticated members—liked to pride itself. Thackeray's knowledge of the rest of Europe was never so deep, although he traveled widely in Germany, Italy, Belgium and Holland, and of course through the Mediterranean. Two places with a particular resonance in his writings deserve mention: Weimar, where he spent a happy six months after leaving Cambridge, learning German and attending the balls and other ceremonies of its little court (he also met Goethe), and Belgium, especially Brussels and Waterloo. As Kalbsbraten-Pumpernickel in *The Fitz-Boodle Papers* (1842–43) and then Pumpernickel in *Vanity Fair*, Weimar figures in his work as a kind of time capsule from the eighteenth century, a quaintly comic miniature court society where Dobbin and Amelia are able to convalesce after the buffetings of fate. Weimar's placing in *Vanity Fair* is strategic, I shall argue, and symbolizes the scaled-down, domesticated, unhistoric lives that await the central characters in post-Napoleonic Europe. Brussels, on the other hand, is the setting for the novel's most spectacular display of worldliness and military-aristocratic glamour. Although Thackeray's chief source for the Waterloo chapters was George Robert Gleig's *Story of the Battle of Waterloo* (1847), the decision to build his novel around the famous battle probably owed much to the visit to the battlefield he made in August 1843 and recorded in *Little Travels and Roadside Sketches*. The account is marked by his characteristic ambivalence: boredom with the British obsession with Waterloo, revulsion from the carnage, impatience that only the officers' names are recorded on the memorial—but also the reluctant recognition that the battle was a legitimate source of national pride:

> Let an Englishman go and see that field, and he *never forgets it*. The sight is an event in his life; and, though it has been seen by millions of peaceable *gents*—grocers from Bond Street, meek attorneys from Chancery Lane, and timid tailors from Piccadilly—I will wager that there is not one of them but feels a glow as he looks at the place, and remembers that he, too, is an Englishman. (505–6)

And if Brussels is the setting for the most spectacular chapters that Thackeray wrote, it is also the setting for one of his quietest, when Henry Esmond discovers his mother's story from Father Holt and goes, "one sunny evening of spring," to visit her grave in the convent cemetery: "I felt as one who had been walking below the sea, and treading amidst the bones of shipwrecks" (*Henry Esmond* [1852] 277–78).

Ireland, the third important area of abroad in Thackeray's writings, was nearer to home, and he shared some of the contemporary perplexity at a country which seemed a baffling mixture of the familiar and the remote, on England's doorstep and yet "far more strange to most travellers than France or Germany can be" (*Paris Sketch Book*, 240). The stereotypes were always at hand, and the fact that his wife's mother, Mrs. Shawe, combined two of the most powerful of them—the mother-in-law and the Irish termagant— may be a factor in his willingness to exploit them in his fiction. But *The Irish Sketch Book* (1843), the product of his second visit in 1842 (his first the previous year had been marked by Isabella's attempted suicide on the boat to Cork), is remarkably free of stereotypes. It is a patient account of a long circuit of Ireland that took him to most of the main centers, north and south, and through much of the most impressive scenery. Contradictory impressions accumulate: the beggars everywhere and the frequent beauty of the women, the shabby buildings and the magnificent scenery, the sectarian bitterness and political violence, but also the charm and courtesy he meets almost everywhere, so that Thackeray is driven to pay the Irish the supreme compliment of declaring that, "I have met more gentlemen here than in any place I ever saw" (119). He reflects upon but does not attempt to resolve these contradictions into the kind of racial theory about Ireland beloved of Victorian ethnographers, and his comments on the condition of the country arise out of observation rather than presupposition. The gathering famine is brought home by the beggars who hobble up when Thackeray is describing the peaceful pastoral setting of Cork:

> One is old and blind, and so diseased and hideous, that straightway all the pleasure of the sight round about vanishes from you—that livid ghastly face interposing between you and it. And so it is throughout the south and west of Ireland; the traveller is haunted by the face of the popular starvation. It is not the exception, it is the condition of the people. (86)

Such observations intimate a grasp of the social and economic crisis of the time which the book as a whole backs off from acknowledging explicitly. Similarly, although Thackeray is wisely reluctant to generalize about the country as a whole, there is a persistent element in his observations which almost adds up to a symbol of the Ireland he saw—the recurrent motif of the grandly planned but shabby or unfinished building: "The whole country is filled with such failures; swaggering beginnings that could not be carried through; grand enterprises begun dashingly, and ending in shabby compromises or downright ruin" (83). Sometimes this comes across as a contrast between the neoclassic grandeur of Ascendancy public buildings and the mundane life rattling around within them, like the Exchange in Dublin, where he notes "a pert statue of George III, in a Roman toga, simpering and turning out his toes; and two dirty children playing, whose hoop-sticks caused great clattering echoes under the vacant sounding dome" (20)—a brilliantly suggestive image of a colonial society in decline. More usually it is a matter of the Irish aspiring to more than they can complete:

> Mill-owners over-mill themselves, merchants over-warehouse themselves, squires over-castle themselves, little tradesmen about Dublin and the cities over-villa and over-gig themselves, and we hear sad tales about hereditary bondage and the accursed tyranny of England. (232)

The fact that such over-reaching might itself be a symptom of mental bondage to England does not seem to have occurred to Thackeray, although his observations suggest it. In these ways *The Irish Sketch Book* touches on a familiar metaphor for a colonial society, the unfinished or grandly declining house, which later writers were to make use of in imagining Ireland.

The Irish Sketch Book is probably the best of Thackeray's travel writings, certainly the most thorough and thoughtful; and it promised a much more interesting work of fiction than the Irish novel he published the following year, 1844. Insofar as *Barry Lyndon* derives from his Irish experience, rather than from the Irish fiction of Charles Lever and Samuel Lover, it can only be described as a retreat into stereotype. The idea of a self-condemning rogue's narrative may have come from reading Captain Freeny's memoirs in the Galway inn, but the character of the boastful, reckless Barry owes much more to literary convention than to anything encountered during Thackeray's visit to Ireland. The eighteenth-century setting has the effect of dehistoricizing the narrative (a paradox familiar to readers of Thackeray's "historical" fiction), replacing the contradictory historical Ireland he visited with a kind of picaresque Hibernian playground where he could resurrect the situations and moral atmosphere of the eighteenth-century novels he loved. Ireland in *Barry Lyndon* functions much as Paris does in the *Yellowplush Papers*, as a place where the normal constraints of English domestic fiction do not apply, and thus an appropriate location for the exploration of ruthless, violent, and otherwise immoral behavior, and for the development of anti-Romantic perspectives which would have been seen as "cynical" in an English setting. Abroad is used less for itself than as a sanction for moral experiment. The same is true of the extensive European material in the novel. Barry's involvement in the Seven Years War, first on the English and then on the Prussian side, enables Thackeray to expose the pointlessness of a war whose causes Barry scarcely understands, as well as the irrelevance of patriotism to most of what goes on in warfare, and the brutality of battle itself. This is done not by rhetorical heightening but, as in "A Gambler's Death," by the very flatness of the first-person voice, revealing both its moral poverty and the randomness of accident:

> I hate bragging, but I cannot help saying that I made a very close acquaintance with the Colonel of the Cravates, for I drove my bayonet into his body, and finished off a poor little ensign, so young, slender, and small, that a blow from my pig-tail would have despatched him, I think, in place of the butt of my musket, with which I clubbed him down. I killed, besides, four more officers and men, and in the poor ensign's pocket found a purse of fourteen louis d'or, and a silver box of sugar plums, of which the former present was very agreeable to me. (70)

Impressive as such moments are, however, *Barry Lyndon* never rises above its relentlessly negative purpose. Although it is the most geographically ambitious of the early novels, its foreign settings remain inert backgrounds against which a predictable display of villainy is played out. Many of the same elements are present in *Vanity Fair*—a morally dubious central protagonist, an anti-heroic purpose, an historical setting at the time of a major European war, a critique of the pursuit of wealth and fashion—and yet the result is a major novel of European scope and stature. The transformation is not easily accounted for, but one explanation seems to be that whereas in the early work abroad functions as a kind of imaginative excursion for Thackeray, enabling him to handle dangerous material and exercise his anti-Romanticism, in *Vanity Fair* it becomes integral to his vision of England in its historical evolution and modern destiny. The geographical and historical distancing of *Barry Lyndon* prevented any real engagement with the Victorian reader's experience; the closer range of *Vanity Fair* drew on a war still in living memory, permitting Thackeray to bring abroad home, as it were, and, by showing how "the eagles of Napoleon Bonaparte" might cast their shadow over "a little corner of the parish of Bloomsbury, London" (211), to write the English *War and Peace*.

One of the marvels of *Vanity Fair* is the way it manages to pull together the very diverse creative strands of the previous ten years, and among these is the consciousness of abroad discussed hitherto in this essay. India figures in the stout person of Jos Sedley, Collector of Boggley Wollah, and as the scene of Dobbin's exile with his regiment. Something of the essence of *The Paris Sketch Book* is to be found in Becky, with her artist father, opera-girl mother, skill at play, and freedom from the inhibition of English manners. Ireland is more generously embodied in the O'Dowds than it had been in *Barry Lyndon*. The expedition that Thackeray made to Brussels and Waterloo expands into Amelia's invasion of the Low Countries, the battle itself, and Jos's escape. *Vanity Fair* even finds room for the embryonic Victorian tourist, as Mr. Osborne travels to see Waterloo, making "that well-known journey, which almost every Englishman of middle rank has travelled since" (339), and as Amelia, Dobbin, and Georgy visit Pumpernickel.

The novel's wide geographical reach is inseparable from its historical subject. By choosing Waterloo and its aftermath as his setting, Thackeray reactivated his own and his readers' memories of the European empire which England had played a major part in destroying, in the "great Imperial struggle" (221) against Napoleon. England entered that war as a great imperial power herself, and its outcome was to lead ultimately to the consolidation of the British Empire as a great mercantile enterprise, in contrast to the European empire which Napoleon had tried to establish by force of arms. Something of this large geographical and historical shift is suggested in the novel, through the prominence given to the merchants Sedley and Osborne (period figures, but relevant to the 1840s as well), and in Dobbin's long service, post-Waterloo, in India. But *Vanity Fair* is chiefly concerned with Europe, and with the significance of that engagement with, and retreat from, Europe which Waterloo meant for the early-Victorian middle classes.

Napoleon and France as the source of a subversive Republican energy are never very far away in the first half of the novel. From the moment when Becky throws Johnson's *Dictionary* out of the carriage window and declares "*Vive la France! Vive l'Empereur! Vive Bonaparte!*" (14), it is clear that wider cultural issues are at stake than simply the outcome of a military campaign. The social upstart is aligned with the Corsican upstart, the marital campaign with the martial, in the effort to penetrate an old society run on the Johnsonian principle of "subordination." Words like "enemy," "invasion," and "campaign" itself are given a delightfully comic double edge in the run-in to the famous battle. Becky catches English fashionable society on the hop just as Napoleon, escaping from Elba, catches the armies of the Allies off guard, and as they both converge on Brussels the culturally subversive implications of this dual French invasion are kept continually before the reader. Thackeray's knowledge of French culture and history, his feeling for its potentially liberating otherness, the new satirical grasp of the English class system evident in *The Book of Snobs* (1846–47), and his skepticism about conventional notions of heroism, all come together here in chapters of the most sustained brilliance he ever wrote.

And yet, paradoxically, Waterloo changes everything in the novel. The refused battle, which takes place offstage and only filters in through the high comedy of Jos Sedley's panic-stricken flight from Brussels, casts a long, melancholy shadow over the second half of *Vanity Fair*. The galloping energies of the first half give way to a sense of lives becalmed in the wake of a climactic event, as Amelia looks back with selfish longing, Dobbin pines for Amelia in India, and early-Victorian tourists like Mr. Osborne start making their pilgrimages to a national shrine. Even Becky's pursuit of fashion is a pursuit "under difficulties," out of step with the momentum of her society (her career as a "sharper" begins, fittingly, in Paris), an increasingly precarious struggle against the social odds. It is almost as if history had come to an end at Waterloo. As John Sutherland says,[5] there is an "odd impression of social tranquility" in the second half of *Vanity Fair*—odd, because the years after Waterloo were in fact a time of great social turbulence in England. In one way this tranquility is appropriate to the increasingly domesticated and middle-aged lives the main characters are seen leading, but it also suggests how much Thackeray's imagination was dominated by the old world of Regency glamour and military heroism whose passing is the grand epic subject of *Vanity Fair*. The defeat of Napoleon is the end of a whole movement in English civilization for him, not, as it is for Tolstoy in *War and Peace*, the start of a national resurgence. His characters live in the lengthening shadows of the past, not in the new dawn of bourgeois consolidation.

This may help to explain why the lives of the main characters should seem to many readers so inactive after Waterloo, and why their wanderings abroad should seem so aimless: they are living in the aftermath of history. And here Thackeray's introduction of Weimar as Pumpernickel at the end of the novel is marvelously apt. For Pumpernickel is a society out of historical synchronization, an eighteenth-century court society untouched by the Napoleonic upheaval, with its baroque fountains, unfinished gardens planned after the Versailles model, and toy-town army, which "consisted of a magnificent band that also did duty on the stage" of the local theater and hussars who are never seen on horseback, for "what was the use of cavalry in a time of profound peace?—and whither the deuce should the hussars ride?" (804). It is a little world progressing from *ancien regime* courtliness to *Biedermeier* gentility without the intervening cataclysms that have shaken the major European powers—a fitting location, then, for Amelia to discover the true worth of the faithful Dobbin, a character who combines the courtly honorableness of the old world with the delicacy of feeling and incipient domestication of the early-Victorian family man. It is here that Dobbin and Amelia enjoy what the narrator describes as "perhaps . . . the happiest time of both their lives" (792), an observation which follows immediately after the famous, if ambivalent, salute to "my friend the major" as that rare thing, a true gentleman.

The Pumpernickel chapters provide an appropriately antique image both of the tranquilized Europe which these two survivors have inherited and of the lives they will live within it: lives decorative and dignified but not useful in any specifically modern sense. And these chapters also point forward to questions which Thackeray's subsequent novels are much concerned with attempting to answer. If Pumpernickel is a holiday from history, where in history can the good man and woman live honorably and productively? What work can the gentleman do when he puts away his uniform, and where is the good society to be found? Not in Victorian England, at any rate, would seem to be the answer given by *The Newcomes* and *Philip*. *Pendennis* takes a typical gentleman out of uniform and into the Victorian age, but largely ducks the question of work by making him an elegant belletrist. As he grew older Thackeray seems to have found modern Europe an increasingly inhospitable environment for the good-man-as-gentleman, and the closer he came to the present the more he was driven back to the past for an image of redeeming virtue. Increasingly, too, his imagination turned from Europe to Empire. In *The Newcomes* it is Colonel Newcome's military service in imperial India which more than anything else marks him out as the one true gentleman in a society of upstarts, and in *Henry Esmond* and *The Virginians* the line of gentlemanly decency crosses the Atlantic to resurrect the good society in pre-revolutionary America. This is the last important area of abroad in Thackeray's writings, a once and future kingdom which might, these novels fitfully suggest, provide the nucleus of a widening Anglo-Saxon commonwealth.

When Thackeray went to America to lecture, in October 1852 and again three years later, he did so as a man middle-aged in years and more than middle-aged in attitude and expectations. He lacked the radical hopes that Dickens had brought with him ten years previously, and so did not experience the bitterness of disillusionment which makes the American chapters of the latter's *Martin Chuzzlewit* so sharply etched. His purpose was the modest one of earning capital for his family as an insurance against his death, and his itinerary was modest also, confined on the first visit to the major cities of the East, with forays south to Richmond and Charleston. On his second visit, traveling up the Mississippi to St. Louis, he encountered the raw America which had so appalled Dickens, and was shocked: "I see a sort of triumphant barbarism, a sordid greed everywhere."[6] But for the most part he moved among the cultivated eastern establishment, and kept his thoughts about the rest to himself. It is significant that he felt most at home in the cities of the aristocratic South.

"Here is the future," he wrote on returning from his first visit, "here is the great English empire to be when the Gauls and Cossacks may have trampled out our old freedom."[7] Thackeray could only imagine such an empire retrospectively, by inventing a mythical past in which America might figure as a kind of purified family extension of England. *Henry Esmond* promises such a trip back to the future for its exiles from history, Rachel and Harry, who take with them to Virginia (appropriately) a revulsion for the Old World and its ways and just a hint of sympathy for the republican future. But when we meet their grandchildren in *The Virginians*, they seem indistinguishable from the Englishmen in that novel. There is little life in the antithesis between New World and Old because, it seems, Thackeray had a very weak sense of what was new or different about the New. Castlewood in Virginia is as feudal as Castlewood in Hampshire—more so, indeed, since its prosperity is founded on slave-owning. Harry Warrington is not presented as a particularly American hero: rather, he is simply another version of the typical Thackerayan prodigal, reckless but generous-hearted, like Pendennis or Philip. His brother, George, studious and melancholy, is a reincarnation of Henry Esmond. *The Virginians*, which promises the most functional use of abroad in Thackeray's fiction, turns out to have the weakest sense of place. The cultural differences exploited in the earlier fiction are softened and diffused when it comes to America, turning the transatlantic setting into an extension of England and of that cozy, literary, slightly sentimental version of the eighteenth century which had such a fatal attraction for Thackeray.

An unkind critic might speculate that *The Virginians* was a calculated bid to capture an audience on both sides of the Atlantic. A more just verdict would be to say that Thackeray's reluctance to give offense as Dickens had done, an honorable enough motive, fatally weakened his ability to engage creatively with genuine cultural differences. Dickens's vision of America in *Martin Chuzzlewit* may be hostile and unfair, but at least it recognizes the radical otherness of America and the way the two societies were and are separated, as the famous wisecrack has it, by a common language. It is a short step, after all, from Dickens's Hannibal Chollop and Elijah Program to the world of Twain's *Huckleberry Finn*. Thackeray's America is intolerably bland, and insofar as *Esmond* and *The Virginians* attempt to mythologize "the great English empire to be," their vision is less imperial than English-Speaking-Union: what they envisage is a WASP Arcadia without a sting. The progress from Europe to America in Thackeray's use of abroad is, therefore, a story of topographical extension and imaginative contraction. Although he liked to toy with the idea of a new Castlewood to redeem the old, he remained a satirist rather than a visionary, and it was the ills of the Old World that stimulated his imagination, not the promise of the New.

NOTES

All references to Thackeray's writings are to the Oxford Thackeray, ed. George Saintsbury, 17 vols. (London: 1908).

1. *Abroad: British Literary Travelling Between the Wars* (New York and Oxford: 1980) 38.
2. See John Pemble, *The Mediterranean Passion: Victorians and Edwardians in the South* (Oxford: 1987) 72.
3. *The Letters and Private Papers of William Makepeace Thackeray*, ed. Gordon Ray (London: 1945–46) 2.182.
4. See *Thackeray: Prodigal Genius* (London: 1977) 103–8.
5. "Introduction," *Vanity Fair*, World's Classics edition (Oxford and New York: 1983) xix.
6. *Letters* 3.553.
7. *Letters* 3.181.

Ford Madox Brown, *The Last of England* (1854)

THE STRANGE CHARM OF "FAR, FAR AWAY": TENNYSON, THE CONTINENT, AND THE EMPIRE

Susan Shatto, University of Edinburgh

One of the many disappointments Tennyson felt at the end of his long life was that his passion for traveling had never been satisfied: he had made almost twenty journeys to the Continent and Scandinavia, including visits and revisits to what he called countries "of colour,"[1] but he had never been to a tropical island or to any exotic place.

Although he was an impetuous traveler—"He talks of going abroad instantly," wrote Arthur Henry Hallam in 1832—he was also an indecisive one: "The Laureate talked of going to the Levant, to West Indies, Cornwall or Brittany," but "he never definitely makes up his mind what he will do until the last." Assailed by restlessness in his twenties, and in his thirties by restlessness, depression, and ill health, he looked toward travel as a possible antidote, but more often than not he was prevented from going by the want of a companion, or money, or both: "He complained so of his hard lot in being forced to travel alone, that I took compassion on him, & . . . I am going," Arthur Hallam wrote of their Rhine journey in 1832. And throughout the 1840s Tennyson grumbled about his frustrated longing to visit Italy: "I shall never see the Eternal City, nor that dome. . . . I have no money for touring"; and "I am going to bolt as soon as ever I can and . . . I would go to Italy if I could get anybody to go with me which I can't and so I suppose I shant go which makes me hate myself and all the world."[2]

Temperamentally, of course, Tennyson was not suited to traveling.

113

Chronically lazy, helpless, and forgetful, he needed to be taken care of by his friends, who served him not merely as companions but as couriers and valets, "doing everything," as he himself confessed. He was also painfully susceptible to any form of personal inconvenience and he disliked foreigners—as much as the filth, fleas and vile food he associated with them. His hostility toward the French, Russians, and Irish was shared by most of his countrymen, but his abomination of Americans resulted from the hordes of them whose curiosity intruded on the seclusion of his house on the Isle of Wight. His prejudice against the Swiss seems to have been largely based on their iodine-deficient appearance: "The Swiss people—no words can describe their lowness in the scale of man, gain greedy, goitred, miserable-looking poor devils. The serfs of Russia, I doubt not, are princes to these republicans."[3]

And yet he traveled. Between 1830 and 1883 he made six visits to France, three to Switzerland, three each to Italy and the Low Countries, two visits each to the Rhine region and Norway, and one each to Denmark and Portugal. Moreover, the figure of the traveler, usually represented as a voyaging mariner, is recurrent in his poetry. The reasons why traveling seems to have been as necessary to Tennyson as tobacco relate to his need to write poetry and to what he needed to see and feel like in order to feel like writing it. What he needed most was inspiration, as Henry Taylor recognized in 1860: "He wants a story to treat, being full of poetry, with nothing to put it in."[4] Taylor might as well have said "scene" as "story," for in traveling to foreign lands, and in reading about them in books of travel, geography, and history, Tennyson sought new scenes.

The scenes to which he responded with the deepest intensity of perception were those which evoked a sense of distance—in the form of the past, be it historical or personal, or in the form of the remote and exotic:

> It is what I have always felt, even from a boy, and what as a boy I called the "passion of the past." And it is so always with me now; it is the distance that charms me in the landscape, the picture and the past, and not the immediate today in which I move.

He explained on another occasion that this enchantment had occurred in his first years of life:

> Before I could read I was in the habit on a stormy day of spreading my arms to the wind and crying out, "I hear a voice that's speaking in the wind," and the words "far, far away" had always a strange charm for me.[5]

His early-formed passion to escape from "the immediate today" to "far, far away" may be associated with the fear of their father which he shared with his brothers and sisters: during Dr. Tennyson's worst fits, the young Alfred, with a terror intensified by his awareness of having inherited his father's physical and mental frailties, would rush at night from the rectory to the churchyard and throw himself down among the graves, wishing to be dead. Nearly fifty years ago W.D. Paden traced the sources of the oriental images and subjects which proliferate in Tennyson's adolescent poetry to the books in his father's library. Moreover, although Paden was writing before the unhappy biographical details of life at Somersby Rectory had been published, he interpreted the exotic tendency in the poetry as an indication of the unusual degree to which Tennyson's sensual appetites had been suppressed and repressed by the constricted circumstances of a childhood spent in the atmosphere of idealism, piety, and terror generated by his exacting but unstable father.[6]

Mixing with the exotic in Tennyson's youthful poetry are other elements which also continue to recur in the poetry of his maturity: images of discovery, voyaging, adventure and expansion, of retreat or withdrawal, and of apocalypse, violence, and death. Always, there are undercurrents or expressions of disillusion, disappointment, loss, grief, loneliness, and despair. Between the ages of fifteen and seventeen he composed a poem which embodies many attitudes which remain constant throughout his work— attitudes toward the familiar countries of the Continent and the stranger and unknowable places in the wider world. The poem was "Timbuctoo," a piece of blank verse on the chosen subject for the Chancellor's Gold Medal at Cambridge in 1829. Although he later dismissed the poem as a "wild and unmethodized performance,"[7] it won the gold medal and was much admired by his contemporaries.

The germ of the poem, on the battle of Armageddon, had been composed around 1826, and Tennyson merely wrote a new beginning and ending—not troubling to compose an entirely fresh work in the fading style preferred for prize poems, heroic couplets. He derived the exotic scenic details for both "Armageddon" and "Timbuctoo" from a variety of books by and about travelers to South and North America, the Orient, the Middle East, and Africa. A mixture of facts, legends, and fantasies, Tennyson's sources, and his use of them, have been examined by W.D. Paden in *Tennyson in Egypt* (1942). What remains to be discussed is the topicality of Timbuctoo in 1829 and how the poem's rendition of the fabled city of the dark continent prefigures much of the later poetry.

While commerce, colonialism, and scientific inquiry may have motivated the European explorers who began to penetrate the interior of Africa from the late eighteenth century onwards, what excited their imaginations were the romantic myths and legends of vast riches, bizarre fauna and flora, grotesquely formed savages, ghastly cruelty, and lustful women. The location of the most fascinating of all places, Timbuctoo, was vaguely known to be near the source of the Niger, a river as mysterious and unexplored as Timbuctoo itself. What was known for sure was that the city had been a wealthy center of trade since the sixteenth century, and nineteenth-century European governments recognized that the country to first discover and lay claim to Timbuctoo would win prestige, a valuable trading center, and a dominant role in the African interior.

Between 1805 and 1826 Britain lost three large and expensive expeditions which had set out to discover Timbuctoo: those of Mungo Park in 1805 and Hugh Clapperton and Alexander Gordon Laing in 1826. In August 1826 Laing actually reached the city, at the junction of the River Niger and the Sahara Desert, but he was killed by the Moslem inhabitants, the rest of his party was never heard from, and reports of both his failure and Clapperton's did not arrive in Britain until April 1828. It is hardly surprising that in mid-December of that year the newsworthy and still mysterious African city, a gift to poetry if ever there was one, was announced as the subject for next year's Chancellor's Gold Medal.[8]

For the faintly South American setting of "Armageddon" Tennyson substituted allusions to Africa in the new opening and conclusion. So "Timbuctoo" opens with the poet atop a mountain on the shores of the Mediterranean gazing southward toward Gibraltar and the coast of north Africa and musing on the "legends quaint and old" (16) about the fabled cities of Atlantis and Eldorado. Raising his voice and crying out, he asks the African continent if it enfolds an equally beautiful city, or "is the rumour of thy Timbuctoo / A dream as frail as those of ancient Time?"(60–61). This inquiry marks the end of the newly composed introduction, and henceforward, up to the grafting on of the new conclusion, the poem incorporates the old "Armageddon," the essence of which is a trance induced by an angel— the first of many poetic accounts of the mystical experience which occurred to Tennyson throughout his life and which formed the basis of his personal faith.[9] In the context of the new poem, the poet's trance becomes a gesture of withdrawal, an inward-turning and depressive response occasioned partly by his awesome act of confronting the actuality of the vast and unknown continent and partly by his anxiety that its legendary city may be only a frail dream. A dream is, in fact, what Timbuctoo is shortly to become, for the angel reveals himself to be the Spirit who courses through "the great vine of *Fable*" and forewarns the poet that "the time is well-nigh come"

> When I must render up this glorious home
> To keen *Discovery*: soon yon brilliant towers
> Shall darken with the waving of her wand;

Darken, and shrink and shiver into huts,
Black specks amid a waste of dreary sand,
Low-built, mud-walled, Barbarian settlements.
How changed from this fair City! (238–45)

A fable of the Romantic poet anticipating the destruction of his own imaginative life as the advances of civilization and rationalism encroach upon the myths which inspire him, "Timbuctoo" is the first expression in Tennyson's poetry of the idea of the undermining of faith by materialism, an idea which recurs most notably in *In Memoriam* (1850), *Idylls of the King* (1855–85) and "Locksley Hall Sixty Years After" (1886). In this respect "Timbuctoo" is also reminiscent of a poem composed in 1827 about the conquest of Peru by Pizarro, "Lamentation of the Peruvians." When British imperialism was at its height fifty years later, Tennyson composed two other poems—"Columbus" and "The Voyage of Maeldune" (both 1880)—which re-explore the theme of European colonialism subverting the innocence of barbarian societies.

Tennyson in the South

At the time of writing "Timbuctoo," Tennyson had traveled no farther from his childhood home in Lincolnshire than London, but in 1830 he made his first trip abroad, to the south of France, accompanying Arthur Hallam on a romantic mission to take money and dispatches to Spanish revolutionaries in the Pyrenees. While Hallam's reasons for going were political, Tennyson's were poetical and psychological. Tennyson's response to the Mediterranean was one he shared with most other British travelers, for whom the South was a realm of tranquillity, freedom, and oblivion—an escape from painful states of mind, from the constricting morality of Victorian religion, and, not least of all, from the cold, dark, and wet British climate. Sunshine intensified the sensations of expansion and liberation: Tennyson longed to visit Italy, for example, because it was "the land of the sun, where men . . . come up more vigorously than in other latitudes"; as an old man too infirm to travel to the Mediterranean, he still felt the ache of nostalgia when he remembered how he used to feel "half-crazed for larger light."[10] His passion for the South was unashamedly sensual and, when he was obliged to remain in England, amounted to painful longing:

You ask me, why, though ill at ease,
Within this region I subsist,

117

Whose spirits falter in the mist,
And languish for the purple seas.

Yet waft me from the harbour-mouth,
Wild wind! I seek a warmer sky,
And I will see before I die
The palms and temples of the South.
                    ("You ask me, why, though ill at ease," 1–4, 25–28)

I lingered yet awhile to bend my way
To that far South, for which my spirits ache,

                    ("Sonnet [I lingered yet awhile]," 1–2)

His passion for the South also derived from its seeming to be haunted with reminiscences and associations. As Benjamin Jowett observed of him, "He always had a living vision of Italy, Greece and the Mediterranean"—because like other educated Victorian travelers he looked at the landscapes through the eyes of the Greek and Roman writers whom he had known by heart since childhood. His intimacy with classical literature, together with his knowledge of Romantic poetry and Gothic fiction, profoundly influenced his preconceptions of the South and made his satisfaction largely dependent on recognition.[11]

His satisfaction with recognizing in the southwest of France the barren landscape of his imagination resulted in three poems with both classical and Romantic associations: "Mariana in the South" and "Fatima" (both influenced by fragments of Sappho) and "Oenone" (all published 1832, revised 1842). In their desolation and single-minded commemoration of their lost lovers, the female figures in these poems descend from the Romantic character of Crazy Jane, the girl who went mad after being abandoned by her lover and who was frequently depicted by Romantic writers and artists.[12]

Arthur Hallam's account of the origin of "Mariana in the South" is useful as an indication of the tone that characterizes the figures in all three poems. He describes how during his journey with Tennyson in 1830 en route to the Pyrenees, "We came upon a range of country just corresponding to his preconceived thought of a barrenness . . . and the portraiture of the scenery in this poem is most faithful."[13]

The "range of country," according to Tennyson, lay between Narbonne and Perpignan, a forty-mile route adjacent to the coast to the north of the eastern end of the Pyrenees. In his Handbook for Travellers in France (1843), John Murray observes of this most southerly corner: "The country . . . is very dreary; large part of it white naked rock: trees very scarce" (336). Of Perpignan, Murray notes that the British visitor will be struck by the Spanish character of the town, with its "semi-Mooresque buildings, its houses furnished with wooden balconies," and its inhabitants resembling more closely their neighbors in Spain than their own compatriots (337). The Spanishness of Perpignan seems responsible for the evocation in "Mariana in the South" of dark, brooding, exotic southerness. As for the route between Narbonne and Perpignan, Murray's description confirms Hallam's remark about the poem's fidelity to the scenery:

> The road is very uninteresting, skirting . . . bare rocks without trees or herbage; only a few bristly plants, and tufts of . . . heath . . . and on the l., the salt lagoons, or shallow lakes . . . bordered with mud and sand. The district is unhealthy, owing to the miasma from this marshy tract. . . . A small stream often dried up . . . is crossed by the road. (336–37)

The hostility of this antisocial landscape is enhanced in "Mariana in the South" through an emphasis on evanescent qualities such as "glaring sand," "stony drought and steaming salt," and "all the furnace of the light / Struck up against the blinding wall" (8, 40, 55–56). Indeed, the elimination of concrete physical features is a characteristic of Tennyson's revision of the 1832 text for the 1842 volume of *Poems*. In the text published in 1842, for instance, there are no features as sharply defined as the "barren hill," "pointed rocks," and "crag sharpshadowed" of the earlier version, and the particularized "dry salt-marshes" of 1832 become unsubstantial "steaming salt" in 1842. The revised text also excludes any description of the landscape as bare (1832 has "barren hill" and "bare of green"), leaving the reader to infer barrenness from the poem's near silence on the subject of flora.

The Levantine southernness of "Fatima" is conveyed predominantly through the intense heat of the sun and the eroticism, or sexual abandonment, which this provokes in the female narrator, for whom the sun comes to mean both tormentor and lover. (The poem is a good example of what John Pemble has described as the Victorians' widely held belief that morals deteriorated as the weather improved.) In "Oenone" the mood of abandonment that characterizes the deserted wife of Paris on her entrance into the poem is expressed in the contrast between her wakefulness and the unnatural stillness that overcomes the natural world in the South when the sun is at its peak:

> For now the noonday quiet holds the hill:
> The grasshopper is silent in the grass:

The lizard, with his shadow on the stone,
Rests like a shadow, and the winds are dead.
The purple flower droops: the golden bee
Is lily-cradled: I alone awake. (24–29)

In this passage and in "Mariana in the South" and "Fatima," the firm physical features of the landscape are subordinated to evanescent qualities used to enhance the feeling of loneliness. The capturing of fugitive moments which are associated with isolation implies an immanent anxiety about inevitable and irrevocable abandonment. Tennyson's visit to the Pyrenees with Hallam served to remind him that love itself is a fugitive moment, as is a journey with a beloved friend. It is not surprising that loss, grief, and loneliness are the anxieties which haunt these poems, and the presentiment of abandonment was borne out when Hallam died in 1833.

Tennyson twice returned to the Pyrenees hoping to recapture the emotions he had invested in the landscape in 1830. In 1861 and again in 1874 he walked once more through the valley of Cauterets—a valley remarkable, as Murray's *Handbook* describes, for its "savage grandeur" and "contrast of rugged, gloomy wildness in the foreground, with the sunny richness beyond of groves, pastures, and cornfields" (301). Here in 1861 he was inspired to write a short pantheistic poem, reminiscent of the closing sections of *In Memoriam*, about hearing the voice of Hallam in the sound of the torrent which rushes through the valley's narrow gorge: "All along the valley, stream that flashest white, / Deepening thy voice with the deepening of the night . . ." (1–2). The sight and sound of rough water always exercised a peculiar fascination for Tennyson, and the frequent recurrence in his poetry of torrents, cataracts, and boisterous seas is far more than a Romantic trait. It may be that proximity to rough water helped him to attain the same metaphysical feeling of loss of individuality leading to union (or reunion) with what he called "boundless being" that he experienced when he put himself into states of trance.[14]

Certainly, if he expected to find rough water on his tour of the Rhine country in 1832, he was disappointed, and on the whole his second and last Continental trip with Hallam seems to have been less successful than the first. They found the scenery of the Rhine disappointing as far as Cologne (all tourists were of this opinion), and Tennyson complained because the weather was not hot enough; indeed, a letter of Hallam's suggests that Tennyson had a curious preconception that the Rhine lay in the South: "Our journey has not been to me unpleasant; but Alfred swears the Rhine is no more South than England, & he could make a better river himself! . . . He has written no jot of poetry."[15] He did find pleasure, however, in the Byronic scenery of the upper Rhine, and he and Hallam followed in the footsteps of Byron's Childe Harold in climbing the highest summit of the Seven Hills, the Dragon Rock or Drachenfels:

> The castled crag of Drachenfels
> Frowns o'er the wide and winding Rhine,
> Whose breast of waters broadly swells
> Between the banks which bear the vine,
> And hills all rich with blossom'd trees,
> And fields which promise corn and wine

(Childe Harold's Pilgrimage 3.55)

Byron's lyric to Augusta, with its wistful final couplet, "But one thing want these banks of Rhine,— / Thy gentle hand to clasp in mine!" is echoed in *In Memoriam*, and the echo enriches the confused emotions the poet feels as he bids farewell to his brother, embarking for the Rhine on a wedding tour:

> You leave us: you will see the Rhine,
> And those fair hills I sailed below,
> When I was there with him; and go
> By summer belts of wheat and vine (98, 1–4)

The echo recurs, but with a different effect, in the opening stanza of "The Daisy" (1855), the poem that records Tennyson's passionate response to visiting Italy for the first time, in 1851, with his wife, a year after their marriage:

> O love, what hours were thine and mine,
> In lands of palm and southern pine;
> In lands of palm, of orange-blossom,
> Of olive, aloe, and maize and vine. (1–4)

The Mediterranean flora, place names, and monuments that ornament the poem and sound like an incantation function as metaphors for the pleasurable physical and aesthetic sensations enjoyed and shared by the couple. While the rhyme scheme and meter jointly convey moods of gaiety and exhilaration, quiet moments for the meditative traveler are provided by recurrent medial caesuras, which function in the text like tablets inscribed "SISTE VIATOR": "Or rosy blossom in hot ravine, / Where oleanders flushed the bed / Of silent torrents, gravel-spread" (32–34). The length of the poem—twenty-seven stanzas tracing the couple's journey to Florence, the Italian Riviera, and back home across the Alps—reflects the expansive and vitalizing effect of Italy on the poet's imagination. What Jowett described as Tennyson's "living vision" of Italy really came to life during this tour, the reality corresponding to his ideal, and he was satisfied.

Of course, the concluding stanzas of "The Daisy" reveal that the poet is recollecting his experiences under circumstances of great contrast. Now alone and in Edinburgh, he chances to find in a book lent by his wife a dried specimen of the prosaic and domestic flower of the title, a memento of their journey: "I plucked a daisy, I gave it you. / It told of England then to me, / And now it tells of Italy" (87–89). As he describes the feelings evoked in him by the daisy, the poem becomes representative of the most recurrent theme in Tennyson's poetry, the power of the remembered past to allay the pain, sterility, and loneliness of the present:

> And I forgot the clouded Forth,
> The gloom that saddens Heaven and Earth,
>   The bitter east, the misty summer
> And gray metropolis of the North.
>
> Perchance, to lull the throbs of pain,
> Perchance, to charm a vacant brain,
>   Perchance, to dream you still beside me,
> My fancy fled to the South again. (101–8)

Tennyson and the Empire

Tennyson's familiarity with the world beyond the Mediterranean was limited by the qualities of his inward-looking character—self-absorption, self-interest, and self-preservation. Even though his appointment as Poet Laureate in 1850 obliged him to write occasional pieces on public events and international issues, he did not welcome the obligation, and his curiosity about the expanding world of the British Empire remained minimal.

Whereas the depiction of the European South in Tennyson's poetry is informed by the first-hand observations he made on his travels, the depiction of the wider world generally derives from two kinds of myth, one inherited from the Romantic tradition and the other generated by contemporary culture. The kind of myth employed depends upon whether the subjects are distanced by history or imagination, or whether they pertain to contemporary events. The use of these antithetical myths is most evident in the poems that feature exploration or that portray the non-European inhabitants of the exotic places that provided fields for colonial expansion.

Colonialism and the non-Christian, non-white "barbarians" whom it "civilized" (according to European notions) are subjects given a Romantic treatment in poems with historical or imaginative foundations. For example, the belief that corrupt European civilization will annihilate the idyllic life led by the native inhabitants of exotic places is implicit in early poems such as "Timbuctoo" and "Anacaona" (1830) and explicit in "Lamentation of the Peruvians" (1827), "Columbus" (1880), and "The Voyage of Maeldune" (1880). In "Columbus," a dramatic monologue based on Washington Irving's biography of the discoverer of the New World, Columbus is embittered and disillusioned not merely because he has been slighted by Spain, but also because he feels responsible for the despoliation of innocence: "Ah God, the harmless people whom we found / In Hispaniola's island-Paradise!" (177–78). In "The Voyage of Maeldune," based on an Irish legend, a group of brave men bent on revenging a death sail from island to island, brawling among themselves and killing each other, and leaving behind them in each place destruction and death.

As Columbus's reference to "harmless people" suggests, the native inhabitants depicted in colonial poems with an historical or imaginative origin are types of the Romantic "Noble Savage," who are invariably naked and brown and live on islands in a state of happy innocence. Thus Columbus wistfully recalls "those happy naked isles" of Hispaniola (169)—the same islands, in fact, ruled by the historical Haitian queen Anacaona, "Wantoning in orange groves / Naked, and dark-limbed, and gay" (5–6). "Anacaona" portrays the queen and her maidens welcoming the Spaniards from their ships: "Naked, without fear . . . / Waving a palm branch, wondering, loving, / Carolling 'Happy, happy Hayti!'" (61, 63–64). So as not to spoil the mood of joyously innocent eroticism, there is no mention in the poem of the historical fact that Anacaona was afterwards killed by the Spaniards.

Victorian travelers in hot climates admired and envied dark complexions, considering them healthy and sexually attractive.[16] Tennyson himself was so naturally swarthy that he was often mistaken for a foreigner, so the note of envy which is obvious in his depictions of dark-skinned "Noble Savages" might seem, at first, surprising. But what is envied is the absence of physical and moral constraints, for in his poetry the recurrent figure of the dark-skinned savage is a metaphor for sexual freedom which is innocent because it is untroubled by a Christian conscience. Moreover, many of Tennyson's sexy savages are depicted either swimming in or floating on the sea, the symbol by which he often represents the subconscious (and thus liberated) mind. There are, for example, the surfing South Sea islanders alluded to in *In Memoriam* (37: 15–16),[17] the "Dark faces pale" of the Lotos-eaters whose boats greet Odysseus, and those metonymical relations of the Lotos-eaters, "the naked limbs and flowers and fruit" which greet the sailors in "The Voyage" (composed 1836).

The feelings of envy with which such unrealizable escapist fantasies are charged explain in part the antagonism toward dark-skinned peoples to which Tennyson gave vent in "Locksley Hall" (1842). The violence with which the narrator recoils from his tropical fantasy is an example of how hatred can be the reaction against envy:

There the passions cramped no longer shall have scope and breathing space;
I will take some savage woman, she shall rear my dusky race.

Iron jointed, supple-sinewed, they shall dive, and they shall run,
Catch the wild goat by the hair, and hurl their lances in the sun;

Whistle back the parrot's call, and leap the rainbows of the brooks,
Not with blinded eyesight poring over miserable books—

Fool, again the dream, the fancy! but I *know* my words are wild,
But I count the gray barbarian lower than the Christian child.

I, to herd with narrow foreheads, vacant of our glorious gains,
Like a beast with lower pleasures, like a beast with lower pains!

Mated with a squalid savage—what to me were sun or clime?
I the heir of all the ages, in the foremost files of time— (167–78)

His reaction is also representative of the widely held opinions about race which had developed by the 1840s as a result of a growing popular interest in ethnology and which, as the Empire expanded in the century, profoundly influenced British attitudes toward the dark-skinned populations of Britain's overseas possessions. Ethnologists discredited the Romantic belief in racial egalitarianism and in the savage who was nobler than the European, maintaining that race was the sole cultural determinant and that there was a great discrepancy of intellect between the Anglo-Saxon race at the top of the scale and the dark-skinned populations at the bottom. As Tennyson had long believed in the theory of gradual, progressive evolution, and that the spiritual aim of mankind was to "Move upward, working out the beast, / And let the ape and tiger die," he could readily subscribe to the supposedly scientific evidence of ethnology.[18]

Never an independent thinker, Tennyson shared many other prevailing beliefs and prejudices, including the intensely emotional nationalism which characterized all of nineteenth-century Europe and the xenophobia which the British felt particularly for France and Russia. Francophobia had resulted from the French Revolution and the Napoleonic wars and was rekindled first in 1848 by the revolution in Paris and then in 1851 by the

124

coup d'état with which Louis Napoleon revived the French Empire. Russo-phobia developed in the early nineteenth century after nearly three hundred years of consistently friendly relations between Britain and Russia. Emerging from the Napoleonic wars as the pre-eminent powers in Europe, the countries were cast in the role of rivals with competitive imperial ambitions, and the British formed certain hostile stereotypes and notions about Russia and the Czar. By the 1840s this hostility had matured and would help to foment the popular support for Britain's role in the Crimean War.[19]

Tennyson's instinctive conservatism, love of freedom, hatred of tyranny and fear of social disorder made it easy for him to appropriate as his own the national anxieties about France and Russia. In numerous poems composed in the 1830s ("English War Song," "National Song," "Buonaparte," "Hail Briton!," "I loving Freedom for herself," "You ask me why . . .," "Of old sat Freedom on the heights," and "Love thou thy land, with love far-brought"), he gave vent to the fierce patriotism and fiercer xenophobia which would again be fueled by the political events of the 1850s, when they found expression in his jingoistic poems of 1852 (such as "Britons, guard you own," "Hands all round!," "Rifle Clubs!!!," and "Riflemen Form!").

All these poems, and indeed all of Tennyson's strictly political statements, are marked (and marred) by prophetic, exclamatory, and bellicose tones, evidence that they served him as a field on which to release the feelings of physical violence and activity which his chronically fearful and indolent temperament prevented him from expressing in real life. What redeems Tennyson's other poems of the 1850s in which nationalism and xenophobia figure (such as the "Ode on the Death of the Duke of Wellington," "The Charge of the Light Brigade," and *Maud*) is that political issues and sentiments are only marginal or implicit and were not the occasion of composition.

Maud (1855), for example, the most important poem of this period, originated as a love story, and the subsidiary themes concerning domestic politics and the Crimean War were introduced only as foils for the emotions generated in the mentally unstable narrator by his love for Maud.[20] Anxious that he should be seen to write a poem about contemporary life, Tennyson made use of new sections to deal with two major preoccupations of the day, the Crimean War and the growth of commerce, or free trade, during times of peace. Partly on account of the aggressive and bellicose manner in which these subjects are treated, Tennyson's opinions about them were widely misunderstood upon publication, and he took pains to dissociate his own attitudes from those of the unstable narrator, explaining that he himself was neither against commerce nor in favor of war.

One attitude which he seems to share with the narrator, however, is that the competition and brutality engendered by a commercial society can be redeemed through active participation in the integration of new regions into the expanding British economy.[21] The hope that free trade, by uniting the nations of the world, might actually prevent war is voiced by the Poet in the "Epilogue" (1885) to "The Charge of the Heavy Brigade":

> I would that wars should cease . . .
> And some new Spirit o'erbear the old,
>   Or Trade re-frain the Powers
> From war with kindly links of gold. (10, 13–15)

Tennyson's best known expression of the widely held Victorian belief that enterprise is the main instrument of expansion and international harmony occurs in the boyhood dream of the narrator in "Locksley Hall" (1837–38):

> For I dipt into the future, far as human eye could see,
> Saw the Vision of the world, and all the wonder that would be;
>
> Saw the heavens fill with commerce, argosies of magic sails,
> Pilots of the purple twilight, dropping down with costly bales . . .
>
> Far along the world-wide whisper of the south-wind rushing warm,
> With the standards of the peoples plunging through the thunder-storm;
>
> Till the war-drum throbbed no longer, and the battle-flags were furled
> In the Parliament of man, the Federation of the world. (119–28)

A year after writing "Locksley Hall," Tennyson expressed the same sentiments in the form of a song composed by his alter ego, Leonard, the poet in "The Golden Year" (1846; composed 1839):

> And slow and sure
>   Comes up the golden year.
> "When wealth no more shall rest in mounded heaps,
> But smit with freër light shall slowly melt
> In many streams to fatten lower lands . . .
>   "Fly, happy happy sails, and bear the Press;
> Fly happy with the mission of the Cross;
> Knit land to land, and blowing havenward
> With silks, and fruits, and spices, clear of toll,
> Enrich the markets of the golden year. (31–34, 42–46)

The most overt equation of free-trade and imperialism appears, appropriately, in the ode "On the Jubilee of Queen Victoria" (1887):

> Fifty years of ever-broadening Commerce!
> Fifty years of ever-brightening Science!
> Fifty years of ever-widening Empire! (52–54)

The belief which informs all these passages, a belief shared by nearly all Victorians, is that the establishment of commercial relations with foreign countries would bring about an international collaboration resulting in a common concern for peace and liberal reform and uniting the enlightened groups of disparate communities.[22] Tennyson's support for the policy of imperialism derived from his conviction that a powerful and unified Empire constituted the only protection against one of his greatest fears, a social and materialist revolution which would overwhelm the world. Thus in many poems composed in the latter part of the century, when some politicians argued that liberation of the colonies was socially and economically desirable, Tennyson urges Britain to preserve her imperial unity and resist attempts to break up the Empire. Indeed, in "To the Queen" (1873), the epilogue to *Idylls of the King* in which he points out the relevance of his Arthurian cycle to contemporary life, he implicitly likens the threatened dissolution of the Empire to the dissolution of the Round Table.

The exclamatory and patriotic tones of Tennyson's statements about the Empire belie the doubt expressed elsewhere that the glorious hopes for expansion, prosperity, progress, and universal harmony can ever be realized: the optimism of Leonard's song about the coming golden year is at once deflated by his realistic companions, and the "vision of the world, and all the wonder that would be" in "Locksley Hall" is merely the irrecoverable boyhood dream of the disillusioned narrator. More generally, the apparent hopefulness implied in the determination of Tennyson's mariners to set forth on yet another journey ("Ulysses," "Columbus," "The Voyage," "Merlin and the Gleam") hardly conceals that their earlier journeys ended, if not in total failure, at least in disappointment.

In the light of these voyages of discovery—Tennyson's recurrent metaphor for the attempt to find a purpose in life—it is curious that he should have chosen the same image for the poem he was invited to write as a prefatory sonnet for the first number of a new journal, the *Nineteenth Century* (1877). In the conceit, the staff of the journal are the crew of the newly chartered craft. They are veterans of previous voyages, and some have lost their faith. There are some among them who are idealists, and these are described in the final lines of the sonnet:

> And some are wilder comrades, sworn to seek

If any golden harbour be for men
In seas of Death and sunless gulfs of Doubt.

Asked to write a prefatory sonnet to the *Nineteenth Century*, Tennyson seized the opportunity to write, with the despondent foresight of a disappointed Romantic, an epilogue to nineteenth century expansion itself.

NOTES

Quotations from Tennyson's poems (except *In Memoriam* and *Maud*) and information about their composition are from *The Poems of Tennyson*, ed. Christopher Ricks (London: 1969); quotations from the other poems and information about them are from *Tennyson: "In Memoriam,"* ed. Susan Shatto and Marion Shaw (Oxford: 1982) and *Tennyson's "Maud": A Definitive Edition*, ed. Susan Shatto (London: 1986). The letters of Tennyson and Hallam are quoted from *The Letters of Alfred Lord Tennyson*, ed. Cecil Y. Lang and Edgar F. Shannon Jr., 2 vols. (Oxford: 1982–) (cited as *Letters*) and *The Letters of Arthur Henry Hallam*, ed. Jack Kolb (Columbus, OH: 1981). Tennyson's comments are quoted from *The Works of Alfred, Lord Tennyson*, ed. Hallam, Lord Tennyson, Eversley Edition, 9 vols (London: 1907–8) (cited as *Eversley*).

1. *The Letters of Arthur Henry Hallam* 601.
2. *The Letters of Arthur Henry Hallam* 597; *Letters* 2.261; *The Letters of Arthur Henry Hallam* 604; *Letters* 1.179, 281.
3. *Letters* 2.241, 1.264.
4. *Letters* 2.258.
5. James Knowles, "Aspects of Tennyson: II (A Personal Reminiscence)," *Nineteenth Century* 33 (1893): 170; *Eversley* 7.375.
6. Martin 25; W. D. Paden, *Tennyson in Egypt: A Study of the Imagery in His Earlier Work* (1942; New York: 1971) 1–16.
7. *Letters* 1.109.
8. Galbraith Welch, *The Unveiling of Timbuctoo: The Astounding Adventures of Caillié* (London: 1938); Brian Gardner, *The Quest for Timbuctoo* (London: 1968); Hallman B. Bryant, "The African Genesis of Tennyson's 'Timbuctoo,'" *Tennyson Research Bulletin* 3 (1981): 196–202; A. Dwight Culler, *The Poetry of Tennyson* (New Haven and London: 1977) 22–23. Bryant states that the discovery of Timbuctoo by Caillié in 1828 and the publication of Caillié's journal influenced the choice of subject for the Prize Poem, and he implies that Tennyson had read the journal before writing his poem (200). But Caillié made his first oral report of Timbuctoo in Tangiers in September 1828, and his *Journal d'un Voyage à Temboctou . . .* (3 vols.) was not published in France until 1830, the same year it was published in an English translation (2 vols., London) (see *British Museum Catalogue*). The evidence that the subject of the poem was announced in mid-

December 1828 is given by Paden 139 (citing the entry in the *University Calendar*) and Culler 256 (citing *The Times*).

9. Paden 71.
10. See John Pemble, *The Mediterranean Passion: Victorians and Edwardians in the South* (Oxford: 1987) 51–109; *Letters* 1.178; "To Ulysses" (1889) line 29.
11. Pemble 114–28; *Memoir* 1.340–1; Pemble 128.
12. Crazy Jane is discussed by Elaine Showalter, *The Female Malady: Women, Madness and English Culture, 1830–1980* (London: 1987) 11–14.
13. *The Letters of Arthur Henry Hallam* 401.
14. *Eversley* 3.217.
15. *The Letters of Arthur Henry Hallam* 616.
16. Pemble 123–24.
17. For Tennyson's literary source for these lines, see *Tennyson: "In Memoriam"* 200.
18. Philip D. Curtin, *The Image of Africa: British Ideas and Action, 1780–1850* (Madison, WI: 1964) 328–31, 363–87; *In Memoriam* 118.27–28.
19. John Howes Gleason, *The Genesis of Russophobia in Great Britain* (Cambridge, MA: 1950) 1–8, 276–77, 284–85, 289. My comments on Tennyson's politics are indebted to three essays: Charles Tennyson, "Tennyson's Politics," *Six Tennyson Essays* (London: 1954) 39–69; F.J. Sypher, "Politics in the Poetry of Tennyson," *Victorian Poetry* 14 (1976): 101–12; Elizabeth A. Francis, "Tennyson's Political Poetry, 1852–1855," *Victorian Poetry* 14 (1976): 113–23.
20. *Tennyson's "Maud": A Definitive Edition* 32.
21. John Gallagher and Ronald Robinson, "The Imperialism of Free Trade," *The Economic History Review* 2nd ser., 6 (1953): 1–15; John Gallagher and Ronald Robinson, *Africa and the Victorians: The Official Mind of Imperialism* (London: 1961) 1–26.
22. Gallagher and Robinson 3.

THE DICKENS WORLD

Andrew Sanders, Birkbeck College, University of London

It is sometimes hard to determine whether or not Charles Dickens ever relaxed. As his published letters demonstrate, he was a very active daily correspondent, even on Christmas Day. His journalist's instinct meant that even his holidays, his vacation rambles, and his tours abroad became the stuff of essays, articles, and scenes in his novels and short stories. In many ways, London's greatest delineator always took something of London with him wherever he went. Dickens, who, unlike most other English writers, found the noise and activity of the city an active stimulus to his work, was often restless without the restlessness of the city around him. He wrote home from Lausanne in August 1846 to express his dismay at the paucity of busy streets in Switzerland:

> I can't express how much I want these. It seems as if they supplied something to my brain, which it cannot bear, when busy, to lose. For a week or a fortnight I can write prodigiously in a retired place . . . and a day in London sets me up again and starts me. But the toil and labour of writing, day after day, without that magic lantern, is IMMENSE !! (*Pilgrim Letters* 4.612)

A month later he still found himself troubled by this physical hiatus in his creative life and complained to Thomas Mitton that, "There are no streets and crowds of people here, to divert the attention. My head suffers" (*Pilgrim Letters* 4.623–24). Dickens always seems to have been most stimulated, and therefore at his happiest, when diverted by, or writing about, cities which were as distracting as London. He loves Paris, admires Boston and New York, and, more detachedly, relishes both Genoa and Naples. He was clearly bored by Lausanne, and he found the placid decay and the market gardens among the ruins of Rome irritating (even though the view of the city

131

from the Campagna had at first stirred the cockney in him to think of London).

Dickens's restlessness, evidenced in his shifting the furniture around in his numerous hotel rooms as much as in his periodic changes of home, clearly found some further release in travel. As a consistent social and political progressive he derived both pleasure and satisfaction from the relative efficiency of Victorian travel by railway, steam-packet, and Atlantic steamer. Getting from London to Paris in a mere eleven hours in the 1850s struck him at once as a realization of an *Arabian Nights* fantasy and as a vivid contrast with the discomforts of the old *diligences* ("all the summer dust . . . all the winter mud . . . the Frenchman with the nightcap . . . who always fell upon me when he went to sleep . . . snoring onions"). But though the sensation of travel and the excitement of being in a foreign place broadened Dickens's mind, both also served to confirm his prejudices. He generally found his fellow countrymen as irritating as travelling companions as he found them in their native island. A wonderfully crass Englishman at the Holy Week ceremonies in Rome seeks noisily for evidence of a mustard pot on the table during a re-enactment of the Last Supper in *Pictures from Italy* (1846); a rich Englishman (typed as "Monied Interest") bound for Paris in "A Flight" insistently reiterates the opinion that the French are "no go" as a nation because they are revolutionary and "always at it" (*Reprinted Pieces*, 481); the English travelers in *Little Dorrit* (1855–59) are either as blinkered as Mrs. General ("It is essential that all persons of polite cultivation should see with other people's eyes, and never with their own") or as stupid as Mr. Sparkler (436). Dickens sees the evidence of too much history and tradition in Italy, and of too little in the United States. He flatters the France he clearly loved, but nearly every French character to appear in his fiction proves to be some kind of villain. He goes into raptures about Mont Blanc ("It is impossible to imagine anything more noble and beautiful than the scene"), but then, according to his biographer, John Forster, turns to longing for Paris again (*Pilgrim Letters* 4.656; Forster 441–42). Other Victorians may have contemplated the Alps and found a spirit of serenity; Dickens turns from the mountains in one of his letters and remarks, "I have no doubt that constant change, too, is indispensable to me when I am at work" (*Pilgrim Letters* 4.656).

By the middle of his career Dickens had traveled widely in two continents, Europe and North America; in the 1860s he contemplated visiting a third, Australia (a continent which he nonetheless peopled with fictional characters as both forced and voluntary emigrants). He visited continental Europe as a private man and as a holiday-maker, but he used his experiences to make a travel book (*Pictures from Italy*) and a series of essays for his journals. He visited America as a celebrity and as a determined sightseer, but in describing the sensitive young Republic in *American Notes* (1842) and *Martin Chuzzlewit* (1843–44) he succeeded in ruffling feathers. The world beyond western Europe and North America figures only minimally in his work, and though representatives of Britain's colonial influence turn up on occasion, like Major Bagstock from India in *Dombey and Son* [1848], or Neville and Helena Landless from Ceylon in *The Mystery of Edwin Drood* [1870], Dickens knew these countries only at second or third hand. Like Mr. Sapsea, the insular native of Cloisterham in *Edwin Drood*, although he had not gone to foreign countries, foreign countries came to him "in the way of business," and he too improved on his opportunities (25).

The emphatic oriental theme which runs as a tantalizing thread through *The Mystery of Edwin Drood* probably originated in Dickens's formative reading of the *Arabian Nights* as a boy. These tales kept his fancy, like David Copperfield's, alive and spurred "the hope of something beyond" (48) the limits of place and unhappy times. The "beyondness" of these stories seems always to have been associated with the exotic and the wonderful, with magic and luxury. When David Copperfield compares Mr. Peggotty's boat to "Aladdin's palace, roc's egg and all," readers catch hints of the force of this "romantic idea" (25). Dickens also reverses this oriental imagery when it suits his fictional purposes. In *Hard Times* (1854), Mr. M'Choakumchild is compared to Ali Baba's slave, Morgiana, as he looks into all the child vessels ranged before him in the schoolroom to see what they contained; rather than stirring the childish imagination, the teacher attempts to kill outright "the robber Fancy lurking within" (6). The fatalistic and magical elements in the *Arabian Nights* are recalled in a tragic mood in *A Tale of Two Cities* (1854). Like Agib, the son of Cassib, in the "Third Calendar's Tale" of the *Arabian Nights*, Dickens's Charles Darnay is drawn mysteriously and irresistibly to the "Loadstone Rock" of his destiny, and at the very end of the novel morally distorted revolutionary Paris is seen as somehow enchanted, like the ape in the "Second Calendar's Tale." Paris too awaits a formula which will turn it back into its proper shape (bk. 3, ch. 15). The *Arabian Nights* embodied the essence of the rich and strange, but though they provide some of Dickens's most striking imagery and continued to feed his creative imagination, he never seems to have sought to travel in the Middle East. It is possible that his disillusionment with other fancied places like America ("this is not the Republic of my imagination") and Rome ("not the Rome of anybody's fancy, man or boy") precluded the risk of further disappointment (*Pilgrim Letters* 3.156; *Pictures from Italy* 365).

The *Mystery of Edwin Drood* opens with an oriental dream, but it is an opium dream which confuses English Cloisterham with Constantinople or Baghdad. Waking up is painful, but necessary. Dickens's awareness of a wider world often seems to consist of an initial exploration of a fancy, succeeded by a period of readjustment provoked either by delight or distaste. He was an instinctive traveler and, had he further cultivated the art, he might have become a great travel writer. He was certainly no little Englander. When his accounts reveal a man pricked into anger, or stimulated into curiosity, or simply thrilled, it is because impressions are translated into words and a succession of details form themselves into a whole. The wider world was no dream to Dickens and it is essential in reading his work to distinguish between his imaginative relish for the exotic and his realist's stubborn, commonsensical feeling of how things really are. If Dickens abroad remains a cockney Dickens, it is because his imaginative and his critical faculties went hand in hand. He was fascinated by the multifarious-ness of the urban culture of the nineteenth century and as a traveler he continues to observe the ramifications of the same multifariousness. The complexity and contradictoriness of early Victorian London provided him with an ideal starting point.

The title of *Pictures from Italy* is both a challenge and a compliment to Italy. It offers sketches of a peregrination through a land of pictures; it may reject much of what had conventionally been seen as "picturesque" but it also seeks to observe freshly and not with the borrowed eyes of *Little Dorritt's* Mrs. General. Dickens may well emerge from his book as blink-ered, Whiggish, and English Protestant, but his pose forms part of his determination to suggest that Italy has a future and that its "noble people" may be raised up from the ashes of an ambiguous past and a decadent present.

That Dickens responded more to Italian cities than to Italian landscapes might be predicted. As with the descriptions of English fields, meadows, and gardens in his novels, he is often bland when picturing useful or fertile tracts of land. He is better at mountains, but, townsman as he is, there is more of a hint of their inconvenience than of their sublimity. In *Pictures from Italy* the high Apennines seem "as bare and desolate as any Scottish moors" and "as barren, as stony, and as wild, as Cornwall" (360–62). Dickens may pay conventional compliments to the Alps, may find the Simplon "stupendous," and may write of "the lonely grandeur" of her summits, but there is nothing in his work to compare with the careful, ecstatic rhythms of Ruskin (348–49). The account of the travelers' arrival at the convent of the Great St. Bernard at the opening of Book 2 of *Little Dorrit* also conveys an impression of unrelieved coldness, solitude, and loneliness. Silence imposes itself on the weary climbers up "the broken staircase of a gigantic ruin" (420). The novelist scarcely seeks to convey exhilaration at the point in his subdued story of 1855–57, but there is a sense in which his own evident lack of elation in the earlier travel book informs the novel. A similar response can be observed as David Copperfield finds the "awful solitudes" speaking to his bereft heart as he crosses the Alps after the death of Dora. As he descends to a valley, however, the renewal of human contact begins the process of consolation. Cottages dot the lower slopes and Swiss shepherds sing:

> All at once, in this serenity, great Nature spoke to me; and soothed me to lay down my weary head upon the grass, and weep as I had not wept yet, since Dora died! (698)

The mood of emotional restoration is reinforced as David discovers letters from Agnes waiting for him at the inn. David may assert that, on Agnes's advice, he seeks out Nature, and that he "never sought in vain," but it seems that his earlier solitude is increasingly replaced by human company. He makes "almost as many friends in the valley as in Yarmouth," and he avoids the snows by wintering in Geneva (699).

It is significant that one of Dickens's finest verbal impressions of European landscape comes not in *Pictures from Italy* but in the nearly contemporary *Dombey and Son*. Carker's fevered journey across France in Chapter 55 of the novel must derive in part from the novelist's impressions of his own travels to and from Italy in 1844–46. The account of Carker's experiences is, of course, molded to suit the state of his mind, but Dickens's short, breathless phrases admirably reflect the sensation of movement. Times and weather conditions change; long country roads give way to the clatter of small towns, the small towns to Paris, Paris to the Channel coast. It is the continental equivalent to Mr. Dombey's haunted railway journey to Leamington in Chapter 20, and, like it, underneath the impression of an individual's response we sense something of Dickens's own stimulation. Instead of contemplation, we have a series of flashing images. Accounts of travel are generally missing from *Pictures from Italy*, for here the sense of movement is conveyed through a succession of places rather than roadside views. The "pictures" are for the most part portraits, genre scenes, and townscapes, not landscapes.

The 1844 journey to Italy was by way of Paris. Although Dickens does not include a full account of his two days in the French capital in *Pictures from Italy*, the impact of the city was "immense." He told Count D'Orsay that he had found it "the most extraordinary place in the World"; his eyes had ached and his head had grown giddy as "novelty, novelty, novelty" came swarming before him (*Pilgrim Letters* 4.166). Even after two weeks in Italy, Dickens still recalled the impact of Paris with enthusiasm; he had walked "in and out, up and down, backwards and forwards" in its streets, and almost every house and person he passed "seemed to be another leaf in the enormous book that stands wide open there" (*Pilgrim Letters* 4.167). His image is striking. Cities are like books and books can be made of cities. Only

Venice, of all the Italian cities he visited, was to stir him as much. Nevertheless, the "novelty" of Genoa did eventually work favorably upon him. On one level his main Italian base reminded him of the slums of London. He compared the Strada Nuova and the Strada Balbi (the two grandest thoroughfares in the port) to Drury Lane and Wych Street in their narrowness, though he conceded that both were *"filled with palaces of noble architecture"*; the city's byways recalled Field Lane in Holborn, and, taken as a whole, "of all the mouldy, dreary, sleepy, dirty, lagging, halting, God-forgotten towns," Genoa seemed "the uttermost superlative" (*Pilgrim Letters* 4.163, 169). His first impressions were not steady, however, for there proved to be much to fascinate him: "I can sit down in a church, or stand at the end of a narrow Vico, zig-zagging uphill like a dirty snake: and not feel the least desire for any further entertainment" (*Pilgrim Letters* 4.169). He later admitted to finding "many hours of happiness and quiet," sensations which are unlikely to have been stirred by St. Giles. Dickens's reaction to Naples is similar. He first found the city filthy and full of beggars, its picturesqueness being a mere veneer on its poverty, but, as with Genoa, the life of the streets enthralled and endlessly amused him.

With the notable exception of the Coliseum, Rome proved disappointing. The city's theatricality, especially its ecclesiastical theater, gives rise to some of the funniest scenes in *Pictures from Italy*, and Dickens admits to being "giddy" with delight at the Carnival, but generally there seem to be too many churches, too many religious, and too much of an air of decay. Lacking a solid classical education (though, of course, he had more than simply the rudiments of Latin), he was only modestly inspired by antiquities. The Vatican and Capitoline statute evoke "wonderful gravity and repose," but generally Roman remains appear to him to be violently stained with ancient blood. Every ruin, however moving in its "transcendent melancholy," is haunted by "the dark ghost of its bloody holidays" and by the shadow of "its awful self, immovable" (407–8). Dickens's often-quoted remark to Forster on his return journey to Rome in 1853 that the electric telegraph wires passing through the Coliseum were like a sunbeam through its "cruel old heart" has often been interpreted as an example of his philistinism (Forster 583). The remark should, however, be qualified by a recall of the "enchantment" worked by the ruin during the novelist's first visit. He went there continually and could never see enough of it; he viewed it "by daylight, moonlight, torchlight, and every sort of light" and described it as both "tremendous" and "awful" (*Pilgrim Letters* 4.282). Despite his suspicion that modern Romans would have been happy to see the monument in use again, he asserted that he had never in his life been so moved by any sight "except perhaps by the first contemplation of the Falls of Niagara" (Forster 369).

Very much of Dickens's ambiguity about modern Italy was conditioned by his antipathy to the outward forms of Roman Catholicism and by his progressivist, Protestant conviction that the nation was worse off for its historic enslavement to Popery. As the deeply prejudiced *A Child's History of England* forcefully suggests, he believed that the Reformation had consigned Popes, monks, relics, and indulgences to the lumber room of history. Italy proved, in many cases, to be that lumber room. The views on Italian art expressed in *Pictures from Italy* stem from related prejudices. Unlike the agnostic George Eliot, who assiduously followed the advice of guidebooks and art historians on her visits to Italian churches and galleries, Dickens relied more on his instincts and on his keen but untrained eye when he formed opinions of painters and paintings. Yet again, his proves to be a subjective rather than a cultivated sensibility, one which refused to be cowed by tradition, precedent, and accepted opinion. In his travel book he asserts his credentials as an amateur of painting and as *l'homme moyen sensuel*:

I am not mechanically acquainted with the art of painting, and have no other means of judging of a picture than as I see it resembling and refining upon nature, and presenting graceful combinations of form and colours. (345–46)

While rejecting baroque excess and a great deal of exclusively Catholic imagery, he seems to have found certain pictures by Raphael, Titian, Tintoretto, Andrea del Sarto, and Van Dyck "natural," "graceful," and consequently impressive. He was revolted by distortion (Guilio Romano at Mantua), distressed by sprawling decay (Coreggio's "labyrinth of arms and legs" [359] at Parma) and worried by assertive male nudity (Raphael's *Fire in the Borgo* Michaelangelo's *Last Judgment* at Rome).[1]

The two pictures to which Dickens responded most warmly were both in Venice. Perhaps it was here, clearly his favorite Italian city, that his artistic sensibility was at its most acute and his anti-Catholicism was relaxed by memories of the city's independent history. He was impressed by that most Catholic of pictures, Titian's *Assumption* (then in the Accademia), a painting which he found "perfection," but he was most taken by Tintoretto's frescoes in the Doge's Palace. On these he wrote to Forster during his second Italian visit:

There are pictures by Tintoretto in Venice more delightful and masterly than it is possible sufficiently to express. His Assembly of the Blest, I do believe to be, take it all in all, the most wonderful and charming picture ever painted. (Forster 586)

137

This is praise indeed from such a willful critic, but it was not an opinion that was then widely shared by connoisseurs (Ruskin's firm advocacy of Tintoretto was relatively new and it is unlikely that Dickens had heeded it in 1845). The impact of the pictures must have been enhanced by the feeling of animation and the "graceful combination of form and colours" which Dickens experienced in the surrounding townscape of Venice, the city of his "Italian Dream." Here, uniquely, the fantasies of the *Arabian Nights* seemed to be dreamily embodied even, as in the cases of the Piazza and the interior of St. Mark's, to be outclassed. Venice beggared description in its "absorbing loveliness"; the Doge's Palace was "more majestic and magnificent in its old age, than all the buildings of the earth, in the high prime and fulness of their youth" (331); St. Mark's proved to be "unreal, fantastic, solemn," and even though the prison adjoining the palace (to which Dickens was drawn by his customary instinct for such structures) "flowed the same water that filled this Dream." Significantly, though, this dreamy city is, unlike the other cities of *Pictures from Italy*, virtually unpopulated. Venice seems to have encapsulated everything Dickens most loved in Italy, except its street life; it also contained reminders of everything he suspected. The city is a "dreamy, beautiful, inconsistent, impossible, wicked, shadowy, damnable old place" and Dickens is bowled over by it (*Pilgrim Letters* 4.220). Nevertheless, it is the shadows which surface again when the novelist treats the city in fiction. When the Dorrit family arrive in this "crowning unreality" of Europe, that string of adjectives may well have been in his mind as they move into a second Marshalsea on the Grand Canal.

Dickens's Venice is a city trapped by its transcendent beauty and by its sinister past. His Paris, both more accessible to him and more consistently a favorite, was very much a city redeemed from its immediate past. It was also living out a peculiar destiny in Dickens's present. The novelist's affection for France and the French was conditioned by his knowledge of its recent history, a history which both depressed and inspired him. In February 1848 he wrote enthusiastically to Forster concerning the revolution which had toppled Louis-Philippe and established the Second Republic. After an adulatory paean in French, Dickens signs himself "CITOYEN CHARLES DICKENS" (*Pilgrim Letters* 5.257). The use of the title "Citoyen" here is no mere play with the idea of temporary foreign nationality, but rather an acceptance of the nomenclature of the first Revolution which, as he later noted in *A Tale of Two Cities*, had compulsorily replaced the title "Monsieur." That first Revolution was evidently much in his thoughts throughout his life. It had possibly formed the subject of boyhood discussions with a father directly involved in naval affairs after the long revolutionary wars with France; it was a subject treated so memorably by Carlyle in a book which Dickens claimed in 1851 to have read five hundred times (*Nonesuch Letters* 2.335)! From Carlyle came the prejudices that the culture of the *ancien regime* consisted of little more than a "leprosy of unreality" and that pre-revolutionary society had been effete and over-stratified. None of these aspects was likely to have appealed to the nonsense liberal in Dickens. As an admirer of the principles of the American Revolution, he was also convinced that France's revolution had taken a dangerous route in 1791 and that the September massacres and the Reign of Terror suggested the unhappy depths to which human nature might fall. He was also persuaded that those excesses were a response to earlier repression and cruelty. As we see them in *A Tale of Two Cities*, the streets of Paris are blood-stained. They were streets that Dickens knew well, but in his description of the modern city there is no ghost to parallel those haunting the ruins of Rome. Paris was a city transformed, and that transformation is the one looked forward to in Sydney Carton's visionary hope of "a beautiful city and a brilliant people risen from the abyss."

In his dying vision Carton also sees the Place de la Concorde as "fair to look upon" and freed of the "disfigurement" of its guillotine and its revolutionary trappings. The disfigurement might also be that of the twisted society which had produced both the guillotine's victims and those who applauded their death. Despite its latter-day poverty (of which, surprisingly, Dickens says very little), the city he knew seemed to have grown away from the oppression and injustice of the past. Its nineteenth-century revolutions were liberal and liberating, not a redressing of grievances toppling over into new injustice (though he was reserved about the regime of Napoleon III). Paris was to him a fantasy of light and pleasure, not the focus of his political concerns.

Dickens's feeling of elation in 1844 remained a constant element in each of his return visits to Paris. Twenty years later he puts into the mouth of Mrs. Lirriper something of his continuing delight:

> And of Paris I can tell you no more my dear than that it's town and country both in one, and carved stone and long streets of high houses and gardens and fountains and statues and trees and gold, and immensely big soldiers and immensely little soldiers and the pleasantest nurses . . . and clean table-cloths spread everywhere for dinner and people sitting out of doors smoking and sipping all day long . . . and every shop a complete and elegant room, and everybody seeming to play at everything in this world. And as to the sparkling lights my dear after dark, glittering high up and low down and on before and on behind and all round, and the crowd of theatres and the crowd of people and the crowd of all sorts, its pure enchantment. ("Mrs. Lirriper's Legacy" 422)

139

At the end of this gushing tribute we come back again to the word "enchantment." Paris is magical, and compared to it London is mundane; it is differently ordered, and in its "novelty, novelty, novelty" it has a different appeal. Dickens, who spent so many summers in "Our French Watering Place" (Boulogne-sur-Mer), was always inclined to slip southwest to the capital. If we seek for the real alternative to the centrality of London in Dickens's experience, it is Paris. In his fiction, however, the Revolutionary past gives a violent edge to the contrast of the two cities. Somehow, modern, unmagical London was too real an inspiration to him ever to be eclipsed.

Dickens deals with America both in fiction and in his earlier travel book, *American Notes* (1842). Both books have been widely discussed.[2] In both there is evidence of amused affection and of antipathy. There is very little room for enchantment. The America he had once imagined, a land without aristocracy, privilege, and the cloying institutions he despised in England, proved not to be fulfilled in the reality he observed, and his awakening was painful. Dickens wrote to his actor-friend, Macready, on March 22, 1842, after two months in the United States:

> This is not the Republic I came to see. This is not the Republic of my imagination. I infinitely prefer a liberal Monarchy—even with its sickening accompaniments . . . to such a Government as this. In every respect but that of National Education, the Country disappoints me. The more I think of its youth and strength, the poorer and more trifling in a thousand respects, it appears in my eyes. (*Pilgrim Letters* 3.156)

This disappointment, expressed so stingingly, is not the result of a temporary tetchiness but of a profounder awareness that perhaps there were no ideal republics, past, present, or to come. He wanted America to be different from England, but he didn't like the differences he saw. He was also judging by English standards. Dickens may well have molded his imagined republic in his own image, larger than life, but expressive of his own aspirations to generosity, liberty, excitement, earnestness, and self-help. The imagined creature proved to have gone its own way; given its freedom, it had chosen a very individual expression. Dickens's spleen derives from the shock that the atrophied states of Europe were not to be counteracted by the dystrophy of the United States of America.

There is, however, ample evidence that Dickens relished his time in America and that he felt himself amongst friends (many of them close friends). Perhaps because he relaxed so readily in an English-speaking country, he damned its shortcomings and laughed at its foibles much as he treated the parallel defects of his homeland. As G.K. Chesterton so properly remarked, *"Martin Chuzzlewit* may be a caricature of America. America may be a caricature of England."[3] It must also be remembered that Dickens offers fulsome praise when he deems a person, an institution, a system, a town, or even a landscape, worthy of his praise (and there are many occasions where good deeds shine out of the often naughty world of *American Notes*). Much of his trouble lay in the fact that the lionized Dickens went out of this way during his first visit to attack American attitudes to the law of copyright, and to be outspoken about the particularly touchy subject of slavery in the southern states. When he wrote *American Notes* he knew that he would offend American sensibilities; he merely compounded his sin by writing the American chapters of *Martin Chuzzlewit*.

Transatlantic sensitivity to criticism by a foreigner was already a raw nerve after the unfavorable comments of Frances Trollope and Harriet Martineau on the darker side of the pursuit of liberty. Dickens, distressed by the anomalies he had seen, was not out to be a model of tact. To a man of his generation, "that accursed and detestable system" of slavery was a red rag to a liberal bull in 1842; but later one can only sympathize with his horrified amusement at finding that a New Yorker would not sit next to two quadroon women ("God damned cusses of niggers") at one of his readings in 1868. His violent reaction against the power of the American press is rather more puzzling, given the fact of his own journalistic experience, his propensity for self-advertisement, and his genuine enough delight in being lionized. He seems to have been taken aback on his first arrival in Boston by a dozen editors leaping onto his boat before it was moored and "tearing violently up and beginning to shake hands like madmen" (*Pilgrim Letters*, 3:33). By virtue of the fact of his celebrity he was adulated by the newspapers and he was often criticized (especially over the copyright bee in his bonnet). He got his own back in *Martin Chuzzlewit* by inventing a series of uncomplimentary titles for fictional New York papers—the *Sewer*, the *Stabber*, the *Family Spy*, the, *Private Listener*, the *Peeper*, the *Plunderer*, the *Keyhole Reporter*, and the *Rowdy Journal*.

Dickens's disillusionment with America is nowhere better exemplified than in the account of Martin Chuzzlewit's unhappy attempt to become a man of affairs in the misnamed settlement at Eden. Eden was almost certainly based on Cairo, Illinois. "Dismal Cairo" appears in *American Notes* as "a hotbed of disease, an ugly sepulchre, a grave uncheered by any gleam of promise: a place without one single quality in earth or air or water, to commend it" (171). It is not simply that this "Eden" is not Paradise; it is that Cairo is not a city. Cairo is a denial of promise, not the Promised Land. Dickens was not really appalled by frontier America, he was ill at ease with it. He may wonder at the speed at which Cincinnati had risen out of the

141

forest like "an Arabian Night city," but he generally failed to respond to a civilization in its raucous infancy.

The metropolitan in Dickens did not relish the American frontier and its cultural implications. He also detected that many of his potential readers shared his prejudice. As a scrupulous and deliberate visitor to America, Dickens seeks out the familiar, or the variations on the familiar—the schools, the prisons, the experimental factories, the charities—and he tends to judge them by what he knows and what he dislikes. His mind was, however, fired by movement, not stillness; by an excess of life, not emptiness; and by the present, not the potential. He is restless in Europe when a history he dislikes distorts the present and its oppressed masses; he is vexed in America when a present he distrusts seems to be molding the future and cultivating an unpeopled wilderness. When thinking of Dickens in a wider world it is, however, crucial to remember that he molds the Europe and the America he saw into provinces of what Humphry House called "The Dickens World," one which is "quite unlike any other world there has ever been."

NOTES

Quotations from Dickens's novels are from the following editions: *David Copperfield*, ed. Nina Burgess (Oxford: 1981); *Hard Times*, ed. George Ford and Sylvére Monod (New York: 1966); *Little Dorrit*, ed. Harvey Peter Sucksmith (Oxford 1979); *The Mystery of Edwin Drood*, ed. Margaret Cardwell (Oxford: 1972); *A Tale of Two Cities*, ed. George Woodcock (Harmondsworth, Middlesex: 1985). Quotations from *American Notes and Pictures from Italy* and *The Uncommercial Traveller and Reprinted Pieces* and *Christmas Stories* are from the Oxford Illustrated Edition (London: 1947–58). Quotations from the letters are from *The Letters of Charles Dickens*, Pilgrim Edition, 5 vols. to date (Oxford: 1965–): Vols. 1 and 2, ed. Madeline House and Graham Storey; Vol. 3, ed. Madeline House, Graham Storey, and Kathleen Tillotson; Vol. 4, ed. Kathleen Tillotson; Vol. 5, ed. Graham Storey and K.J. Fielding; and from *The Letters of Charles Dickens*, ed. Walter Dexter (London: 1938). Quotations from John Forster, *The Life of Charles Dickens* are from the 1928 edition, ed. J.W.T. Ley (London).

1. For Dickens's attitudes to Italian art see Leoneé Ormond, "Dickens and Painting: The Old Masters," *The Dickensian* 79 (1983): 130–51.
2. The most recent and most detailed discussion is Sidney P. Moss's *Charles Dickens's Quarrel with America* (Troy, NY: 1984). See also Michael Slater, *Dickens on America and the Americans* (Austin, TX: 1978).
3. G.K. Chesterton, *Charles Dickens* (London: 1928) 108.

MATTHEW ARNOLD: EUROPEANISM AND ENGLAND

Park Honan, University of Leeds

At the heart of Matthew Arnold's best writing, one senses an acute awareness of Europe. His idea of "criticism" is that nothing in the art, politics, religion, or social structure of a modern nation can be well understood unless we compare—and for a British critic useful comparisons are to be drawn with France, Germany, Italy. His *Essays in Criticism* (1865) compares European with English writers; his idea of "culture" in *Culture and Anarchy* (1869) is rooted in German ideas. His education books draw contrasts between England and Europe (the best of them, *A French Eton* [1864], does so even in its title). In religion he contends with French and German theology. Even his funniest social satire (in *Friendship's Garland* [1871]) arises from his taking a blue-eyed, pipe-smoking Prussian over to London and Reigate. "Do you suppose," his Baron Arminius insults the Londoners, "we should tolerate in France, Germany, Switzerland, Italy, your London corporation and London vestries, and London as they make it?" (*Works* 5.21).

Yet his involvement in Europe is more vital than any of this suggests. Arnold became the most influential Victorian critic and helped to form a modern sensibility, in England and America, because he expressed a new attitude of feeling and reflection. That attitude arises largely from his awareness of Europe, and I think that his achievement becomes clearer when we keep his interest in Europe in view. How and why did Europe influence him in his early years and later? How did he "use" Europe? It is easy in answering these questions, perhaps, to be too academic and arid; we are concerned not only with an intellect but with love, faith, grief, the feelings and awarenesses of a very unusual man in his developing regard for the richness of European history and culture.

It is fair to say that Europe hovered over his cradle—to delight and fascinate him. Soon after his birth at Laleham-on-Thames on December 24,

1822, Matthew Arnold was listening to his father's stories taken from Greek legends. He had wall-prints of the Alps to see, foreign coins kept in a cabinet of "Mt. Etna" wood to touch, and a small history of France by "Mrs. Markham" (the pen name of a relative) to read. Many of his ideas about Europe were in the long run influenced by his father, Dr. Thomas Arnold (1795–1842). Legends about Dr. Arnold's mental narrowness have been fostered by works such as Thomas Hughes's *Tom Brown's Schooldays* (1857) and Lytton Strachey's *Eminent Victorians* (1918), but Dr. Arnold, though not an original thinker, had a hungry, open mind for new ideas about history and theology and a passion for Europe; on two of his twelve visits abroad, his eldest son, Matthew, was to join him. The quality of Dr. Arnold's mind is evident in his books. Through his lectures, letters and essays, he became the most influential opponent of J.H. Newman and the Oxford "High Church" or Tractarian movement in the late 1830s. Influenced by S.T. Coleridge and by Prussian scholars (as we shall see), Dr. Arnold advocated a liberal or "broad" Church of England; he brought comparative approaches to his classrooms at Rugby and recommended recent or new German and French books.

Matthew was also affected by his mother's fondness for Europe, and probably by his sister Jane's interest in Germany. "When you see the Jura," wrote Mrs. Arnold, "think of me." His early poems echo an elegiac note in his mother's pocket diaries and journal. He would discuss Goethe with his sister, Jane. These feminine influences may be related to the intelligent subtlety of his regard for France and Germany; in any case, his mature views are free from a heavy Saxon earnestness, and remain mobile, flexible, developing. Very early, to impress his mother and sister and younger brothers, he began to pose as a European sophisticate. So at fourteen when he first visited France— and to his parents' despair bought his first monocle en route, in London—he inscribed a travel journal to his brother Pig or Didu (Edward) and then tried very hard to be French, chic, and observant. His journal depicts the dress of a French postilion; he overworks his favorite adjective at Chartres Cathedral: its outer stonework was "most beautiful," but "beautiful as this was" the inside carvings "seemed to me more beautiful still." Then he sees Paris, "a capital," as Matthew wrote, "in fashion elegance public buildings & inferior to none." He sees something aesthetic, one feels, in nearly everything at Paris: a live giraffe, the shops, the "Aegyptian Porphyry" at the Louvre, the ices, wine, food, and hotels. Later he told his mother that "we" in England "have more to learn from France than from any other nation," mainly "because she is so unlike ourselves."[1]

France seems to haunt him. What he responds to in the 1830s is its visual, Celtic, Catholic, colorful aspect, perhaps, its pleasantness and pathos.

Later—to leave his youth for a moment—he would see that the French Revolution of 1789 was that violent break with the past or death-blow in France to the older power of Church, kings, and medievalism that left the country bereft and yet free to develop her rational civic order, her excellent school system, her new laws and outlooks. He would gather data in France on school-inspecting tours for the British government. He would be an anomaly as an Englishman there—a tall, smiling dandy and epicure, simple in manner and fluent in French, a questioning, listening man, with none of the usual Francophobia, who could express a Parisian view of the Franco-Austrian war "perfectly" in his early (and politically naive) pamphlet on "England and the Italian Question" (1859). But Arnold kept seeking in France. His subject was usually not France, but England-and-France or what there was in this nation that his countrymen might emulate. "What makes me look at France and the French with such inexhaustible curiosity and indulgence," he wrote, "is this,—their faults are not ours, so we are not likely to catch them; their merits are not ours, so we are not likely to become idle and self-sufficient from studying them" (*Works* 5.33–34). No nation or person, he felt, can afford the illusion of self-sufficiency, and if we would save ourselves (or our societies) from tragic error we must heed the "unlike." He was to learn from French belles lettres, but also from French critics, historians, philosophers, civic officials, teachers, and pupils. His talents and penchants—such as his fondness for detail, his desire for overviews and principles that freed him from the tyranny of detail, and his instinct for comparison—helped him to use well what he saw and heard even as he pored over French books, newspapers, *Revue germanique et français*, or *Revue des Deux Mondes*.

At school he did well in French, delighting in translating, and read more modern textbooks in the Sixth Form at Rugby than other English schools were then using: François Guizot's *Histoire de Revolution de l'Angleterre* (1826–27) and F.A. Mignet's *Histoire de la Revolution Francaise* (1824). In London, Dr. Arnold met Guizot, and Matthew was clearly impressed by his father's friendships. Though his father knew John Keble and other biblical scholars at Oxford, few of those Englishmen had kept pace with Dr. Arnold's Prussian intellectual friends such as Barthold Niebuhr, the historian (1776–1830), or Christian Bunsen (1791–1860), who replaced Niebuhr as Prussian diplomatic minister at Rome.

Niebuhr and Bunsen in effect demonstrated that Europe was a time-machine for England. Anyone at Oxford who knew the most advanced Europeans might perceive ideas which, sooner or later, would change England. Niebuhr drew new analogies between past and present societies. Bunsen followed Schleiermacher and a few other astute Germans in avoiding a narrow, literal view of biblical truth and in testing the fertile, suggestive qualities of myth. "Papa worked in the direction of these ideas of Bunsen and Schleiermacher," Arnold wrote in 1867, and was "the only deeply religious man" who had the culture for it (*Letters* 1.442); he told his mother in 1869 that "papa's immense superiority" to the Oriel set was in being so "European" as to get out of the narrow medium in which "his English friends lived" (*Letters* 2.5).

These remarks exaggerate his father's uniqueness, perhaps, and have the look of family piety. They are unfair to Newman of Oriel[2]—and to others at Oxford who were alert to Europe. But they are sincere remarks; and Matthew, in commenting in later life on his father's significance, looked back through his grief over Dr. Arnold's sudden death in 1842. That loss had turned Matthew Arnold to Europe for help, and made him a more effective poet.

He had just completed his first, carefree year at Oxford when his father died; Matthew was then nineteen. As Dr. Arnold had believed in dedicating oneself to a calling, so Matthew settled on poetry as his prime vocation. As his father had sought to meet Europeans, so he, in his debonair way, soon went abroad to applaud the French actress Rachel and to meet George Sand. Thus far as a poet he had favored English and classical topics, writing about Mycerinus, Alaric the Visigoth, Cromwell, Shakespeare, Bishop Butler, or Wellington. Failing in his own view to find a deep basis in conviction and emotional warmth for his verse, he was now drawn in the 1840s to what he called the European "sentimental school" of writers.

Their writings included Goethe's early lyrics and novelette *The Sorrows of Young Werther*; much of Tieck, Novalis, and Jean Paul Richter in Germany; Ugö Foscolo's Italian *Letters of Ortis*; Chateaubriand's *Rene*, and the Swiss writer Senancour's remarkable *Obermann* (1804), which purports to present the letters of a disillusioned, seeking wanderer in the Alps. Such works may exalt the values of love and faith—only to make use of the desolate state of mind of a hero who has lost faith or who is crushed in love. They at times employ a special mode of impassioned, reflective writing. Madame de Staël called it the mode of *"la passion reflechissante"*—passion, in bitter isolation, which exists to judge itself and the world with severe clarity.[3]

The sentimentalists were, in one respect, Arnold's antidote to the Bodleian Library, or to his excessive reading. His sonnets on Butler and Emerson rid the poet of the mental burden of their books: and the hero of *Empedocles on Etna* seems choked by too much data, too much intellectual food. Arnold's "culture" in *Culture and Anarchy* would involve a paradoxical way of keeping the mind free of subservience to books, though still nurtured by them.

The sentimentalists, then, relieved him; they released his feeling and perhaps helped him to sympathize with Wordsworth's complaint that modern life develops the selfish, canny brain at the expense of the feelings. "Others will strengthen us to bear," Arnold wrote in "Memorial Verses: April, 1850" when Wordsworth died, "But who, ah! who, will make us feel?" (67). In Europe's Catholic agricultural societies he would find qualities of feeling that industrial England lacked, and would read much beyond "the sentimental school" in his pursuit of European perspectives. But the sentimentalists seemed especially useful to him in their almost elegiac concern for faith.

Arnold, so far as we know, did not lose his faith and never went through the typical Victorian religious crisis; but, if in the 1840s he could credit a vague deity (later a Spinozan one), he had had his childhood belief in a personal, intervening God chipped away. As he says in his "Stanzas from the Grande Chartreuse,"

> rigorous teachers seized my youth,
> And purged its faith, and trimmed its fire. (67–68)

In this respect, he was in the position of many other young English and European intellectuals. He thought the sentimentalists might help him incorporate his yearning and unease into his poetry; further, he seems to have felt, they could help him to depict the Western condition of waning, inadequate faith after the failure of the medieval Catholic unity of mind and heart—a failure, he believed, which was signaled by the Reformation and later by the French Revolution, with its echoes in the Revolutions of 1848. So he aimed to picture his own and Europe's spiritual loss, and hence the modern condition of mind. That aim was not naive or ungenerous, and—to the amusement of his friends—a love affair helped him achieve it. He knew the exiled Claudes, French Protestants from Germany who had moved to Liverpool and summered in the Lake District. As Mrs. Claude says, her son Louis was "occupé à faire *des riens,*" and her daughter Mary was too headstrong to attend a "point de reunion," but at least the pale, dark-blue-eyed Mary Claude acted in Schiller's plays at home, and read and imitated Foscolo, Goethe, and her favorite, Jean Paul Richter. As a follower of European sentimentalists, Mary was as "beautiful" a girl as Hartley Coleridge (for one) had seen. She took tea with the "Clougho-Matthean set" (Arnold's Oxford friends), joined young men for "scrambles" and outings at night, and once became lost on the fells. Her fondness for midnight walks, her use of the daisy as a symbol of religious isolation in her children's stories, her refusal to attend church, though learning to dance "in defiance of the godly," made her a timid, appealing rebel. Mary Claude had relatives in the Swiss Alps. Her friend Anne Clough had visited Swiss Thun, which is associated with legends of Minnesingers. The details of Mary's relationship with Matthew are largely undocumented, but in the summer of 1848, we know that she left Ambleside. That September, Matthew Arnold hoped to meet a pair of "blue eyes" at the Hotel Bellevue at Thun near a turquoise lake and Bernese Oberland peaks. The "blue eyes" did not appear, and in November one of his sisters wrote a "long letter" that amused Tom Arnold, in New Zealand, because it concerned "Matt's romantic passion for the Cruel Invisible, Mary Claude."[4]

She becomes Marguerite—a name reminiscent of alpine daisies, or *marguerites des pres*, in *Obermann*, which remind the hero of Europe's past and the lost illusion of God. Borrowing and even translating from Goethe, Arnold retreated to the Alps alone in 1849, and in the next few years wrote a number of reflective lyrics which he grouped as his "Switzerland."[5] Most of the Marguerite lyrics seem impersonal, touching, interesting, and also gauche; but this embarrassing broken-off affair with Mary Claude, the exile baptized at Friedrichstadt's French Reformed Church, seems to have helped him to write one superb lyric as an exercise in *passion-reflechissante*. This is "Yes! in the sea of life," called at different times "To Marguerite—Continued" and, alluding to Foscolo's book, "To Marguerite, in returning a volume of the Letters of Ortis." Replying to Foscolo's story about a bitter, estranged hero, Ortis, Arnold adopts lovely imagery of sea and islands to suggest that our isolation is a condition of life. Yes, Ortis was isolated, but so are *we all*:

> Yes! in the sea of life enisled
> With echoing straits between us thrown,
> Dotting the shoreless watery wild,
> We mortal millions live *alone*.
> The islands feel the enclasping flow,
> And then their endless bounds they know. (1–6)

The islands are metaphors for the human spirit, but they also remain geographical. The poem's "sounds and channels" suggest the English Channel. The lines for the islands' desire,

> For surely once, they feel, we were
> Parts of a single continent! (15–16)

point to a unity in geological time before there was a Channel, and to the Catholic unity of England and Europe before the Tudor severance. The word "severance" has various implications. Each of us is severed from nature, spiritually severed from others, and severed in a European sen-

148

timentalist sense if feeling is now divided from thought, and if modern thinking withers modern feeling. For all this, as our Hebraic and Christian beliefs slowly lose hold in modern life, we may say that a pagan God of Fate is responsible. What other deity could have divided us?

> A God, a God their severance ruled!
> And bade betwixt their shores to be
> The unplumbed, salt, estranging sea. (22–24)

In this and other poems, Arnold is sensitive to the landscape and geography of his nation and of Europe. Just as Berkshire is vivid and real in "The Scholar-Gipsy" and "Thyrsis", so the Swiss Alps are evoked in "Parting" —a poem which moves beyond its borrowings from Goethe to do something new. The Alps with their rushing winds, torrents, and stark white ice-walls suggest the speaker's forceful need to blot out society, to escape it:

> Hark! fast by the window
> The rushing winds go,
> To the ice-cumbered gorges,
> The vast seas of snow! . . .
> There the avalanche thunders
> The hoarse torrent dumb. (25–28, 31–32)

But his memories of a "wet bird-haunted English lawn" and of "sweet blue eyes" (19, 37) suggest the inescapable appeals of love, commitment, and perhaps social responsibility. English and alpine memories rush in a broken sequence until, with a calmer yearning, the poet tries to resolve them.

It would be wrong to assume that Arnold's best lyrics depend only on the "sentimental school" since he borrowed far and wide, but sentimentalists lend phrases, imagery, symbolism, or feeling to much that he wrote before 1860. Often his Europeanism is wholly subsumed, as in his use of Senancour's *Obermann* in his two Oxford elegies; but he is never better than when evoking an Englishman's sense of modern Europe. In "Dover Beach," as the speaker bids his lady to come to the window on a calm night above Dover's cliffs, a French beacon is literally seen from England:

> on the French coast the light
> Gleams and is gone; the cliffs of England stand,
> Glimmering and vast, out in the tranquil bay.
> Come to the window. (3–6)

That surprising "window" opens on the Channel and on history, too. The

French light gleams as did the *siècle de lumière* or Enlightenment, which divided France from her past. A noise of waves at Dover's beach is ontological in suggesting sad, inevitable facts of being, and in reminding the speaker of the plight of Sophocles's Philoctetes, cruelly abandoned by friends on an island where he hears only melancholy waves. The speaker thinks of the modern withdrawal of the Sea of Faith. Thus the poem's movement is from the present back to the Greek Aegean and from medieval Europe back to England's hectic present, in which religious belief retreats as if to the sound of the night wind down naked shingles of the world. If lovers at Dover would be "true," the fact of modern spiritual life is that

> we are here as on a darkling plain
> Swept with confused alarms of struggle and flight,
> Where ignorant armies clash by night. (35–37)

In a world devoid of love, joy, faith, even help from pain, one may not expect to find constancy. The historical paradox is that while Catholic France may remind the viewer of an age of faith, its *lumière* of rationalism has divided everyone from faith's certainty. Europe's problem suggests a hopeless dilemma, a division in man, as if his spirit hovered between two shores neither of which he might reach. Faith may return, but we lack it now; there is no way back into the past, and no way forward. "Dover Beach," then, is rooted in two perceptions about our condition. One is that Europe's loss of religious confidence is not a passing misfortune, but a tragic deprivation, if nothing we know about *now* supplies what we lack. The second perception is that the psyche may be permanently in a state of unease, division, and tension.

Arnold makes poetry not only out of religious and psychological dilemmas, but also out of his quest to resolve them; he seeks answers in Europe's past and present. One of his best lyrics of quest, "Stanzas from the Grande Chartreuse," is almost wholly autobiographical, based on a journey and complex experience in the high Isere. He may have thought too little of his wife's dislike of the cold (not long after they married) when he took her to the freezing monastery of the Carthusians late in September 1851. He and his wife rode up on mules along a precipice with the Guiers Mort River below—as if they were passing by death. At a gate near slate roofs topped with reminders of the Crucifixion, he was divided from his wife, who spent the night "in a small house," while he watched the monks' Ceremony of the Pax. At last he went into a dark, bleak cell: "The cells!" he writes, "—the suffering Son of Man / Upon the wall" (45–46).

He asks himself, in his poem, what he, as a rational Briton, is doing among Europe's Carthusian monks:

The House, the Brotherhood austere!
—And what am I, that I am here? (65–66)

It is a good question. Seeking self-possession, he has come to a source of
French faith for calm, wholeness, self-control. He had written in a note
about the medieval outlook that one can be interested in "the dark ages"
because, then, man had "thrown off the burden of his over-stimulated,
sophisticated, artificialized, false-developed miserable nervous sceptical self
and begun life anew."[6] He asks the monks to shield him:

> Take me, cowled forms, and fence me round,
> Till I possess my soul again;
> Till free my thoughts before me roll,
> Not chafed by hourly false control! (93–96)

These lines are not primarily religious in implication, but pragmatic. They
arise from a creative writer's desire for both the control and the depth of
feeling needed for art. The objection which "wounds and perplexes me from
the religious side," Matthew Arnold wrote in a note, is that "feeling and the
religious mood are eternally the deepest being of man."[7] Europe, in its
instinctive age of faith, had formerly offered a chance to know the self's
"deepest being." The monastery of the Isère is of value, then, although its
faith, at present, is a "dead time's exploded dream"; here, at least, one is put
in closer touch with oneself. He realizes the failure of visionaries who have
done nothing to replace the monastery's faith. We still lack a compelling
authority for our spiritual lives. He summons up Byron, Shelley, and the
author of *Obermann*—all of whom might have instructed us. Yet what did
Byron's knowledge of Europe do to make him wiser, or Shelley's of Italy?
There is a double-edged quality to Arnold's complaints—the lovely form of
his accusations suggests that a few poets achieved *some* self-integration (or
transcended their fracturedness) through beauty of language:

> What boots it, Shelley! that the breeze
> Carried thy lovely wail away,
> Musical through Italian trees
> Which fringe thy soft blue Spezzian bay?
> Inheritors of thy distress
> Have restless hearts one throb the less? (139–44)

Arnold is modest when comparing himself with poets of the past. He implies he is more febrile, uncertain, and divided than others. He would shel-
ter himself in faith to unite his heart and intellect; he would aspire, as an

intellectual, to the "high white star of Truth," and would also yield to sentiment to lament the failures of visionaries. He cannot do all of that. But if a French monastery shows him his confusions, Europe may afford a strange, unexpected clarity about the self. Each of us is a mass of volition, promptings, and aims: the psyche's hint may be that we are more complex than we know. If so, the information that the British present gives us about ourselves is not enough. Europe in cultural richness and connections with the past belongs to us, or correlates with much in us: hence there is no mere display of cosmopolitan knowingness, for example, in Arnold's uses of Marcus Aurelius, Eugenie de Guerin, Heine, Joubert, or Spinoza to describe the modern spirit in *Essays in Criticism*.

In his verse he had developed a sensitive voice, an attitude of alert awareness to the important past. As an essayist he would try to convey a sense of the past when dealing with matters present. Arnold's attitude is in part elegiac, or compassionate about what is no longer viable. "Dissolvents of the old European system of dominant ideas and facts we must all be, all of us who have any power of working," he writes in *Essays in Criticism*; "what we have to study is that we may not be acrid dissolvements" (*Works*, 3:109–10). Not to be "acrid" is to appreciate in what is obsolete or no longer viable, or in what we are helping to destroy, something that refreshed or helped mankind. Even in Europe's outmoded, literal belief in a heaven of pure love there was a rich nourishing of imagination, an effect missing in our rational outlook. In "The Church of Brou" he attributes just that older, naive idea of heaven to the sixteenth-century duke and duchess who lie entombed near Bourg-en-Bresse. They exist now only in their affecting, lifelike tomb effigies:

> So rest, for ever rest, O princely Pair! . . .
> Where horn, and hound, and vassals, never come . . . .
> Or if ye wake . . .
>   let it be on autumn nights, when rain
> Doth rustingly above your head complain (1–33)

And if the statues then open their stone eyelids, they will hear the Angels' wings in the lovely wind:

> And on the lichen-crusted leads above
> The rustle of the eternal rain of love (45–46)

"The Church of Brou," one feels, is not an "acrid dissolvement" because it displays something deeply touching and haunting in the naivety and impossibility of an old belief.

In maturing as a prose writer, Arnold at first had virtually turned his prose against his poetry, in a sense had used Europe's facts against Europe's feeling. In a brilliant "Preface" to his *Poems* (1853), he was concerned to explain why he would not reprint his fine *Empedocles on Etna*. He considered this poem as depressing, though he argues in a way that highlights that which he would suppress. Empedocles, he says, belongs to a melancholy era, when "the dialogue of the mind with itself has commenced," when "we hear already the doubts, we witness the discouragement, of Hamlet and of Faust" (*Works* 1.1). But he had depicted that era in his Marguerite lyrics, in "Dover Beach," in "Grande Chartreuse." He had evoked it with considerable feeling in "Stanzas in Memory of the Author of 'Obermann'" with its superb view from the Gemmi Pass above Switzerland's Leukerbad (Baths of Luke):

> Behind are the abandoned baths
> Mute in their meadows lone;
> The leaves are on the valley paths,
> The mists are on the Rhone—
>
> The white mists rolling like a sea!
> I hear the torrents roar.
> —Yes, Obermann, all speaks of thee. (5–11)

But Senancour's Obermann may be sad company for a School Inspector, after all. Matthew Arnold in the 1850s often came home exhausted; his own boys were ill. One Arnold son died in a crib; another son died of a cardiac complaint, and when a third boy, "Budge," died Arnold broke down before schoolchildren. He was then seeing English schools without heat, floors, or textbooks, where a young teacher might be in charge of eighty children. To improve the chaos in British education, he gladly accepted the chance to visit schools abroad, and so wrote his *Popular Education of France* and his *A French Eton*. These exercises made him a comparative critic, who was taking in social facts which poetry cannot adequately report and which, certainly, the European sentimentalists avoided. Arnold in effect rebuked the German sentimentalists "Tieck, Novalis, Jean Paul Richter" in his essay "Heinrich Heine," and then (1863) exalted his old guide Goethe and claimed that the poet Heine was Goethe's truest successor (*Works* 3.108).

In brief, he turned with increasing urgency to prose to achieve tasks he felt beyond the capacity of his poetry. In *Essays in Criticism* (using the word "essay" to mean "attempt—specimen") he meant, in 1865, to illustrate European viewpoints and sensibilities that had no exact counterparts in England. Even so, he showed off a new urbane, contrasting method. In nine essays he takes up modern or recent French Catholics, a pagan emperor, German poets, a Dutch philosopher, Hebraic values, the uses of a French Academy of letters; and the present functions of criticism. Typically in an essay at first called "A French Coleridge," he introduces a writer who was an anachronism by 1865, not widely known abroad, and almost unheard of in England: Joseph Joubert was an invalid, a Jesuit-trained Neoplatonist, an unambitious, reflective French Catholic. Arnold reveals him through biography, comparison, quotation, contrasting Joubert and Coleridge, Byron, and Chateaubriand. He does not overpraise Joubert, who was "a little too ethereal," but shows that his amenity and delicacy are lacking in England (*Works* 3.196). Again, in "Heinrich Heine," he relates the career of an exiled German-Jewish poet to show how Heine's free play of mind rejected every "stock" notion. With French wit and ardor, and German sentiment and culture, Heine struggled against "*Philistinism*," or against those who invoke merely outworn notions against reason, or who will not value ideas "irrespectively of the practical conveniences" of those ideas (*Works* 3.113).

Goethe seems to preside over the "Heine" piece, and indeed over the rest of the *Essays*. Later, in 1872, Arnold was to say that four writers from whom he had learned certain ruling ideas, methods, and habits were Newman, Wordsworth, Goethe, and Sainte-Beuve. Arnold had heard Wordsworth in old age complain in that Goethe's verse was "not inevitable enough," and yet Arnold in 1853 could rank this German as "the greatest poet of modern times, the greatest critic of all times" (*Life* 196–205). He had delved into the sixty volumes of his mentor's *Ausgabe Letzter Hand* and, for instance, had translated and copied out, almost in full, Goethe's essays of advice for young poets ("Fur junge Dichter" and "Noch ein Wort fur junge Dichter"). In all, he saw Goethe as a poet and critic who had struggled from error and folly to the serene wisdom of his talks in old age with Eckermann (in *Conversations* or *Gesprache mit Goethe*). And yet, still, Arnold's comments on him could be negative. Critical and very chilly about him at times, Arnold through his adult life deeply engaged with him, and in that sense paid him homage. (Indeed, he admitted that one of his final estimates of Goethe, in "A French Critic on Goethe," [1878], was expressly ambivalent or a "double judgement.")[8]

Sainte-Beuve, whom he met in Paris, was of a very different value to Arnold. This gossipy Frenchman might idly take street-girls home to his grubby rooms, but he wrote *Lundi* (or Monday) essays for the Paris *Constitutionnel* with such unaffected ease that he seemed "a man discharging with delight the very office for which he was born."[9] From him, Arnold learned lessons in lightness, fluency, ease, and also learned more about biographical methods in criticism. He was amused by Sainte-Beuve without being any more slavishly impressed by him than by Goethe's more intellectually fertile works.

His reactions to Goethe and Sainte-Beuve illustrate his need for views, hints, and refreshment from diverse sources. It is just this need or principle that is a central theme of *Culture and Anarchy* (1869). Arnold's idea of culture derives in large part from Goethe's and Herder's notion of *Bildung*, or the process of seeing anew, changing and developing. His book has an easy, flexible, cosmopolitan quality enriched by travel abroad; he is humorous and exploratory. Our politicians "educate," says Arnold, and then, referring to himself, we "pretend to educate no one, for we are still engaged in trying to clear and educate ourselves" (*Works* 5.229). He implies that we can never have enough light, and so ought to be eager to take in foreign viewpoints. We cannot absorb all the best that has been "thought and said," but can know some of it, to turn "a stream of fresh and free thought" upon our accepted notions. For him, no author is absolutely satisfactory and comprehensive in dramatizing or describing a human truth. Needing perspectives from diverse sources, we may find that our terms of discourse are not valid; useful truth may lie in the interaction between several terms, such as "culture and anarchy," or "Hebraism and Hellenism." He uses the latter pair to comment on Western history, England's present, the human psyche. Victorian England, as Arnold felt, had leaned too far toward moral strictness and needed more of the clearness, ease, and radiance of Hellenism. That verdict suggests the influence of Arnold's travels in France and Italy, and his feeling about a Latin ambiance he missed in Britain. But he does not make the mistake of judging one nation wholly by another: he slaps no perfunctory verdict down upon any locale or person. His Hebraism and Hellenism are best in hinting of a mixture of impulses and values in Western life.

What he most opposes is a provincial infatuation in one's views. Critics can be narrow, and an infatuation mixes in with English verdicts about Shakespeare, he believed. The critic ought to dwell "much on foreign thought"; there is only one world-river of poetry and our nations for intellectual and spiritual purposes "are one great confederation" (*Life* 329, 388). Yet he looked across the Channel for subtle instruction. When he traveled to the United States, he did more than compare its society in the 1880s with what he knew at home; America too may be partly judged on Europe's scale. In "A Word More about America," he praises that nation's laws, resources, and federal system but finds it lacking in manners, beauty, and a pleasantness he had known on the continent. An English person of taste "would rather live in France, Spain, Holland, Belgium, Germany, Italy, Switzerland," he believed, though he felt Americans would improve and admired the forthright, alert talk of American women. Still the test of America's intellectual maturity would be whether it had "learnt to assimilate independently the intellect of France and Germany and the ancient world as well as of England" (*Works* 10.217; 5.81). He had aimed at just that assimilation in his own writing.

One benefit of his Europeanism was to release him from some aspects of the mind-set of his present, from the hard surface qualities of thought and prose style in works written in a newly technological era. The historian Macaulay's prose, Arnold says in "A French Critic on Milton" (1877), is only "a style brilliant, metallic, exterior; making strong points . . . [but] not, with the soft play of life, following and rendering the thing's very form and pressure." Or he finds the criticism of Edmond Scherer, who was trained at Geneva, "that home of large instruction and lucid intelligence," lacking in the delight and suppleness of Sainte-Beuve's manner (*Works* 8.174) We may be impressed by the brilliance of a writer, he implies, and may only know the defects of that supposed brilliance through bold, delicate comparison.

However, his Europeanism has defects. He is a poor guide to Italy. In a section on Italy in his last education book he calls the Renaissance "a literary movement"[10]—as though the paintings of Raphael, Da Vinci, Titian, and Correggio; the sculpture of Donatello or Michelangelo; or the architecture of Lombardi and Bramanti were of little importance. His account of Italian history in the same book is bizarre and self-contradictory. But he uses the Italians, who are "preeminent in feeling the power of beauty," in his reasonable campaign to widen middle-class attitudes and to show that the British social class has "a defective type of religion, a narrow range of intellect and knowledge, a stunted sense of beauty" (*Works* 8.288; 9.276). Italians are capable of an intellectual seriousness that is even lacking in France, as he says in reviewing Ernest Renan's *La Reforme intellectuelle et morale de la France* (1871) (*Works* 7.48). If Arnold is wrong in some details about Italy, one feels that he is sensitive to aspects of its culture that could benefit England. When he says that the English theater of his own day is "perhaps the most contemptible in Europe" (*Works* 8.294), we do not feel that he retreats from British problems. Europe gave him confidence and perspective to judge his nation well, and informed his work with a delicate, alert attitude that still refreshes.

NOTES

Quotations from Arnold's prose are from *The Complete Works of Matthew Arnold*, ed. R.H. Super, 11 vols. (Ann Arbor, MI: 1960–77). Quotations from Arnold's poetry are from *The Poems of Matthew Arnold*, ed. Kenneth Allott (London: 1965). Quotations from Arnold's letters are from *Letters of Matthew Arnold 1848–1888*, ed. G.W.E. Russell (New York and London: 1895).

1. Arnold's early travel journal survives at Balliol College, Oxford; he visited France for the first time with his parents in a ten-day tour in August 1837.

2. Arnold's ideas and methods and sensibility were deeply influenced by Newman, as Arnold himself acknowledged. But, if he thus insists on the importance of his father as a "European," he does not do so only to please his mother. Dr. Arnold had sought out European scholars as friends; he had visited Europe at least twelve times and had shown that knowledge of the Continent comes from seeing, hearing, talking with, feeling with, and so relating to its best minds while observing its cultures. His father's example helped to send Arnold many times abroad.

3. Arnold's unpublished 1851 diary shows him reading Mme. de Staël, Chateaubriand, and Goethe's Swiss letters at the same time. In her *De la littérature considerée dans ses rapports avec les institutions sociales* (Paris: 1800) 1.311–13, Mme. de Staël had noted in Goethe's *Werther* and Chateaubriand's *Rene* a mode of intense reflection by an isolated, perceiving hero. The Swiss letters in Senancour's *Obermann* are written in a similar mode: his isolation, despair, and stoicism drive Obermann to use his feeling as a way of discovering truth about the self and the world. Arnold was much taken by *Obermann*, but even his early "Stanzas" are critical of that book's author, Senancour; and "To Marguerite— Continued" replies to the sentimentalist Foscolo. Arnold began to free himself from the "sentimental school" while being influenced by it in the years between 1847 and 1853. His *Empedocles on Etna* shows in part how grandly useful the influence was.

4. See Park Honan, *Matthew Arnold: A Life* (New York: 1981) 144–58, cited hereafter as *Life*.

5. See R.E. Becht, "Matthew Arnold's 'Switzerland': The Drama of Choice," *Victorian Poetry* 13 (1975): 35–45.

6. Undated note, Yale University manuscript.

7. Undated note, Yale University manuscript.

8. James Simpson's comprehensive *Matthew Arnold and Goethe* (London: 1979) suggests that Arnold, while rating him highly, freed himself from Goethe's useful image, too, by criticizing and deflating him, revising his judgments of Goethe's poetry or mind.

9. He thus compares Sainte-Beuve with the graver, less flexible, if still useful critic Edmon Scherer in "A French Critic on Milton" in *Works* 8.175.

10. Neither the heat nor his poor informants, when he was inspecting Italian schools, explain his historical inaccuracies in "Italy" in his *Schools and Universities on the Continent* (1868); he did not make such mistakes in its "Germany" section, which he felt was the most helpful part of his book.

HISTOIRES DE VOYAGE: THE ITALIAN POEMS OF ARTHUR HUGH CLOUGH

Simon Gatrell, University of Georgia

> O land of Empire, art and love!
> What is it that you show me?
> A sky for gods to tread above
> A soil for pigs below me!

Italy seems to have released some sort of creative spring in Arthur Clough. He went to Rome in April 1849 and to Venice in the autumn of 1850, and the inventory of poems that derive directly from these Italian holidays is impressive: *Amours de Voyage*, "Easter Day, Naples, 1849," "Say Not the Struggle Naught Availeth," "O Land of Empire, Art and Love," and "Dipsychus"; indeed one might go so far as to say that there is very little else besides *The Bothie of Tober-na-Vuolich* that ranks in the highest level of his achievement. It is the purpose of this essay to offer some account of what Italy meant to Clough, and why his best poetry was conceived there.

The poem whose opening also opens this essay is usually known by its first line, but Clough once gave it the title "Resignation, to Faustus,"[1] and though the poem provides the most direct statement of his response to Italy, it is apparent that Clough also thought of it as a response to the poem by his friend Matthew Arnold called "Resignation—to Fausta."

In fact, Italy plays a crucial role in Clough's response to Arnold. Arnold's poem, set for the most part in the English Lake District, suggests that ordinary people must be resigned to obscurity because their lives are so short and the world about them so vast and enduring; a quiet mind is the

159

best they can hope for. Clough accepts the need for resignation in our lives, but rejects any scale of reference larger than man. Our duty is to experience the world to the full, and in Italy it becomes clear that to do so we must be resigned to the smell and feel and sight of the filth beneath our feet because it is part of the condition of life that allows us also to experience a sky above us fit for gods to tread. In England this truth is harder to come by, because in the north the whole process of the birth and growth of the pure and beautiful from the richly vile is so slow and struggling; dirt can be kept at a distance more easily because less swiftly and openly decaying and festering. Clough notes that in Italy,

> scarcely bound by space or time,
> The elements in half a day
> Toss off with exquisitest play
> What our cold seasons toil and grieve,
> And never quite at last achieve (54–58)

Life and death and life follow so swiftly on each other's heels that they are scarcely distinguishable; out of death and decay and corruption comes new life so rapidly that there is scarcely a moment to regret the loss before there is a new beauty to replace it, battening on the remains of the old. A society that strives to be aseptic like the middle and upper classes of England (the tourist classes of Clough's time) may preserve itself clean and cool and healthy, but only at the expense of virtuosity and richness in its response to life.

Clough epitomizes what it is that makes Italy as he experienced it so different from the chilly north, in the punning couplet:

> O richly soiled and richly sunned,
> Exuberant, fervid, and fecund! (35–36)

Italy is everything that England, that the Lake District, is not. But the same principle applies everywhere, and Clough uses a botanical analogy to broaden the reference of his point:

> In forest-shade in woodland bower
> The stem that bears the ethereal flower . . .
> From mixtures fetid foul and sour
> Draws juices that those petals fill. (46–50)

What seems self-evident in Italy, is, if you think about it, also part of life farther north.

160

More significantly, though, Clough goes beyond the vegetative aspects of his subject. It is an easy observation to make that life is swifter to flourish and decay and die in a hot climate; it is less evident that:

> In such a clime, who thinks, forgives;
> Who sees, will understand; who knows,
> In calm of knowledge find repose,
> And thoughtful as of glory gone,
> So too of more to come anon,
> Of permanent existence sure,
> Brief intermediate breaks endure. (70–76)

For English tourists the sight, day after day, of inescapable combinations and swift successions of such extremes of pureness and filth, beauty and ugliness, life and death, soon provokes thought. Once they begin to reflect upon the significance of what they have seen, they begin to understand what is hard for northern puritan minds to grasp, that dirt does not eliminate fineness, that one death is not universal death. This understanding leads to a general forgiveness of the processes of nature, of the existence of pain, sickness, even death; and this understanding, once accepted as true knowledge, will form a satisfying place of rest from the dislocations, the uncertainties, the anxieties of the modern world. This is Clough's resignation. If, as seems to be the case, this mixture of the fair and the vile, this frantic interchange of death and rebirth, is a fundamental principle of nature, then it cannot be evil:

> O Nature, if indeed thy will,
> Thou ownest it, it is not ill! (77–78)

At the end of the poem Clough blends the filth of the street, the glory of the sky, and the artistic perfection of the Corinthian column into an acceptance of all as essential parts of what a later poet was to seek as "unity of being":

> With resignation fair and meet
> The dirt and refuse of thy street
> My philosophic foot shall greet,
> So leave but perfect to my eye
> Thy columns set against thy sky! (84–88)

It is Nature that Clough addresses here, quite comfortable in accepting the human crafted work of art as a work of hers, distinct from her own beauty, but existing within it.

It seems that Clough found the creative abundance of Italy stimulating to his own creativity, and it seems impossible to escape a comparison with two poets of an earlier generation who also produced their finest work while in Italy--Byron and Shelley. All three men were powerfully drawn to republican ideas, eager for the destruction of social, economic, and religious oppressions; and as Byron and Shelley were in Italy during the abortive Carbonari risings in 1820, so Clough was in Paris in the spring of 1848, and in Rome in 1849, two months after the proclamation of the Roman Republic by Mazzini.

But to draw this comparison is also to mark the chasm that separates the Victorian from the Romantic. Byron in Ravenna was actively involved with the Carbonari in 1820, and though disillusioned with what he considered their feebleness and bad judgment, was later still prepared to commit himself to the cause of Greek independence. Clough remained an observer in Paris as in Rome, and, though sympathetic, was always restrained in his enthusiasm and quick to turn to skepticism. Byron and Shelley were thirty years closer to the revolution of 1789 and found it easier to believe in the fulfillment of nationalist and republican dreams.

A paragraph from a letter to Matthew Arnold's brother, Tom (who was in New Zealand), dated February 24, 1849—just over a month before Clough left England for Rome—gives a rapid insight into his attitudes both to his Paris experience and his forthcoming trip:

> Today, my dear brother republican, is the glorious anniversary of the great revolution of 48, whereof what shall we now say? Put not your trust in republics nor in any institution of man. God be praised for the downfall of Louis Philippe. This with a faint feeble echo of that loud last year's scream of *à bas Guizot* seems to be the sum total. Or are we to salute the rising sun with Vive l'Empereur and the green liveries? President for life I think they will make him, and then begin to tire of him. Meantime the Great Powers are to restore the Pope! and crush the renascent (alite lugubri) Roman republic[2] of which Joseph Mazzini has just been declared a citizen. The said J.M. has written two long letters to the Spectator attributing the Italian disaster entirely to the damper of the national enthusiasm caused by the Piedmontese interference—which is possible, yet of course he would say so. I fear his own pets now dominant in Rome and Tuscany are not strong enough for the place. Yet some heroic deeds ought to come of them, if they are worth anything.

Despite the resigned skepticism of "Put not your trust in republics nor in any institution of man," Clough could still think of himself as a republican; and his skepticism about their future is balanced by the temperate anticipation of "some heroic deeds" from the citizens of the new Roman Republic.

He must have traveled to Italy with mixed feelings: on the one hand excitement at the thought of visiting the city that was for his class and race the embodiment of civilization, and on the other a deep interest in the future of the fragile republican state.

Clough arrived in Rome as the French prepared to besiege the city, and during his stay began to write *Amours de Voyage*, a poem that centered on a man much like himself, a young, unmarried intellectual, traveling alone, in Rome for the first time at the moment when the Roman Republic is forced to fight for its life. Claude is not Clough, and yet there is a strong autobiographical element in the poem, not so much in terms of what happens to Claude (indeed it seems very probable that part of his experiences were based on those of Matthew Arnold elsewhere in Europe[3]), but in the analysis and speculation that Claude offers concerning the three strands of his life in Rome (and subsequently elsewhere in Italy)—art, war, and love.

Claude was consciously designed by Clough as a representative type of Victorian tourist, just as the Meagleses and the Dorritts (never forgetting Mrs. General) were by Dickens. At first Rome disappoints him. A traveler like Claude would have been led by education and by the reports of earlier writers to expect more obvious splendor and less rubbish. But gradually, with the assistance of John Murray's guidebook, and through the kind of serious study which alone could justify a mid-Victorian man leaving his responsibilities at home, Claude learns to discriminate between rubbish and excellence; and it is reasonable to suggest that most of his views on Roman art and architecture reflect Clough's.

Clough too, as his letters make clear, was a careful observer of the struggle between the French and Neapolitans and the Romans. His sympathies, as has already been observed, would have been with the Republic, but he came only slowly to identify with the defenders of the city. He was at first suspicious of Mazzini and unprepared to become emotionally involved with what his reason told him was bound to be a lost cause; but by 3 June he could write to Tom Arnold: "These blackguard French are attacking us again. May the Lord scatter and confound them."[4]

Claude has no previous record of support for republican causes, as he is careful to point out in Canto 2, letter 1: "I, who . . . never beheld a / New Jerusalem coming down dressed like a bride out of heaven / Right on the Place de la Concorde . . .",[5] but he too becomes emotionally committed to the Romans, so that "Will they fight?" of Canto 2, letter 3 becomes " we are fighting at last" of Canto 2, letter 5.

Neither Clough nor Claude goes beyond emotional involvement, however; the Victorian gentleman abroad is incapable of the heroic romantic (or Romantic) gesture. There can, though, be no certainty that Claude's entertaining debate on whether or not he could lay down his life for the "British female" also reflects one of Clough's own concerns. It is also quite difficult to determine whether or not Clough formed any romantic attachment during his weeks in the city; if he did, no evidence survives. It is, however, Claude's relationship with Mary Trevellyn that emerges as the most significant element in the narrative.

For much of the poem he denies that he is in love with her, maintaining a perpetual cool flirtation of the most unromantic kind, and justifying his behavior with an analysis of the nature of sexual attraction that builds on an earlier poem of Clough's "Natura Naturans". Eventually the Trevellyns (a family group with some similarities to the Dorrits) escape Rome for Florence, and though Claude had intended to go with them, at the last minute some inquiries from a third party about his intentions toward Mary offend his fastidious sensibilities, and he remains in the city. Claude refuses to be "circumscribed into action," and his retreat into contemplation of the Ludovisi collection and Vatican marbles echoes hollowly against the accompanying noise of the Romans acting to the last to try to preserve their republic.

The remainder of the poem chronicles the unlucky attempts of Claude to track down the Trevellyns, once Mary's absence has convinced him that he does indeed love her. Canto 4 is only 83 lines long, but is packed with futile journeying across the face of northern Italy. However, his failure to find Mary Trevellyn leads Claude in the end to an earned resourceful resignation. One among several details that might illustrate the development of this strength in the hitherto vacillating and hypersensitive man has a curious echo in a celebrated travel book of three years earlier. While in Florence, having given up the chase, Claude writes thus to Eustace:

> Moping along the streets, and cursing my day, as I wandered
> All of a sudden my ear met the sound of an English psalm tune.
>
> Comfort me it did, till indeed I was very near crying.
> Ah, there is some great truth, partial very likely, but needful,
>
> Lodged, I am strangely sure, in the tones of the English psalm tune.
> (Canto 5, letter 5, 88–92)

In *Notes of a Journey from Cornhill to Grand Cairo* (1846), Thackeray wrote of his feelings on hearing English church music in Jerusalem: "It was affecting to hear the music and language of our country sounding in that distant place . . . it was the music that was the most touching, I thought, the sweet old songs of home."[6] Claude though is tougher, less sentimental than Thackeray, for in the next section of the letter he writes:

Almost I could believe I had gained a religious assurance,
Found in my own poor soul a great moral basis to rest on.
Ah, but indeed I see, I feel it factitious entirely;
I refuse, reject, and put it utterly from me;
I will look straight out, see things, not try to evade them:
Fact shall be fact for me; and the Truth the Truth as ever
Flexible, changeable, vague, and multiform, and doubtful.
(Canto 5, letter 5.96–102)

At the end of the poem Claude paraphrases the famous passage from St. Paul's first epistle to the Corinthians:

Not as the Scripture says, is, I think, the fact. Ere our death-day,
Faith, I think, does pass, and Love; but Knowledge abideth.
Let us seek knowledge . . .
Knowledge is hard to seek, and harder yet to adhere to.
Knowledge is painful often; and yet when we know, we are happy.
(Canto 5, letter 10.197–201)

And the reader of Clough can make the connection between this poem and "O Land of Empire." It has taken the combination of all of Claude's experiences in Italy to drive him to this tough conclusion—a conclusion which we may fairly believe also to have been Clough's—one which is not without hope, even though Claude continues the letter almost in parody:

Seek it, and leave mere Faith and Love to come with the chances.
As for Hope, —tomorrow I hope to be starting for Naples.
(Canto 5, letter 10.202–3)

Claude's is not the only voice in *Amours de Voyage*. We hear briefly from two of the Trevellyn sisters; but more importantly there is an unnamed voice (perhaps that of a narrator, perhaps that of Clough in-the-poem) which offers the reader, in elegiacs that open and close each canto, a different perspective on Italy.
The poem begins with an invocation that also recalls elements of "O Land of Empire":

Over the great windy waters, and over the clear crested summits
Unto the sun and the sky, and unto the perfecter earth,
Come, let us go,—to a land wherein gods of old time wandered,
Where every breath even now changes to ether divine.

Nowhere in *Amours de Voyage* does Clough make clear the fetid and sour

165

side of the Roman scene (though in his first letter from Rome the hero Claude does call Rome "rubbishy," as Clough himself did in a letter to his mother soon after his arrival[7]) here the ballast to this ethereality is a different one. The speaker goes on to cast doubts upon the value of the whole enterprise:

> Come, let us go; though withal a voice whisper, "The world that we live in,
>   Whithersoever we turn, still is the same narrow crib;
> 'Tis but to prove limitation, and measure a cord, that we travel;
>   Let who would 'scape and be free go to his chamber and think;
> 'Tis but to change idle fancies for memories wilfully falser;
>   'Tis but to go and have been."—Come, little bark, let us go!

"Think" and "know": such important words in Clough's writing, such important activities in his life. And Claude proves the accuracy of the whispering voice, though, like Clough, he had to do the traveling to perceive the truth, and he discovered many incidental beauties on the way.

Clough's other great Italian poems, "Easter Day" and "Dipsychus," have a close relationship with *Amours de Voyage*, closer than appears in their currently available form. It has always been clear from the opening of "Dipsychus" that Dipsychus himself lays claim in some sense to authorship of "Easter Day," but what is now obscured is that Claude too has a circumstantial claim to "authorship" of "Easter Day." The later of the two manuscripts of "Easter Day," the one from which all published texts have been taken, was, in fact, headed "Naples, August 1849." From this piece of evidence it is not unreasonable to deduce that Clough (who did not himself visit Naples in 1849) had Claude in mind as the inferred writer of the poem, the Claude whose last words at the end of *Amours de Voyage* were of journeying to Naples.[8]

It would also follow that there is a close identity between Dipsychus and Claude; and before considering the Venetian poem, there are a couple of passages eventually cancelled (one might say censored) from the final copy for *Amours de Voyage* that should be taken into account. It is not hard to see that Claude and Dipsychus have much in common; what these cancelled passages show is that Claude at one time had also a certain kinship with the Spirit. For instance, there is a cynicism about the state of England that barely surfaces in the poem as we have it—or only perhaps in Claude's comments on the Trevellyns. In the first and longest draft of the whole poem, Canto 2, letter 9 (the letter in which Claude wishes that the "nice and natural people" of Rome could be "allowed this chance of redemption" in Mazzini's republic), ended thus:

When God makes a great Man he intends all others to crush him:
Pharaoh indeed, it is true, didn't put down Moses, but then that
Happened in barbarous times ere polity rose to perfection,
Ere the World had known bankers and funds and representation.
Rise up therefore ye Kings and ye, ye Presidents—Ah well
What is the use of all this? Let me sing the song of the shopman
And my last words like his let me shout with the chorus of journals.
Oh happy Englishmen we! that so truly can quote from Lucretius
Suave mari magno—how pleasant indeed in a tempest
Safe from the window to watch and behold a great trouble of others.
O blessed government ours, blessed Empire of Purse and Policemen,
Fortunate islands of order, Utopia of—breeches pockets,
O happy England, and oh great glory of self-laudation.[9]

The writer of this passage is evidently kin to the speaker of "How pleasant it is to have money" in scene 4 of "Dipsychus," though there is a bitter irony that is far from the Spirit's comfortably self-satisfied tone. And it is perhaps worth noting that Clough here latches on to something that Joseph Conrad later emphasized in *Heart of Darkness*, the security of an empire based on the policeman at the corner, and its distance from the fertile southern worlds.

Nor was Claude particularly convinced of the divine right of his country to power and influence:

Even though England and France by a Nemesis possibly righteous
Should in the issue succumb to the terrible cossack they talk of,
Why, I don't know. For the Czar may indeed be the Lord's own
    annointed,
Out of that people that walketh in darkness a great light issue,
Out of that Galilee come a new Era; or anyway England
France and the like may be the things the Creator is sick of; the
    Planet
Certainly still would revolve on its axis. What does it matter!
Though England fall and France; Europe turn one Russia in Europe
Men would live I suppose, the earth would turn on its axis.
Runagates would still visit Rome, and would stare and wonder as
    usual,
And the Pope be retained as Custode of Vatican marbles.[10]

These examples, which show a side of Claude's personality that hardly surfaces in the poem as we nowadays read it, help to resolve the question that is always raised about the relationship between Dipsychus and the Spirit. Once it is recognized that—potentially at least—Claude contains elements of the Spirit's nature within him, and it is accepted that the link through "Easter Day" identifies Claude and Dipsychus closely, then it seems clearer that the Spirit is an integral element in Dipsychus's personality, that "Dipsychus" really is to be read as an internalized debate between aspects of the same personality.

Though Dipsychus's hypnotic barcarole in the gondola could have been sung nowhere else, for the most part Venice appears to be no more than a slightly exotic background to his poem. After all, there are prostitutes, rude foreigners, famous buildings, crowds, and so on in a hundred cities. Is there anything about Venice that makes it a particularly appropriate setting for "Dipsychus"?

Two English writers whose names are particularly associated with Venice, and who are invoked in the poem, give the basis for an answer. Scene 5 of the poem begins with the Spirit's enquiry:

> What now? The Lido shall it be?
> That none may say we didn't see
> The ground which Byron used to ride on,
> And do I don't know what beside on.

Byron had by 1850 become a tourist attraction, featured in Murray's guidebooks, but when he was living in Venice the city was associated in the literate English mind with riotous and corrupt excess—a reputation which the visits of successive waves of Victorians did nothing to diminish. This is how Shelley saw the city when he first visited Byron there in 1818:

> I had no conception of the excess to which avarice, cowardice, superstition, ignorance, passionless lust, and all the inexpressible brutalities which degrade human nature, could be carried, until I had lived a few days among the Venetians.[11]

And John Pemble, in his excellent study, *The Mediterranean Passion: Victorians and Edwardians in the South*, has a series of quotations from subsequent visitors who regarded Venice as the most vivid current example of the decay of greatness through moral degeneracy—against which, implicitly at least, they could hold up their own empire of virtue.[12] Clough certainly makes use of this reputation, though it is not clear from the poem how fully he accepted it. The gaiety of the crowd, for instance, in the Public Garden in scene 2 is more strongly felt than its licentiousness.

Ruskin was as certain as anyone of the degeneracy of modern Venice, but in *Seven Lamps of Architecture* (published before Clough visited the city) he began his systematic glorification of its gothic architecture, of the medieval craftsmen that produced it, and of its basis in religious and moral ideals. The Spirit, not surprisingly, is unimpressed by Ruskin's enthusiasm. In scene 4, immediately after his song about the pleasantness of the possession of money, he continues:

> Come, leave your Gothic, worn-out story,
> San Giorgio and the Redemptore;
> I from no building, gay or solemn,
> Can spare the shapely Grecian column . . .
> The Doge's palace though, from hence,
> In spite of Ruskin's d----d pretence,
> The tide now level to the quay,
> Is certainly a thing to see.
> We'll turn to the Rialto soon;
> One's told to see it by the moon. (204–29)[13]

The Spirit, though not averse to expressing an opinion of his own, is (like Claude at times) ever the tourist, ever the essence of conventional wisdom, doing what his guidebook tells him to (when he was interesting himself in the hoofprints of Byron's horse, Dipsychus was off for a bracing bath in the Adriatic). It is, though, worth remembering that a Corinthian column was chosen by Clough to represent beauty in "O Land of Empire," and what the Spirit presumably finds offensively pretentious in Ruskin is his association of religious faith and social duty with architecture. Thus the contrast that the poem proposes between Ruskin the moral aesthetician and Byron the amoral hedonist might stand for the extremes Clough found mingled in the personalities of representative educated Victorian gentlemen and of their exemplar in the poem, Dipsychus/Spirit —mingled, too, in his own personality.

The topography of Venice is, of course, unique. The inversion of the normal state of affairs that is so integral a part of the Venetian experience— where the main streets are water and only narrow alleys debouching into sudden piazzas are dry land—can lead to strange responses, of which Dickens's hallucinatory dream-vision in his *Pictures from Italy* (1846) is only the most extreme. In scene 10, Dipsychus sees the maze of Venetian alleyways and bridges as an image for his life:

> Aimless and hopeless in my life I seem
> To thread the winding byways of the town,
> Bewildered, baffled, harried hence and thence,

All at cross-purpose ever with myself,
Unknowing whence from whither. (75–79)

The city is entirely flat, and it is only in the campanile spire or the distant
Alps (beloved of Dipsychus, inevitably) that the mind can find a symbol of
aspiration; and Dipsychus's self-analysis continues:

Then, in a moment,
At a step, I crown the Campanile's top,
And view all mapped below: islands, lagoon,
An hundred steeples and a million roofs,
The fruitful champaign, and the cloud-capt Alps,
And the broad Adriatic. (79–84)

But this vision of life mapped out from a position of absolute certainty, of
complete knowledge, soon fades, and he finds himself again bearing "the
workday burden of dull life / About these footsore flags of a weary world"
(88–89).

In the end Dipsychus succumbs to his Spirit's insistence, not through
intellectual conviction, but through intellectual and emotional weariness.
Claude (who is and is not Clough), whose stoical acceptance of his inade-
quacies in the face of the world is matched by his determination to seek
knowledge, to live to the full the intellectual life, has now, in Dipsychus
(who is also Clough and not Clough), capitulated to the worldly wisdom
offered by his Spirit. It was believed by the mid-Victorians that Venice was
in imminent danger of returning, once and for all, to the Adriatic,[14] and in its
approaching disintegration the city provides a fitting emblem of Dipsychus's
final collapse before the iron rule of common sense propounded by the
Spirit.

It is impossible to ignore the autobiographical elements in the fabric of the
Italian poems, and it is hard not to believe that Dipsychus's pact with his
Spirit does not also represent the conclusion of years of intellectual and
spiritual conflict for Clough. The poetic sequel, at any rate, to the poems
written in Italy were the limp *Mari Magno* narratives, and the subsequent
pattern of Clough's life was formed by engagement and marriage to a
woman who epitomized the conventional Victorian.

Clough needed to travel out from England to be able to understand clearly
what it was he wanted to write, and these journeys seem also to have been
necessary for him to see himself with any clarity. The public garden in
Venice at the feast of the Assumption is as far from Hampstead Heath on
August Bank Holiday as can be imagined, and one can see much farther
around large questions when one views them from a distance.

170

The Italian setting of these great poems reveals sharply the peculiarly English nature of the anxieties and problems that are debated in them; and it does seem that it was only Italy that could give Clough this perspective. He was in Paris for five weeks in 1848, and there is nothing to show for it; later he was in America for much longer, and again there is nothing significant to show for it. Italy, to end as I began, is a land of vanished Empire, of art, and of love, and in it Clough found the impulse to speak to a land of growing empire, of little art,[15] and little love—to speak to England of what it is to be young, intelligent, sensitive, and English. Without the god-like sky and the fecund soil, Clough, I think, would never have been able to see or express with such clarity these insights into the dilemmas that confronted him, and those like him.

NOTES

Quotations from Clough's poems are mostly from *The Poems of A.H. Clough*, eds. H.F. Lowry, A.L.P. Norrington and F.L. Mulhauser (Oxford: 1951). There are several respects in which this edition is not adequate, particularly in its reluctance to print all of Clough's poetry, and to note all of the variants to it; references to the text of *Amours de Voyage* are from the edition of the poem by Patrick Scott (St. Lucia, Queensland: 1974), an edition of superior authority to the Oxford text. Clough's letters are quoted from *Correspondence of Arthur Hugh Clough*, ed. F. Mulhauser, 2 vols. (Oxford: 1957).

1. This is the heading for the second manuscript version of the poem; most commentators have noticed the relationship between the two poems. One wonders in passing, with Richard M. Gollin ("The 1951 Edition of Clough's *Poems*," *Modern Philology* 60 [1962]: 120–27), why the editors of the standard edition did not adopt this title. Gollin also points out that there are twelve lines in one of the two extant manuscripts of the poem that appear neither in the published text of the Oxford edition (64–66), nor in the notes to it (481).

2. This is an adaptation of a line from the third of Book 3 of Horace's odes, "Troiae renascens alite lugubri" (the renascent Troy, accompanied by disastrous omens), and powerfully reinforces Clough's skepticism. The letter is in *Correspondence* 1.244.

3. Eugene August ("*Amours de Voyage* and Matthew Arnold in Love," *Victorian Newsletter* 60 [1981]: 15–20) suggests that Arnold's unsuccessful assignation in 1848 with Mary Claude in a Swiss hotel, well known to the Arnold-Clough circle, may have provided Clough with romantic material for *Amours de Voyage*. The coincidence of names is otherwise certainly very remarkable.

4. *Correspondence* 1.256.

5. The passage ironically echoes part of a letter that Clough wrote to Tom Arnold about his early days in Paris in 1848: "I was in extreme enjoyment—walked

about Jerusalem and told the towers thereof with wonderful delight" (*Correspondence* 1.214–5).

6. Chapter 13: "Jerusalem."
7. *Correspondence* 1.252.
8. This connection with Claude also provides the most satisfactory answer to the question: why did Clough see Naples as the appropriate site for "Easter Day"?
9. Scott 53–54.
10. Scott 73.
11. *The Complete Works of Percy Bysshe Shelley*, ed. Roger Ingpen and Walter E. Peck (London and New York: 1926) 9.335.
12. John Pemble, *The Mediterranean Passion: Victorians and Edwardians in the South* (Oxford: 1987) 232–35.
13. It is an interesting sidelight on the editing (by Clough's wife) that when "Dipsychus" was first published in the privately printed *Letters and Remains of Arthur Hugh Clough* (1865), the line "In spite of Ruskin's d----d pretence" was replaced by "In spite of doctrinaire pretence." Whether she was frightened of Ruskin or "d----d" or both is uncertain.
14. Pemble 232.
15. Matthew Arnold, in often quoted summaries in letters addressed to Clough, makes it clear how little he believed England was currently an Empire of art:

> Reflect too, as I cannot but do here more and more, in spite of all the nonsense some people talk, how deeply *unpoetical* the age and all one's surroundings are. Not unprofound, not ungrand, not unmoving:—but *unpoetical*.

> My dearest Clough these are damned times—everything is against one—the height to which knowledge is come, the spread of luxury, our physical enervation, the absence of great *natures*, the unavoidable contact with millions of small ones, newspapers, cities, light profligate friends, moral desperadoes like Carlyle, our own selves, and the sickening consciousness of our difficulties: but for God's sake let us neither be fanatics nor yet chaff blown by the wind. . . .

> (*The Letters of Matthew Arnold to Arthur Hugh Clough*, ed. H.F. Lowry [1932; Oxford: 1968] 99, 111.)

THE DYNAMICS OF CROSS-CULTURALISM IN CHARLOTTE BRONTË'S FICTION

Sally Shuttleworth, University of Leeds

From Charlotte Brontë's earliest writings onwards, the realm of the "foreign" functions as a site of imaginative projection. Although her primary engagement with the world of "abroad" occurs in her two Belgian novels, *The Professor* (1846) and *Villette* (1853), written after her two-year stay in Brussels, the imaginative landscape of her adolescent writings reveals a prior preoccupation with the notion of alternate lands. Angria, the geographical locus of her late juvenilia, combines the terrain of Yorkshire with the burning skies of Africa and the seductive lushness of a Mediterranean climate. Social and political issues of the day are played out in an atmosphere of heightened romanticism, bearing all the trappings of the Victorian engagement with the exotic. The travels of Mungo Park, *The Arabian Nights*, and the political reporting of contemporary newspapers are all blended together. Verdopolis, the early capital of Angria, possesses the mills and furnaces of an English northern city, and undergoes the same social unrest, strikes, and agitation for social change and political reform.[1] Its enemies of order, however, are a diverse blending of elements which draws together various strands of Victorian social fears. In Brontë's mythic land, the lower-class "mob," which figured so largely in mid-century political rhetoric, joins forces with the acclaimed enemies of English nationalism, the French, and two representatives of alien "uncivilized" cultures, the Arabs and the Ashantee.[2] All are symbolized in the figure of their leader, that Byronic reincarnation of Napoleon, Rogue Percy. As in Brontë's later writing, social and political issues are projected onto a personalized, psychological plane.

In Charlotte's Angria, the wars between England and France are recast as a struggle between two individuals: Zamorna (son of the Duke of Wellington) and Percy. Social and political questions of allegiance, obedience, and the dynamics of power are played out in the highly eroticized sphere of romance. (Although both figures are endowed with numerous devoted mistresses, their primary romance is, arguably, with each other.) The African setting and dramatization of the Ashantee people is used as a vehicle to explore English feelings of simultaneous attraction and repulsion toward the seemingly "foreign." Thus the narrator speculates that Zamorna must have had a deep and fixed hatred of the rebel Ashantee prince Quashia (who had been raised in his own family) to have ordered the death of this "man in whose person all the virtues of savage life were so nobly united, even though it cannot be denied that he possessed likewise many of its concomitant vices."[3] At once part of the family and yet unknown and alien, noble and yet vicious, Quashia, the representative "savage," embodies the disruptive political and sexual energies which so troubled the Victorians. (In one of the Roe Head fragments, Quashia is envisioned in a drunken stupor in the highly symbolic sanctum of the queen's bedroom.)[4] Charlotte's mythic land enacts in bolder form the Victorian appropriation of images of the exotic "Other" in order to articulate responses to threatening elements within their own culture.

After Charlotte's "Farewell to Angria" (at the age of 23), the exotic disappears, in the main, from her fiction, with the notable exception of her creation of Jane Eyre's shadowy double, the "mad" Mrs. Rochester, whose West Indian origins function as a displaced explanation of disturbing female sexuality. The major fiction follows the pattern of the juvenilia in exploring social and political issues through the medium of highly charged psychological interaction. Brontë is still very much engaged with the "foreign," but her focus now lies with specific European cultures, preeminently those of Belgium and France. Questions of character definition, gender, and class are set in relation to this cross-cultural nexus. The novels conform to two basic patterns. Either, as in her two Belgian novels, *The Professor* and *Villette*, English culture is transported into, and tested against, a foreign milieu; or, in the pattern followed by *Jane Eyre* (1847) and *Shirley*, (1849) elements of foreign culture are placed within an English setting, offering a grid against which to measure indigenous social and gender relations.

This shift of focus in Brontë's fiction is clearly related to her own experience of living abroad. From February 1842 until November 1842, when they were recalled to Haworth by their aunt's death, Charlotte and Emily were enrolled as pupils at the Hegers' school in Brussels. Charlotte then returned by herself, this time in the capacity of teacher, from January 1843 until late December. The experience undoubtedly had a profound impact upon both her life and fiction. In particular, it gave rise to her intense emotional engagement with M. Heger, which clearly stimulated her fictional preoccupation with the dynamics of cross-culturalism and teacher-pupil interaction. The seeming close correlation between events in Brontë's life and those in her Belgian novels has tempted many critics in the past into offering reductive readings of these works. Clear distinctions must be made, however, between Brontë's life and her fictional creations. This essay will move outside the narrow focus of biographical concerns to consider the imaginative engagement with ideas of "abroad" and the narrative functions of cross-culturalism in Brontë's fiction.

For the first-person narrator of *The Professor*, William Crimsworth, the experience of moving to Belgium is both liberating and threatening. He is released from the tyranny of his uncle and brother, but finds himself in a strange land, with only his wits to support him. Unlike the later Lucy Snowe, he already speaks French, so is neither helpless nor cut off from communication, though his first experiences reinforce his alien status: he understands neither the Flemish maid nor the rapid French of the Belgian gentlemen he encounters. His initial attempts at teaching are thus governed by caution: "It would not do yet to trust my unpractised tongue with the delivery of explanations" (63). Crimsworth's lack of status and tenuous command of the language seem to exacerbate his tendency, already evident in England, to turn his relations with others into battles in which he struggles for the advantage and upper hand. His whole narrative, indeed, operates as a fierce self-justification, a vindication of his own character and actions, whose urgency is never fully explained.

Crimsworth approaches the task of describing the people of Belgium as if he were a naturalist classifying the species of a new area. Drawing on theories of physiognomy and phrenology that were current at the time, he delineates the character of all he meets from a reading of their external features.[5] No doubts or afterthoughts enter to trouble his assertive judgments; he rests confident in his powers of definition. The scientific aura of the vocabulary he employs reinforces his belief in his own objectivity, and his superiority to the world he is studying. His attitude mirrors that of late eighteenth and early nineteenth-century travel literature and the writings within the newly emerging discipline of anthropology. Where the anthropologists were writing from a Euro-centric perspective, however, for an audience who shared their beliefs that "primitive" cultures represented the childhood of man, Crimsworth is directing his gaze toward other European cultures.[6] His evident national chauvinism functions as a troubling element in the narrative. In part it acts as an indictment of his self-satisfied character; but, without overt challenge, it also seems to carry a degree of authorial endorsement.

Crimsworth risks verdicts, not only on individuals, but on a whole race; thus he sums up the "character of the youth of Brabant": "Their intellectual faculties were generally weak, their animal propensities strong; thus there was at once an impotence and a kind of inert force in their natures" (67). From national character he jumps swiftly to national history, using his readings of the boys' features as an explanation of "the political history of their ancestors. Pelet's school was merely an "epitome of the Belgian nation" (68). Crimsworth's arrogance is quickly set in place, however, by ironic juxtaposition. His dismissive summary of Belgian history is immediately followed by his complaints against the French Pelet for not treating his Flemish ushers with respect. Admittedly, he maintains, they were Flamands, "and both had the true Flamand physiognomy, where intellectual inferiority is marked in lines none can mistake," yet they were still men, "and I could not see why their being aboriginals of the flat, dull soil should serve as a pretext for treating them with perpetual severity and contempt" (69). By attempting to display his own liberality, Crimsworth only condemns himself further. Although the Flamands are admitted into the category of men, their aboriginal habitat seems to place them more on the level of worms.

Few individuals or races seem to escape the lashings of Crimsworth's tongue: Aurelia, a "half-breed between German and Russian," is ignorant and slovenly; the Belgian Adele is "Gorgon-like"; while Juanna Trista, of mixed Belgian and Spanish origin, displays a phrenological profile so frightful he wonders how "any one, looking at the girl's head and countenance, would have received her under their roof" (100–1). His love is therefore reserved for Frances, whom he identifies at first sight as being "the type of another race . . . less jocund, material, unthinking" (124). Half English and half Swiss, Frances possesses the added advantage of a pure English accent, without much grounding in the language. She is thus a perfect candidate for his pupil/bride. The relationship between Crimsworth and Frances anticipates that between Louis and Shirley, and M. Paul and Lucy Snowe in *Villette*. In each case the courtship is founded not solely on the master-pupil relationship, but also on the acquisition of a foreign language. The master introduces his female pupil into his own language, using its discipline as a way of governing and dominating her behavior. This repeated pattern forms one aspect of Brontë's fascination with bilingualism, an accomplishment which she suggests can be both liberating and imprisoning.

Bilingualism sets Crimsworth free. It enables him first of all to defy the tyranny of his brother in the counting house, and secondly to escape from the constraints of English society, where his social position is both limited and clearly defined, to the anonymity of a foreign culture which eventually allows him to make his fortune. He can thence return to England with independent wealth to take up his "rightful" position in the social hierarchy.

For Jane Eyre too, bilingualism is liberating: her skill at French enables her at last to leave Lowood, to take up a career as teacher. Lucy Snowe, by contrast, embarks on her voyage to Labassecour without any knowledge of French, and finds her initial experiences suitably daunting. Her rise, however, from her initial humble position of nursery maid to that of teacher is due in large part to her swift acquisition of French. In her relationship with M. Paul it is noticeable that her bilingualism gives her a distinct advantage. Locked within one language, M. Paul is reduced to a sense of impotence when forced to allow Lucy to distribute the English prizes. English always represents to him a threatening area beyond his control.

The primary function of bilingualism or language acquisition in courtship, however, is to establish male dominance. In learning English, Frances submits herself entirely to Crimsworth's control. Once having made the transition from pupil to wife, French becomes her mode of rebellion; in her "elfish freak" she does "ample justice to the pith, the point, the delicacy of her native French, in which language she always attacked me" (258). Crimsworth's response is first to imprison her bodily and then to make her "read English to me for an hour by way of penance" (258). In *Shirley*, the same structure is in evidence. Louis finally achieves dominance over Shirley by making her recite the same French text which had marked her submission to his authority in adolescence. Her capitulation is entire: "When he ceased, she took the word up as if from his lips: she took his very tone; she seized his very accent; she delivered the periods as he had delivered them: she reproduced his manner, his pronounciation, his expression" (558). Shirley's own voice is entirely submerged; she has taken over not only Louis's native language but his very articulation.

Henceforth the androgynous Shirley, lord of the manor and cavalier to Caroline, ceases to exist, and in her place we have the pining captive of the book's conclusion, with the foreign brothers, Louis and Robert, "divid[ing] Brairfield parish betwixt us" (736). Caroline too participates in this rout. When having problems with her French grammar, part of her training in femininity as conceived by Hortense, it is to Robert that she goes to "get the rough place made smooth by his aid" (88). Frances, Shirley, Caroline, and Lucy Snowe are all willing pupils in their master's hands, ready to enter eagerly into his language and cultures.

Another model of the pupil-teacher relation is offered in *Jane Eyre*, where St. John Rivers tries to impose on Jane the same subjugation he has exerted on his own faculties. She is to learn at his hands not his native language, but the alien "Hindostanee." St. John's desire to travel to India as missionary is represented in the novel not as a specifically Christian or charitable act, but rather as evidence of his will to power. Jane under his tutelage loses her "liberty of mind," falling "under a freezing spell" (508). Unlike her counterparts, however, she can declare "I did not love my servitude" (508). She frees herself and takes on instead the role of tutor, translating the world for the blind and mutilated Rochester. As Jane's case suggests, in each of these pupil-teacher situations, Brontë is less concerned with the specific content of the foreign language and culture being imbibed than with the psychological dynamics that accompany foreign acculturation. Cultural difference is used as a model through which to explore gender division and interaction.

Bilingualism and cross-culturalism also function in the novels to undermine rigid social categorizations. Crimsworth's assertive judgments on the basis of racial characteristics are upset by the enigmatic figure of Yorke Hunsden, who, like the later Hiram Yorke of *Shirley*, refuses to fit into a neat, definable category. Hunsden is immediately identified by Crimsworth as both English and Gallic; his features are the only ones he designates as "indescribable," and indeed, Crimsworth finds *"his* face, the most original one Nature ever modelled" (206). Hunsden's cross-cultural characteristics, his strange mannerisms, and his immersion in French and German culture are linked, in Crimsworth's eyes, to an ambiguous gender identity. His perusal of Hunsden's foreign library is immediately followed by an analysis of the contrast betwen Hunsden's feminine lineaments and his massive frame, which suggests to Crimsworth "incompatibilities of the 'physique' with the 'morale'" (35).

With Hiram Yorke, the emphasis falls less on cross-gender attributes than on his disturbing political stance—the incongruity, for Tory eyes, of a mill owner who espouses radical views. Brontë is clearly fascinated by this "French-speaking Yorkshire gentleman" who switches so effortlessly between "broad Yorkshire," "pure English," and perfect French (53, 50).[7] Alone of all the characters, he has two chapters devoted to an explanation of his character and history. In an attempt to lay to rest his worrying traits, Brontë returns to Crimsworth's technique of character reading: Mr. Yorke receives a detailed phrenological analysis which effectively transforms his cultural and social ambiguity into a symptomatic effect of his peculiar phrenological configuration.[8] His challenging social stance is thus reduced to a question of physiology.

Hunsden is less easily disposed of. His presence in the closing scenes of *The Professor* hints at the problematic nature of the English idyl Crimsworth claims to have established. Crimsworth's violent shooting of his son's dog, Yorke, a gift from, and emblem of, Hunsden, suggests the cost to be exacted in his attempt to bring Victor up as a strict Englishman and Etonian. He aims to raise his son in the brutal English tradition of "whipping" the "offending Adam" out of him: "he will be cheap of any amount of either bodily or mental suffering which will ground him radically in the art of self-control" (271). Hunsden, for whom Victor shows a decisive partiality, recommends by contrast a more liberal approach, representative of the more enlightened continental philosophy of education from which Brontë herself benefited under the tutelage of M. Heger. Victor's spirit, Hunsden maintains, should not be curbed.

A further critique of English constraint and repression is offered by Hunsden's portrait of Lucia, a figure who reveals, in Frances' analysis, Hunsden's own limiting adherence to English convention. Frances paints a picture of the glamorous Lucia's life, which is opposed in all respects to her own willing subservience to the role of English wife and mother. The Italian Lucia, she maintains, is a figure who has broken her chains and found a career on the stage: "The face is that of one who has made an effort, and a successful and triumphant effort, to wrest some vigorous and valued faculty from insupportable constraint" (266). Unlike the later figure of Vashti with whom Lucy Snowe identifies, Lucia is not represented as demonic; her ability to break through social constraint to achieve free self-expression is judged entirely laudable. As enigmatic foreign figure, she stands as emblem of female potentiality repressed and denied in English culture. In Brontë's later narratives such emancipation is looked at with a more troubled eye.

Brontë's next two works, *Jane Eyre* and *Shirley*, are both cast entirely within an English setting, but in each novel elements of foreign culture play a definitive role in the analysis of gender and class relations. Although English, Jane Eyre writes as an alien within her own culture. At Gateshead Hall she is considered something less than human; she is not "natural," a "bad animal," a "rat" (6, 8). In her own eyes she is a "discord . . . I was like nobody there . . . a heterogeneous thing . . . an interloper not of her race . . . an uncongenial alien" (13–14). Her story, which is that of her gradual assimilation into a recognized social position in English culture, is deliberately set against two foreign archetypes of female development: the French model of Rochester's mistresses, embodied in miniature in her pupil, Adele, and in the darker image of sexual voracity represented by the imprisoned Creole wife of Rochester who, like Jane, haunts the third story of Thornfield Hall. The French model represents no great threat; based on typical English prejudices regarding French frivolity it can easily be surmounted by Protestant earnestness. The association with the Creole, since less overt, is not so easily dismissed.

Recent feminist criticism of *Jane Eyre* has drawn attention to the ways in which imagery and narrative structure insistently relate Jane and Bertha, Rochester's "angel" and "demon."[9] The duality is that constantly invoked by Victorian medical texts which spoke of the frightening passions which lay behind female modesty and decorum, ever waiting to erupt.[10] Models of explanation were frequently racist: women, like children, were considered to be under greater control of the body than men, and were thus viewed as closer to the "primitive" races.[11] The structure of explanation was one which dominated Victorian anthropology, while in its popular forms it created an indelible association between female sexuality and black races.[12] Jane's response to this threat is that of Victorian social ideology: ever tighter self-control. The contrast between the representation of the Italian Lucia and the Creole Bertha is marked: both attempt to ovethrow social constraint and to achieve self-expression, but whereas the European Lucia's attempt is celebrated, Bertha's violation of English decorum results in her categorization as "fiend." While Lucia stands for Frances as an image of lost potential, Bertha represents to Jane an unhealthy manifestation of sexual passion which must be exorcized before she can be received into her rightful place as wife and mother in upper-class English society.

In *Shirley* there are no ghost-like doublings, but rather literal character divisions, in the four-part relations of Shirley and Caroline, Louis and Robert. The whole is played out this time in a nexus of Anglo-Belgian relations which operates, fundamentally, to explore the intricacies of class politics. With the figure of Hortense, and her attempt to create Belgian housekeeping at Hollows Mill, we are offered the comic side of the problems involved in cross-cultural assimilation. At a deeper level, the foreign birth and dual nationality of Robert Gerard Moore permit Brontë to offer a cultural explanation for the problem of class antagonism explored in the novel. Robert is two characters in one. His English name, Robert, is associated with the "dreamer," and the realm of home and leisure, and the European name, Gerard, with the hard dog of the counting house and the world of "mill and market" (287). His failure to respond to his workers, Brontë suggests, is due in large part to his foreign birth and his lack of understanding of Yorkshire folk and custom. His specific cultural origins are less important than his foreign status; assimilation, Brontë seems to imply, brings greater understanding and thence a resolution of social conflict. By focusing on the question of cross-culturalism, Brontë sidesteps the charged issue of class division. As in her previous novels, however, the conclusion undermines the suggested images of resolution. Just as Hunsden's foreign influence disturbs Crimsworth's English idyl, and the image of St. John Rivers' passionate discontent in India mars Jane's picture of domestic happiness, so Robert's vision of industrial ravagement of the land places a question mark over the neat conclusion of *Shirley*.

With *Villette*, Brontë turns once more to a foreign setting. Like Crimsworth, Lucy Snowe finds her transition to a foreign culture liberating, setting her free from the stifling confinement of her English life represented by her existence with Miss Marchmont when "two hot close rooms . . . became my world" (30). Alone and virtually penniless, she moves into an environment where, unlike England, her status cannot easily be defined, or future possibilities be closed off. The process of transition is more daunting for her than for Crimsworth, bearing all the hallmarks of a mythic entry into a dark new world or afterlife. As she is rowed out to the ship at night, Lucy thinks of "the Styx, and of Charon rowing some solitary soul to the Land of Shades" (68). Her arrival in Labassecour does little to dispel her fears; the landscape is less attractive than Crimsworth's vision, being "bare, flat, and treeless" and, like a savage Eden, traversed by "slimy canals [which] crept, like half-torpid green snakes" (81). Her sense of exhilaration is matched by ceaseless anxiety: "The breathing of that beast of prey was in my ear always; his fierce heart panted close against mine. . . . I knew he waited only for sun-down to bound ravenous from his ambush" (82). Once Lucy arrives in Villette her fears are literalized. Following her devastating loss of her luggage, and her rescue by Dr. John, she is pursued through the streets by the two "dreaded hunters" (86) whose presence—by underlining the perils to which a woman without home, connections, or even native language was exposed—suggests the extraordinarily daring nature of Lucy's enterprise. On finding Madame Beck's, it is her very foreignness, her conformity to Madame Beck's image of the intrepid "Anglaises," that saves her from the fate that might have met her in a London street.

Brontë's analysis of cross-culturalism is less specifically directed in her final novel than in *The Professor*. It is not to Belgium and Brussels that Lucy moves, but to Labassecour and Villette. While the tilting of the novel deliberately foregrounds the theme of foreign cultural experience, the fictional construct of "Villette" allows Brontë to consider this issue within a more broadly European context. Unlike Crimsworth, Lucy does not view her surroundings with the eye of a natural historian or anthropologist. Her concern is less to categorize from an external, seemingly objective standpoint, than to explore the effects on her own psyche of her immersion in this alien medium. Crucial to her analysis is the disparity between Roman Catholic and Protestant systems of education, a theme which, while touched on in *The Professor*, with the figure of the "automaton" Sylvie, rendered mindless by the control of the church, was never fully developed. In Brontë's own responses to foreign education, the question of religious difference had also loomed large. One of her earliest letters from Brussels records that "the difference in country and religion makes a broad line of demarcation between us and all the rest"[13]; and in a later tirade against Catholicism and its impact on the Belgian pupils, she speaks in vehement terms of having "the brand of Protestantism and Anglicism upon us."[14] Catholicism seemed to crystallize for her all the threatening aspects of the foreign.

Lucy's puzzled responses to Madame Beck's system of education at first seem mildly approving. She judges her approach to the physical and mental

181

well-being of her pupils "easy, liberal, salutary, and rational: many an austere English school-mistress would do vastly well to imitate it" (101). Yet at the same time that she praises Madame Beck's capacity to teach without overburdening her students, and to keep them in the peak of spirits and health, Lucy also expresses reservations about Madame Beck's disciplinary system, her activities of surveillance. Madame Beck herself, she avers, "seemed to know that keeping girls in distrustful restraint, in blind ignorance, and under a surveillance that left them no moment and no corner for retirement, was not the best way to make them grow up honest and modest women" (100). The charge at first seems curious. Why should the ability to retire from surveillance, and hence hide thoughts and actions, create greater honesty or modesty? As the narrative progresses, the associative nexus of these terms is revealed: at stake is the clash between two cultures which, for Lucy, focuses on the different value systems of Protestantism and Catholicism. "Honesty" and "modesty," in Lucy's Protestant perspective, are equated with fierce self-control and the ability to conceal inner thoughts from the prying eyes of the Catholic Church.

Catholicism is associated for Lucy with this ever-vigilant system of "espionage," the "surveillance of a sleepless eye," symbolized by the 'mystic lattice" of the Roman Catholic confessional (592). Some of Lucy's most intense emotional responses are evoked by her encounters with Catholicism. She flees, burning hot and heart throbbing, from the nightly "lecture pieuse" with its "dread boasts of confessors, who had wickedly abused their office" (163). Her true mental breakdown is signified not by her initial tortured state of delirium, but by her entry into the confessional, her voluntary revelation of the innermost secrets of her psyche to the eyes and ears of the Catholic church. At issue here is not simply a religious difference, but the dominant social and economic ideologies of Victorian England: individualism and self-control.

To understand Lucy's vehement antagonism to the Catholic Church, we must place the novel in its contemporary context. Brontë's earlier antagonistic responses to Catholicism were reinforced by the cultural climate of the early 1850s. From November 1850 through the period of the writing of *Villette*, the newspapers were full of reports of "papal aggression" in response to the perceived intervention of the Pope in British affairs. The Brontë's local Tory paper, *The Leeds Intelligencer*, carried weekly accounts of stealthy "Romish encroachments," arguing that "the Protestant spirit of the country and the resolute independence of Englishmen will sooner or later be roused to the discomfiture of those who dream of reimposing an intolerable civil and spiritual bondage upon us."[15] To add fuel to this patriotic fervor, Leeds was also one of the centers of the shift toward Catholicism in the Protestant church, the "perverts of St. Saviour's," as *The*

Leeds Intelligencer termed them. An oration by Newman was greeted as evidence of "how a mind that has surrendered itself to the limbo of authoritative teaching, that has abandoned its own powers of reasoning to an alien infallibility, and has cast off the responsibility of thinking for itself, may become emasculated."[16] The tirade places the image of the "automaton" Sylvie in a nationalistic context. Catholicism was regarded as a threat to control, both on the national, patriotic level, and also at the individual, psychological level. Outraged responses to the perceived "Romish" threat functioned both to focus and reaffirm the ideologies of self-control so central to the social and economic system of Victorian England.

The anti-Catholicism of *Villette* draws on these nationalistic sentiments, and vehement defenses of Protestant autonomy, but as in Jane Eyre's fierce assertions of self-determination, there is also one more element in play—the sexual. Lucy's fear of disclosure focuses preeminently on the sphere of sexual desire, whether in connection with her love for Dr. John, and her precious "buried letters," or in her growing relations with M. Paul, which the church, in the person of Pére Silas, actively tries to disrupt. The buried Catholic nun who haunts the text operates, like the mad Creole wife in *Jane Eyre*, to suggest the cost exacted for the open demonstration of sexual desire (while Bertha is imprisoned for her "unchaste" behavior, the nun was buried alive "for some sin against her vow"). Only if Lucy, like Jane, retains "Protestant" "honesty and modesty" will she be successful in the realm of love.

With the open declaration of love between M. Paul and Lucy, the threat of Catholicism seems miraculously to dissolve. Unlike Crimsworth, Lucy chooses to remain the rest of her life in Belgium/Labassecour which, in spite of her anti-Catholicism, continues to be her land of opportunity. As foreigner, she can acquire social status and prosperity as mistress of a school that would be difficult to achieve in England. Labassecour has also offered her the possibility of romance. Lucy was as little likely to draw the sexual interest of Dr. John, the archetypal Englishman, as was a piece of furniture. Only to the fiery M. Paul, who looks without the eyes of English prejudice, is she a figure of romance. M. Paul, however, with his "Spanish face" and passionate gestures, is not a typical product of Labassecour culture. His emotional excesses and lack of self-control align him rather with Latin culture, whose negative female form was earlier imaged by the Creole, Bertha Mason.

The pattern of courtship between M. Paul and Lucy is still that of master-pupil, but Lucy displays none of Shirley's willing submission; she retains to the end the advantage of bilingualism. As a passionate, socially powerful figure, M. Paul is Lucy's desired "Other"; through her emotional battles with him and the experience of conflict they engender, she strengthens her own sense of self-definition. With his declaration of love, however, opposition ceases. Like Bertha, therefore, who also represented a threat to autonomy, he is removed from the scene, this time by water rather than by fire. Lucy remains in Labassecour whose attractions for her, arguably, reside less in any specific cultural attributes than in its non-Englishness. As foreigner, she can affirm and strengthen her own sense of self through her experience of difference. Far from being absorbed and defined by her surrounding culture, she remains outside its parameters, an intrepid "Anglaise" in a foreign land.

Throughout Brontë's work, the realm of the "foreign," whether imported into England or experienced abroad, functions as a medium through which she can explore aspects of indigenous Victorian culture. Different facets of the foreign are shown to be simultaneously liberating and menacing, offering glimpses of an escape from social confines, but also threatening to dissolve the socially ingrained certitudes of selfhood. Thus Crimsworth firmly insists on his essential distinction from all the European characters and physiognomies he encounters in Belgium, and Jane Eyre returns to Rochester only after she has come to terms with the troubling image of femininity suggested by her foreign double, Bertha Mason. In both *The Professor* and *Villette*, residence in Belgium/Labassecour permits the protagonist to develop a stronger sense of selfhood through opposition to the prevailing culture. Yet in many of the courtships Brontë explores, the reverse process occurs: the woman, surrendering her identity to the man's, adopts his alien language. In all the novels, cross-culturalism operates as a way of exploring the social construction of gender relations, and also of sexual self-definition, as in the case of Jane Eyre's rejection of the two alternate foreign models of femininity. Yet the alignment of her self and Bertha, implicit in the construction of her narrative, suggest an underlying investment in the Victorian ideology which linked women to the "lower" races. This pattern is repeated in *Villette*, where the cretin stands as a dreaded image of the breakdown of "civilized" feminine self-control.

Although Brontë leaves behind the "burning climes" of her juvenilia, with its stark images of cultural and racial difference, her European novels still employ encounters with the foreign to explore, in a more subtle register, problematic elements within English culture. While *Shirley* is the only novel which seems explicitly to use cultural difference to explore social and political questions, in each novel, as in the juvenilia, these concerns are mediated through the analysis of psychological interaction. Thus Lucy's virulent response to Catholicism is framed by Victorian social ideologies of self-control, on both a national and individual level. Brontë's engagement with the world of "abroad" in her fiction suggests the diverse ways in which foreign culture acted for the Victorians, as for us today, as a way both of exploring disturbing elements within one's own culture, and of sharpening the lines of definition of social and psychological identity.

NOTES

Quotations for Brontë's novels are from these editions: *Jane Eyre*, ed. Jack and M. Smith (Oxford: 1969); *The Professor* (1900; New York: 1973); *Shirley*, ed. H. Rosengarten and M. Smith (Oxford: 1979); *Villette*, ed. H. Rosengarten and M. Smith (Oxford: 1984).

1. See, for example, the story "The Bridal," in *The Miscellaneous and Unpublished Writings of Charlotte and Patrick Branwell Bronte*, ed. T.J. Wise and J.A. Symington, (Oxford: 1936–38) 1.210–11.
2. For a detailed account of the "Ashantee" rising, see "The Green Dwarf" in *Legends of Angria*, ed. Fannie E. Ratchford (New Haven: 1933). The struggles between the British and the Ashanti tribes of Ghana for control over the Gold Coast figured prominently in newspaper reports throughout the period of the juvenilia.
3. "A leaf from an Unopened Volume," *Miscellaneous Writings* 1.318.
4. See Christine Alexander, *The Early Writings of Charlotte Brontë* (Oxford: 1983) 148.
5. For further discussion of the impact of physiognomy and phrenology on Brontë's fiction see Ian Jack "Physiognomy, Phrenology and Characterisation in the Novels of Charlotte Bronte," *Bronte Society Transactions* 15 (1970): 377–91; and S. Shuttleworth, "Psychological Power and Social Definition: Phrenology in the Works of Charlotte Bronte," *Beneath the Great Divide: Essays on Science and Literature, 1700–1900*, ed. J. Christie and S. Shuttleworth (forthcoming, Manchester Eng.).
6. The belief in a developmental line, linking "civilized" and "primitive" culture was, in itself, a liberal position at this era. Thus a review of J.C. Prichard's *The Natural History of Man*, run in 1844 by *Frasers*, a periodical to which the Brontës subscribed, pours scorn on the idea that there was any relation between the descendants of the "Adamitic race" and the "lower tribes of the human animal" who remain, for the reviewer, more closely associated with the baboon than with Western man (*Frasers Magazine* 30 [1844]: 537–49).
7. The impetus for the portrait clearly came from the father of Brontë's friend, Mary Taylor, whose household offered to the adolescent Brontë a new world of foreign culture and alien political views. As with the Brussels experience, however, the relationship between the fictional construct and biography is not one of parallelism, but the more oblique one of motivating impulse.
8. Although phrenology continues to figure in Brontë's writing, this is the only place, outside of Crimsworth's self-serving text, where its vocabulary is used to offer a fixed and unchanging character assessment. M. Paul, in *Villette*, is more true to the spirit of phrenology in offering an open verdict on Lucy's potentiality.

9. See, for example, E. Showalter, *A Literature of Their Own: British Women Novelists from Brontë to Lessing* (Princeton: 1977); and S. Gilbert and S. Gubar, *The Madwoman in the Attic: The Woman Writer and the Nineteenth-Century Literary Imagination* (New Haven: 1979).
10. Thus J.G. Millingen speaks of pent-up forces of female emotion: "Like a smouldering fire that has at last got vent, her passions, when no longer trammelled by conventional propriety, burst forth in unquenchable violence" (*The Passions: or Mind and Matter* [London: 1848] 157–58).
11. For an interesting discussion of the assumptions behind this notion see N.L. Stepan, "Race and Gender: The Role of Analogy in Science," *Isis* 77 (1986): 261–77.
12. For further exploration of this point see S. Gilman, "Black Bodies, White Bodies: Toward an Iconography of Female Sexuality in Late Nineteenth-Century Art, Medicine, and Literature," *Critical Inquiry* 12 (1985): 204–42. Gayatri Spivak offers a rather different interpretation to my own of the relationship between *Jane Eyre* and imperialism in "Three Women's Texts and a Critique of Imperialism," *Critical Inquiry* 12 (1985): 243–61.
13. *The Brontës: Their Lives, Friendships and Correspondence*, ed. T.J. Wise and J.A. Symington (Oxford: 1933) 1.68.
14. *The Brontës* 1.260.
15. *The Leeds Intelligencer* 5 April, 1851.
16. Ibid.

LESSONS OF HISTORY: RUSKIN'S SWITZERLAND

Elizabeth Helsinger, University of Chicago

John Ruskin made twenty-eight trips to Switzerland, one nearly every other year for fifty-five years. At twenty he recorded in his diary that the Alps, with Venice, were his "two bournes of Earth," a phrase he quoted forty years later in his autobiography, *Praeterita*.[1] The thought is further varied and elaborated: Geneva and the Alps are one of the "centres of my life's thought," a "school," a "kingdom" to see and possess "by the law of love," "the Holy Land of my future work and true home in this world" (*Works*, 35.156, 321, 167, 508). The terms of his passionate praise are revealing of the special meaning Switzerland possessed for Ruskin. If he began as a visitor, his repeated returns made Switzerland a center in his mental and emotional geography. Yet it was never his home. Despite attempts to settle there in the 1860s, his home remained the place to which he addressed his daily letters, his parents' house in England.[2] The kingdom that can be possessed only by the eyes and the heart, the Holy Land glimpsed in a vision of the future—in these terms Ruskin confirmed at the end of his traveling life the meaning that his earlier words, reencountered as he read over his diaries, may have suggested. As a "bourne of Earth," Switzerland was both an ultimate destination and a place beyond the reach of the English visitor. It was a place of spiritual pilgrimage, to be attained only after death. To live there was not possible, any more than it would be possible to live in the land that Hamlet imagines in the lines that echoed through nineteenth-century uses of the word:

> The undiscover'd country, from whose bourn
> No traveller returns.[3]

Much of *Praeterita* is concerned with accepting Switzerland as permanently out of reach. It was indeed out of reach for Ruskin himself after 1888;

by the time he wrote the last pages of *Praeterita* he had been brought home, sick in mind, from what was to be his last trip abroad. His treatment of it must have also been an effort at protection: he had come to hate the ordinary English visitor to whose influence he attributed the railroads and hotels that were transforming the Swiss landscapes he remembered. The Switzerland evoked in *Praeterita* cannot be defaced because it exists only in memory sustained by Ruskin's lyrical prose. But he was above all making peace with his dead parents. The Switzerland of *Praeterita* is the idyllic place he visited with them in his youth, not the place he tried to live in alone, deserting them and England in their old age. If *Praeterita* is a story of Paradise lost and regained, as one perceptive reader has suggested,[4] then "this mountain Paradise" (35.114) is regained as idyllic memory through filial sacrifice, an act of belated obedience to his father. Acknowledging that "I am more thankful, through every year of added life, that I was born in London" (35.320), Ruskin tells England and his parents that if Geneva has been his "bourne of Earth," England was his place of origin—to which, unlike Hamlet's traveler, he has returned:

> And although, in the course of these many worshipful pilgrimages, I gathered curiously extensive knowledge, both of art and natural scenery, afterwards infinitely useful, it is evident to me in retrospect that my own character and affections were little altered by them; and that the personal feeling and native instinct of me had been fastened, irrevocably, long before, to things modest, humble, and pure in peace, under the low red roofs of Croydon, and by the cress-set rivulets in which the sand danced and minnows darted above the Springs of Wandel. (35.33)

But *Praeterita* is the end of the story. This "dutiful offering at the grave of [his] parents" (35.12), as Ruskin called his autobiography, suppresses much of the tension not only between parents and son, but also between home and abroad that structured his life. The attraction of those centers abroad is evident even as he renounces them in *Praeterita* (Venice absolutely, Switzerland, partially—to be regained as a memory).[5] But one has to go outside *Praeterita* to understand both what those centers abroad meant for Ruskin, and why his return home has—as it does—a more than biographical interest.

The return was first announced in his inaugural lecture for the Slade Professorship of Art at Oxford, in 1870. Accepting the post was a recommitment of his energies to England, after a decade in which he defined Switzerland as the locus for his work.[6] The lecture reverses the relationships between home and abroad that had sustained Ruskin in the preceding three decades of his life. It is a call to the young Englishmen he is addressing not to go abroad to find what England lacked—be that high mountains or high

188

art—but to cultivate England so that they might take it with them and go out to establish an Empire. Ruskin's call was heard, albeit only in part, by a young Oxford student, Cecil Rhodes, who later remembered Ruskin's "Inaugural Lecture" as one of the shaping influences of his life.[7]

And this is what [England] must either do, or perish: she must found colonies as fast and as far as she is able, formed of her most energetic and worthiest men;—seizing every piece of fruitful waste ground she can set her foot on, and there teaching these her colonists that their chief virtue is to be fidelity to their country, and that their first aim is to be to advance the power of England by land and sea. . . .
But that they may be able to do this, she must make her own majesty stainless; she must give them thoughts of their home of which they can be proud. The England who is to be mistress of half the earth, cannot remain herself a heap of cinders, trampled by contending and miserable crowds; she must yet again become the England she was once, and in all beautiful ways,—more: so happy, so secluded, and so pure. (20.42–43)

Those wistful words—"so happy, so secluded, and so pure"—take us once again back to *Praeterita*, recalling both the England of Ruskin's earliest memories and the Switzerland that he shared with his parents. Both are the model for the "thoughts of home" that must sustain the Englishman in his new destiny abroad.

There is a destiny now possible to us—the highest ever set before a nation to be accepted or refused. . . . Will you, youths of England, make your country again a royal throne of kings; a sceptred isle, for all the world a source of light, a centre of peace; mistress of Learning and of the Arts:—faithful guardian of great memories in the midst of irreverent and ephemeral visions . . . ? (20.41)

The England envisioned here is the "faithful guardian" of all that Ruskin had discovered in Switzerland and Italy: the heritage of Western European civilization. These are the terms in which he described the Venice and Switzerland of Europe's past: Venice, the mistress of the seas and of the arts; Switzerland, "the centre of religous and social thought, and of physical beauty, to all living Europe" (35.321). His return to England, then, was indeed a Paradise regained: the memories not only of his own but of Europe's youth were henceforth to be anchored in, and guarded by, the paternal and maternal presences of the family and the nation.
This picture of Ruskin the apologist for imperialism is, however, as incomplete as that of Ruskin the obedient son. For whether Ruskin sought

in Switzerland his own past or England's, what he found was far more problematic than *Praeterita* or the "Inaugural Lecture" suggest. It is the story omitted in *Praeterita* and at Oxford that I would like to examine.

To begin at the beginning: what did it mean for an Englishman to visit Switzerland in the early Victorian years?[8] To travel geographically and temporally, but not too far. Visiting Switzerland had none of the connotations of travel to Italy: for most travelers, it was neither a cultural nor a spiritual pilgrimage. Travel *through* Switzerland had a long history, but travel *to* it was rare before the 1760s. Almost as soon as the English discovered Switzerland, however, their visits took on all the characteristics of modern tourism. Though it was still just possible, in the 1830s, to explore beyond the reach of guidebooks and hotels, most visitors to Switzerland were tourists. Among them were Ruskin and his parents.

Ruskin knew three generations of Swiss tourists and belonged to the middle one. The reopening of Europe to travelers after the Seven Years' War coincided with two cultural phenomena that brought the first wave of English visitors to Switzerland. In 1760 Rousseau's *La Nouvelle Heloise* set new directions for the novel by making a sense of place inseparable from the sentiments of its characters. Literary Europeans for the next century went seeking the passion of Julie and St. Preux to her garden at Clarens and his rocky retreat at Meillerie, on the shores of Lake Geneva. Of equal importance for the English, enthusiasm for the landscape sublime, reaching its first height, encouraged Thomas Pars, Francis Towne, John Robert Cozens, Wordsworth, and many more travelers to look with new expectations at Swiss glaciers, mountains, and waterfalls. The French Revolution and Napoleonic Wars stopped the growing tide of English visitors only temporarily. Turner, Shelley, and Byron, arriving just after Napoleon's departure, were the avant-garde of a second generation of English tourists in Switzerland. By the 1820s and 1830s these new visitors were overwhelmingly middle class. They followed well-marked routes to places already half-familiar from the travel poetry of Byron and Rogers and the illustrations of Prout and Turner.

For Ruskin's generation, Switzerland was first of all a place of sublime natural scenery. It was also one of the last places in Europe where remnants of a genuinely pastoral life supposedly persisted, savored before the Revolution by famous French and English residents including Voltaire and Gibbon. Then, too, Switzerland was the country of legendary patriotic struggles to defend political and religious autonomy; the exploits of William Tell (dramatized by Schiller) everywhere shape the traveler's consciousness in Murray's first Swiss guidebook of 1838. Finally, of course, Switzerland remained the historical path to Italy, the path not only of pilgrims, travelers, and now of tourists, but also of armies—Hannibal's, and Napoleon's.[9]

190

Within Ruskin's lifetime, however, Switzerland acquired a different fame and attracted a new kind of visitor—the climber.[10] Alpinists were often impatient with the mountain aesthetics of those who had never ventured on the high peaks. They spoke, instead, in a language where sport carried strong imperialistic overtones, of virgin mountains and the challenge of conquest, where one no longer climbed for the view but rather looked in order to climb higher. In the 1850s and 1860s, the early days of the British Alpine Club, Switzerland briefly recovered for the climber the freshness of the unknown. But climbing, which as Ruskin foresaw quickly produced its own kind of tourism, had less appeal for those who had grown up on Byron and Rousseau. Ruskin's bitter, funny descriptions of the gymnastic antics of the climbers leave no doubt that he remained a Romantic tourist.[11]

Yet he was, of course, more than a tourist. The sheer number of his visits, and the span of years they cover, constitute a different experience. Switzerland made Ruskin acutely aware of the laws of change. His repeated returns to the same scenes became the occasion for a history of his own responses, cryptically noted in his diaries. Switzerland itself, observed from year to year, seemed no less fluid. The most memorable of his accounts—for both nineteenth- and twentieth-century readers—are the celebrations of mountain glory in *Modern Painters* I and IV, based on intensive study of the Alps in the 1830s and 1840s. These books impressively extend the sensibilities of the romantic tourist, supplementing sublimity with science. They also do something more: they teach the Romantic tourist to read the sublime forms of mountains as the records of a natural history still being written, as the curving shapes and lines of natural forces creating an ever-changing landscape. (Ruskin's powerful attachment to James Forbes's theories of glacial movement is part of the same dynamic vision of mountains as both form and energy.) When he turned his attention in the 1850s from Swiss mountains to Swiss towns, his preoccupation with visible traces of change persisted: in his drawings, bridges, roads, and towers replaced granite outcroppings and cleavages as the clues to Swiss political and religious history.

But the lines of change visible in Swiss towns pointed to some deeply troubling conclusions. As in Venice, so in the Swiss cantons Ruskin saw a gradual fall from an original purity as the shape of human history: the hotels and railroads of a modern, commercial Switzerland left large blanks in his drawings because he could not bear to record them. A further difficulty was the unresolved question of the influence of place on mind, a proposition that Ruskin, following Romantic predecessors from Wordsworth to Madame de Staël, had assumed in his theocentric theories of natural beauty in *Modern Painters* II and in his studies of Gothic architecture in *The Stones of Venice*. The histories of lives lived in the shadow of the Alps, including his own, suggested a more complex and problematic relationship. Perhaps that is why

191

Ruskin never wrote the later books on Switzerland he planned—a history of Swiss towns, a history of European medieval Christianity (*Our Fathers Have Told Us*). But fragments of Swiss history are scattered throughout his writings after 1856, interwoven with biography and autobiography. It is through these fragments—including Ruskin's drawings—that I would like to explore Ruskin's Switzerland. Though he remained a romantic traveler, in these excursions through Switzerland into the painful territory of human history, Ruskin abandoned Wordsworth for less optimistic fellow-travelers and guides: Byron, Rousseau, and Turner. In Ruskin's eyes—as in those of many other Victorians—these Romantics took a less comfortable view of the European civilization that England had inherited than Ruskin allowed when he returned to England in 1870.

When he first set out with his family for Switzerland in 1833, however, he did not foresee the directions these guides would take him. The Ruskins followed the footsteps of the most famous Romantic tourist in search of pastoral villages and landscape beauty and sublimity. Though Prout's lithographs had whetted their appetites for European towns, it was Byron who fixed their expectations of Swiss lakes and mountains. Other influences came quickly—Turner's vignettes, Saussure's natural history, William Brockedon's travel books, Shelley's "Mont Blanc," James Forbes on glaciers—but Byron retained his priority.[12] His part in Ruskin's experience of Switzerland grew more rather than less as Ruskin found in Byron lessons of self-consciousness and historical consciousness he had not read in the 1830s.

In the 1840s Switzerland chiefly meant the excitement of high mountains to Ruskin; it was on visits in 1842, 1844, 1846, and 1849 that his studies of geology and mountain form led him to the discoveries of curvilinear structure that he set forth in *Modern Painters* IV. But in the same years his diaries record the beginnings of a reciprocal study of self and place, made necessary by the sometimes painful consciousness that his visits were acquiring a history of their own. In 1841 he is overjoyed to find that neither he nor Switzerland has changed. Geographical return is also temporal return, and the revisit prompts him to articulate both something about himself ("my old joy in the Alps") and something about Switzerland ("most thorough Swiss it was . . . complete, unsophisticated Swiss pastoral feeling").[13] In 1844 he finds Switzerland the same but himself changed—his childhood freshness of response subtly diminished.[14] By 1846 the perception of passing time as loss moves him to value traces in the landscape of past times—others' as well as his own—that once had no part in his mountain enthusiasms. Switzerland, he concludes, is dear because it is neither "strange" to him nor "without history"; American mountains would leave him cold.[15] In 1849 he explores the effort of will required to respond even to loved places: "I put my *mind* into the scene. . . . I repeated 'I am in *Switzerland*' over and over again, till the name brought back the true group of associations—and I felt I had a soul, like my boy's soul, once again."[16] Mind and language convert loss to gain, preserving and recalling events and feelings of the past that have become a necessary part of Ruskin's present response to places. Byron already knew this, as Ruskin remembered years later. "Though he could not teach me to love mountains or sea more than I did in childhood," he noted in *Praeterita*, Byron "first animated them for me with the sense of real human nobleness and grief." Byron and his poetic creation, Childe Harold, preceded Ruskin as self-conscious travelers exploring changes in the self through travel.

"He taught me the meaning of Chillon and Meillerie," Ruskin goes on, referring neither to descriptions of natural beauty nor to associations with Rousseau's fictions but to the historical past of the political prisoner and Rousseau himself: "Byron told me of, and reanimated for me, the real people whose feet had worn the marble I trod on" (35.150–51). Through Byron, Ruskin first gained access to the other Switzerland to whose appeal both Byron and Schiller had responded: Switzerland as the site of representative European struggles for political and religious autonomy, celebrated in "The Prisoner of Chillon" and the third canto of *Childe Harold* III. From 1856 (a passage in *Modern Painters* III) until the end of his public career, Ruskin invokes Switzerland again and again as an example of political and religious virtue.[17] The stories of the pastoral, Catholic Forest cantons in the fourteenth and fifteenth centuries, successfully banding together to defend themselves against foreign interference, and of Protestant Geneva, establishing her independence in the sixteenth, rebuke the areligious and politically unstable nations of the nineteenth century—and demonstrate to the English that Protestants have no monopoly on such virtue. Ruskin compares the heroes of these Swiss struggles with those of Greece at Thermopylae; Switzerland becomes for him a second *locus classicus* for the Western European heritage that should pass to England—another small country whose constitutional government and shared religious faith should endow it with the strengths and virtues of the Swiss cantons and the Greek city-states. Switzerland is Greece, plus Christianity: small communities unified in faith and the desire for political autonomy, in which justified wars of defense provide opportunities for personal heroism. It is this Switzerland that Ruskin celebrates as "a complete centre of the history of Europe."[18]

Where Switzerland becomes the classic ground from which to exhort and rebuke contemporary England, the meaning of her history seems clear. But a closer look at the inhabitants of the Alps, especially in the nineteenth century, raised questions not easily answered. Ruskin's new concern with the human history of Switzerland is early expressed in a change in the dominant metaphors he applies to mountains. In *Modern Painters* I, his figures are anatomical: mountains are the bones of the earth. In *Modern Painters* IV, they are architectural: mountains are cathedrals, places of human habitation and worship. The desire to praise mountains as responsive to human needs, particularly psychological and spiritual, leads Ruskin to set aside one conclusion of his earliest work on Switzerland. In *The Poetry of Architecture* (1838), he had concluded that scenery had little effect on the Swiss, judging from the lack of harmony between Swiss houses and their landscape settings. *Modern Painters* IV celebrates a nature fitted to the mind of man—but not without considerable difficulty. In *The Poetry of Architecture*, the unimaginative order and practicality of Swiss houses had pleased Ruskin but seemed incompatible with the sublime scenery surrounding them. In *Modern Painters* IV, the peasants of the Valais, the Alps just south of the Rhone valley, pose a related but more troubling problem. They are not exalted but sunk into dull torpor by their mountain-cathedrals. Their villages are slovenly, their faith based on fear and superstition, their bodies and minds distorted by goiter and cretinism.

Though Ruskin offers many explanations for the gloom of the Valaisan peasants, their bleak lives survive in his prose to trouble his newly humanized and historicized response to the magical name, Switzerland. The mountain gloom he could not wholly dispel he recognized as another tie between himself and less hopeful Romantics than Wordsworth. With Rousseau, Shelley, Turner, and Byron, he wrote in 1880, he shared his sensitivity to the "morbid . . . mystery and softness" of material beauty and his "unaccountable affection for 'Rokkes Blak' and other forms of terror and power," but with them too his "profound conviction, that about ninety-nine hundredths of whatever at present is, is wrong" (34.342–43).

Ruskin assumed in Rousseau the links between mind and place of which Byron had written. On his visit in 1816 with Shelley, Byron discovered in the alternately wild and placid beauty of the lake near Clarens not only Julie and St. Preux but their creator, the "self-torturing sophist, wild Rousseau," "he who threw / Enchantment over passion."[19] In Ruskin's "'Rokkes Blak'" and beauty morbidly mysterious and soft, the landscape of Lake Leman is once again reflected, its power to shape sensibility implicitly acknowledged. Though Rousseau stood at the head of the chain of Romantic visitors who linked him to this Swiss spot, Ruskin did not read Rousseau until 1849. Rousseau's reputation in England had been low since Burke's devastating attacks on his political ideas and personal egotism. The author of *The Social Contract* and *The Confessions* was seldom read; even the sentimental novelist was highly suspect.[20] Looking at *La Nouvelle Heloise* for the first time, Ruskin recorded the general distrust when he noted that "it has given me as much pleasure as surprise considering the way it is abused" (19.xxiii). But by 1862 he wrote his father, "I know no one whom I more entirely resemble than Rousseau. . . . I judge by the *Nouvelle Heloise*, the *Confessions*, the writings on Politics, and the life in the Ile St. Pierre" (18.lxii). Lonely in voluntary self-exile in Switzerland, beginning a second ill-received book of social criticism, Ruskin felt a resemblance to be feared as well as welcomed. Rousseau returned Ruskin to the mountain gloom of the Valaisan peasant and its troubling implications for social as well as psychological history.

Rousseau's St. Preux, in a famous chapter of his novel, discovers in the mountains of the Valais an unspoiled pastoral community, with no use for money or for literacy.[21] Though Rousseau's Valaisan peasants reflect the rugged wildness of their country, their lives are not bleak; they possess a modern-day version of that happy strength through simplicity which, Rousseau argued in his *First Discourse*, allowed Persians to triumph over Lydians, Greeks over Persians, Spartans over Athenians, Romans over Greeks, Goths over Romans, and, finally, Swiss over Austrians in the days of William Tell.[22] Ruskin repeats Rousseau's list of historical examples in his 1858 "Inaugural Address" at the Cambridge School of Art, but for Ruskin, Rousseau's conclusion is profoundly disturbing. What is the use of culture, he asks, if "the liberty of Europe [is] first asserted, the virtues of Christianity best practised, and its doctrines best attested, by a handful of mountain shepherds, without art, without literature, almost without a language, yet remaining unconquered in the midst of the Teutonic chivalry, and uncorrupted amidst the hierarchies of Rome" (16.189–90)? Rousseau's Valais, eighty years before Ruskin saw it, like the medieval Swiss cantons around the Lake of Lucerne that Ruskin is describing here, suggests the exalting influence of mountains on habits and tempers, but Ruskin was committed to a belief in their influence on minds, expressed in language, literature, and art. Swiss history seemed to Rousseau and Ruskin to confirm a lesson of classical history, that language, literature, and art, like money, corrupted social virtues; the strongest communities produced the slightest art. By 1860, as Ruskin wrote the concluding pages of *Modern Painters*, Rousseau's Switzerland called the value of that seventeen-year work into question. "I have many inquiries to make," Ruskin sadly wrote as he described again the achievements of the early Swiss communities, "many difficult passages of history to examine, before I can determine the just limits of the hope in which I may permit myself to continue to labour in any cause of Art" (7.423).

He had already begun his inquiries in 1854. His project—to write a history of Switzerland through its towns, illustrated by his own drawings— was a sign of his growing conviction that the history of places is as important as their natural beauty. Studying the visual aspect of these towns, Ruskin read Swiss history in their architecture of walls, towns, gates, and houses in its mountain setting, seeking visual clues to the reciprocal influence of mind

J.M.W. Turner, *The Lake of Zug* (1843)

J.M.W. Turner, *Goldau* (1843)

and place. The challenge posed by Rousseau gave his project new urgency. Ruskin's efforts to accept Rousseau's Switzerland inform a *Modern Painters* V passage describing the Swiss pine as an influence on and an emblem of Swiss character. There the orderliness of Swiss architecture that had disturbed him in 1838, and the stubborn unimaginative consistency of Swiss habits that he had read as mental torpor in 1856, are reinterpreted as virtues analogous to those of the pine. The "serene resistance, self-contained" of the perfectly upright pine against mountain wildness is matched by the "obstinate rectitude" and "undeceivable common sense" of the Swiss (7.105, 112). The expressions of this implicitly place-influenced temper of mind are not artistic or literary but political and social. Elsewhere Ruskin insists that the Swiss cantons first assert "the liberties of Europe," and "the idea of equitable laws" (16.190). Stubbornly defending their political and religious autonomy, they provide Europe with examples of a nationalism wholly defensive (5.415, 18.464 29.338). The cooperation of barons, burghers, and peasants in their collective endeavor mold a social hierarchy where the responsibilities of each group are defined by communal laws (35.508–17). In the fragmentary notes on Swiss history scattered through his later books, written and projected, the failure of mountain landscapes to inspire great art or literature in their inhabitants is not denied.[23] Accepting Rousseau's lesson that mountain aesthetics belong not to healthy but to ailing communities, Ruskin turns the energy of his discomfort to exploring the uses of culture compatible with social health—in his histories of medieval Christian communities in Switzerland and Italy (*Our Fathers Have Told Us*) and in the educational projects of the St. George's Guild.

Ruskin made himself accept Rousseau's Switzerland, inscribing himself in *Praeterita*, with Rousseau and Calvin, among those whom Geneva had taught (35.321). But the strain of traveling toward two "bournes of Earth" took its toll. The austere Swiss towns among the high mountains that were Ruskin's first love rebuked the glories of Venice that were his second. In the 1860s Ruskin avoided Italy and tried to make Switzerland his only home. Separated from both his parents and from Rose La Touche, the young girl with whom he had fallen obsessively in love, trying to give up art for social criticism and Italy for Switzerland, Ruskin brooded on his "intense resemblance" to that "self-torturing sophist, wild Rousseau." "I cannot help wondering," he wrote his mother in 1866, "if the end of my life is to be in seclusion or in ill temper like his" (18.xxxviii). Writing the history of Switzerland under Rousseau's tutelage, Ruskin found the biography of his teacher threatening to become his own.

But the man whose biography Ruskin was least able to separate from Swiss history or the story of his own life was, of course, Turner. Turner shared Ruskin's divided allegiance to Geneva and to Venice. The sense of

Switzerland that Ruskin deciphered in Turner's drawings was, like Ruskin's own, profoundly historical; like Ruskin's too, it changed over time. Turner's six trips to Switzerland began in 1802; after a long-delayed return in 1836, Turner went back every year from 1841 through 1844. Tracing Turner's response to Swiss scenery, first in *Modern Painters* V and then in the *Catalogue Notes* of 1878, Ruskin followed his own preoccupations with Swiss history while he wrote in fragmentary form the biography of Turner he had long planned. By 1878 he recognized that the intertwined stories of Switzerland and Turner unfolding in his notes to Turner's drawings also formed (in Ruskin's phrase) "a little autobiography" (13.488)—one far gloomier, however, than *Praeterita*.

Ruskin discovered Turner's Switzerland in three stages. In 1833 he came back from his first Swiss trip to find Turner's vignettes to Rogers, reflections of Turner's own first visit. In the early 1840s, he was overwhelmed by Turner's late Swiss watercolors, finished impressions of the last repeated journeys. And in the mid-1850s, he discovered yet another aspect of Turner's Switzerland in his final sketchbooks, part of the Turner Bequest with which Ruskin spent long hours alone in the basement of the National Gallery. The impact of each successive discovery is reflected both in Ruskin's drawings and in his prose. From imitations of visionary alpine vignettes he shifted under the influence of the late watercolors to careful topographical drawings of Turner's subjects, following him first, in 1845, to the Pass of St. Gothard, and finally, in the late 1850s, to the Swiss towns that Turner too had repeatedly sketched.

Though Ruskin always praised first the natural drama of rocks and air in Turner's Swiss work, he was more and more struck, especially after he had seen his sketchbooks, by Turner's attention to architectural signs of human presence. Discussing *The Pass of Faido* (on the St. Gothard route) in *Modern Painters* IV, for example, Ruskin points out how the road and coach in the right foreground, the old bridge in the distance, and the ruined gallery on the far left side of the valley suggest the traveler's difficult prior passage over the high peaks, a crucial element in the sublimity of the scene (6.33–40). By the time he finished *Modern Painters*, Ruskin was still more certain that "the pass of the St. Gothard, especially, from his earliest days, had kept posses-sion of his mind, not as a piece of mountain scenery, but as a marvellous road." *The Pass of Faido*, he went on, "was wholly made to show the surviving of this tormented path" (7.435n). Ruskin had been convinced of Turner's concerns by his sketches of towns like Bellinzona, the southern terminus of the route over the St. Gothard. The road is a principal feature of these views, sometimes as the traveler might perceive it, sometimes as used by the town's inhabitants, who in one sketch are shown lining it as a procession advances. Turner is equally interested in signs of earlier history,

199

the dominating remains of the fortresses built by nobility from three kingdoms to guard the passage to Italy. The sketches capture the social and political significance of the town's mountain setting.[24]

Ruskin's own Swiss town drawings study from different points of view the architectural landmarks Turner depicted, as Ruskin tries to decipher not only their place in the history of minds and landscapes but also their meaning for Turner. Ruskin's bridges, like the covered wooden bridge at Lucerne on which he worked for months in the fall and winter of 1861 (and again on later visits), seem to extrapolate the bridges in Turner's more comprehensive views.[25] Ruskin too insists on the significance of roads and rivers as elements in a humanized landscape, using startling projection and rapid recession to explore his—and Turner's—perceptions. His many drawings of the towers of Fribourg supplement Turner's sketches of a town whose historical importance Ruskin later explained in *Praeterita*. Sacred and secular towers are here for Ruskin a visible record of the town's unique foundation as an autonomous bourgeois civic power created and protected by the rival powers of church and nobility. Fribourg's hill-guarded valleys shape and express its story.[26] Yet the account in *Praeterita* omits the gloom that shaped Ruskin's work on Lucerne's bridge or Fribourg's towers, the sense of dissolution and loss that seem to eat away the page, leaving bridges and towers stranded in a disappearing landscape that they can no longer safely traverse or protect.[27]

Into the last pages of *Modern Painters* V Ruskin compressed all that he had not yet said about Turner, under the myth of Apollo and the Python. Like the sun-god who can never wholly defeat his enemy, in Ruskin's story Turner's celebrations of natural beauty cannot dispel his consciousness of defeated human effort. The myth is played out in two locations, Venice and Switzerland—Turner's Venice drawings discussed in the text, his Swiss ones in the increasingly lengthy footnotes. The Swiss drawings "are nearly all made," Ruskin explains, "for the sake of some record of human power, partly victorious, partly conquered. . . . [Turner] seems to have gleaned the whole of Switzerland for every record he could find of grand human effort of any kind; I do not believe there is one baronial tower, one shattered arch of Alpine bridge, one gleaming tower of decayed village or deserted monastery, which he has not drawn" (7.435–36n). The meaning of the Swiss drawings is summed up in two watercolors, the footnote counterparts of the Hesperid Aeglé and the Sybil Deiphobe, Ruskin's emblems in the text for Turner's fragile art and Venice's fading beauty. *Goldau*, the site of a destructive avalanche, and its companion, the neighboring *Lake of Zug* with its village of Arth, are for Ruskin the twin emblems of human power defeated by mountains, and human effort, especially the political struggles of the early Swiss cantons, inspired by them. *Goldau* is a sunset; *Zug* a sunrise:

The crimson sunset lights the valley of rock tombs, cast upon it by the fallen Rossberg; but the sunrise gilds with its level rays the two peaks which protect the village that gives name to Switzerland; and the orb itself breaks first through the darkness on the very point of the pass to the high lake of Egeri, where the liberties of the cantons were won by the battle-charge of Morgarten. (7.438–39n)

Sunrise and sunset, human effort and defeat are balanced here, but Ruskin's tone in these last pages is elegiac. What does he mourn? Turner's serene visions of Lake Lucerne are indeed, as Ruskin noticed, matched by his repeated depictions of the tormented path of human progress through the surrounding mountains. But Turner's late drawings do not suggest that Swiss mountains foster social virtues incompatible with the art inspired by Italian light. It was Ruskin who opposed Switzerland to Italy in these pages. His footnotes impinge on his text until the diminished voice of Venice, that "whisper . . . through the deep hearts of nations" (7.440), finally disappears. Though he means to write biography, there is virtually no distance between himself and his subject at the end of *Modern Painters*. The eclipse of Venice by Switzerland, while faithful to the pattern of Turner's last travels, is more significant as a figure for Ruskin's coming struggle to leave the glories of Italian art for the hard lessons of Swiss history. Ruskin's mountain gloom, reinforced by Rousseau, makes these pages of Turner's life an elegy for Venice.

In 1878, just before his first serious madness, Ruskin finished the catalogue notes to an exhibition of his Turner drawings; two months later, recovering, he wrote the notes to an additional show, "Mr. Ruskin's Own Handiwork Illustrative of Turner." The work he chose to hang beneath Turner's portrait, described in the last entry of the Turner catalogue, was Turner's serene and beautiful *Fluelen*, the village at the southern end of Lake Lucerne where the St. Gothard road begins. The focal work of the second exhibition was also Turner's—the *Pass of Splugen*, which had been given to Ruskin during his illness. Separating Turner's two favorite, contrasting Swiss subjects—Lake Lucerne and the mountain pass—Ruskin implicitly acknowledges a distance between himself and Turner he did not see in 1860. The Turner exhibition concludes with mountain beauty. Though that beauty is historicized and humanized, the signs of struggle—like William Tell's chapel, just out of sight in the *Fluelen*—seem to have dissolved in air and light. In the *Splugen* around which Ruskin's show is arranged, history still marks the landscape that has shaped it. The tall tower on the rock, Ruskin explains, is a solitary baron's tower, a reminder of the League of the Grisons to defend the autonomy of the valleys (13.516). The rocks beneath it, deeply eroded, are in sympathy with "the decline of all human power, in their own

John Ruskin, *Fribourg* (1859)

John Ruskin, *The Walls of Lucerne* (c. 1866)

dissolution . . . the dark plain being itself only the diffused wreck of the purple mountains that rise from it, rounded like thunder-clouds" (13.517). The bitterness of loss strongly infects these notes, occasioned now by Ruskin's sense, twenty years after *Modern Painters*, that the Switzerland he and Turner, Byron and Rousseau once saw is rapidly disappearing, its beauties and its lessons destroyed by hotels and railways. But here the drawing that is Ruskin's emblem for human effort and loss is attached to his own story, not to Turner's. The revision of *Modern Painters* V suggested by the opposed drawings is completed in Ruskin's notes. In the catalogue for his own drawings, Ruskin quotes entire the last pages of *Modern Painters*, this time printing the Swiss footnotes as part of the text. The changes are absolutely appropriate: not only is the loss mourned there more Ruskin's than Turner's, but Switzerland is inseparable from the main text of Ruskin's story.

The strongest evidence of Ruskin's fascination with the interactions of place and his own mind is the silent evidence of his Swiss drawings. Not all are illustrations of Turner. As Paul Walton has pointed out, Ruskin's disregard of conventional composition is more striking in these drawings than Turner's.[28] In some, long trails of wall and town zig-zag across the page horizontally, as in the 1866 *Walls of Lucerne*, or vertically, as in an 1863 sketch of Baden.[29] These compositions are most striking for what they leave out. There are no remnants of the rectangular stages or windows that constitute earlier ideas of pictures. We are left with what seem to be the connected movements of a highly selective eye. Behind that eye we sense an equally selective mind, tracing resemblances and making omissions; here, linking the signs of Lucerne's or Baden's past across the blank spaces of their present, the hotels and railways Ruskin did not want to look at.

In other drawings all trace of an horizon disappears; in a visual field where up and down lose their normal meaning, new patterns emerge, most often felt as centripetal and centrifugal forces simultaneously pulling all things to a central focus and dissolving them into sudden emptiness, as in the whorl of houses of a [*Village near*] *Lucerne* (1856).[30] The lines of force that organize the *Lucerne*, or a still more disconcerting *View of Fribourg from Above* (1859)[31], where detail obsessively clear is abruptly washed away, again seem to express both the energetic interaction of land with buildings that attempt to anchor and control a natural landscape, and their powerfully disorienting effect on the mind that tries to comprehend what it sees. Both are Ruskin's themes: the influence of place on mind and mind on place that constitutes, for him, history, biography, and autobiography. The lessons of travel that these Swiss drawings record are not those that Ruskin taught to Oxford students in the "Inaugural Lecture" or offered to his parents in *Praeterita*: that England can become, for him and for the world, the center that

Switzerland was—"so happy, so secluded, and so pure." But their unsettling visions of a center that will not hold are, more than Turner's *Goldau*, *Zug*, or *Splugen*, the emblems of Ruskin's Switzerland.

NOTES

1. *The Diaries of John Ruskin*, ed. Joan Evans and John H. Whitehouse (Oxford: 1956), 1.183; *The Complete Works of John Ruskin* (Library Edition), ed. E.T. Cook and Alexander Wedderburn, 39 vols. (London: 1903–12), 35.296. The original edition of *Praeterita* gave the phrase as cited; Cook and Wedderburn, looking at the diary entry, thought "bournes" was meant to be "homes" and so printed it; Evans and Whitehouse restored "bournes" in their edition of the diary. "Bournes" is certainly the less common word, but for reasons that I shall argue below, its connotation of "ultimate destination" rather than origin seems more appropriate for the way Ruskin thought of Venice and Switzerland.

   Although there are several studies of Ruskin's associations with Venice (particularly in connection with *The Stones of Venice*), his lifelong ties to Switzerland have rarely been examined. Elisabeth Gertrud Koenig makes a beginning in her *John Ruskin and die Schweiz* (Bern: 1943). On Ruskin and Venice, see especially Jeanne Clegg, *Ruskin and Venice* (London: 1981), which does for that city what I have tried to do here on a much smaller scale for Switzerland: to study the history of a relationship between a man and a place to which he continually returns.

2. A few letters from this correspondence were published in Cook and Wedderburn's edition; the originals (for 1861–63) are in the Beinecke Library at Yale. The full sequence provides moving testimony to Ruskin's loneliness and isolation during these prolonged stays in Switzerland. Despite his long attachments to the place and his desire to settle there, the ties to home were unbreakable, however painful at times.

3. *Hamlet* 3.1.79–80. According to the O.E.D., most nineteenth-century uses of the word, obsolete until revived in the eighteenth century, were influenced by these lines.

4. Bruce Redford, "Ruskin Unparadized: Emblems of Eden in *Praeterita*," *Studies in English Literature 1500–1900* 22 (1982): 675–87.

5. For the renunciation of Venice, see 35.156 and 372.

6. Ruskin never completely gave up his ambitions to reform England even in the 1860s, when he felt most alienated from his English audiences. And in the two preceding decades he had also spent extended periods at work in Switzerland and Italy—in the 1840s, in the Alps, and in the early 1850s, in Venice. Nonetheless, he came closest to accepting the status of spiritual and physical exile when he spent long periods in Switzerland in the 1860s; the Slade Professorship, and the establishment of the St. George's Guild at Sheffield and the public letters of *Fors Clavigera*, mark the end of that exile.

7. See Basil Williams, *Cecil Rhodes* (London: 1921) 41–42. Although Rhodes did not arrive at Oxford until 1843, he subsequently came very much under Ruskin's influence and must have read the earlier lecture.

8. On English travel to Switzerland, see Arnold Lunn, *Switzerland and the English* (London: 1944), and (for a more anecdotal account), G.R. de Beer, *Alps and Men* (London: 1932). C.E. Engel, *La littérature alpestre en France et en Angleterre au XVIIIe et XIXe siecles* (Chambery: 1930), is also a good introduction. *Murray's Handbook for Travellers in Switzerland* (1838) probably gives the best idea of the British tourist experience of Switzerland in Ruskin's youth.

9. William Brockedon's *Illustrations of Passes of the Alps* (1828: acquired by the Ruskins in 1834) pays considerable attention to this aspect of Switzerland.

10. For the early days of British alpinism, see Leslie Stephen's *The Playground of Europe* (1871; Oxford: 1946) and the collection of essays first published in 1859 and 1862, *Narratives Selected from Peaks, Passes and Glaciers* (Cambridge: 1910). Two key books from the slightly later period of more athletic (and to Ruskin, less acceptable) climbing are John Tyndall's *Hours of Exercise in the Alps* (1871) and Edward Whymper's *Scrambles Amongst the Alps* (1871).

11. Ruskin attacked the athletic tourist on several occasions; for example, in "Of Kings' Treasuries" (1864), he accused the English of having "despised Nature": "The Alps themselves, which your own poets used to love so reverently, you look upon as soaped poles in a bear-garden, which you set yourselves to climb and slide down again, with 'shrieks of delight'" (18.89–90). See also 5.320.

12. Samuel Prout's *Facsimiles of Sketches in Flanders and Germany* (1833) stimulated the Ruskins' first continental traveling, fixing their expectations of European villages and towns (including Switzerland). Byron's most important Swiss poems include "The Prisoner of Chillon," Canto III of *Childe Harold's Pilgrimage*, and (for its setting), "Manfred." John James Ruskin read Byron aloud to his family while Ruskin was growing up: in 1833 he acquired the 17-volume *Works of Lord Byron* (with Thomas Moore's *Life*), just published by Murray, with illustrations by Turner and others. (Two of the vignettes are Swiss views.) Ruskin also acquired in 1833 the edition of Samuel Roger's *Italy* illustrated with vignettes by Turner and Stothard that included a number of Swiss scenes. In 1834, the family bought Brockedon's *Passes of the Alps* and (at Ruskin's special request) Horace Benedict de Saussure's *Voyages dans les Alps* (1779), a classic work of travel and natural history that remained one of Ruskin's favorite books. He was later influenced by James Forbes's *Travels Through the Alps of Savoy* (1843).

13. *Diaries* 1.196, 203.

14. *Diaries* 1.277, 291.

15. *Diaries* 1.325.

16. *Diaries* 2.381.

17. In 1858, for example, he wrote of it as the place where "the liberty of Europe [was] first asserted, the virtues of Christianity best practiced, and its doctrines best attested" (16.189). In 1860 he praised the Forest Cantons as "the foremost standard-bearers among the nations of Europe in the cause of loyalty and life"

(7.111). *Praeterita* praises Geneva as "the centre of religious and social thought, and of physical beauty, to all living Europe" (35.321). Several times he used the victory of the Swiss over the Austrians as an example of how true liberty and religion are "generally" victorious over attacking nations (5.415, 18.464—in a defense of just wars; 16.189, 29.338). At other times he used the resistance of the Catholic Forest Cantons to Protestant efforts to impose their religion (Zwingli's salt tax) as a reminder to Protestants that they were not always the defenders of religious autonomy (18.538, 17.355–57, 23.111). The chapter on pastoral Catholicism intended for *Our Fathers Have Told Us* ("The Bay of Uri") would, apparently, again have praised the Catholic faith of the Forest Cantons (33.186–87).

Ruskin's many references to the Swiss heroes of liberty William Tell and Arnold von Winkelried include his discussion of the legend of Tell as the means by which the Swiss "expressed their imagination of resistance to injustice" (22.270) and his characterization of Tell as "the Heracles of Switzerland" (22.259). For comparisons of the battle of Morgarten to Thermopylae and of Arnold to Leonidas, see *Modern Painters* V (7.231–32), *The Eagle's Nest* (22.258–59), and the Preface to *Bibliotecha Pastorum* (31.24). The passages on Swiss history in *Praeterita* focus on wise leadership rather than heroism, but praise a series of Swiss towns as patterns of social cooperation between barons, burghers, and clerics (35.508–17).

18. *John Ruskin: Letters from the Continent*, ed. John Hayman (Toronto: 1982) 28.
19. *Childe Harold* III, stanza 77. See also accounts by Shelley and Byron of their visit in Shelley's letter to Hogg of 18 July 1816 (*Shelley and His Circle 1773–1822*, ed. Kenneth Neill Cameron, 8 vols. [Cambridge, MA.: 1961–86] 4.719); and Byron's letter to John Murray of 17 June 1816 (published in Moore's *Life*, which the Ruskins owned; *The Life, Letters, and Journals of Lord Byron*, ed. Thomas Moore [London: 1892] 388).
20. For Rousseau's reputation in England, see Edward Duffy, *Rousseau in England: The Context for Shelley's Critique of the Enlightenment* (Berkeley: 1979); Jacques Voisine, *J.-J. Rousseau en Angleterre a l'epogue Romantique* (Paris: 1956); and Henri Roddier, *J.-J. Rousseau en Angleterre au XVIIIe siecle* (Paris: 1950).
21. Part I, Lettre 23, "Sur le Valais."
22. Jean-Jacques Rousseau, *The First and Second Discourses* ed. Roger D. Masters (New York: 1964) 51–52. Rousseau ends this sequence of examples: "A group of poor mountaineers, whose greed was limited to a few sheepskins, after taming Austrian pride crushed that opulent and formidable House of Burgundy which made Europe's potentates tremble. . . . Let our politicians deign to suspend their calculations in order to think over these examples, and let them learn for once that with money one has everything, except morals and citizens." The parallels with Ruskin's argument in the Cambridge "Inaugural Address" of 1858 are sufficiently close to make it virtually certain that Ruskin was drawing directly on Rousseau.
23. See especially 16.189–90, 7.110–14 and 423–31.
24. See, for example, the three sketches of Bellinzona (1842 and 1843) reproduced in

Andrew Wilton's *J.M.W. Turner: France, Italy, Germany, Switzerland* (New York: 1982), plates 111–13 (British Museum TB cccxxxii–25, cccxxxvi–15, ccclxiv–343).

25. Ruskin's *Old Bridge at Lucerne* [*Kapellbrucke*] is at the Ashmolean Museum (E116); it is reproduced in Cook and Wedderburn 6.394 (plate A) and Paul H. Walton, *The Drawings of John Ruskin* (Oxford: 1972), plate 81. Another drawing of the bridge is at the Ruskin Galleries, Bembridge, Isle of Wight (1372; undated). Cook and Wedderburn list several other sketches of the same bridge in their catalogue.

26. For examples, see the drawing at the Fogg Museum (1928.12); another at Brantwood (listed as 917 in the catalogue, but the drawing displayed under this number is—or was—different); a third in the Cunliffe Collections (see *Connoisseur*, 1969); a fourth engraved and reproduced in *Modern Painters* IV (6.46, plate 24). There are also numerous larger views of the town with its towers. Ruskin discusses the history of Fribourg on 35.514.

27. See Ruskin's letters to his father from Lucerne and Altdorf during the autumn of 1861 (Beinecke Library, Yale University), especially those of 17 October, 22 November, and 27 November.

28. Walton 92.

29. *The Walls of Lucerne* is at the Ruskin Galleries, Bembridge (1376). It is reproduced in Walton, plate 66; Cook and Wedderburn 5.xviii (plate G); and Helsinger, *Ruskin and the Art of the Beholder* (Cambridge, MA: 1982), plate 21. The 1863 *View* of Baden is reproduced in Cook and Wedderburn 36.456 (plate 19).

30. Ruskin Galleries, Bembridge (1375); reproduced in Walton, plate 69.

31. British Museum (1901-5-16-4), reproduced in Walton, plate 68, and Helsinger, plate 22.

ROBERT BROWNING
AND ITALY

Jacob Korg, University of Washington

Although he is recognized as one of its major Victorian interpreters, Robert Browning's purposes in visiting Italy and incorporating Italian scenes and characters in his poetry were private ones. He first went to Italy in 1838 with the intention of working on *Sordello*, hoping that the scenes where its actions had taken place in the thirteenth century would inspire him to complete the poem he had been laboring at for nearly five years. But he was far more strongly impressed by Italy's present than by its past, and wrote *Pippa Passes*, a play set in contemporary Italy, before returning to his long historical poem.

By the time of his second visit, in 1844, Italy had begun to acquire a new significance for him. During this inverval, he attempted to gain recognition by working energetically at his poems and plays, but felt that he was adrift, an outsider, unable to reach an audience. He felt smothered by the influences around him, where opinions were all like his own; he did not know "what men require," and he believed that literature had entered a period of inertia. His letters of this period show that he felt himself to be facing artistic defeat. He said that accomplishment was possible only by following the example of others who had left England, but he never seems to have considered this seriously at this time. Instead, he visited Italy again as a way of refreshing himself—"for my head is dizzy and wants change," and when he returned, continued to think of going back.

It was during his courtship of Elizabeth Barrett that the idea of Italy as a permanent escape from the stifling influences of England as well as a haven for their marriage took form. Between 1846 and 1861, which he spent, with many interruptions, in Florence and Rome, his attachment to Italy grew stronger. After Mrs. Browning died he was forced to live in England in order to educate his son, but often said that he wished it were possible to return to Italy, and in later years spent most of his holidays in Venice, and even went back for a visit to Asolo, the scene of *Pippa Passes*.

The descriptions of Italian life, landscape, historical figures, and social scenes that entered his poetry as a result of these journeys were vivid and perceptive, and his readers responded to them. But Italy was more than a subject for Browning. It was a powerful influence, which changed his way of thinking and writing. His consciousness of it widened the horizons of his thought and experience, and led to a growth in his poetic resources that had a significant influence, in turn, on the history of English poetry. Henry James recognized both Browning's power to create a sense of the physical presence of Italy and the support this concreteness lent to the poems in which it appeared. In his talk on "The Novel in 'The Ring of the Book,'" James acknowledges the faults and disproportions of Browning's great poem, and then turns to its compensating qualities:

> Another force pushes its way through the waste and rules the scene, making wrong things right and right things a hundred times more so— that breath of Browning's own particular matchless Italy which takes us full in the face and remains from the first the felt, rich, coloured air in which we live.[1]

In Italy Browning of course found the attractions that had always seduced English travelers and residents—the color and vitality of daily life, the inspiring presence of great works of art and architecture, and the sense of a long and varied history. As the first volume of J.A. Symonds' *Renaissance in Italy* shows, and as many visitors observed, the records of Italian history with their innumerable conflicts, achievements, and intrigues are unsurpassed as reflections of human passions and motivations. Traditionally, Italy was regarded by the English as a land of dramatic contrasts, where the evil energies exemplified by Machiavelli and the Borgias existed side by side with the refinement, artistic vision, and spiritual fervor visible in Renaissance art. Many travelers from England and America commented on the vitality of Italian life in both the past and the present, observing that it contained far more incident and variety than their own cultures did.

The attitude of English people toward contemporary Italy was uncertain, for they sympathized with a country occupied by powers they considered dangerous, France and Austria, but were suspicious of Italy's Catholic heritage, hostile to the power, especially the secular power, of the Church, and were skeptical of Mazzini's republican principles and Garibaldi's violent methods. Browning shared many of these views, but differed from many English people in supporting Italian nationalism enthusiastically, and feeling a special sympathy with the country's poor, a sentiment which led him to become a close observer of the daily life of the common people.

One of the values Italy offered Browning was a sense of unlimited space within which his imaginative powers could expand to achieve a firmer sense of his own identity. The liberating effect that the Italian past and present had on him owes something to his feeling that Italians themselves were indifferent to the beauties of their landscape and to the glories of their history and art, so that the opportunity of celebrating them was left to foreigners like himself. He had complained of the "creeping, magnetic, assimilating influence" of English intellectual life, and welcomed the discovery that contemporary Italy, in contrast, was barren of ideas; that Italians felt but did not think. Freed from the commitments and competition of England, he was able to deploy his ideas freely over a scene whose inhabitants, "those tantalizing creatures," had "such a facility of being made pure mind of," as he wrote to Elizabeth Barrett. Looking back at the years he had spent in Italy, he wrote, "I felt alone with my own soul there."[2] In *The Ring and the Book*, he says that after reading the record of a vivid and passionate episode of Italy's past in the collection of documents called the Old Yellow Book, and going out on the terrace of Casa Guidi to overlook the nearby church and the street below, "I turned, to free myself and find the world."

However, he did not simply adopt Italian values and attitudes, but, on the contrary, insisted that his approach to Italy was based on his own individuality. He may have overstated the case when he wrote to Elizabeth Barrett, in attempting to console her for her lack of experience, that, "All you gain by travel is the discovery that you have gained nothing, and have done rightly in trusting to your innate ideas—or not rightly in distrusting them, as the case may be," for he added immediately, "You get, too, a little . . . perhaps a considerable, good, in finding the world's accepted *moulds* every where, into which you may run & fix your own fused metal,—but not a grain Troy-weight do you get of new gold, silver or brass. After this, you go boldly on your own resources, and are justified to yourself, that's all."[3] The image suggests that personal convictions are not surrendered in an encounter with an alien culture, but rather "fused," that is, liquefied, so that they can be adapted to new forms without losing their original nature.

Hence, Browning's Italy is not only recognizable as "the elements for which the name of Italy stands" as James put it—that is, as a representation that conforms to the general conception—but also as a partly fictional creation whose value arises less from the facts on which it is based than on Browning's imaginative vitality. Browning was always averse to mere mimesis, and, while he resisted the self-expressive rhetoric of the Romantics, considered it his responsibility to invest his materials with his own thoughts. The method he used to develop *The Ring and the Book* from the records of an old trial— "I fused my live soul and that inert stuff"— expresses a principle that operates throughout his poetry, and applies to the general treatment of Italy in his poems.

However, the process of employing alien realities as a means of self-identification leads logically to a desire for some definitive view of the context within which the self is to be identified. Browning felt that in Italy, with its extremes of virtue and felicity, on the one hand, and wickedness and suffering on the other, he surveyed the whole range of human possibilities. There was simply more to be observed, felt, and responded to in the Italian setting than in any other, and this made it an ideal subject for Browning. Here was material to which Browning, with his powerful aversion to the trite and commonplace, instinctively responded. It is significant, and in line with his tendency to see the infinite within the particular—"the instant made eternity"—that his sense of Italy's general significance should be generated by particular objective events. C.H. Herford observes that in the character of Pippa he saw "an ideal construction, shadowing forth, under the semblance of a single definite bit of life, the controlling elements, as Browning imagined them, in all life."[4] The meeting with the beggar-girl in *Sordello* acquires a general meaning, and leads him to feel that "Venice seems a type of Life," in which can be found "the evil with the good / Which make up Living rightly understood." In Browning's imagination, Italian history and daily life, with their balance of good and evil, were a cosmic metaphor, a symbol of the world. To confront them was "to free myself, and find the world," for they offered an amplitude of vision he could not gain in any other scene.

This fuller understanding enabled Browning to feel that he could correct the views of his sheltered English friends. In a long exchange of letters with the poet, Julia Wedgwood complained that *The Ring and the Book* emphasized the darker aspects of human nature too strongly; she called on Browning to recognize that "love is the principle [sic] thing in this world and the world beyond," and maintained that the depiction of a character like Guido, who displayed no possibilities for good, and did not seem to be a part of God's world, served no moral purpose. In his replies, Browning tried to induce Mrs. Wedgwood to recognize the co-existence of evil with good, "Which make up Living rightly understood," and described the Italian setting of his poem, with all its horrors, as representative of the human condition, saying, "I think this *is* the world as it is, and will be—*here* at least."[5]

What were the constituents of this moral universe, for which Italy could be taken as a surrogate? Much of it is summed up in the varied themes of Browning's first Italian work, *Pippa Passes*, which was based on Browning's personal knowledge of the town where it is set, rather than on the library research used for *Sordello*. The scene between Ottima and Sebald dramatizes sexual lust and murderous hatred in conflict with agonizing flashes of guilt and remorse. Jules (who is French) displays a passionate devotion to art and the beauty of Phene, though his commitment to both is partly misplaced. Luigi, who is planning to assassinate the Emperor, embodies the desperate

212

patriotism of Italian nationalism. The street-girls speak of their poverty, deprivation, and pathetic aspirations. And, finally, the conspiracies aimed at Jules and Pippa and the scenes involving the policemen and the Intendant create the atmosphere of duplicity, mystery, repression, and violence that penetrates the town. Pippa, the prototype of a series of Italian women in Browning's works who combine ignorance with goodness, and helplessness with a strong urge for self-determination, dominates the mood of the play with her piety and cheerfulness.

Pippa Passes should not be taken as a report on nineteenth-century life in Italy—although it accurately records the physical details of the town— for its depiction of Italian wickedness owes much to stock notions. On the other hand, the gentle revolutionary Luigi, the poor girls conversing on the steps, the group of foreign art students, and Pippa herself are fresh material. They reflect an interest in common people and ordinary affairs that now appears for the first time in Browning's work, and which seems clearly to be the result of his fascinated observation of daily life in Italy. In a letter to Elizabeth Barrett, he criticized Mary Shelley's failure to notice such things in her account of her travels in Italy, and asked:

> why don't you tell us that at Rome they eat roasted chestnuts, and put the shells into their aprons, the women do, and calmly empty the whole on the heads of the passengers in the street below; and that at Padua when a man drives his waggon up to a house and stops, all the mouse-coloured oxen that pull it from a beam against their foreheads sit down in a heap and rest.[6]

By using carefully observed details of this kind in his poems as symbols or metaphors, Browning made them perform a double function; they convey a vivid sense of Italy that, as Henry James noted, was unparalleled in its intimacy, and also exploit Italy as a source of poetic meaning. Sometimes the significance attached to them can only be felt, not explained, as when Browning responds joyfully but inarticulately in "By the Fire-Side" to

> the sense of the yellow mountain-flowers,
> And thorny balls, each three in one,
> The chestnuts throw on our path in showers! (51–53)

Or when, after speculating about Ulysses' reactions to the singing of birds on the islands off Sorrento he was supposed to have visited, Browning can only say, "He heard and he knew this life's secret / I hear and I know."

In insisting upon the concreteness of the ordinary features of Italian landscapes, streets, and behavior, Browning's poetry offers something that is fairly distinct from its aesthetic value: a vital and tangible sense of the physical reality of Italy. The effect appears in the "fig-skins, melon-parings, rinds and shucks, / Refuse and rubbish" the starving young Fra Lippo Lippi is forced to eat (84–85); in the view of Florence from a hillside suburb, the peeling frescoes and the torrent of similar details in "Old Pictures in Florence"; and the vignette in *The Ring and the Book* which focuses momentarily on

> marketmen glad to pitch basket down,
> Dip a broad melon-leaf that holds the wet,
> And whisk their faded fresh. (1.97–100)

"The Englishman in Italy" is an entire poem made up of images of this kind, and numerous passages of *The Ring and the Book* use the same resource.

Such passages offer the home-bound reader the pleasures of sightseeing, but also, in their context, function as parts of a poem, embodying serious themes. The dual effect is not limited to localized images. Browning often extends such imagery in a way that vitalizes an entire poem or a long section of one; examples are the use of the church in "The Bishop Orders His Tomb," the landscape in "Two in the Campagna," and the Medici-Riccardi palace that stands near Fra Lippo as he talks to the watch. The most prominent examples, of course, are the Ring and the Book. The Ring is a replica of gold ornaments dug up, as Browning says, from ancient tombs near Chiusi; the Book is a tattered relic that records a forgotten and obscure trial. Each, emerging from the deep Italian past, is at once a memory-laden memento and a vehicle that the poet uses to explain his poetic theory.

Henry James, registering his response to *The Ring and the Book*, has pointed out this double effect of Browning's images. He begins by testifying to the overwhelming effectiveness of the atmosphere Browning creates:

> The old Florence of the late spring closes round us; the hand of Italy is at once, with the recital of the old-world litter of Piazza San Lorenzo, with that of the great glare and the great shadow-masses, heavy upon us, heavy with that strange weight, that mixed pressure, which is somehow, to the imagination, at once a caress and a menace. . . . Something that I want to feel both as historic and aesthetic truth, both as pictorial and moral interest, something that will repay my fancy tenfold if I can but feel it, hovers before me. . . . They press upon me close, those wonderful, dreadful, beautiful particulars of the Italy of the eve of the eighteenth century . . . beautiful, I say because of the quantity of romantic and aesthetic tradition, from a more romantic and aesthetic age, still visibly, palpably, in solution there; and wonderful and dreadful through some-

214

thing of a similar tissue of matchless and ruthless consistencies and immoralities.[7]

Both "pictorial" and "aesthetic," the Italian details of the poem create vivid sensuous impressions and also participate in the design of the poem; they support this design by projecting the "wonderful and dreadful" ambivalence of a scene where "caress and menace" are simultaneously present.

Characterization is one of Browning's most vital poetic resources, and there is good reason to believe that he learned much of his skill in handling it from Italian experiences. The broad variety of vigorous feelings and attitudes expressed in his lyrics as well as in the dramatic monologues is due to Browning's capacity for identifying himself temporarily with others, playing the part of Keats's chameleon poet. It seems reasonable to suppose that this extraordinary ability owes something to his life in Italy. In spite of his long residence there, and his deep attachment to the country, he did not go native, or pretend to change the views of an English Protestant which he brought to it, but observed what went on around him with an objectivity that could encompass attitudes varying from sympathy to indignation, never verging on the sort of identification that would involve the surrender of his own beliefs. It is easy to imagine that Browning was diversifying and extending his poetic powers, especially his powers of characterization as he went through the travel experience he described in his letter to Elizabeth Barrett, sympathetically receiving alien ideas, testing his own against them, and finally gaining a clearer sense of his own convictions.

Browning knew few Italians; living as an exile, sometimes isolated, and sometimes in a circle of English and American friends, he was compelled to gauge the nature of Italians at a distance, and from his encounters with casual acquaintances, servants, and tradesmen. As a result, many of his Italian characters owe as much to his reading, or to the general tradition of Italy, as they do to observation. The most prominent of his Italian types, the elegant villain, has an obvious literary ancestry in the Machiavellian character of Elizabethan tragedy and the Gothic novel. Yet such figures as the Duke of Ferrara, the Bishop of St. Praxed's, and Guido transcend the pattern: in these characters, a love of beauty, devotion to honor, and a sense of family pride are not incompatible with cruelty and wickedness, and if these apparent inconsistencies seem to be specifically Italian, Browning's underlying implication that Italy is a surrogate for the world leads irresistibly to the suggestion that they are not irrelevant to the rest of mankind.

The English reader is drawn into the world of Browning's Italian people by another peculiar feature of his characterizations. Among the complaints Julia Wedgwood voiced about *The Ring and the Book* was the attitude of "photographic impartiality" Browning adopted toward his wicked characters, his readiness to "hold a brief" for any figure who displayed individuality. This objectivity, which sounds like a virtue to modern readers, prevented Mrs. Wedgwood from entering sympathetically into Browning's poem, but she accurately identified the mechanism that aroused her antipathy. "I cannot bear to see your thoughts on loan to deck out a sleek pedantic buffoon," she wrote, after reading the monologues of Archangelis and Bottinius, "I cannot endure to hear your voice in those Advocates' pleadings."[8] For Browning does often "lend his mind out," as Fra Lippo puts it (306), allowing his worst characters to express his own ideas and patterns of thought with elegance and conviction. By assigning the line "Ah, but a man's reach should exceed his grasp" (97) to a weak character like the title character of "Andrea del Sarto," or, in The Ring and the Book, the defense of Pompilia to a lightweight like Bottinius, Browning ran the risk of confusing inflexible readers like Mrs. Wedgwood, but he also suggested a wealth of ideas to the more open-minded: that there are elements of worth even in unworthy souls, that the good and the wicked are not so easily distinguishable from each other, that lofty or correct principles may mask evil purposes.

When we turn to the virtuous characters of Browning's Italian milieu, we find that he escapes the dictates of tradition, and draws upon convictions based on his experiences; we witness that pouring of one's own metal into new molds that he mentioned in the letter to Elizabeth noted above (26). These figures are usually victims of one kind or another who combine simplicity and natural wisdom; most of them are women. The oppressed Pippa knows enough to trust God, and the foundling Fra Lippo has a better sense of what is right in art than the learned church authorities. Pompilia, though illiterate, finds a way to escape the net in which she has been trapped by the indifferent churchmen and unscrupulous relations who control her fate.

The two men of this group, Caponsacchi and the Pope in The Ring and the Book, are complex characters whose chief traits exceed any limited idea of the specifically Italian. Caponsacchi mingles dandyism and melancholy, spirited gallantry and deep Christian piety, pride of ancestry and self-contempt, but his more central qualities are the noble self-doubts and aspirations of a troubled mind. The Pope displays many surface qualities that give him an Italian coloring, piety of course, and also an earthiness, directness and impatience that correspond with his Neapolitan origin. But, as with Caponsacchi, his most important characteristics are not regional; they are qualities of a sympathetic, righteous, and sensitive mind, and some of them lead him to express ideas that are distinctly out of key with the historical period.

As a group, the sympathetic figures among Browning's Italian characters appear to be familiar human beings rather than representatives of their country, but they do nevertheless convey an impression of Italy through the problems they encounter. All are enmeshed in a maze-like social structure harboring many mysteries formed by custom, state, and church. The wicked characters, we find, are allied to these forces and participate in their conspiratorial programs, while the sympathetic ones can only struggle against them ineffectually because they are unsophisticated and powerless. Pippa, wandering innocently through a village where evil plots are festering, including one against her life, has no idea of what is happening behind the walls, and Luigi in the same poem is naive about the power he is rebelling against. Even the Pope despairs of understanding the tradition of his church and gaining control of it. This is perhaps a foreigner's impression, but it is integral to the view of Italy and Italian national character projected by Browning's work.

Browning's poetry is generally characterized by a keen sense of place, and this is nowhere more conspicuous than in his Italian poems. Most of his Italian settings are in Rome and Florence, but *Pippa Passes* takes place in the obscure town of Asolo. "The Englishman in Italy" describes details of Sorrento, and Venice is an occasional subject. Nearly every one of the Italian poems is anchored to a locality or setting that plays a vital part in it, many of them likely to be known to the English traveler or to those who have read or heard about Italy. But Browning rarely describes them. He leaves the details of their appearance to the reader's knowledge, and uses them to achieve a tone that pervades his whole treatment of Italy—a subtle irony produced by contemplating the difficult lives ordinary Italians lead in the shadow of famous buildings, monuments, and streets.

In *The Ring and the Book*, Guido's execution takes place in the well-known Piazza del Popolo, but instead of describing the scene as a spectacle, Browning dwells on some incidents that occurred as the criminals were being transported through the streets of Rome which reflect the daily life of the city. Similarly, in describing the market square where he discovered the volume that contained the story of his poem, he focuses not on the church of San Lorenzo or the Riccardi-Medici palace that frame it, but on the disreputable second-hand goods displayed for sale. The part of the poem that takes place in Rome refers frequently to such well-known localities as the Piazza Navona, the Piazza Barberini, and the Castel Sant' Angelo, but instead of exploiting their beauty or their historical associations, Browning introduces them as backdrops for a story which has many sordid episodes. He also employs many unfamiliar settings that bring obscure corners of Italian geography into his reader's consciousness. The prime example is Asolo, which is hardly mentioned in the Murray's popular guides of the period. Most of the Roman locales specified in *The Ring and the Book* are places of the kind tourists are sure to see. Others have no particular fame, but are drawn from Browning's sources, and some of the sites mentioned in the poem call attention to aspects of the city's life that foreign visitors are likely to ignore: the Piazza di Monte Citorio, where Pompilia's mother worked as a washerwoman; the New Prisons on the Via Guilia; and the inn at Castelnuovo just outside Rome where Guido overtook the fugitives—all sites drawn from the Old Yellow Book—are among the scenes that tend to modify the image of Rome as a city of art and history. As well, much of the action of *The Ring and the Book* takes place in Arezzo, and Browning's poem emphasizes some of the features of a place that tourists visited comparatively rarely.

Florence, a city well known to English visitors, and Browning's home for sixteen years, appears as a natural setting for many of his Italian poems. Unlike the other Italian locales he employed, Florence figures in Browning's poems as a city of art and history, the two subjects of "Old Pictures in Florence" which are used to call for the liberation of the city from Austrian control. The poem has the form of a semi-playful reproach to Giotto for allowing a lost painting of his to be found by another collector,[9] and refers familiarly to a long series of painters (not all of them Florentines), and to several of Florence's locales. Browning characteristically praises the greatness of Italy's past at the expense of its present as he addresses contemporary Florentines as "you of the little wit" and reproaches them for failing to appreciate the old painters, for allowing their frescoes to deteriorate, and for selling their paintings to foreigners. In Browning's mind this indifference is caused by foreign occupation, for the poem ends by linking hope for the political freedom of the city with the hope for a better awareness of its art. In his buoyant conclusion, Browning predicts that the Austrians will be expelled, and that Florence will then take a proper pride in its art: "Once Freedom restored to Florence, / How Art may return that departed with her" (261–62).

While "Andrea del Sarto" and "Fra Lippo Lippi" are occupied mainly with searching investigations into the nature of art and the characters of artists, Browning grounds each of these figures in particularities whose vividness, as James observed, has independent value as a means of rendering his Italy. Fra Lippo claims consideration from the night watchman because he is a dependent of Cosimo de' Medici, whose handsome palace "caps the corner" (18); its rings have other uses, to a drunken reveler, than "to plant a flag in, or tie up a horse!" (230). He identifies himself as a monk from the Carmelite monastery, and attempts to justify himself because he is the teacher of Masaccio, whose frescoes in the church there show great promise. The picture he plans to paint as penance for his faults was requested by the nuns of Sant' Ambrogio, a church not far from the scene of the poem. He describes the familiar subjects of his paintings, the reactions of the plain-folk people who admire them, and the everyday life of church and monastery; but he also alludes to the Medici and the church officials who disapprove of his paintings. Between them, these intimate glimpses into the life of the time expose an ambiance in which irrepressible natural feelings and sober authority are in perpetual conflict.

There is much less of this in the discourse of the cold, self-satisfied Andrea del Sarto, who refers to Florence and the suburb of Fiesole only in order to congratulate himself on his prosperity, incidentally fixing the scene of his speech with great precision. Browning's way of inserting Fiesole, the convent garden, Michelangelo, Raphael, Da Vinci, and other familiar Italian themes into the texture of his character's thought gives them new life. He also transcends the familiar by shading the well-known historical scene with the silver twilight of a mind which failed to share its brilliance, and again modifying the usual view of Italy and the Renaissance.

Like most Englishmen, Browning depended for his knowledge of the Renaissance and Italian art on Giorgio Vasari's *Lives of the Painters* (which he read in Italian); although he later turned to Filippo Baldinucci's *Notizie de' Professori del Disengo*, Vasari remained his unquestioned authority. He had first seen Italian paintings in the Dulwich Gallery near his home in south London when he was a boy; later, he spent much time in seeing the art of Italian galleries and churches with Vasari as a guide, and, like other foreign residents of Florence, rooted about the city in the hope of turning up forgotten masterpieces. He bought some paintings and hung them in Casa Guidi, hoping they might be by famous artists, but nearly all of these attributions have now been discredited.

During his life in Florence, the presence of its numerous masterpieces had a strong inspirational effect on Browning, urging him to make use of his own talents, although he was not especially perceptive or original in his view of art. However, one aspect of Victorian taste, the Romantic principle that art is primarily self-expression, led him to his real strength—interest in the nature of the artist as it is revealed in his work. This is exhibited, not only in the two painter poems of *Men and Women*, but also in the earlier "Pictor Ignotus" and the later "Parleying with Francis Furini." Poems of this kind use Italian art and artists as the basis for minute analyses of artistic motives and effects. Browning saw in Italian art a vital humanism that he describes in "Old Pictures in Florence" as an advance upon the cold perfection of classical sculpture, an attitude most appealingly expressed in Fra Lippo Lippi's naive contention that it is the artist's purpose to replicate God's world in order to evoke appreciation of it.

The period of Browning's residence in Florence was the time when the merits of the so-called primitives, the Italian painters of the thirteenth and fourteenth centuries, were at last being fully recognized. Browning, like others, at first thought of Italian art in terms of the High Renaissance, but when he saw the work of the earlier painters in Florence, read Vasari's accounts of them, and acquired what he believed to be examples of their work, his taste changed, and he mentioned many of them in "Old Pictures in Florence," contributing to the intense interest in the earlier period which was already underway. However, the values that the most prominent supporters of "primitive" paintings saw in them were mainly spiritual and aesthetic, while Browning regarded them as manifestations of character.[10] This emphasis is continued in later poems. For instance, "Parleying with Francis Furini" praises the seventeenth-century painter for his skill in painting "God's best of beauteous and magnificent / Revealed to earth—the naked female form" (142–43), an attitude which is surprising until one realizes that Browning was defending his son, Pen, whose nudes had been attacked as indecent.

It can be argued that Browning's consciousness of Italy had a profound effect on his ideas about poetry and his way of writing it. One of his most powerful impressions—and he was not alone, of course, in feeling this—was that nineteenth-century Italy was a mere degraded remnant of a glorious past. The majestic Roman ruins and the splendid works of art created in the Renaissance and earlier which attracted foreign tourists were testimonials to a former greatness that seemed to have left no trace on contemporary Italy. Like others, Browning found modern Italians to be generally insensitive and lacking in creative power, though he was much less critical of them than other English observers. Further, most of Italy had for centuries been partitioned and occupied by foreign powers, and had suffered under a wide variety of despotisms until gaining freedom in 1860. As the names given to them show, the notable periods of Italian history, the Renaissance and the Risorgimento, were thought of as times when former glories were recovered, as rebirths of old powers. Browning was close to these, since he was immersed in the art and history of the Renaissance, and lived in Italy during the period leading up to its unification, witnessing some of the struggles that took place. Renewal engendered by passionate imaginative effort was a theme of Italian history and a central preoccupation of the contemporary Italian mind. It was perhaps as a result of his encounter with feelings of this kind that the recovery of the past became a principle of his poetic theory and practice.

In Book I of *The Ring and the Book*, explaining why he feels justified in mingling "fancy" with the "facts" about his subject he has learned from The Old Yellow Book, Browning describes the poet's work as a process of finding forms that once were vital, but are now nearly extinct, and bringing them to life again by renewing men's consciousness of them. This conception of poetry had been in Browning's mind for a long time. He had described his poet-hero in Book I of *Sordello* as one of those who "are fain [to] invest / The lifeless thing with life from their own soul, / Availing it to purpose" (1.490–92). The idea is much more fully developed in the apologia for *The Ring and the Book*, where Browning says of the poet,

> —although nothing which had never life
> Shall get life from him, be, not having been,
> Yet, something dead may get to live again (1. 727–29)

The Ring and the Book of course follows this method, reviving the characters and conflicts recorded in the annals of an old trial, but it was one that Browning instinctively followed elsewhere as well. Many of his poems are based on *données* from more or less obscure passages of history; he generally avoided the Romantic lyric of response to immediate experience, and preferred to resuscitate some near-forgotten anecdote or personality. This process parallels on a small scale the great revivalist movements of Italian cultural and political history.

A second feature of Browning's art which might be attributed to his Italian experience is its dramatic quality. As we have noted, he did not adopt Italian views, but observed customs and attitudes he might or might not approve, keeping his thoughts about them to himself. Browning renders this experience poetically by recording the speaker's words, exhibiting his character and opinions, and silently embodying the reactions of a listener; in his dramatic monologues, we hear the voice of a well-realized speaker and, as a subtext, the vibrations of another consciousness that identifies the author's stance by supporting what is being said or suggesting a more or less ironic reception of it. Often, this second level of meaning tells the truth obliquely, as Browning put it in his conclusion to *The Ring and the Book*, and speaks more powerfully when it moves in silent, ironic opposition to the character's ideas as it does in the speeches of Bishop Blougram and Guido Franceschini than when it parallels the thoughts of Rabbi Ben Ezra or Pompilia. The first example of this mode, "My Last Duchess," is a poem whose setting in Italian history is indispensable to this dual effect, and suggests the possibility that the dramatic monologue replicates Browning's experience in listening to Italians. Many believe that Browning adopted the practice of speaking through a character in order the mask the feelings he had unwisely exposed in *Pauline*, but the form is really an independent poetic genre, and a necessary alternative to the Romantic lyric. Its basic device is, of course, that of allowing an identifiable speaker, often a historical character, to express his views, while letting the reader understand that there is an accompanying level of silent communication between himself and the poet which may confirm, question, or ironically undercut the speaker's discourse.

The form was adopted by Browning's contemporaries, and has acquired much importance in modern poetry. It has opened new poetic possibilities, since it frees the lyric poet from the limits imposed by his own convictions, and enables him to employ the vocabulary, imagery, and ideas of other minds. It has enabled poetry to meet the challenge which the modern phenomenon of the multiple or disappearing self presents to the Romantic lyric, a form based upon the premise of a unified personality. Because it employs such elements as impersonality, realism, and irony, it has encouraged poets writing in other forms to work with new levels of sophistication and new ranges of feeling. While it cannot be said to be in any sense an Italian form, there is good reason to believe that it had its origin in Browning's encounter with the alien manners of Italy.

It is clear that Browning's genius responded to the Italian scene by achieving an unrivaled representation of its surface characteristics. But it also seems likely that certain of his Italian impressions led him to the resuscitation theory of poetry and the objective mode of the dramatic monologue. If Italy influenced him in this way, it must be given credit, not only for providing him with subjects he wanted to share with his readers, but also for playing a part in shaping his distinctive style, and through him, the course of English and American poetry.

NOTES

Quotations from Browning's poetry are from *Robert Browning: The Poems*, ed. John Pettigrew, 2 vols. (New Haven: 1981) and *Robert Browning: The Ring and the Book*, ed. Richard D. Altick (New Haven: 1981).

1. Henry James, "The Novel in 'The Ring and the Book,'" *Quarterly Review* 217 (1912): 79.
2. *Dearest Isa: Robert Browning's Letters to Isabella Blagden*, ed. Edward McAleer (Austin, TX: 1951) 239.
3. *The Letters of Robert Browning and Elizabeth Barrett, 1845–1846*, ed. Elvan Kintner (Cambridge, MA.: 1969) 1.46. Ruskin expresses this same feeling about Italy in more prosaic language. If one becomes involved in personal relationships there, he says, "Of course, things are learnt about the country that way which can be learned in no other way, but only about that part of it which interests itself in you, or which you have pleasure in being acquainted with. Virtually, you are thinking of yourself all the time." (*Praeterita*, Cook and Wedderburn, 35.119).
4. *Robert Browning* (New York: 1905) 50.
5. *Robert Browning and Julia Wedgwood*, ed. Richard Curle (New York: 1937) 136–55.
6. *The Letters of Robert Browning and Elizabeth Barrett* 1.189.

7. James 80–81.
8. *Robert Browning and Julia Wedgwood* 158–59.
9. The subject of this painting was the death of the Virgin, although Browning later mistakenly identified it as the Last Supper. See the unpublished letter quoted in Julia Markus, "'Old Pictures in Florence' Through *Casa Guidi Windows*," *Browning Institute Studies* 6 (1970): 54–55.
10. For detailed accounts of his position, see David J. DeLaura, "The Context of Browning's Painter Poems," *PMLA* 95 (1980): 367–88, and Leonee Ormond, "Browning and Painting," *Robert Browning*, ed. Isobel Armstrong (Athens, OH: 1975) 184–210.

"AT THE ROADSIDE OF HUMANITY": ELIZABETH BARRETT BROWNING ABROAD

Deborah Phelps, University of Delaware

Elizabeth Barrett Browning lived abroad for the fifteen years after her marriage until her death in 1861. Before this she was the self-described "prisoner" of 50 Wimpole Street, London, kept to one room by chronic bronchial illness and paternal restraint. Eloping with Robert Browning, she traveled first to France, then made her home in Florence, returning infrequently and always with trepidation to her father's England (he had disowned her and, for a time, her brothers followed suit). Motivated by these circumstances, and by her husband's preference for the European south, to break with her English past, Barrett Browning's last years were spent in an artistically productive exile in Florence. Most of her major poetry was written abroad, mainly in apartments on the Champs-Elysees or in Florence's Casa Guidi.

The move abroad opened up Barrett Browning's life in that it was an escape from the restraining influence of her father's house. Yet to say that she broke completely with the style of life she had adopted in her Wimpole Street sickroom would be correct only in terms of venue. Her letters indicate that seclusion still figured greatly in her life; she remained more or less an invalid throughout her marriage and travel was always complicated by her precarious health. Abroad, the poet resumed a variation on the enclosed life she had known in England: she kept to her own set of rooms in which she rested and wrote; received selected visitors from Florence's Anglo-American community; and traveled from one apartment in one continental city to another, moving with the season in pursuit of greater physical comfort while retaining the relative isolation she found personally necessary. Florence itself she described as the only place she could be truly happy for it was "cheap, tranquil, cheerful, beautiful, within the limit of civilisation yet out of the crush of it" (*Letters* 2.170). To her friend Mrs. Jameson she wrote: "It seems unnatural to think of you in one room. *That* seems fitter for *me*, doesn't it? And the rooms in England are so low and small that they put double bars on one's captivity" (*Letters* 2.109–10). Once abroad, Barrett Browning's world expanded to include an increased commerce with civilization, yet was still "out of the crush of it." She was, as she remarked in *Casa Guidi Windows* (1848), "at the roadside of humanity" (2.654), close enough to the progress of events, but distanced enough to distinguish her voice from the general uproar.

While life abroad was freer than England's "double bars" allowed, Barrett Browning nevertheless held to seclusion in her marriage exile. Curiously, her particular isolated existence can be seen as a microcosm of the kind of insularity the English abroad were known for. Neither Browning knew many Italians well, and, apart from those in their employ, both refrained from actively seeking them out. Yet both poets crowded their work with Italian figures and locales, and, in Barrett Browning's case, with the contemporary leaders and events of the Franco-Italian political scene. Despite seclusion, her poetic involvement with political and foreign issues had always been apparent ("Crowned and Buried," 1840; "The Cry of the Children," 1843). Yet the revolutions of 1848 and their aftermath roused her sympathies for Italian nationalism and engaged her emotions and intellect in a way they had not been roused before. Barrett Browning's enthusiasm for the cause of freedom and national unity extended to a personal identification with Italy: an 1855 letter is typical: "Oh, we Italians grow out of the English bark; it won't hold us after a time" (*Letters* 2.197).

Significantly, Barrett Browning's interest in the political issues of Italy and of the non-English world in general occurred at a time when the Byronic interest in national liberation had fallen out of fashion in England. This dichotomy appears even more pronounced when her work is compared to Robert Browning's calmer, more distanced treatment of Italian political issues. Born in 1806 (six years before Browning) and coming to poetic maturity when the influence of Byron and Shelley still lingered, Barrett Browning brought to her poetry the Romantic atmosphere of her youth as opposed to her husband's more settled, mid-Victorian tone. This view of abroad engendered an idealistic attitude to national liberation that is ubiquitous in both her public and private writings. The ringing call to action in the cause becomes the signature note of her verse:

> And very loud the shout was for that same
> Motto, 'Il popolo'. IL POPOLO,—
> The word means dukedom, empire, majesty,

226

And kings in such an hour might read it so.

(*Casa Guidi Windows*, 1848, 1.498–501)

The hero worship in the first part of *Casa Guidi Windows* (and other political poems), indicative of the more contemporary influence of Carlyle, additionally fueled her deeply emotional involvement with the Italian cause. A letter of 1859 reiterates the belief in heroic leadership with a characteristic description of Louis Napoleon: "The only great-hearted politician in Europe—but chivalry always came from France. The emotion here is profound—and the terror, among the priests. Always I expected this from Napoleon, and, if he will carry out his desire, Peni and I are agreed to kneel down and kiss his feet" (*Letters* 2.307). Yet the embedded frame of *Casa Guidi Windows* (and of the letters) is of a woman observing the rise and fall of the Italian Risorgimento from behind the windows of a home-bound life, able only to cheer or bemoan the activity in the streets. Although Julia Markus, in her critical edition of *Casa Guidi Windows*, contends that the move abroad enabled Barrett Browning's verse to leave the room of indirect literary experience,[1] the poet admits her own contradictory position as an enclosed champion of action in the "Advertisement to the First Edition": "'From a window,' the critic may demur. She bows to the objection."

In much of the poetry dealing with foreign issues, the dramatic situation consists of an emotionally involved woman prescribing and denouncing, but always sequestered from direct relation to the world of action outside her window. This limit is countered by the almost supernatural, witch-like power that Barrett Browning gives her female speakers. The intensified tone of voice often appears compensatory—as if the poet were fighting against her speaker's limited influence in the world of men by amplifying the individual force of the imprisoned self (which may or may not be explicitly presented). We see a woman attempting to bridge the distance between herself and the world by declaring a public stance, but succeeding only in affecting her immediate surroundings: the home, the child. In this, she is among the least "domestic" of female poets in her use of domestic space. What is at work here, as Sandra M. Gilbert suggests, is the power of a woman creating her own *matria*, or area of feminine influence, but ultimately failing to affect the prevailing patriarchal controls of external circumstances.[2] As an extension of the Victorian convention of the woman in the room (Tennyson's "The Lady of Shalott" and "Mariana"; Christina Rossetti's "Shut Out"),[3] the dramatic situation of Barrett Browning's foreign poetry is expressed in the quotation George Eliot used to introduce Dorothea Brooke in *Middlemarch*: "Since I can do no good because a woman/ Reach constantly at something that is near it." It is the method of

227

this reach, the exercise of the internal will to effect external change, that is most striking in Barrett Browning's work, and her identification with foreign national causes is at its center.

In an early lyric on a foreign subject, "On a Picture of Riego's Widow" (1826), the woman wields influence beyond both spatial and temporal enclosure. Although her husband, the revolutionary leader of the struggle for a constitutional Spain, was executed as a traitor by King Ferdinand, the dead widow oddly triumphs, exuding a proud stoicism from her picture-frame:

> But silent else, thou past away—
> The plaint unbreath'd, the anguish hid—
> More voiceless than the echoing clay
> Which idly knocked thy coffin's lid.
>
> Peace be to thee! while Britons seek
> This place, if British souls they bear,
> 'Twill start the crimson in the cheek
> To see Riego's widow THERE! (33–40)

This "Daughter of Spain," repressed into death and with her image literally confined to frame and wall, nevertheless represents to the political forces of other nations a reminder of the pure commitment to human freedom exemplified by the 1820 Spanish civil rebellions. A symbol of revolutionary ideals, Riego's widow is the first of repeated characterizations in Barrett Browning's verse of women as the struggle personified, as human icons of national liberty. Riego's widow becomes an emblematic standard who has risen above a wife's personal grief to a stance of public, declamatory emotion: scorn, anger, stoic pride. In doing so she represents a powerful admonishing presence: "see Riego's widow THERE!"

The power of this female presence exceeds the sexual. It is a quality Barrett Browning admired in her personal heroines, especially George Sand:

> We see thy woman-heart beat evermore
> Through the large flame. Beat purer, heart, and higher,
> Till God unsex thee on the heavenly shore
> Where unincarnate spirits purely aspire!

("To George Sand: A Recognition," 1844, 11–14)[4]

Like Madame Riego's transcendent presence, the woman in the second part of Casa Guidi Windows (1851) scorns both the betrayal of her political ideals and the feminine nature she believes allowed her to naively idealize the betrayers of the Italian cause:

228

Absolve me, patriots, of my woman's fault
That ever I believed the man was true! . . .
Forgive, that I forgot the mind which runs
   Through absolute races, too unsceptical!
I saw the man among his little sons,
   His lips were warm with kisses while he swore;
And I, because I am a woman, I,
   Who felt my own child's coming life before
The prescience of my soul, and held faith high,—
   I could not bear to think, whoever bore,
That lips, so warmed, could shape so cold a lie.

(2.64–65, 91–99)

In the poem of that title (1856), Aurora Leigh similarly criticizes her sex's deflection from full confidence in art and mind:

We women are too apt to look to one,
Which proves a certain impotence in art.
We strain our natures at doing something great,
Far less because it's something great to do (5.43–46)

Aurora vows to conquer the feminine voice in the attempt to eliminate what she construes as its emotional weakness toward the masculinized tone of unfettered commitment to a higher aim in poetry: "This vile woman's way/ Of trailing garments shall not trip me up:/ I'll have no traffic with the personal thought/ In Art's pure temple" (5. 59–62). Women must exceed the weaker side of their nature in a greater cause.

While the woman's concentrated emotionality within her enclosed realm is vehemently powerful (at least in rhetorical terms), the final result is that she remains confined and thus forever frustrated. However, the implicit point is that this weakness is the sole weapon of her disenfranchisement. Her only outlet is the manipulation, through voice or "domestic" means, of her small sphere of influence. Political involvement is effected in the methods of displaced power noted above, and in what is perhaps the ultimate exercise of the *matria*, the manipulation of the child in sacrificial dedication to the cause. Gilbert touches lightly on the child as emblem of female power,[5] but its use as a matriarchal instrument of action is strongly evident in several important poems.

In the powerful poem "The Runaway Slave at Pilgrim's Point" (1850), the persona is an American slave who has escaped after her black lover is killed and she herself has given birth to her white master's child. Barrett Browning drives home the hypocrisy of American society by bringing the fleeing slave to a scene symbolic of American freedom. The image of woman as slave provides a vivid portrait of entrapment and doomed yearning to break out of the constraints of her world: "I stand on the mark beside the shore . . ./ I look on the sky and sea" (I. 1, 7). In terms similar to the poet's position in *Casa Guidi Windows*, the slave speaks of her imprisonment and the externalized compensatory acts of freedom she could perform:

> Our blackness shuts like prison-bars:
> The poor souls crouch so far behind
> That never a comfort can they find
> By reaching through the prison bars . . .
>
> But, once, I laughed in girlish glee
> For one of my color stood in the track . . .
> And from that hour our spirits grew
> As free as if unsold, unbought

(39–42, 58–59, 64–65)

Surrounded by her captors, the slave's last means of retaliation is the curse: "I only cursed them all around . . ./ from these sands/ Up to the mountains, lift your hands,/ O slaves, and end what I begun!" (227–31). But rhetoric is by no means her only reaction against her position.

The runaway slave is Barrett Browning's most poignant mother. After the birth of her fair-skinned child, she feels immediate mother-love, yet the baby constantly reminds her of her bonds. She smothers the child, "to save it from my curse," and buries it in a deserted forest where "All, changed to black earth,—nothing/ white,—/ A dark child in the dark!—ensued/ Some comfort" (185–87). To protect it against her own curse of the white masters, she murders the child and by this act turns white to black in death. Yet the act is also a protest, an expression of rebellion against the condition of slavery. When she dies, her last comfort is the thought of reunion with her now-black child, "In the death-dark where we may kiss and agree" (251). The murder of the child is the symbolic exertion of frustrated social will: both child and slave will die and travel out toward the emblematic "sky and sea," beyond the restraint of America.

Like the runaway slave's murder of the child, the action of "Mother and Poet" (1861) centers on the sacrifice of the child in the attempt to exert external change within feminine enclosure. Specifically, the children are refashioned into the objects of the mother's sociopolitical hopes—the success of the Italian Risorgimento. The mother, who "was a poetess only last year,/ And good at my art, for a woman, men said" (6–7), has taught her

230

sons patriotism and sent them off to fight for the Italian cause:

> What art can a woman be good at? . . .
> To teach them . . . It stings there! *I* made them indeed
> Speak plain the word *country*. *I* taught them, no doubt,
> That a country's a thing men should die for at need.
> *I* prated of liberty, rights, and about
>   The tyrant cast out.
>
> And when their eyes flashed . . . O my
>   beautiful eyes! . . .
> *I* exulted; nay, let them go forth at the wheels
> Of the guns and denied not. (21–28)

The poem is a monologue of betrayal. Having given her sons to the cause, her patriot's faith is betrayed by their defeat in death. The mother had already ascertained the limits of her own power to act— "What art's for a woman?"—and so exerted what will she could command to infuse her children with the idealism that would eventually kill them. Her relationship to her children is less vicarious identification than it is her own direct offering to the cause. As in the unsexed characterization of Riego's widow and others, the mother's reaction to the deaths resembles the patriot's political disillusionment rather than an expression of maternal loss. Her reiterated curse is the frustrated cry of the betrayed poet/patriot who angrily retracts her services from the leaders of the cause: "When you sit at the feast/ And are wanting a great song for Italy free/ Let none look at *me*!" (3–5). Like Riego's widow or the runaway slave, her self-sacrifice creates a disturbing admonitory presence.

In several other poems supporting Italian and French unification, Barrett Browning's speakers turn in frustrated dejection from external events to the child in the room—if not to literally murder, then indirectly to sacrifice. After she has cursed and retreated from the balcony at the conclusion of *Casa Guidi Windows*, the speaker pins upon the child his mother's dreams of a free Italy:

> my own young Florentine . . .
>
> fix thy brave blue English eyes on mine,
> And from my soul, which fronts the future so,
> With unabashed and unabated gaze,
>   Teach me to hope for, what the angels know
> When they smile clear as thou dost.

231

Stand out, my blue-eyed prophet!—thou, to whom
The earliest world-day light that ever flowed,
Through Casa Guidi Windows chanced to come!

(2. 743, 747–51, 756–58)

By transforming his nationality and thus dedicating the child to the woman's
nationalistic position, the mother strives to make a commitment to international political change. Significantly, Barrett Browning had raised her own
son, Penini, culturally Italian—over Robert Browning's objections.[6] Her
personal identification with Italy extended to her son: "There's an inclination in me to turn round with my Penini and say 'I'm an Italian'" (*Letters*
2.180–81). As in *Casa Guidi Windows*, this motif is put to use in "A Tale of
Villafranca" (1859), where a mother relates the story of the last phase of the
doomed Risorgimento to her son. The poem is a dirge of doused passion:
"My little son, my Florentine . . ./ What matter if we live?" (1. 84). The
identification of the child with the failure of hope for a free Italy, with "this
low world, where great Deeds die" (83), results in his sacrificial dedication
to the cause. Like the conclusion of *Casa Guidi Windows*, where the son's
"brave blue English eyes" engendered hope for the world's support of
Italian liberty, the son of "Villafranca" is transformed from English to
Florentine to Venetian in a ritual of hope for future victory:

They say your eyes, my Florentine,
    Are English: it may be.
And yet I've marked as blue a pair
Following the doves across the square
    At Venice by the sea (73–77)

Yet in the final stanza the mother returns to the present fall of Florence and
attaches her son, again a "Florentine," to the death of the "great Deed" in
frustration of her betrayed hopes. The obliteration of the child through
matricide or nationalistic sacrifice is a major component of the transcendent
power of Barrett Browning's enclosed women. As they transform the role of
mother and become speakers for the cause, the children are similarly
refashioned into the instruments of their limited social will.

    In these political poems, especially "The Runaway Slave at Pilgrim's
Point" and "Mother and Poet," the murdering woman is also a cursing
woman. She not only manipulates the child toward her socio-political ends,
but uses the bitterest force of her voice to effect this desire and express her
frustration over her inability to act directly on the world's stage. The curse is
a controlling feature in poems of complaint against the forces opposing

freedom and national unity. The second part of *Casa Guidi Windows*, written after Barrett Browning's disillusionment with Pope Pius IX and the Grand Duke Leopold, is strung with curses: "Bitter thing I write/ Because my soul is bitter for your sakes,/ O freedom! O my Florence!" (2. 192–94). As the poem continues, this specific denunciation is extended beyond those who have betrayed the Risorgimento to comfortable, non-interventionalist, free-trade England, symbolized by the Great Exhibition, and to the nations of the world in general:

> O magi of the east and of the west,
>> Your incense, gold, and myrrh are excellent!
> What gifts for Christ, then, bring ye with the rest?
> No remedy, my England, for such woes?
>> No outlet, Austria, for the scourged and bound,
> No entrance for the exiled? no repose,
>> Russia, for knouted Poles worked underground,
> And gentle ladies bleached among the snows?—
>> No mercy for the slave, America?—
> No hope for Rome, free France, chivalric France?
> Alas, great nations have great shames, I say
>
> (2. 628–30, 641–48)

Only able to look from her Casa Guidi windows, Barrett Browning demands attention by sarcastically equating her own unheard voice with that of the world's oppressed:

> O gracious nations, give some ear to me!
> You all go to your Fair, and I am one
>> Who at the roadside of humanity
> Beseech your alms,—God's justice to be done.
> So prosper! (2. 652–56)

A complacent age of peace is criticized in imagery similar to that in Tennyson's *Maud* (1855), where Victoria in the Crystal Palace is alluded to as materialistic:

> Peace sitting under her olive, and slurring the days gone by,
> When the poor are hovelled and hustled together each sex, like swine,
> When only the ledger lives (1. 33–35)

In a letter written after a visit to England in 1851, Barrett Browning had similarly remarked: "You do want a place in England for sculpture, and also to show people how olives grow" (*Letters* 2.24). In *Casa Guidi Windows*, the conquering Austrian army overruns Tuscany, "While every soldier in his cap displayed/ A leaf of olive. Dusty, bitter thing!" (2. 370–71). Sharply contradicting the gender expectation of the woman as peaceful bearer of the olive, Barrett Browning declares, in the highly charged voice of the enclosed feminine life, for action over diplomacy.

In the preface to *Poems before Congress* (1860), her most overtly political collection, Barrett Browning warned that here the poetry was "pungently rendered." Indeed, the cursing woman appears here more often, and more intensely, than in previous volumes. "Napoleon III in Italy," a fervid panegyric to the "Sublime Deliverer," is even more of a spirited attack on his foes throughout the Italian states. In this poem she explicitly defines the curse as a reaction by repressed peoples toward the loss of their hopes for a golden age of liberation:

> Some cursed, because at last
> The open heavens to which they had looked in vain
> For many a golden fall of marvellous rain
> Were closed in brass (32–35)

"An August Voice" (1860) jeers at those who would betray Italian liberation by reinstating the Grand Duke: "Remember your Dead on Ticino;/ Be worthy, be constant, be strong—/ Bah!—call back the Grand Duke!" (106–8). The speaker's public stance is declared, but what ultimately remains is the deep frustration embodying the curse. The undramatized, disembodied "august voice," implicitly signifying the speaker's distance, separation, and frustration from direct action in the world at large, marks the particular mode of being possible to the political woman.

The most overt cursing is in "A Curse for a Nation" (1860). The "Prologue" to the two-part "Curse" explains how the poet-speaker was commissioned by "an angel" to write a curse against the American policy on slavery. The poet demurs, protesting in anticipation that to do so would be hypocritical: "My heart is sore/ For my own land's sins: for little feet/ Of children bleeding along the street" (18–20). The angel counters that she is equipped for the role precisely "because thou hast strength to see and hate/ A foul thing done *within* thy gate" (35–36). The poet then answers with what she ironically offers as her ultimate drawback, her sex: "To curse, choose men./ For I, a woman, have only known/ How the heart melts and the tears run down" (38–40). But to the angel, this is no weakness; the intensity of emotion deriving from limited power gives her voice the appropriate qualities:

> "Therefore," the voice said, "shalt thou write
> My curse tonight."
> Some women weep and curse, I say
> (And no one marvels), night and day
>
> "And thou shalt take their part to-night,
> Weep and write.
> A curse from the depths of womanhood
> Is very salt, and bitter, and good."(41–8)

The image of the woman able to act only through harsh words is thus transfigured into a most powerful instrument.

These rhetorical and "domestic" acts of will the enclosed woman performs in her displaced attempt to alter the outside world are motifs that also occur throughout Barrett Browning's longest work, *Aurora Leigh*.

Despite the frequency of travel and activity abroad in *Aurora Leigh*, Barrett Browning's protagonist remains sequestered, first by force, then by choice, throughout the poem's action. Born in Italy, Aurora spends her childhood after her mother's death:

> Among the mountains above Pelago . . .
> God's silence on the outside of the house,
> And we who did not speak too loud within . . .
> So, nine full years, our days were hid with God
> Among his mountains (1. 111, 123–4, 204–5)

After her father's death she is taken to England to live with her aunt with the idea that she learn to live as a proper Englishwoman should: "A sort of cage-bird life" (1.305). But Italian Aurora sickens to near death in England's closed culture where the carefully trained physical landscape oppresses and diminishes the life within:

> The skies themselves looked low and positive,
> As almost you could touch them with a hand,
> And dared to do it they were so far off
> From God's celestial crystals; all things blurred
> And dull and vague. Did Shakespeare and his mates
> Absorb the light here?—not a hill or stone
> Or active outline on the indifferent air. (11. 262–69)

Bereft of the life-force of the more expansive natural scenery of Italy, she searches her limited space for solace and "chanced upon the poets" (1. 845). Reading literature in her "little chamber in the house" (1. 567), she finds life opening up for the first time in England: "I woke, rose up . . . where was I? in the world" (1. 565).

But if poetry gives Aurora the world, she refuses to join it physically. Holding "the whole creation" in her artistic power, she challenges her cousin Romney's utopian social schemes in a defense of her power as a poet:

> And I, incapable to loose the knot
> Of social questions, can approve, applaud
> August compassion, Christian thoughts that shoot
> Beyond the vulgar white of personal aims . . .
>   —Ah, your Fouriers failed,
> Because not poets enough to understand
> That life develops from within.—For me
> Perhaps I am not worthy, as you say,
> Of work like this: perhaps a woman's soul
> Aspires, and not creates: yet we aspire,
> And yet I'll try out your perhapses sir

$$(2.\ 339\text{--}42,\ 483\text{--}9)$$

In this curious declaration of her poetic aims, Aurora reiterates the interior action of the woman in *Casa Guidi Windows*: she will achieve her poetic fulfillment as the roadside commentator on the world who applauds and curses, prescribes and scourges.

Refusing Romney's[7] invitation to mix directly with the oppressed citizenry of her sympathies in a helpmate marriage, and eager to escape her new-found literary fame and the general crush of London society, she flees in relief to the continent. She first comes to Paris, finding the city a mixed bag of idealism and misguided aims, yet vivid with a spirit and beauty unknown in England which is rendered in an image that suggests her own poetic stance: "This poet of nations, who dreams on/ And wails on (while the household goes to wreck)/ For ever, after some ideal good" (6. 54–56). Revelling in her anonymity among the foreign crowds in France, she travels to Italy and, refreshed by the intensity of the natural scene, almost immediately seeks out her father's mountain house. But finding it nearly unrecognizable—alive with the presence of current tenants—she withdraws in horror. The impulse to return to her childhood home of isolation, in contradiction to the expansion of travel, finds Aurora again following her inclination toward the closed life her culture and family bred in her.

The sight of her altered past appears to shock Aurora into resolve; she will now become her own woman. This decision is accompanied by the move to another enclosed space—but this time with a difference:

> I found a house at Florence on the hill
> Of Belloguardo. 'Tis a tower which keeps
> A post of double observation o'er
> That valley of Arno (7. 515–18)

In her poetic tower she can finally attempt to transcend her position of mere observer to that of commander of her own realm. There Aurora continues to muse upon external matters: social inequity (her face-to-face meeting with Parisian poverty is Dickensian in descriptive power), "life and art," and the unfolding mystery of Romney's personal affairs. Though she cares about these issues, she does not act except in the indirect methods of telling her story in verse and marrying a now-damaged Romney. She and Romney confess their mutual idealistic impotence in effecting social change and plan a united effort to alter society through love, faith, and "fewer systems." However, Aurora retains the "roadside" role of her poetic career: she will be the inspirational force whose poetic dreams of a corrected society will be made real through her husband's direct, though now more pragmatic, action. Idealism is not shaken: the moral of *Aurora Leigh* settles on Barrett Browning's customary dictum of action infused with thought derived from the woman's vantage of distance:

> His bride of dreams . . .
> . . . should walk beside him on the rocks
> In all that clang and hewing out of men,
> And help the work of help which was his life.
>
> (9. 797, 800–802)

The comparative treatment of England and abroad in the poem illustrates Aurora's apparently contradictory preference for action in enclosure. Italy signifies a place of emotional and psychological expansion wherein the wild scenery lends a backdrop of liberation to the chosen life of isolation. Conversely, England's lower-toned nature is imbued with a sense of compulsory suppression; it is a place where the only window on the world is an involvement with social issues. There Aurora reacts against the cage she cannot choose to create for herself. She flees to Italy so that she may have the freedom to design a cage of her own from which she may look outward as she desires; an autonomous life that "develops from within" to effect the scene without.

As the Franco-Italian political scene moved toward the disappointment of Napoleon III's failure to follow through in the Italian cause, Barrett Browning's poetry became more stridently intense in its support of Italian nationalism. The digressive, diffused style of *Aurora Leigh* gives way to the sharper, shorter poetry of the poet's last year. The poetry now centers its patriotic focus on remembrance of the cause rather than fervored campaigning. While the tension between the socially sequestered woman and the outside world still results in scenes of powerful if indirect action, the amplified, frustrated voice is often missing. "The Dance" (1860) features Florentine society gathered on a feast day with soldiers "of the liberating nation/ . . . groups of Frenchmen everywhere" (23–24). At an invitation from "the noblest lady present," the soldiers and women dance as the Italians watch in strangely reverent silence: "It might have been a Mass, and not a dance" (40). Stranger still is the reaction of the crowd: "Husbands, brothers, Florence's male youth,/ Turned round and kissed the martial strangers mouth to mouth" (49–50). The sudden burst of political fellowship transforms the dance into an alliance.

That the simple scene of a public dance could evoke such an effect is striking. Barrett Browning points to the catalytic effect of women who symbolically instigate political unification among nations on this social, "feminine" plane. Exposing the political alliance forged by the leaders of the national liberation movement as comparatively weak, Barrett Browning's women triumph as private legislators of public freedom:

> And a cry went up, a cry from all that people!
> —You have heard a people cheering, you suppose,
> For the Member, mayor . . . with chorus from the steeple?
> This was different: scarce as loud, perhaps (who knows?),
> For we saw wet eyes around us ere the close. (51–55)

Only when the female leader, the "noblest lady," makes her request does the external alliance between France and Italy solidify into a true bond of unity:

> And we felt as if a nation, too long borne in
> By hard wrongers,—comprehending in such attitude
> That God had spoken somewhere since the morning,
> That men were somehow brothers, by no platitude,—
> Cried exultant in great wonder and free gratitude. (56–60)

While the women are overtly illustrated as "beauties/ Who lean and melt to music" (7–8) at street fairs, their action in the mock-sexual union of the

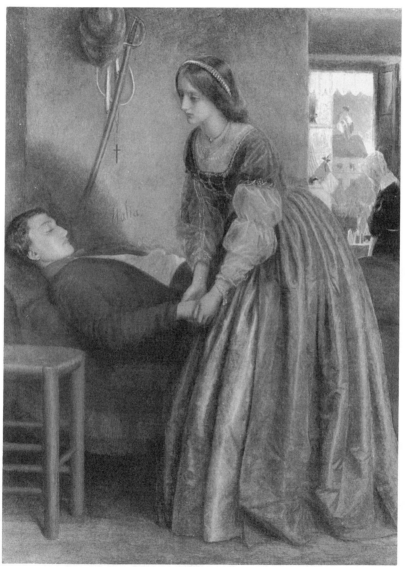

Arthur Hughes, *"That was a Piedmontese ..."* (1860)

dance belies their social enclosure. The Florentine women achieve and even surpass the identical aims of the men.

"A Court Lady" (1860) continues Barrett Browning's characterization of women who conquer their traditional roles in the performance of symbolic political achievement. A grand dame of Milanese society dresses in her finest gown and jewels to visit the wounded Italian forces. Her reiterated nobility and general goodness set the stage for transcendence from society lady to symbol of the cause: "Never was a lady on earth more true as woman and wife,/ Larger in judgment and instinct, prouder in manners and life" (5–6). At the hospital, the Lady, like a social Florence Nightingale,[8] makes the rounds of the wounded by addressing each soldier by the name of an Italian state. The condition of each Italian region can be read in the Lady's varied reactions to the soldiers: maternal pride in Tuscany, smiles for the Lombard, silent tears for Venice. The dying soldier of Piedmont incurs her emphatic patriotic benediction: "That was a Piedmontese! and this is the Court of the King" (54).

Identified as both a matriarchal and national symbol (she "smiled like Italy," was "kind as a mother"), the Lady gives heroic resonance to the event.[9] Typical of Barrett Browning's political women, the Court Lady behaves not in an emotionally feminine way, but patriotically; her words are for the nation-states, not the individual soldiers:

—"Out of the
Piedmont lion
Cometh the sweetness of freedom! sweetest to live or die on."
Holding his cold rough hands,—"well, oh well have ye done
In noble, noble Piedmont, who would not be noble done."
(48–52)

As an icon of Italian freedom, the Lady's action unites the country by freeing each soldier/state into triumphant death. Thus she manages to transcend her societal role as spectator of world events by working within it. The Court Lady's power is, like that of the women of "The Dance," superficially feminine. Yet the implicit action of effecting the maneuvers of national unification on a microcosmic scale is a conclusive example of Barrett Browning's belief in the creatively strong feminine will. In the words of Aurora Leigh: "The works of women are symbolical" (1. 456).

Because a significant portion of her verse centers on detailed events and personages of the European mid-century, Elizabeth Barrett Browning is read today, when she is read at all, largely as a poet of love lyrics. While her political and social poems may not be as immediately accessible, their rhetorical force, always looking outward as it works within, makes a considerable testament to the tension between the Victorian woman's enclosed position and her pained awareness of the world. Barrett Browning's life and art epitomized this tension. As she explained in an unsent letter to the Emperor Napoleon: "It is a woman's voice, sire, which dares to utter what many yearn for in silence" (*Letters* 2.262). Much of her poetic success is a consequence of her fusion of the European struggle for freedom and the intensities of a woman's circumscribed world.

NOTES

Quotations are from *Aurora Leigh*, ed. Cora Kaplan (London: 1978); *Casa Guidi Windows*, ed. Julia Markus (New York: 1977); *The Poetical Works of Elizabeth Barrett Browning*, ed. Harriet Waters Preston (Boston: 1974); *The Poetical Works of Elizabeth Barrett Browning*, ed. Alice Meynell (London: 1918?) for "On a Picture of Riego's Widow"; and *The Letters of Elizabeth Barrett Browning*, ed. Frederick G. Kenyon, 2 vols. (London: 1897).

1. "As a poet, for the first time in her adult life, she was *not* looking at life 'from a window,' but was actually well enough to experience the Italy she had previously only known through literature." The poem connects "immediate experience to a political ideal" (Julia Markus, Introduction, *Casa Guidi Windows*, xxxi–xxxii).
2. Gilbert explains Barrett Browning's *matria* specifically as Italy, "a utopian motherland." She aligns the Italian Risorgimento to Barrett Browning's personal regeneration after marriage and through this structure traces the employment of female energy in *Casa Guidi Windows* and *Aurora Leigh*. Gilbert's feminist reading of these two poems centers largely on the struggle for identity in the female characters, political Italy, and Barrett Browning herself (Sandra M. Gilbert, "From *Patria* to *Matria*: Elizabeth Barrett Browning's Risorgimento," *PMLA* 99 [1984]: 198–200).
3. For a fuller analysis of this theme see Jennifer Gribble, *The Lady of Shalott in the Victorian Novel* (London: 1983).
4. A companion sonnet, "To George Sand: A Desire" (1844), also illustrates Barrett Browning's admiration for the feminine/masculine nature in women:

> Thou large-brained woman and large-hearted man,
> Self-called George Sand! whose soul, amid the lions
> Of thy tumultuous senses moans defiance
> And answers roar for roar, as spirits can (1–4)

5. Gilbert concentrates on Marian Erle's infant in *Aurora Leigh*, seeing the child as a sign of female divinity in creativity (205). Earlier, in a discussion of *Casa Guidi Windows*, Gilbert mentions Barrett Browning's motif of "delivering her children

both in death (as soldiers) and life (as heirs)" in the pursuit of the "community of nations where she belongs," and the redemptive quality of mothers and children in the poem's conclusion (199–200).

6. Robert Browning was uncomfortable with his son's "golden curls and fantastic dress." After Barrett Browning's death he took Penini to England as "a common body." See Gardner B. Taplin, *The Life of Elizabeth Barrett Browning* (New Haven: 1957) 404. For an account of Penini's life after his mother's death, see Appendix I, "What Happened Afterwards to Penini," in Rosalie Mander's *Mrs. Browning: The Story of Elizabeth Barrett* (London: 1980) 127–30.

7. Interestingly, Gilbert points out that while Romney bears a striking resemblance to *Jane Eyre*'s St. John Rivers (see also Taplin, 316–17), as the poem continues he becomes more like Rochester and therefore more Byronic (210 n. 13).

8. In 1855 Barrett Browning wrote: "I know Florence Nightingale slightly. . . . I honor her from my heart. She is an earnest, noble woman, and has fulfilled her woman's duty where many men have failed." (*Letters* 2.188–89).

9. "'The Court Lady' is an individualization of a general fashion, the ladies at Milan having gone to the hospitals in full dress and in open carriages" (*Letters* 2.362).

TROLLOPE: THE INTERNATIONAL THEME

Michael Cotsell, University of Delaware

Anthony Trollope was the greatest traveler among mid-Victorian novelists. He began his writing career during his first residence in Ireland, 1841–51, and returned there to reside at Donnybrook, Dublin, between 1854 and 1859. In addition to extensive travels in Europe, he visited all the most important areas of British expansion except India: the West Indies (1858); North America, five times; Australasia twice (1871 and 1875), the second time via Suez and Ceylon; South Africa (1877). Each of these regions produced a substantial travel book—*The West Indies and the Spanish Main* (1859); *North America* (1862); *Australia and New Zealand* (1873); *South Africa* (1878)—which, as well as providing accounts of his travels, make extended analysis of political and social institutions and their prospects. In his official post-office capacity, he also visited Egypt and the Middle East (1858), though no travel book ensued, and he was one in a pleasure party to Iceland, which did produce a brief, amusing travel book (*How the "Mastiffs" Went to Iceland*, 1878). In 1882 he was again in Ireland, working on the novel *The Landleaguers* (1883), which he was to leave unfinished at his death.

Trollope's work discusses the "world-searching Englishman" (Charles Kingsley's phrase) in many of his manifestations: emigrants who have become Midwestern farmers, or gold diggers in Australia, or who will not work for the salaries paid to blacks in South Africa; South African officials and West Indian plantation owners; and English tourists. His *Travelling Sketches* (1866) provide a sympathetically humorous and perceptive account of the varieties of middle-class English men, women, and children who now set out abroad every year:

> money increases quickly, and distances decrease; wings that a few years
> since were hardly strong enough for a flight over the Channel now carry

their owners safely to the Danube and the Nile; Jerusalem and the Jordan are as common to us as were Paris and the Seine to our grandfathers. (92)

"Upon the whole we are proud of our travelling," he remarks, and, he thinks, rightly so, though he adds, "but yet we must own that, as a nation of travellers, we have much to learn." Nevertheless, the genial tone of the *Travelling Sketches* is instructive, as is its characteristically uncomplaining argument that it is good for English men and women to travel, even if they do not know another language. Critics of tourism should not demand too much: "It is not given to any of us to see the inside of many things" (108). In an age of ready satire on the tourist, Trollope is the least satirical of observers. In the *Sketches*, those who are the least happy travelers, the greatest nuisance to themselves, are the Unprotected Female Tourist, the Man Who Travels Alone (a reader of Byron), and the Art Tourist: those outside the English family, as it were, and precisely the types—we can think of Charlotte Brontë, Byron, and Ruskin—who make of travel abroad an intense and significant business.

This suggests a certain resistance in Trollope to the conventional assumptions of travel and travel literature. A further sign of that resistance is that in his own travel works he rarely indulges in that staple feature of travel writing, enthusiastic description of scenery. He makes a bash at the Niagara Falls and is appreciative of the lakes and mountains of New Zealand, but at the Cape Observatory he declines an offer to view the southern skies with the remark, "In truth I do not care for the stars. I care, I think, only for men and women" (*South Africa* 2.127). In Barbados he makes the characteristically mid-Victorian observation that "it is the waste land of the world that makes it picturesque" (*West Indies and the Spanish Main* 202). Similarly, he describes the difficulties and contrivances of the traveler in remote regions with gusto, but without the glamour of adventure; it is in keeping that he appreciates the jolly insensibility of the Alpine Club. In the novels he is often even more sparing of foreign atmosphere: *John Caldigate* (1879), for instance, gives much less of the feel of being in Australia than Henry Kingsley's fiction. Though his characters have often, like their author, traveled immense distances, there is little evocation of distance in the form or texture of the novels. Thus an early reviewer, Frederic Harrison, was led to remark that Trollope "though a great traveller, rarely uses his experiences in a novel, whereas Scott, Thackeray, Dickens, Bulwer, George Eliot fill their pages with foreign adventures and scenes of travel."[1]

One novel that does derive from Trollope's travels, *The Bertrams* (1859), begun during Trollope's eastern journey and finished in the West Indies, also suggests some of his disquiets. The hero, George Bertram, travels to Jerusalem, expecting to experience a religious emotion, "his heart . . . ready to melt into ecstatic pathos" (1.116). He is at first only disillusioned: the pilgrims at the Tabernacle of the Holy Sepulchre seem to be "the outcasts of the world . . . hardly . . . brothers of his own creed," and, Trollope adds, "such, we believe, are the visits of most English Christians to the so-called Holy Sepulchre" (1.126–7, 128). The view of Jerusalem from the Mount of Olives does produce in Bertram a moment of religious commitment, but he is distracted from it by his interest in a high-spirited and independent young woman, Caroline, who is traveling in a party with her aunt. Caroline and George subsequently become engaged, but through their excessive pride their engagement is broken off and Caroline marries a successful friend of George's, with tragic consequences. Trollope does not make explicit the connection between the opening scenes in the East and the flaws in his two principal characters, but George's wilfulness is manifested in the development of a religious skepticism which owes something to his eastern experiences. The first of Bertram's skeptical works, the *Romance of Scripture*, argues that the authors of Scripture were "Orientals, who wrote . . . with the poetic exaggeration which, in the East, was the breath of life" (2.46–47). Caroline's travels act as an image of her too insistent independence: indeed, the traveling independent woman becomes a type in Trollope's fiction. George and Caroline lack sufficient measure of the spirit of domestic fidelity: their tragedy derives from a certain rootless emotional assertiveness. As a subplot which tells of the long engagement of a poor clergyman suggests, true belief and true values inhere in rooted English social practice, though the need for balance is suggested: the clergyman does not learn to declare his love and deal with his mother's appropriation of his home until he has experienced some of the adventure and freedom of travel abroad in the company of George.

Trollope's feeling for the high value of a rooted English world is evident in the early work of social commentary, unpublished during his lifetime, *The New Zealander*. The title alludes to a passing and rather conventional remark about the Catholic Church in one of Macaulay's reviews (subsequently the subject of an illustration by Doré):

And she may still exist in undiminished vigour when some traveller from New Zealand shall, in the midst of a vast solitude, take his stand on a broken arch of London Bridge and sketch the ruins of St. Paul's.[2]

Trollope rejects this view of the inevitable ruin of England: "What though Nineveh and Babylon fell and Tyre and Carthage," he asks, "are not English morals, English habits, English industry, and English truth still held to be examples for the world?" (3–4). Nor, he adds, repudiating the "Preface" to Ruskin's *Stones of Venice*, has the fall of Venice any necessary message for

England, and he complains that, "Men who know Florence and Rome as well or better than they know London; who are closely intimate with the stones of Venice . . . have never visited Somersetshire and Dorsetshire, and know nothing of the quiet gems which are there" (191). Trollope's rejection of Macaulay and a generation of "sages" (Carlyle's *Latter-Day Pamphlets* is a primary target) is based on his belief in essential and timeless English qualities. *The New Zealander* was written in the early months of 1855, its immediate cause probably Trollope's unhappiness with the violent political discontent provoked by the mismanagement of the Crimean War. By then, he had completed *The Warden* (1855) and was about one-third of the way through *Barchester Towers* (1857); in *The New Zealander*, it is the originals of Barsetshire who epitomize the qualities of his England.

The Barchester novels established an idealized provincial England at the heart of Trollope's imaginative world. They represent, however, only a part of Trollope's early fiction. His first two novels, *The Macdermots of Ballycloran* (1847) and *The Kellys and the O'Kellys* (1848), are set in Ireland; his third, *La Vendée* (1850), deals with the French Revolution. *The Warden* and *Barchester Towers* were followed by *The Three Clerks* (1858) and *Dr. Thorne* (1858), but Trollope then wrote *The Bertrams*, with its eastern theme, a travel book, *The West Indies and the Spanish Main* (1859), and a further Irish novel, *Castle Richmond* (1860). He returned to Barchester with *Framley Personage* (1861), but his next publication was a collection of short stories drawing largely on his travels—the first series of *Tales of All Countries* (1861). *Orley Farm* (1862) is then followed by his travel book *North America* (1862). This pattern of movement between home and abroad continues in his work.

The early Barchester novels were, indeed, written largely from Ireland, and Trollope's career as a novelist had begun there. Writing for Trollope began in exile, as it was subsequently fueled by his journeyings. Ireland appears to have provided him with an opportunity to develop self-confidence, and it was a point of vantage from which essential England could be imagined. But Ireland was itself an important subject. Trollope's first novel, *The Macdermots of Ballycloran*, is a tragic and grotesque tale of the decline of a Catholic gentry family into idiocy and ruin, and of their pitiful resistance to the corrupt local representatives of the Protestant ascendency. With its powerful descriptions of the remote and ruined family estate, it makes an important contribution to the novel of the failing big Irish house established by Maria Edgeworth in *Castle Rackrent* (1800). Though evidence is short, it seems likely that some of Trollope's own pity and self-pity at the failure of his father and at his own miserable youth enter into this novel. His second novel, *The Kellys and the O'Kellys*, also written in Ireland, moves imaginatively in the direction of England. Its principal figures belong to the

Protestant Anglo-Irish gentry rather than the Catholic gentry, and the action is not confined, as it is in *The Macdermots*, to a remote estate, but moves up to Dublin. *The Kellys and the O'Kellys* is also a comedy rather than a tragedy, though grotesque elements remain.

The achievement of *The Macdermots of Ballycloran* points to some of the attraction of foreign subjects for Trollope. They provided not only variety but the chance to present tragedies of cultural conflict imagined with a vividness of description that is unusual in his work. There is an interesting group of novels set in Europe, the first two of which, *Nina Balatka* (1867) and *Linda Tressel* (1868), Trollope published anonymously. He wished to test whether the popularity of his fiction was dependent upon earlier successes; this appeared to be the case, for sales were poor, and the third novel in this series, *The Golden Lion of Granpere* (1872), was published under his name. The choice of a European setting for these works doubtless owes something to the desire to disguise their author, but that explanation does not account for the peculiar strength of *Nina Balatka*. The novel is set in Prague and tells of the love of a young poor Christian girl and a wealthy Jew, Anton Trendelssohn. The lovers are nearly driven apart by the machinations of Nina's prejudiced Catholic relatives, who succeed in persuading Anton that Nina has concealed a document proving his possession of the property inhabited by her and her father. Pushed to this point, Anton, who is otherwise presented as a dignified and loving man, reveals "the hard suspicious greed of the Jew" (2.152); the evocation of the conditions under which the Jews of Prague pursue lives and businesses makes even this reaction understandable. Nina is driven to despair and to consider suicide. Tragedy is narrowly averted in a scene on the bridge across the dark river that runs through the city; few of Trollope's novels so powerfully evoke a setting as *Nina Balatka*.[3] The couple are united, but must leave what is good as well as what is bad in their respective traditions in that "stronghold of prejudice," Prague (2.71), to seek a life in Germany or perhaps in England, where Anton understands that Jews are accepted into society. In *Linda Tressel*, tragedy is not averted: a young girl is driven to despair, illness, and death through the pressure brought on her by her aunt, who holds extreme Protestant beliefs, to marry an older man. Her young lover is, interestingly, a political conspirator, though he is only sketchily presented. In the next of this series of novels, as in the earlier Irish series, Trollope moves toward comedy: *The Golden Lion of Granpere*, the work which appeared under his name, is a facile and easily resolved tale of lovers' difficulties. Yet this series of European novels points to an important aspect of Trollope's later fiction.

Before considering the later fiction, however, a further element in Trollope's relation to the wider world must be considered. Like many of his contemporaries, Trollope saw emigration as a hopeful development, one that might offset the consequences of the meaner aspects of a commercial society. Thus in *The Bertrams* he wrote, "England a nation of shopkeepers! No, let us hope not; not as yet, at any rate. There have been nations to whom buying and selling . . . has been everything; lost nations. . . . But let us hope that no English people will be such as long as the roads are open to Australia, to Canada, and New Zealand" (2.219). Similarly, in *The New Zealander*, though Barsetshire is the touchstone of timeless English values, the triumph of these values over adversity and time depends upon expansion. England herself may decay, Trollope allows, but "the blood and language of Englishmen will be the blood and the language of the dominant race of mankind" forever. Thus, "the New Zealander when he comes will speak in his native tongue to his English guide" (11). There is no guide in Macaulay or Doré: Trollope has in mind a sort of world-federation of English-speaking countries. His title, *The New Zealander*, refers both to the problem Macaulay posed and to the answer to it represented by the settlement colonies.

Trollope (typically) took seriously the commonplace mid-century metaphor for the relation of England to the settlement colonies, the Mother country and her offspring: it is a phrase that repeatedly organizes his discussions in the travel works. The metaphor was widely used to suggest that the progress toward independence of the colonies depended on their arrival at maturity and responsibility, which meant, roughly, that they could operate the English political system in its widest definition. This is the way Trollope uses the phrase in his travel writings. This model of the transmission of family values also operates in his fiction, primarily through an examination of love matches; the transmission of property, social values, and happiness depends on their being made correctly. An unspoken analogy with the relations of cultures and nations underlies his accounts of romance between modestly representative people, enlarging them into an examination of the expanding English world of his time.

Trollope's concern for an extended English world can be seen in his short stories, many of which, as Michael Sadleir recognized, draw on his travels.[4] For instance, in the first series of *Tales of All Countries* (1861), the stories are set in France; Ireland; Spain; Jamaica; Albany, New York; Belgium; Egypt; and France again. Only one, the first French tale, "La Mere Bauche," is tragic. Set in the off-season in the empty grounds of a hotel at the spa town of Pau, it tells of love thwarted by material interest, of a son, overly influenced by his mother, who does not marry the girl who loves him. "The O'Conors of Castle Conor" is a comic tale of a misunderstanding between a young Englishman and his Anglo-Irish hosts: a romantic encounter gets lost in the confusion.[5] "John Bull on the Guadalquivir" is the story of a young Englishman who, traveling to meet his Spanish fiancée, behaves boorishly when he misinterprets the style and appearance of a Spanish grandee; he learns a lesson, but his essential values are defended. "The Courtship of Susan Bell" tells of an American girl who waits for her young man to prove his qualities as an engineer. The "Relics of General Chasse" is a light-hearted look at spinsters in an English "colony" in Belgium; "An Unprotected Female at the Pyramids," a colder tale of a woman using travel to find a husband, is another example of Trollope's use of the independent female traveler. "The Chateau of Prince Polignac" nicely balances the first tale, since it shows a decent French bourgeois reluctantly admitting his profession to the middle-aged Englishwoman he loves: "*Je suis un tailleur.*" To which, after some hesitation, she replies, "And I, also—I will be of the same business" (310–12).

The other story in this collection. "Miss Sarah Jack, of Spanish Town, Jamaica," draws on *The West Indies and the Spanish Main*, the most readable of Trollope's travel works, as well as the shortest. Compared with Carlyle's denunciations of the emancipated West Indian blacks, Trollope's travel book is strikingly urbane and easy-going. He approvingly quotes Carlyle's remark about "the unfortunate nigger gone masterless," and (in some anticipation of V.S. Naipaul) argues that the West Indian blacks are not a people of their own, and that their Christianity is not their own and hence has less real ethical content for them. However, he is not enthusiastic about white officialdom (he writes that Spanish Town is "like a city of the dead" [15]) or the planters (particularly the self-satisfied Barbadians), and he believes that the political future of the islands does not lie with the whites, but with the "colored" or mulatto population of the islands, though he does not greatly admire them either.

The source of the story of Miss Sarah Jack is a little discussion on the notorious practice of flirtation among the daughters of the plantation owners. In Trollope's view, "The doing of anything that one is ashamed of is bad. But as regards flirting, there is no such doing in the West Indies. Girls flirt not only with the utmost skill, but with the utmost innocence also" (166). Trollope himself, he tells us, enjoyed being among the admirers of one Fanny Grey. Similarly, the behavior of Sarah Jack is sanctioned. The belle of a declining post-emancipation plantation society, she appears to be a heartless flirt but, it turns out, is true to her heart. Thus she remains part of Trollope's extended English family: she, and by implication her people, have not been corrupted by the tropics, slave-owning, or the bitterness of subsequent economic decline. This is what concerns Trollope. He can countenance the idea of handing over political authority in the West Indies precisely because his concern is with values and not rule: "And if it be fated that the Anglo-Saxon race in these islands is to yield place to another people, and to abandon its ground, having done its appointed work . . . should not this be enough for any men?" To which he adds: "The present position and prospects of the children of Great Britain are sufficiently noble, and sufficiently extended. One need not begrudge to others their limited share in the population and government of the world's welfare" (82–83).

Such a passage clearly associates Trollope with the confidences of the empire of free trade of the mid-century. Indeed, as regards the rule of non-white populations, he is always pragmatic. It is not that he has much sympathy for the benevolent idealism of the philanthropists. Where, as in Australia or North America, the native population is small or weak enough to have been largely wiped out by white expansion, he accepts the fact with little show of sentiment: in *North America* he writes, "of . . . polishing savages off the face of creation there has been a great deal, and who can deny that humanity has been the greater?" On the other hand, where there is a large nonwhite population, and hence little prospect for the growth of English society, other than as a parody aristocracy (like that of the American South), he shows no concern for its maintenance. Hence he took no interest in India, and visiting South Africa in the 1870s he argued that, as there was no sign of the black population declining, the future was theirs: "South Africa is a country of black men—and not of white men. It has been so, it is so, and it will continue to be so" (*South Africa* 2.332).

Both Trollope's travel writings and the nature of his concerns for an extended England suggest that the settlement colonies would be particularly attractive to him. In fact, they play a relatively minor part in his fiction, though the part they do play is striking. For instance, the novel *John Caldigate* tells of a young English gentleman who takes passage to the Australian goldfields. On the journey out he forms a liaison with a disreputable woman, but, having made his money and broken with her, he returns to England and marries the woman of his choice. His Australian lover and her seedy associates then follow him to England to claim that he married her in Australia: the intention is to blackmail him. What is at issue is whether Caldigate has been irredeemably tainted by his immersion in the rough society of the diggings. Though it is proved that he was not married there, the suffering his English wife undergoes leaves it an open question whether the gold has been worth it.[6]

Trollope's interest in America was also guided by his concern for the extension of English values. Like Charles Dilke, he saw America as part of Greater Britain: as Dilke put it in his "Preface" to *Greater Britain* (1869), "In America, the peoples of the world are being fused together, but they run into the English mould," and, "Through America, England is speaking to the world." Trollope's travel book, *North America*, was provoked by the crisis in relations between Britain and the North over the American Civil War, and was written with memories of the attacks made on American society by his mother and by Dickens:

The writings which have been most popular in England on the subject of the United States have . . . created laughter on one side of the Atlantic, and soreness on the other. If I could do anything to mitigate the soreness, if I could in any small degree add to the good feeling which should exist between two nations which ought to love each other so well, and which do hang upon each other so constantly, I should think that I had cause to be proud of my work. (2–3)

Trollope's appreciations are unfeigned. He sees the Founding Fathers as the antitype of the conquering or rapacious imperial adventurer: "They came here driven by no thirst of conquest, by no greed of gold, dreaming of no western Empire such as Cortez had achieved and Raleigh had meditated" (45). More importantly, Trollope is able to carry that enthusiasm to the Midwest and to the frontier character, as his mother and Dickens had not been able to do. His account of frontier ethics is very much more restrained than that in Dickens's *Martin Chuzzlewit* and again suggests Trollope's distance from English imperial adventure:

Clive and Warren Hasting were great frontier men, but we cannot imagine that they ever realized the doctrine that honesty is the best policy. . . . "It behoves a frontier man to be smart, sir." . . . Such is the prevailing idea. And one feels driven to ask oneself whether such must not be the prevailing idea with those who leave the world and its rules behind them, and go forth with the resolve that the world and its rules will follow them. (195)

Nevertheless, it is clear that, despite his balance, Trollope has arrived at a point of discomfort. At the boundary of Greater Britain he has again failed to find English values. His subsequent remark that he would not like to see his children grow up on the frontier is a typically familial response.[7]

Trollope admired the settlement colonies and America because they provided a more hopeful life for many English-speaking peoples: of the emigrant to America he wrote, "I defy you not to feel that he is superior to the race from whence he has sprung in England or Ireland" (204). He was, however, uncomfortably aware that English life was liable to be transformed abroad. In *The Bertrams*, two military widows returning from India and on the lookout for husbands are treated genially, but it is clear that they have assumed another and lesser set of values. The chilling short story "The Journey to Panama" (in *Lotta Schmidt*, 1867) tells of the death of a beloved wife on a journey through the Panamanian jungle, and shows how pained Trollope was by the exposure of English domestic affections to hostile conditions in remote places. Thus in his fiction, except in his short stories, he rarely follows the English in their world-searching.

251

Instead, in a development of earlier tales of the cultural borders, he brings the foreigners to England: Europeans like Count Pateroff and Sophie Gordeloup in *The Claverings* (1867) and European Jews such as Melmotte in *The Way We Live Now* (1875) and Lopez in *The Prime Minister* (1876); Phineas Finn, the Irishman in *Phineas Finn* (1869) and *Phineas Redux* (1874); and a whole host of Americans, primarily women characters who owe a great deal to his interest in the young American, Kate Field. In this enlargement which is a major, perhaps a defining, characteristic of his late fiction, he brought together the regions of his imagination: the intense points on the cultural borders and frontiers—European, Irish, and imperial—where the questions of adequate values and social relations were strikingly posed, and the English center which was to him the center of all values. The fictional advantages of bringing the foreign home are obvious (and parallel Henry James's arguments for a European setting for his fiction): here the issues could be tested with all the detail and immediacy of the intimately known, and with the emotional reality of what most concerned him and his English readers. The result is a fiction which, though it leans finally to upholding the values of the English center, gives an unprecedented sense of the experience of those outside, of their struggles to affirm themselves, their search for values, their rejection or acceptance. Trollope's earlier outsiders were those outside a certain class; in his later work, he develops his treatment of the outsider to an examination of international relations which represents his recognition that the expanding world of the English was bringing them into new and tenser relations with the world beyond.

Among American characters, the Senator in *The American Senator* (1877), a minor character in the novel that bears his title, is a caricature, in the Dickensian vein, of the rhetorical institutional American: his part in the novel is to show incomprehension of English society. On the other hand, Trollope introduces independent and sympathetic American women into *He Knew He Was Right* (1869); *The Way We Live Now*; *The Duke's Children* (1880); *Dr. Wortle's School* (1881); and his last (unfinished) novel, *The Landleaguers* (1883). In each case, what is at issue is the suitability of their marriage to English gentlemen. Winifred Hurtle, in *The Way We Live Now*, though treated with increasing sympathy, is too tainted by frontier life for such a marriage, and at the novel's end is exiled to California. In *He Knew He Was Right*, *The Duke's Children*, and *The Landleaguers*, the marriage is allowed, but it is nevertheless possible to feel, particularly in the latter, that Trollope's appreciation of his heroines' independent and frank style is under some strain. *Dr. Wortle's School* is the strongest novel in this vein: an English clergyman, believing (as she does) that the brutal husband of an American lady is dead, marries her. But the husband is not dead and the couple bring their secret back to England and the school where Dr. Wortle is headmaster: it falls upon him to defend them and in so doing to stand up against all that is false in English society.

One of the earliest treatments of Americans in Trollope's fiction, *The Way We Live Now*, is the most hostile (it is interesting that the novel was written on Trollope's return from Australia). *The Way We Live Now* is in the vein of the great Victorian international novel which includes *Vanity Fair* (1847–48) and *Little Dorrit* (1855–57), and goes on to *Daniel Deronda* (1876), Meredith's *One of Our Conqueror's* (1891), and Gissing's *The Whirlpool* (1897). Where it differs from its predecessors is in the extent to which it shows English society penetrated by alien forces. In *Vanity Fair*, there is the Frenchified Becky and the knock-on effect on English lives of Napoleon's return; the London of *Little Dorrit* is haunted by the villainous Rigaud; but the London of *The Way We Live Now* is dominated by unscrupulous American and European speculators, whose deceptive promises of the financial rewards of expansion (the South Central Pacific and Mexican Railway) have corrupted the greater part of the English aristocracy: frontier smartness has come home. Heading the speculators is the Californian Hamilton K. Fisker, and the European Jew, Augustus Melmotte, an interesting combination, but not, at first, an obvious one. The novel is best understood as Trollope's attack on imperialism. As is noted above (p. 6), the term came into English usage in reference to the combination of demagoguery, the prestige of international adventurism, and the excitements of rampant speculation of France's Second Empire. By the mid-1870s, Disraeli's opponents were applying the term "imperialist" to him. The immediate model for Melmotte was a particular notorious financier, but behind him, and behind the novel's whole satire, is Disraeli. Trollope suggests that imperialism is not about the expansion of England, but, rather, its penetration. He shows an England dominated by the plutocracy of imperialism: Cecil John Rhodes before his time. Smartness is finally banished to America, but the tragic defiance of the massive and vulgar Melmotte leaves a powerful impression.

Trollope was indeed unhappy with Disraelian imperialism in the 1870s and 1880s, and in late editions of *South Africa* he criticized the rapidity of annexation in the scramble for southern Africa. Nor was he happy with the development of relations with Ireland, and Ireland again became a preoccupation in his later fiction.[8] In *Castle Richmond* (1859), he had dealt with the Irish Famine, though it appears only as a background, and Trollope entirely justifies the behavior of the Anglo-Irish landowner. The Phineas Finn novels are the greatest achievement of Trollope's Irish fiction, dealing sympathetically with an Irish politician divided in his feelings between England and Ireland, but, of course, they largely move the fiction from the representation

253

of Ireland to the representation of its representation in the English parliamentary system. Two of his novels, however, *An Eye for an Eye* and *The Landleaguers*, return to the Irish scene, and bring together a number of Trollope's discomforts with England's position in relation to the wider world.

An Eye for an Eye (1879) is a fable of relations between England and Ireland, which, in tragic intensity and evocation of scene, recalls *Nina Balatka*. Its narrative frame of a mad Irishwoman in an English mental institution who repeats "'it was an eye for an eye'" starkly defines a vengeance and confinement destructive to both sides. The story tells of one of Trollope's very ordinary young gentlemen who goes to the west of Ireland and finds it romantic, a scene for adventure. This feeling is communicated in the descriptions—unusually developed for Trollope—of the sea cliffs: the descriptions are, however, a sign of a false eye for a false abroad. In this environment, the young man falls in love with a Catholic girl, and makes her pregnant, but when he discovers that he has become the heir to an English earldom he knows with an absolute and almost dumb conviction that he cannot marry her. Only at this point, as he seeks to escape his Irish involvements, does unromantic Ireland appear, in the figure of the girl's drunken father, Captain O'Hara, and in a succession of shabby town scenes. The young man is fiercely denounced by the local Catholic priest, who reveals the essential irresponsibility of his earlier romantic attitudes. In an act in which, with his simple, limited sense of honor, he almost acquiesces, he is pushed by the girl's infuriated mother off the romantic cliffs where he has conducted his affair; it is she who ends up in the mental institution. The sense, especially toward the novel's end, that everyone is acting in a numbed way, as though subject to forces that exceed the personal, is acute. As well as being a fine novel about English relations with Ireland, *An Eye for an Eye* is Trollope's most thorough critique of the characterization of the non-English as a field for romance and adventure.

His last, uncompleted novel, *The Landleaguers* (1883), was provoked by the Phoenix Park murders of 1882. It portrays an English family almost under siege at their landed property in County Galway. The youngest son of the family, the boy Florian, has fallen under local influences and "turned Catholic." Thus, though he knows who has flooded his father's meadows and ruined the improvements of thirty years, he lies about his knowledge. With a chilling logic, it becomes clear that Florian will never recover his Englishness or be really forgiven: when he is shot by an Irish conspirator, something like relief prevails. One of the novel's heroines, the daughter of the English family, falls in love with Captain Yorke Clayton, a policeman who lives the dangerous life of a hunter of Irish conspirators: he is the "woodcock," a living target. In Clayton, Trollope creates an imperialist hero

254

in the aggressive and militaristic vein. Even more disturbing is Trollope's sympathetic presentation of the deep inward fury of the Orangeman, Black Daly, when the Catholic peasantry disturb the hunt of which he is Master. The policeman, the woman who loves him for his life of action, the angry Orangeman: the novel's characters extol the ethos of violent rule—as though Carlyle's Cromwell were rising up in Trollope's calmer world.

The Joneses are an English family and, though Trollope introduces chapters of political reflection that suggest that the Irish crisis can be ridden out, their isolation in Ireland, protected only by the police, points toward the impossibility of any English future there. Another concomitant of putting an English family in Ireland at the narrative center is that some of its members live "abroad" in England. The novel's other narrative line follows the eldest son in his pursuit of an attractive American girl who is trying to establish a career as a singer in London. There his apparent rivals are a Whig Lord, who is a connoisseur of the arts, and a Jewish financier cum promoter (Mahomet Moss): the young Englishman is almost as abroad in London as he is at home. To complicate matters further, the American father of the girl is a supporter of Fenianism, and even succeeds in entering the House of Commons as an Irish representative (though, as with Melmotte, his tenure is short). Here Trollope recognizes an historical irony that can also be perceived in Dilke's *Greater Britain*, for, even as Dilke championed the United States as part of Greater Britain, he warned that fraternal relations were threatened by the very nature of the population that America was absorbing: "All great American towns will soon be Celtic" and hence hostile to Britain, and thus the "one great question" is, "Who are Americans to be?"[9]

Trollope's answer in *The Landleaguers* is ambiguous. It is clear that the novelist's late fiction derives much of its strength from his development of an international theme. It will also be clear that in his work the theme owes much of its intensity to a political awareness which is absent from the work of the master of the high Victorian international novel, Henry James.[10] Behind Trollope's achievement in novels like *The Way We Live Now*, *Dr. Wortle's School*, or *The Landleaguers* lies the perception that his earlier peaceable vision of an expanding English world can no longer be sustained. Barchester had been, from its inception, an alternative to a London which Trollope mistrusted, the London which he had shown corrupted by cosmopolitanism in *The Way We Live Now*. He had sought to connect England's provincial verities to an expanded English world, but in *The Landleaguers* his province of values is a threatened enclosure in a surrounding alien hostility, its representatives more out of place in London than mobile internationals. It is not that he approaches Macaulay's vision of ruin, imagining an American Fenian gloating over the ruins of the world's capital. He does, however, combine his intense feeling for the excellence and value of essential English social organization and his tough and informed experience of the world beyond England to produce a fiction that makes a sustained examination of a new and disturbing sense of England's place in the world. In it, neither the character of the returning New Zealander, nor that of the population waiting to greet him, is assured.

NOTES

Quotations from Trollope's fiction are from the following editions: *The Bertrams*, 3 vols. (1859; New York: 1981); *Tales of All Countries*, First Series (1861; New York: 1981); *Nina Balatka*, 2 vols. (Edinburgh and London: 1867); *An Eye for an Eye*, 2 vols. (1879; New York and London: 1979); *The Landleaguers*, 3 vols. (1883; New York and London: 1979). Quotations from his other prose works are from these editions: *The New Zealander*, ed. N. John Hall (Oxford: 1972); *The West Indies and the Spanish Main* (London: 1859); *North America*, 3 vols. (Leipzig: 1862); *Travelling Sketches* (London: 1866); *South Africa*, 2 vols. (London: 1878).

1. Frederic Harrison, *Studies in Early Victorian Literature* (1895), quoted by Michael Sadleir, *Anthony Trollope: A Commentary* (Boston and New York: 1927) 176.
2. Macaulay, "Ranke's *History of the Popes*," *Edinburgh Review* 145 (1840): 228.
3. Trollope remarks that both *Nina Balatka* and *Linda Tressel* were written "very quickly but with a considerable amount of labour . . . after visits to the towns in which the scenes are laid,—Prague and Nuremburg. . . . There was more of romance proper than had been usual with me. And I made an attempt at local colouring, at descriptions of scenes and places, which has not been usual with me" (*An Autobiography* [Berkeley and Los Angeles: 1947] 171).
4. Sadleir 176–77.
5. "The O'Conors of Castle Conor," like "Father Giles of Ballymoy," a story in the *Lotta Schmidt* collection (1867), is based on Trollope's own experiences in Ireland (*Autobiography* 53).
6. Trollope's other Australian work, the short novel *Harry Heathcote of Gangoil* (1874), tells of a struggle between gentry settlers and ex-convicts. Set in the bush, it has much of the atmosphere that *John Caldigate* lacks.
7. Trollope's subsequent response to California is recorded in a letter to the *Liverpool Mercury* (1875) collected in *The Tireless Traveller*, ed. Bradford Allen Booth (Berkeley and Los Angeles: 1941).
8. See J.H. Davidson, "Anthony Trollope and the Colonies," *Victorian Studies* 12 (1969): 305–30.
9. Charles Wentworth Dilke, *Greater Britain: A Record of Travel in English-Speaking Countries During 1866 and 1867* (London: 1869) 199.
10. The possible influence of Trollope on James is discussed in John Halperin's "Trollope, James, and the International Theme," *Yearbook of English Studies* 7 (1977): 141–47.

GETTING OUT OF THE EEL JAR:
George Eliot's Literary Appropriation of Abroad

Deirdre David, University of Maryland

In George Eliot's last novel, *Daniel Deronda* (1876), a group of upper-class English people sits at lunch. It is November 1865 and the talk turns from roulette to recent events in Jamaica. And why not? The Morant Bay rebellion in October 1865, which Governor Eyre had suppressed with a ferocity that shocked even the fiercest supporters of colonial rule, was a controversial topic in the English press. Among others, John Stuart Mill and Herbert Spencer wanted Governor Eyre tried for murder; his admirers, including Thomas Carlyle, John Ruskin, Charles Kingsley, and Tennyson, wanted him commended for his courage. Characteristically reticent about disputatious political matters, Eliot publicly had nothing to say. Also characteristically, she appropriated a contemporary political issue as elaboration of the social and moral realism for which she had been celebrated since the publication of *Scenes of Clerical Life* in 1857.

If we place this brief scene in *Daniel Deronda* in the larger context of George Eliot's persistent and pervasive literary appropriation of abroad for social and moral me ning, we will see that the different responses of the characters at lunch reflect her long-held views about the proper meaning of abroad in English life. The lunch party is composed (primarily) of Gwendolen Harleth; her mother; the man to whom she has recently become engaged, Henleigh Grandcourt; and Daniel Deronda. Gwendolen says nothing, for she is preoccupied with imagining Deronda's response to her engagement; Gwendolen's mother observes that her father had an estate in Barbados but that she has never been to the West Indies; Grandcourt declares that the "Jamaican negro" is "a beastly sort of baptist Caliban"; and Deronda confesses that he has "always felt a little with Caliban" (376). Gwendolen's silence signifies an indifference to the foreign scene that Eliot always found reprehensible; she was equally critical of the mindless understanding of most things in terms of income exhibited in the response of Gwendolen's mother. Without embarrassment, Grandcourt expresses the dislike of natives and missionaries based upon the perception (not unfounded) that English missionaries tended to be more aligned with their converts than with their Queen; Eliot places his languid malevolence far beyond the scope of her moral correction. Deronda's remark suggests the generous sympathy for suffering outsiders that he manifests throughout the novel and which, of course, Eliot describes with great affinity.

Primarily, then, it is the attitudes of Gwendolen and her mother to which Eliot implicitly directs her social criticism. Her English readers need to know more about Jamaica, indeed more about the wider world, not necessarily to abhor or to approve the actions of a colonial governor but to understand both their smallness and their importance in the larger scheme of things.[1] As Eliot points out elsewhere in *Daniel Deronda*, she is writing at a time when "women on the other side of the world would not mourn for the husbands and sons who died bravely in a common cause, and men stinted of bread on our side of the world heard of that willing loss and were patient"(159)—the cataclysmic events of the American Civil War and its devastating influence upon the English cotton mills. Eliot's literary idea of abroad is bound to that expansive moral teaching indelibly associated with her life and career as sagacious intellectual novelist: to understand correctly those things signified by her deployment of the foreign scene widens the individual perspective, diminishes the sovereignty of the ego, and creates greater sympathetic understanding of one's own culture and the wider Victorian world. The lunch party chat in *Daniel Deronda* is, in the words of the narrator, "polite pea-shooting."

In his *Life of George Eliot* (1890), Oscar Browning is puzzled that Eliot, "who was always most happy and most productive under the circumstances of foreign life, should have lived so much in England."[2] Browning attributes this peculiarity to George Henry Lewes's ineradicable affection for London, and this may be so. One thing is certain, however; if we look back over Eliot's life, it becomes clear that after the momentous visit to Germany with Lewes in 1854 (she had boldly left England in the company of a married man), her pleasure in Continental travel instituted regular journeys abroad as a feature of their life together. It would seem that being away from England was, for Eliot, an occasion for expanded intellectual and emotional possibility, an opportunity to be free of domestic constraint. Her sense of liberation began with her very first trip abroad in 1849.

The father whom she had defied with her uncompromising refutation of

Christian doctrine died in May 1849, and in June of that year Eliot left provincial Coventry in the company of her free-thinking friends, Charles and Caroline Bray. The Brays deposited her in Geneva for the winter at the lodgings of M. and Mme. D'Albert-Durade, where she was exhilarated (and occasionally frightened) by her new-found liberation. She returned to England in March 1850, left again in 1854 on that decisive trip to Germany, and her life with Lewes until his death in 1878 was punctuated by many visits, usually of two to three months' duration, to the countries she writes about most frequently in her letters, essays, and novels—namely Germany and Italy—and by less frequent journeys to Switzerland, France, and Spain. In essence, it is Germany and Italy (or to be more precise, those states that eventually constituted these two nations) that govern her imaginative world of abroad—in the nineteenth-century popular English mind, one the country of intellectual discipline and dispassionate scholarship and the other the country of artistic genius and passionate feeling. Refining these popular views of German and Italian culture with the tact that we expect from her expansive mind, Eliot appropriates them for her own literary effect.

The future translator of Strauss's *Das Leben Jesu* (1844) and Feuerbach's *Das Wesen des Christentums* (1854) began to study German in 1840 when the influence of Thomas Carlyle stimulated English intellectual interest in German thought. But, as Thomas Pinney observes in his introduction to Eliot's essays, though she "shared Carlyle's 'awful sense of the mystery of existence', the Germany she discovered was not his" (7). Where Carlyle was attracted to the writings of the idealist philosophers, she was drawn to the work of the historical critics of the Bible. When she left England with Lewes in 1854, her translations of Strauss and Feuerbach had enlisted her as a leading intellectual in the school of secular, humanistic criticism that drew its inspiration from the German Higher Criticism.

Eliot and Lewes traveled first (and briefly) to Antwerp and Brussels and then on to Germany, specifically to Weimar where Lewes spent three months gathering information for his biography of Goethe (*The Life and Works of Goethe*, 1855). Initially, Weimar seemed to Eliot rather too much like "the back streets of an English provincial town," disappointingly unlike the "Athens of the North" she had imagined it to be. But this was merely the impression of a first morning's walk, and the discovery of chestnut-lined avenues, the "labyrinthine" beauties of the park, and the associations with Goethe, Schiller, and Herder established Weimar as securely and pleasingly un-English. Weimar will comfort those, Eliot observes, "weary of English unrest, of that society of 'eels in a jar', where each is trying to get his head above the other" (*Essays* 84). Belonging to the genre of travel essay, her writings about Weimar anticipate the expansive interrogations of English culture and society that we encounter in almost all her fiction from *Scenes of*

259

Clerical Life to *Daniel Deronda*. England may have been the premier "workshop of the world," but in Eliot's view its inhabitants were enthralled by commercial success, entranced by their own imagined superiority, and, as the eel image suggests, fatally engaged in the competitive individualism that was the driving ideology of a powerful middle class.

When she returned to England in 1855, the influence of Germany was clear. In January 1856, for example, the *Westminster Review* published her long appreciation of the life and work of Heinrich Heine, and in July of the same year the *Westminster* also published what is probably the most significant of her writings dealing with German culture, especially in relation to her fiction. This review essay, "The Natural History of German Life," a strongly appreciative assessment of the work of Wilhelm Heinrich von Riehl, is excellent evidence of how Eliot derived from German thought many of the aesthetic values she articulates and manifests in her fiction.

Her essay is based upon discussion of new editions of two books by Riehl, *Die Bürgerliche Gesellschaft* (1851) and *Land und Leute* (1853). Eliot strongly endorses Riehl's suggestions for observing "the People as they are," whether from a sociological or literary perspective: his work is exemplary, in her view, for a sympathetic study of the lower classes. At the present, "a true conception of the popular character" is unavailable. Distorted by those who believe "the relations of men to their neighbours may be settled by algebraic equations" or sentimentalized by those who practice an "aristocratic dilettantism which attempts to restore the 'good old times' by a sort of idyllic masquerading," the "People" remain misrepresented (*Essays* 272). For Eliot, English attitudes toward the lower orders are either inflexibly governed by mechanical formulas or sentimentally ordered by antiquated noblesse-oblige. It is to abroad, quite specifically to German culture and society, that the English should look for moral guidance in their artistic representation of, and political dealings with the lower classes. Responsibly sympathetic understanding of "ordinary" people is a familiar emphasis in Eliot's fiction: the narrator in "Amos Barton" assures us that "you would gain unspeakably if you would learn *with me* [my italics] to see some of the poetry and the pathos, the tragedy and the comedy, lying in the experience of a human soul that looks out through dull grey eyes, and that speaks in a voice of quite ordinary tones" (81).

The tone of the Riehl essay, its commanding appropriation of German thought as a form of aesthetic and social criticism, displays Marian Evan's achieved transformation from intelligent provincial scholar to authoritative metropolitan intellectual. In 1865, established as the literary celebrity "George Eliot," author of *Scenes of Clerical Life*, *Adam Bede*, *The Mill on the Floss*, and *Romola*, she published her last important essay on German culture, "A Word for the Germans." Strongly influenced by the trend of categorizing the moral and intellectual qualities of different nations that was related to contemporary fascination with racial and national traits, the essay aims to correct English misreadings of German life. Eliot unambiguously castigates "John Bull" for his misconceptions of the Germans. She laments the fact that to the materialistic English, Germans are fuzzy metaphysicians given to obfuscating terminology unreadable at one's club. Culling examples from her extensive readings in German thought, she counters such misguided notions by celebrating the superior nature of German intellectual life: every serious thinker has "recourse to German books"; the footnotes of every "good French or English book that appears, whether in scholarship, history, or natural science, are filled with references to German authors." She continues:

> Take away the Germans, with their patience, their thoroughness, their need for a doctrine which refers all transient and material manifestations to subtler and more permanent causes, and all that we most value in our appreciation of early history would have been wanting to us. (*Essays* 389)

Patience, thoroughness, the preference for ideas that transcend the transient and the material—Eliot's condensed image of nineteenth-century German culture is central in her literary imagination. Initially, this may seem improbable if we think merely in terms of setting; with the exception of *Romola*, Eliot's historical novel set in Renaissance Florence, and large parts of *Daniel Deronda* set on the Continent, all of Eliot's major fiction is situated in England. But we do not discover the dense presence of German culture in her novels so much in physical setting as in its function as the fertile source of social and moral criticism, in the way Eliot executes a literary appropriation of the foreign scene for social and moral meaning. It will not seem odd, then, if we turn to the novel most often associated with Eliot's intellectual beginnings in the English Midlands—not one where we would expect to encounter anything German. Yet *The Mill on the Floss* implicitly embodies the ideas expressed in her nonfictional writings about German culture.

After devoting the first three books to the narrative of Maggie and Tom Tulliver's childhood, Eliot opens Book 4 by abruptly shifting the reader's perspective from flourishing St. Ogg's (the river town that is central in the lives of the Tullivers and their relatives) to a decrepit France. Adopting that distinctive narrative tone that embraces her reader in shared experience, in common moral and cultural attitudes, she assumes we have journeyed down the river Rhône and noted the ruined villages that stud the banks, the sign of a lost but unlamented world:

> Strange contrast, you may have thought, between the effect produced on

us by these dismal remnants of commonplace houses, which in their best days were but the sign of a sordid life, belonging in all its details to our own vulgar era; and the effect produced by those ruins on the castled Rhine, which have crumbled and mellowed into such harmony with the green and rocky steeps, that they seem to have a natural fitness, like the mountain-pine.(237)

The explicit contrast between Rhône and Rhine is between French "dismal remnant" and German "natural" ruin, but, as closer examination of the opening of Book 4 of *The Mill on the Floss* reveals, Eliot's juxtaposition also discloses her social criticism of English worldliness.

Associating the fragmented, disjunctive ruins of Rhône villages with contemporary Victorian communities ("our own vulgar era"), the narrator shows that both the decayed society of the Rhône and the flourishing society of St. Ogg's are governed by rules of commonplace materialism. The people of St. Ogg's, if not condemned to Ruskinian river gloom, are certainly less than glorious; what is glorious is the medieval Teutonic spirit that built the splendid Rhine castles. Inheriting "a sublime instinct of form," the grim robber-barons of the Rhine "thrill" Eliot's narrator with their vibrant grandeur. We begin to see that Eliot invests the Rhine (Germany) with a quite particular literary meaning.

The Rhine castles, she says, belong in the literature—and it can be no other than the epic genre—that recounts the departure of great emperors from "their Western palaces to die before the infidel strongholds in the sacred East" (237). The dismal ruins on the Rhône, through imaginative association with Eliot's "own vulgar era," may, therefore, be associated with the popular novel, the dominant genre of Eliot's time and the one given to that mechanical and sentimental representation she excoriates in her essay on Wilhelm von Riehl. What's more, if we see Tom Tulliver unavoidably complicit with the values of St. Ogg's (and by association with the world of ruined Rhône villages), then it is Maggie Tulliver whom we must see as imaginatively associated with German culture and with epic literature. Maggie is a tragic emblem of Eliot's deep affection for the cultural life she discovered in Germany, a symbolic representation, perhaps, of Eliot's pessimism about the eel-like nature of English society. An intellectually ambitious young woman, by turn exhilarated and depressed by her vital intelligence, is affiliated by her creator with the European culture that influenced her own intellectual life more than any other, and that permitted her own escape, through the translations of Strauss and Feuerbach, from a world not unlike that of St. Ogg's.

In her struggles to transcend the material conditions of her life, in her passionate search for meaning beyond the world of perennial stock-taking,

THEY "DO" COLOGNE CATHEDRAL.

"They 'Do' Cologne Cathedral," from Richard Doyle, *The Foreign Tour of Messrs Brown, Jones and Robinson* (1854)

whether it be in terms of the linens and "chiny" cherished by her mother and her aunts or the land fiercely possessed by her father and her uncles, Maggie Tulliver is a compelling antithesis of all that is connected with Rhône villages. She is a figure associated with the epic builders of Rhine castles, with the poetic adventurism of people who experienced a "living, religious art and religious enthusiasm." But where Marian Evans left her provincial origins to become a literary celebrity and seasoned European traveler, Maggie Tulliver remains a moving representation of thwarted intellectual ambition. It is in Eliot's last novel, *Daniel Deronda*, that a character as sensitively intelligent as Maggie Tulliver and more directly associated with German culture is allowed to live—though not in England. This, of course, is the Deronda we have already encountered at lunch in November 1865.

Critics have long argued about the unity of *Daniel Deronda*, the novel most frequently mentioned in discussion of Eliot's fascination with the foreign scene. It begins in a German spa, takes its central characters to Italy for the definitive experiences of their lives, and concludes with the departure of the hero for Palestine. For some readers, the novel is fatally flawed by its two narratives, one to do with Gwendolen Harleth's education in renunciation of the self (finally made possible through the death of her husband in Genoa) and the other with Daniel Deronda's reconciliation with his Jewish mother and assumption of Jewish identity (also experienced in Genoa); for others, the two stories are intimately linked, so thoroughly enfolded with each other in terms of theme and structure, of English and Continental meanings, that their separate but unified status constitutes the greatness of Eliot's last novel. Whether one sees *Daniel Deronda* as split or unified, it is undeniably critical of English upper-class society and sympathetic to what Eliot saw as the more conservative, less competitive values of German society—here given a specifically Jewish meaning. But it is in the wider European world that Deronda discovers his identity as the grandson of Daniel Charisi.

It is in Frankfurt (early in the novel) that Deronda enters a synagogue and is noticed by Joseph Kalonymos, devoted friend of his grandfather and keeper of the Deronda family papers. It is to Mainz (at the end of the novel), after the devastating meetings with his mother in Genoa, that Deronda goes to reforge the natural ties she has sought to break. Understanding *Daniel Deronda* as a whole (which is what Eliot always wanted her readers to do), one begins to perceive that Eliot's novel represents the rejection of narrowly English identities and allegiances and examines the contention between two sets of values: male/German/Jewish and female/Italian/non-Jewish. In effect, we begin to see that *Daniel Deronda* associates German culture with the scholarly, interpretive world of the father, and Italian culture with the artistic, fervently emotional world of the mother.

264

In Mainz, Kalonymos recounts to Deronda the history of the Charisi family, Italian Jews brought many generations ago to Germany. The Charisi story is the narrative of Jews who dwelt "in wealth and unity," whose Jewish brains "fed and fattened . . . the learning of all Germany"—that is until Deronda's grandfather returned to Italy as a young man and married an English "Jewess of Portuguese descent" (790). Knowing that his daughter despises the rituals and restrictions of her patriarchal religion, he marries her to her cousin, the last survivor of his German family. But in her career as a singer, in her history as a dramatically attractive and passionate woman, she deliberately attaches herself to everything not Jewish, and, by association, not German. Emerging from an alien, exotic world, she tells a story of wanting "to live a large life, with freedom to do what every one else did," of disgust with a religion that thinks it "beautiful that men should bind the *tephillin* on them, and women not" (693). Our awareness of the different meanings of European countries in Eliot's literary imagination allows us to see an informing relationship between Deronda's temperamental preference for the contemplative world of his father and Eliot's long-sustained alliance with German culture. Deronda's mother represents a passionate, wayward opposition to the values Eliot praised in her 1865 essay, "A Word for the Germans": patience, thoroughness, and a need to refer "all transient and material manifestations to subtler and more permanent causes" (*Essays* 389).

At this point, it is illuminating to go back to one of the earliest works in Eliot's canon, "Mr. Gilfil's Love-Story" (published nineteen years before *Daniel Deronda*), and discover that this narrative, while set in an English country house, also presents a disruptive female character whose passionate nature anticipates some of the willfulness of Deronda's mother. Set in the late 1780s, the second of Eliot's *Scenes of Clerical Life* chronicles the love of a country parson for an Italian orphan, Caterina Sarti, the talented ward of a local aristocratic family. She is distinguished by a "rare contralto," a voice that gives expression to "her love, her jealousy, her pride, her rebellion against her destiny." The love is reserved for the heir to the estate and the rebellion directed against the class imperatives that dictate marriage to someone more suitable for the daughter of an Italian "*primo tenore* of one short season" who, like many Italian singers, Eliot notes, "was too ignorant to teach" (149).

Linking English domestic drama and European politics, Eliot makes explicit connections between Caterina's passionate, revolutionary nature and the cataclysmic events in French history at the end of the eighteenth century that led to the closing of the Continent to English travelers until after the final defeat of Napoleon in 1815. In registering the domestic "state of things" at Cheverel Manor in 1788, Eliot declares, "In that summer, we know, the great nation of France was agitated by conflicting thoughts and passions, which were but the beginning of sorrows. And in our Caterina's little breast, too, there were terrible struggles" (147). Moreover, in describing how the impassioned Caterina rushes "noiselessly, like a pale meteor, along the passages and up the gallery stairs" (inflamed with jealousy of the woman Anthony Cheverel plans to marry), and in emphasizing how "those gleaming eyes, those bloodless lips, that swift silent tread, make her look like the incarnation of a fierce purpose, rather than a woman" (211–12), Eliot draws on the extensive English nineteenth-century equation of political revolution and unconquered passion. Eliot's Italian orphan, incited by jealousy to a kind of revolutionary rage, recalls Dickens' swirling crowds in *A Tale of Two Cities* (1859), caught in "the raging fever of a nation," or Carlyle's personification of "Maternity" in *The French Revolution* (1837), desperate for bread to feed her children and driven to the streets in a fury. Eliot's first works of fiction, then, disclose the views of German and Italian culture that she expressed (in explicit or symbolic terms) until the end of her career. We have seen that the theories of representation of Wilhelm von Riehl are manifested in Eliot's solicitation of the reader's sympathy for the lives of the ordinary and the dull. "Mr. Gilfil's Love-Story," with its focus on an impassioned, uncontrollable Italian woman, foreshadows the rebellious female challenge presented in *Daniel Deronda*.

In Eliot's later fiction, the Italian settings are based upon the observation permitted by travels to Florence and Rome. Before having Gwendolen Harleth and Daniel Deronda meet their respective fates in Genoa, she chose late fifteenth-century Florence for *Romola* and set in Rome one of the most memorable scenes in *Middlemarch*. In *Romola*, Eliot seeks to educate her nineteenth-century reader in the trans-historical similarities between Medici Florence and Victorian England; in *Middlemarch* she seeks to educate those same readers in the correct historical imagination. Both novels reveal Eliot's attempts to broaden the English mind, to instruct her English readers in understanding the wider world so they might be liberated from that debasing struggle "where each is trying to get his head above the other" that she derided in her 1854 writings about Weimar.

Eliot first visited Florence in May 1860. She spent another month there in the spring of 1861, making notes for the novel about Savonarola (Lewes suggested the idea for an historical novel about the Italian monk whose life is inextricable from a history of Florentine politics); she was "buried in the Middle Ages" in July and September, and in October she began the writing of *Romola*.

The minutely observed scenes of Florentine life and character that we find in this novel manifest Eliot's meticulous research, and at times *Romola* seems a vivified Renaissance canvas, the most visual, painterly of her novels. Burnished with golden color, crammed with movement, Florence is animated by Eliot with the sights and noises of "old clothes-stalls, the challenges of the dicers, the vaunting of new linens and woollens, of excellent wooden-ware, kettles, and frying pans" (57). In the manner, say, of the mid-fifteenth-century Florentine painter Paolo Uccello, she peoples the city-state with gesticulating barbers, haggling goldsmiths, comic peasants, and plotting politicians, who crowd the bridges, swell the narrow streets, and seem to spill over the edges of her novelistic canvas as the Medicis are expelled from power, Savonarola enjoys a brief period of protection from Charles VIII of France, and Romola, the pre-Raphaelite heroine who seems to step from a Rossetti painting, experiences the disappointment of her intellectual ambitions and the treachery of her handsome Greek husband. Romola is consoled in her unhappiness by the words of Savonarola; she is taught to renounce the self for the greater social good.

"We cannot but think," declared the anonymous reviewer of *Romola* in the *Westminster Review*, "that this long and elaborate disquisition . . . is set forth by George Eliot too much in the colours of the nineteenth century." Eliot's "Proem" to the novel lends credence to this view, describing as it does a Renaissance "night-student" of 1492 who, in his intellectual ambition, resembles one of Eliot's most gifted, unhappy, and characteristically Victorian characters: the physician Tertius Lydgate in *Middlemarch*. The Renaissance student has been "questioning the stars or the sages, or his own soul, for that hidden knowledge which would break through the barrier of man's brief life, and show its dark path, that seemed to bend no whither, to be an arc in an immeasurable circle of light and glory" (43). The search for a "hidden knowledge" that will illuminate the darkness of man's "brief life" anticipates Lydgate's ambitious medical research: he wants "to pierce the obscurity of those minute processes which prepare human misery and joy, those invisible thoroughfares which are the first lurking-places of anguish, mania, and crime" (*Middlemarch* 194). In *Romola*, Eliot appropriates the historical past and the foreign scene for literary, moral effect: in writing about Renaissance Florence, she wishes her readers to see their similarity to and their difference from a fifteenth-century Italian city-state.

She develops this idea of the mixture of cultural sameness with historical difference when she characterizes the Renaissance student as having inherited a

> strange web of belief and unbelief; of Epicurean levity and fetichistic dread; of pedantic impossible ethics uttered by rote, and crude passions acted out with childish impulsiveness; of inclination towards a self-indulgent paganism, and inevitable subjection to that human conscience which, in the unrest of a new growth, was filling the air with strange prophecies and presentiments.(48)

267

Aiming to represent in a more neutral way the Italian values that are negatively associated with disruptive female passion in *Daniel Deronda* and "Mr. Gilfil's Love-Story," Eliot shows that fifteenth-century Florence is not that different from Victorian England (as the *Westminster* reviewer suspected). By opposing "belief and unbelief," "Epicurean levity and fetichistic dread," rigid "ethics" and "crude passions" in the consciousness of a Renaissance student, Eliot implicitly represents the cultural paradigms of her own era.

Through the narrative of Romola's subjection to Savonarola's teaching, Eliot's novel instructs her readers in the urgent need to renounce selfish desire for the social good. Romola's worthy but unfeasible dream of becoming as learned as Cassandra Fedele (an important woman humanist) is chastened in an important chapter entitled "An Arresting Voice." This is the voice that impedes through proclamation of a destiny different from the one imagined or desired: it is the voice of the Annunciation, a subject of enduring fascination for Eliot. In an unfinished and undated fragment, "Notes on the Spanish Gypsy and Tragedy in General," Eliot writes of how the subject of *The Spanish Gypsy* was suggested to her by a painting of the Annunciation, probably by Titian, in the Scuola di San Rocco at Venice (which she first visited in June 1860). *The Spanish Gypsy*, Eliot's verse drama published in 1868, recounts the renunciation required by the daughter of a gypsy king; Fedalma, who has been brought up in the household of Spanish aristocrats, must, in her words, "take this yearning self of mine and strangle it"—that is to say, she must give up forthcoming marriage to Count Silva and assume responsibility as leader of her tribe. In her notes, Eliot goes on to describe how the subject of the Annunciation had "always attracted" her. Historical necessity obviously makes Savonarola Italian, but Eliot invests his secularized annunciative voice with so much of the disciplining power that we find in the patriarchal culture of *Daniel Deronda* that imaginatively he may be allied with the German law resisted by Italian will in her last novel. As we know, Deronda's mother manages to thwart her father's wishes, at least for some twenty-five years; Romola's resistance is milder by virtue of Eliot's historical realism. Undeniably, it was easier for a mid-nineteenth-century woman to become a singer/actress than it was for a Renaissance woman to become a humanist scholar, unsettling as it is for us to discover Romola at the end of the novel tutoring her dead husband's illegitimate son in Petrarch while his mistress decorates an altar devoted to Savonarola. In sum, *Romola* shows that Renaissance politics bear some resemblance to those of Victorian England, and that Eliot's jostling, eel-like readers might well stretch their historical imaginations and find inspiration in Savonarola's emphasis on self-renunciation. Let us now consider how *Middlemarch*, published in the early 1870s and celebrated for its fidelity to the provincial manners and morals of the late 1820s and early 1830s, is also about the historical imagination—indeed, by implication, about the wider world.

Almost immediately after her initial arrival in Rome on her first visit there in 1860, Eliot wrote to her publisher, John Blackwood, that her "Rome unvisited" (the city of her imagination and the "scene of varied broken grandeur") was violated by an "ugly, flat city"(*Letters* 3.284). At once articulated with a stunning realism and invested with strong symbolic resonance, the Rome of *Middlemarch* is the terrifying place of Dorothea Brooke's honeymoon; it is also the place where she begins to acquire an historical perspective less tainted by the myopic religiosity that led to her marriage.

Married to Casaubon, the man of her innocent choice, Dorothea finds herself six weeks after her wedding "beholding Rome, the city of visible history, where the past of a whole hemisphere seems moving in funeral procession with strange ancestral images and trophies gathered from afar" (224). Dorothea does not possess the historical imagination that allows one properly to understand this city: "To those who have looked at Rome with the quickening power of a knowledge which breathes a glowing soul into all historic shapes, and traces out the suppressed transitions which unite all contrasts, Rome may still be the spiritual centre and interpreter of the world" (225). But Dorothea is a girl "brought up in English and Swiss Puritanism, fed on meagre Protestant histories and on art chiefly of the hand-screen sort," and, in her recent marriage to a man some twenty-eight years older than herself, "plunged in tumultuous preoccupation with her personal lot" (225). The ability that "traces out the suppressed transitions which unite all contrasts" originates in the historical imagination which can journey beyond the self and beyond English culture and society.

That Dorothea is on her honeymoon and that she is crying is all that can be said: Victorian social and literary convention permit no more explicit allusion to her sexual experience. Yet Eliot's description of the effect of Rome upon Dorothea is structured in such a way that it also suggests the sexual reality of her marriage. Eliot's literary appropriation of Rome in *Middlemarch* serves to symbolize virtually unnarratable, virtually unspeakable, events. Long before writing *Middlemarch*, she had engaged in a similar, but private, appropriation of abroad to signify a problematic event—perhaps the most significant of her life.

Ten days before she left England in July 1854 in the company of George Henry Lewes, Marian Evans prepared her old Coventry friend Sara Hennell for the forthcoming revelation of her bold public union with a married man: "I shall soon send you a goodbye, for I am preparing to go to 'Labassecour'" (*Letters* 2.165). Labassecour is Charlotte Brontë's name for Belgium in her 1853 novel, *Villette*. It is also the fictional country where the English Protestant heroine, Lucy Snowe, struggles with bitter isolation in an alien

Catholic culture, achieves professional independence as mistress of her own school, and, in all likelihood, does not marry the man who loves her (the ambiguous ending suggests he dies in a shipwreck). Labassecour, to all readers of *Villette*, means the foreign site of woman's feeling, the place of a psychological misery so intense it shocked Matthew Arnold into declaring that Brontë's mind was full of "hunger, rebellion, and rage".[3] It is the place of an erotic awakening so charged with passionate longing that Harriet Martineau announced, "All the female characters, in all their thoughts and lives, are full of one thing, or are regarded by the reader in the light of one thought—love."[4] What is interesting about Marian Evan's reference to Labassecour is that she deploys a fictional place to signify (at this moment in her life) the publicly unspeakable. Labassecour, freighted with the emotional, erotic meaning given to it in Bronte's novel, signifies the beginning of Eliot's illicit sexual union with Lewes.

Eliot's literary coding of her departure for Germany with a married man suggests how in *Middlemarch* she makes strategic use of a foreign setting. Let us see how this strategy works in the Roman scene. The "gigantic, broken revelations of that Imperial and Papal city" are "thrust abruptly" upon Dorothea; the "weight of unintelligible Rome might lie easy on bright nymphs" but Dorothea has "no such defence against deep impressions; ruins and basilicas, palaces and colossi, long vistas of white forms, the vast wreck of ambitious ideals, sensuous and spiritual" are "urged" upon her. The language of thrusting, of weight, of deep impressions urged upon the sexually naive Dorothea, symbolizes the shock of sexual initiation. Casaubon may be intellectually impotent but the symbolic effect of Rome upon his wife suggests that he performs his marital duties with the weighty punctiliousness with which he does everything else. When Dorothea's much more sexually knowing sister remarks that she does not like the way he eats his soup, she intimates an intuitive knowledge of his sexual behavior. Eliot's descriptions of Rome also intimate Dorothea's recent, precise experience.

The scene in Rome where we find Dorothea crying six weeks after her wedding concludes with Eliot's oft-quoted observation that if we were to feel the tragedy of ordinary human life, it would be unbearable, it would be like " hearing the grass grow and the squirrel's heart beat, and we should die of that roar which lies on the other side of silence." We need to be "well wadded with stupidity" to survive (226). And yet *Middlemarch*, together with all of Eliot's writing, asks us *not* to wad ourselves with stupidity, asks us to hear the roar, to sharpen our vision and get a feel of "all ordinary human life." To do this, we must acquire "the quickening power of a knowledge" that Eliot deems necessary to piece the "broken revelations" of Rome together; we will possess what most of those at the lunch party in *Daniel Deronda* lack. This imagination will enable us to understand the wider world, the paradoxical insignificance and importance of the individual self in the larger scheme of things. Helped by Eliot's appropriation of the foreign scene for creation of social and moral meaning, we will wriggle free of our eel-inhabited jar and make links, see connections. We will understand Jamaican politics, the American Civil War, German scholarship, and many other things besides, as integral to English culture and society.

Middlemarch, a novel firmly rooted in the rural reality of the Garth farm, the jolly hospitality of the Vincy drawing-room, the bleak spaces of Casaubon's household, also teaches us about the wider world—in a very real sense about abroad. In asking her readers to look back forty years, to make those links and see those transitions, Eliot facilitates sympathetic understanding of a world outside the mid-Victorian self. If Eliot helps her reader to this understanding, then it is interesting that the character who eventually helps Dorothea to develop "the quickening power of a knowledge which breathes a growing soul into all historic shapes, and traces out the suppressed transitions which unite all contrasts" is only *half* English. Described by the worldly Mrs. Cadwallader as a "troublesome sprig" who should have been sent to India, Will Ladislaw is in some ways a little like Eliot herself.

As the son of an English mother and a Polish father, as the dependent of Casaubon, as sometime-artist and then political journalist, Will Ladislaw is external to Middlemarch upper-middle-class society. It is appropriate that at the end of the novel he and Dorothea move to London, that place where the intellectually industrious Marian Evans found cultural recognition. Despite the eventual social acceptance, indeed reverence, of "George Eliot," in some ways Marian Evans remained a privileged outsider, iconized as the sibylline sage, the "feminine" intellectual whose delicate woman's body contained a powerful "male" mind. She is clearly of a different moral and talented order than her character, Will Ladislaw, yet she makes him similar to herself in his sensitive, enthusiastic acceptance of a wider world. Long traveled in the realms of Europe and European literature, Eliot is the uninvited guest at that lunch party in *Daniel Deronda*, urging her readers to journey beyond the narrow compass of their own existences, to travel to Weimar, Mainz, Genoa, Florence, Rome, the Rhône Valley, the Rhine river banks, even to Jamaica. If we possess the passport of Eliot's "quickening power of a knowledge . . . that traces out the suppressed transitions," we will see that the social and moral meanings in her work derive from, and are expressed through, the fertile presence of the wider world in her literary imagination.

NOTES

Quotations from Eliot's works are from the following editions: *Adam Bede*, ed. Stephen Gill (Harmondsworth, Middlesex: 1980); *Daniel Deronda*, ed. Barbara Hardy (Harmondsworth, Middlesex: 1967); *Middlemarch*, ed. W.J. Harvey (Harmondsworth, Middlesex: 1965); *The Mill on the Floss*, ed. Gordon S. Haight (Oxford: 1980); *Romola*, ed. Andrew Sanders (Harmondsworth, Middlesex: 1980); *Scenes of Clerical Life*, ed. David Lodge (Harmondsworth, Middlesex: 1973); *Essays of George Eliot*, ed. Thomas Pinney (New York and London: 1963). Quotations from the letters are from *The George Eliot Letters*, ed. Gordon S. Haight, 9 vols. (New Haven, CT: 1954–78).

1. Eliot's concern is with English attitudes to the foreign scene, not with the plight of the colonized. In general, she inclined to celebrate European culture over that of the non-European world: in 1867, for example, shortly after her return from Spain, she declared that the pictures in Madrid and Seville were "enough to justify western civilization, with all its faults, and transcend any amount of diaper patterns even if they were coloured as the Moors coloured. Not that I mean to be irreverent to the Orientals, but I am thankful that Europe has been filled with ideas over and above what they ever possessed" (*Letters* 4.351).
2. Oscar Browning, *Life of George Eliot* (London and New York: 1890) 40.
3. *The Letters of Matthew Arnold*, ed. George W.E. Russell (New York and London: 1896) 1.34.
4. Martineau's review of *Villette* appeared in the *Daily News*, 3 February 1853, and is reprinted in *The Brontes: The Critical Heritage*, ed. Miriam Allott (London and Boston: 1974) 171–74.

SELECT BIBLIOGRAPHY OF SECONDARY WORKS

1. Travel and travel writing

Bethke, Frederick John. *Three Victorian Travel Writers: An Annotated Bibliography of Criticism on Mrs. Frances Milton Trollope, Samuel Butler, and Robert Louis Stevenson*. Boston: 1977.

Cox, Edward Godfrey. *A Reference Guide to the Literature of Travel: Including Voyages, Geographical Descriptions, Adventures, Shipwrecks, and Expeditions*. 3 vols. Seattle: 1935–49.

Galton, Francis. *The Art of Travel or Shifts and Contrivances Available in Wild Countries*. 1855. Newton Abbot, Eng.: 1971.

Greenhill, Basil, and Ann Giffard. *Travelling By Sea in the Nineteenth Century: Interior Design in Victorian Passenger Ships*. London: 1972.

Kirkpatrick, F.A. "The Literature of Travel, 1700–1900." *Cambridge History of English Literature*. 15 vols. New York and London: 1907–17. 14.265–283.

Pimlott, J.A.R. *The Englishman's Holiday: A Social History*. 1947. Hassocks, Eng., and New York: 1976.

Pudney, John. *The Thomas Cook Story*. London: 1953.

Shattock, Joanne. "Travel Writing Victorian and Modern: A Review of Recent Research." *Prose Studies* 5 (1982): 151–64.

Swinglehurst, Edmund. *The Romantic Journey: The Story of Thomas Cook and Victorian Travel*. London: 1974.

Vaughan, John. *The English Guide Book, c. 1780–1870: An Illustrated History*. Newton Abbot, Eng.: 1974.

Verax, Victor [George Grave]. *Cautions for the First Tour: Or the Annoyances, Shortcomings, Indecencies, and Impositions Incidental to Foreign Travel*. London: 1863.

Wilson, Mona. "Holidays and Travel." *Early Victorian England, 1830–1865*. Ed. G.M. Young. 2 vols. London: 1934. 2.283–314.

Woodruff, D. "Expansion and Emigration." *Early Victorian England, 1830–1865*. Ed. G.M. Young. 2 vols. London: 1934. 2.349–410.

2. Science and Travel

Beer, Gillian, *Darwin's Plots: Evolutionary Narrative in Darwin, George Eliot, and Nineteenth-Century Fiction*. London: 1983.

Brockway, Lucile H. *Science and Colonial Expansion: The Role of The British Royal Botanic Gardens*. New York: 1979.

273

Howarth, O.J.R. *The British Association for the Advancement of Science: A Retrospect 1831–1921*. London: 1922.

MacLeod, Roy, and Peter Collins, eds. *The Parliament of Science: The British Association for the Advancement of Science 1831–1981*. London: 1981.

Markham, Clements R. *The Fifty Years' Work of the Royal Geographical Society*. London: 1881.

Morrell, Jack, and Arnold Thackray, eds. *Gentlemen of Science: Early Years of the British Association for the Advancement of Science*. Oxford: 1981.

Secord, James A. "King of Siluria: Roderick Murchison and the Imperial Theme in Nineteenth-Century British Geology." *Victorian Studies* 25 (1982): 413–42.

Stafford, Barbara Maria. *Voyage into Substance: Art, Science, Nature and the Illustrated Travel Account, 1760–1840*. Cambridge, MA and London: 1984.

Tallmadge, John. "From Chronicle to Quest: The Shaping of Darwin's *Voyage of the Beagle*." *Victorian Studies* 23 (1980): 324–45.

3. Empire

Anderson, Olive. *A Liberal State at War: English Politics and Economics During the Crimean War*. London and Melbourne: 1967.

Bell, Leonard. "Artists and Empire: Victorian Representation of Subject People." *Art History* 5 (1982): 73–86.

Carrington, Charles Edmund. *The British Overseas: Exploits of a Nation of Shopkeepers*. Cambridge: 1950.

Clarke, I.F. *Voices Prophesying War 1763–1984*. London and New York: 1966.

"Colonial and Imperial Themes." Vol 13 of *Yearbook of English Studies* (1983).

Curtin, Philip D., ed. *Imperialism*. New York: 1971.

Gallagher, John, and Ronald Robinson. "The Imperialism of Free Trade." *Economic History Review* 2nd ser. 6 (1953): 1–15.

Green, Martin. *Dreams of Adventure, Deeds of Empire*. London: 1980.

Hobsbawm, Eric, and Terence Ranger, eds. *The Invention of Tradition*. Cambridge, Eng., and New York: 1983.

Hyam, Ronald. *Britain's Imperial Century, 1815–1914: A Study of Empire and Expansion*. London: 1976.

Kiernan, V.G. *The Lords of Human Kind: European Attitudes Towards the Outside World in the Imperial Age*. London: 1969.

Koebner, Richard, and Helmut Dan Schmidt. *Imperialism: The Story and Significance of a Political Word, 1840–1960*. Cambridge: 1965.

Spivack, Gayatri Chakravorty. "Three Women's Texts and a Critique of Imperialism." *Critical Inquiry* 12 (1985): 243–61.

Thornton, A.P. *Doctrines of Imperialism*. New York: 1965.

Thornton, A.P. *The Imperial Idea and Its Enemies: A Study in British Power*. London and New York: 1959.

Woodcock, George. *Who Killed the English Empire?: An Inquest*. London: 1974.

4. France

Campos, Christophe. *The View from France: From Arnold to Bloomsbury*. London and New York: 1965.

Coville, Alfred, and Harold Temperley, eds. *Studies in Anglo-French History During the Eighteenth, Nineteenth, and Twentieth Centuries*. Freeport, NY: 1967.

Faber, Richard. *French and English*. London: 1975.

Green, F.C. *A Comparative View of French and British Civilization (1850–1870)*. London: 1965.

Hall, John Richard. *England and the Orleans Monarchy*. London: 1912.

Marlowe, John. *Perfidious Albion: The Origins of Anglo-French Rivalry in the Levant*. London: 1971.

Maxwell, Constantia. *The English Traveller in France, 1698–1815*. London: 1932.

Starkie, Enid. *From Gautier to Eliot: The Influence of France on English Literature, 1851–1939*. New York: 1960.

5. Germany

Ashton, Rosemary. *The German Idea: Four English Writers and the Reception of German Thought 1800–1860*. Cambridge and New York: 1980.

Fuerst, Norbert. *The Victorian Age of German Literature: Eight Essays*. University Park, PA: 1966.

Haines, George. *German Influence upon English Education and Science, 1800–1866*. New London, CT: 1957.

Kennedy, Paul M. *The Rise of Anglo-German Antagonism, 1860–1914*. London and Boston: 1980.

Mander, John. *Our German Cousins: Anglo-German Relations in the Nineteenth and Twentieth Centuries*. London: 1974.

Morgan, Bayard Quincy, and A.R. Hohlfeld, eds. *German Literature in British Magazines, 1750–1860*. Madison, WI: 1949.

Schmitt, Bernadotte Everly. *England and Germany, 1740–1914*. Princeton, NJ: 1918.

Sontag, Raymond James. *Germany and England: Background of Conflict, 1848–1894*. New York and London: 1938.

6. Russia

Cross, Anthony G. *The Russian Theme in English Literature from the Sixteenth Century to 1980: An Introductory Survey and a Bibliography*. Oxford: 1985.

Gleason, John Howes. *The Genesis of Russophobia in Great Britain: A Study of the Interaction of Policy and Opinion*. Cambridge, MA: 1950.

Middleton, K.W.B. *Britain and Russia: An Historical Essay*. London and New York: 1947.

7. Iceland and the North

Allen, Ralph Bergen. *Old Icelandic Sources in the English Novel*. Philadelphia: 1933.

Loomis, Chauncey C. "The Arctic Sublime." *Nature and the Victorian Imagination*. Ed. U.C. Knoepflmacher and G.B. Tennyson. Berkeley, Los Angeles, and London: 1977. 95–112.

Tomasson, Richard F. "'Iceland on the Brain.'" *American Scandinavian Review* 60 (1972): 380–91.

8. Switzerland and the Alps

De Beer, Gavin Rylands. *Travellers in Switzerland*. London and New York: 1949.

Levine, George. "High and Low: Ruskin and the Novelists." *Nature and the Victorian Imagination*. Ed. U.C. Knoepflmacher and G.B. Tennyson. Berkeley, Los Angeles, and London: 1977. 137–52.

Lunn, Arnold. *Switzerland and the English*. London: 1944.

Nicolson, Marjorie Hope. *Mountain Gloom and Mountain Glory: The Development of the Aesthetics of the Infinite*. Ithaca, NY: 1959.

Robertson, David. "Mid-Victorians Amongst the Alps." *Nature and the Victorian Imagination*. Ed. U.C. Knoepflmacher and G.M. Tennyson. Berkeley, Los Angeles, and London: 1977. 113–36.

Schmid, Walter. *Romantic Switzerland, Mirrored in the Literature and Graphic Art of the 18th and 19th Centuries*. Bern and Hallwag, Switz.: 1965.

9. Italy

Beales, Derek Edward Dawson. *England and Italy, 1859–60*. London and New York: 1961.

Churchill, Kenneth. *Italy and English Literature, 1764–1930*. Totowa, NJ: 1980.

Hamilton, Olive. *Paradise of Exiles: Tuscany and the British*. London: 1974.

McIntire, C.T. *England Against the Papacy, 1858–61: Tories, Liberals, and the Overthrow of Papal Temporal Power During the Italian Risorgimento*. Cambridge and New York: 1983.

Martini, Paola Maria. "The Image of Italy and the Italian in English Travel Books: 1800–1901." Diss. U. of Washington, 1983.

Mead, William Edward. "Italy in English Poetry." *PMLA* 23 (1908): 421–470.

Parks, George Bruner. *The English Traveller to Italy*. Stanford, CA: 1954.

Pine-Coffin, R.S. *Bibliography of British and American Travel in Italy to 1860*. Florence: 1974.

Praz, Mario. "Rome and the Victorians." *The Hero in Eclipse in Victorian Fiction*. Trans. Angus Davison. London and New York: 1956.

Wollaston, George Hyde, ed. *The Englishman in Italy: Being a Collection of Verses Written By Some of Those Who Have Loved Italy*. Oxford: 1909.

10. The Mediterranean and Greece

Gutteling, Johanna Frederika Cornelia. *Hellenic Influence on the English Poetry of the Nineteenth Century.* Folcroft, PA: 1972.

Pemble, John. *The Mediterranean Passion: Victorians and Edwardians in the South.* Oxford: 1987.

Turner, Frank M. *The Greek Heritage in Victorian Britain.* New Haven, CT: 1981.

11. The Middle East

Bevis, Richard, ed. *Bibliotheca Cisorientalia: An Annotated Checklist of Early English Travel Books on the Near and Middle East.* Boston: 1973.

Daniel, Norman. *Islam and the West: The Making of an Image.* Edinburgh: 1960.

Gournay Jean-Francois. "Travel Narratives and British Imperialism in the Near East." *Politics in Literature in the Nineteenth Century.* Lille, France: 1974. 113–34.

Hollenbach, John W. "The Image of the Arab in Nineteenth-Century English and American Literature." *The Muslim World 62* (1972): 195–208.

Kohn, Hans. *Western Civilization in the Near East.* Trans. E.W. Dickes. London: 1936.

Said, Edward. *Orientalism.* London: 1978.

Searight, Sarah. *The British in the Middle East.* London: 1969.

Shaffer, E.S. *"Kubla Khan" and the Fall of Jerusalem: The Mythological School in Biblical Criticism and Secular Literature, 1770–1880.* Cambridge, Eng., and New York: 1975.

Simmons, James C. *Passionate Pilgrims: English Travelers to the World of The Desert Arabs.* New York: 1987.

Wortham, John David. *British Egyptology 1549–1906.* Newton Abbot, Eng.: 1971.

12. India

Bearce, George Donham. *British Attitudes Towards India, 1784–1858.* London and New York: 1961.

Brown, Hilton, ed. *The Sahibs: The Life and Ways of the British in India as Recorded by Themselves.* London: 1948.

Edwardes, Michael. *Bound to Exile: The Victorians in India.* London: 1969.

Garratt, Geoffrey, ed. *The Legacy of India.* Oxford: 1937.

Hoskins, Halford Lancaster. *British Routes to India.* New York: 1928.

Ingram, Edward. *In Defence of British India: Great Britain in the Middle East, 1775–1842.* London and Totowa, NJ: 1984.

Kincaid, Dennis. *British Social Life in India, 1608–1937.* London: 1939.

Oaten, Edward Farley. *A Sketch of Anglo-Indian Literature.* London: 1908.

Sencourt, Robert. *India in English Literature.* 1925. Port Washington, NY: 1970.

Singh, Bhupal. *A Survey of Anglo-Indian Fiction.* London: 1934.

Stokes, Eric. *The English Utilitarians and India.* Oxford: 1959.

Woodruff, Philip [Philip Mason]. *The Men Who Ruled India.* 2 vols. London: 1953–54.

Yapp, Malcolm. *Strategies of British India: Britain, Iran, and Afghanistan, 1798–1850.* Oxford and New York: 1980.

13. The Far East

Appleton, William Worthen. *A Cycle of Cathay: The Chinese Vogue in England During the Seventeenth and Eighteenth Centuries.* New York: 1951.

Arberry, A.J. *British Orientalists.* London: 1943.

Brewster, Dorothy. *East-West Passage: A Study in Literary Relationships.* London: 1954.

Edwardes, Michael. *East-West Passage: The Travel of Ideas, Arts and Inventions between Asia and the Western World.* London: 1971.

Meester, Marie E. de. *Oriental Influences in the English Literature of the Nineteenth Century.* Heidelberg, Germ.,: 1915.

Wint, Guy. *The British in Asia.* London: 1947.

Yokoyama, Toshio. *Japan in the Victorian Mind: A Study of Stereotyped Images of a Nation, 1850–80.* London: 1987.

14. The Pacific

Pearson, Bill. *Rifled Sanctuaries: Some Views of the Pacific Islands in Western Literature to 1900.* Auckland, NZ, Oxford, and New York: 1984.

Smith, Bernard William. *European Vision and the South Pacific, 1768–1850: A Study in the History of Art and Ideas.* Oxford: 1960.

15. Africa and the West Indies

Barker, Anthony J. *The African Link: British Attitudes to the Negro in the Era of the Atlantic Slave Trade, 1550–1807.* London: 1978.

Curtin, Philip D. *The Image of Africa: British Ideas and Action, 1780–1850.* Madison, WI: 1964.

Gallagher, John, Ronald Robinson, with Alice Denny. *Africa and the Victorians: The Official Mind of Imperialism.* London: 1961.

Perhan, Margery Freda, and Jack Simmons. *African Discovery: An Anthology of Exploration.* London: 1942.

Rotberg, Robert I., ed. *Africa and its Explorers: Motives, Methods, and Impact.* Cambridge, MA: 1970.

Temperley, Howard. *British Anti-Slavery, 1833–1870.* London: 1972.

16. The Settlement Colonies

Donaldson, Ian, and Tamsin Donaldson, eds. *Seeing the First Australians*. Sydney and Boston: 1985.

Friedrich, Werner P. *Australia in Western Imaginative Prose Writings 1600–1960*. Chapel Hill, NC: 1967.

Healy, John Joseph. *Literature and the Aborigine, 1770–1975*. New York: 1979.

Goodwin, Craufurd D.W. *The Image of Australia: British Perception of the Australian Economy from the Eighteenth to the Twentieth Century*. Durham, NC: 1974.

Lansbury, Coral. *Arcady in Australia: The Evocation of Australia in Nineteenth-Century English Literature*. Melbourne: 1970.

Lyon, Peter, ed. *British and Canada: Survey of a Changing Relationship*. London: 1976.

Madden, A.F., and W.H. Morris-Jones, eds. *Australia and Britain: Studies in a Changing Relationship*. London and New York: 1980.

Williams, Margaret. *Australia and the Popular Stage, 1829–1929*. Melbourne and New York: 1983.

17. The Americas

Allen, Walter, ed. *Transatlantic Crossing: American Visitors to Britain and British Visitors to America in the Nineteenth Century*. London: 1971.

Berger, Max. *The British Traveller in America, 1836–1860*. New York and London: 1943.

Bowen, Frank C. *A Century of Atlantic Travel, 1830–1930*. London: 1930.

Conrad, Peter. *Imagining America*. New York: 1980.

Gordon, George Stuart. *Anglo-American Literary Relations*. London and New York: 1942.

Honour, Hugh. *The European Vision of America: A Special Exhibition to Honor the Bicentennial of the United States, Organized by the Cleveland Museum of Art with the Collaboration of the National Museum of Art, Washington, and Reunion des Musées Nationaux, Paris*. Cleveland and Kent, OH: 1975.

Jones, Joseph Jay. "British Literary Men's Opinions About America, 1750–1832." Diss. Stanford U, 1934.

Lease, Benjamin. *Anglo-American Encounters: England and the Rise of American Literature*. Cambridge, Eng., and New York: 1981.

McNeil, R.A., and M.D. Deas. *Europeans in Latin America, Humboldt to Hudson: Catalogue of an Exhibition Held in the Bodleian Library, December 1980–April 1981*. Oxford: 1980.

Maurer, Oscar. "'Punch' on Slavery and Civil War in America 1841–65." *Victorian Studies* (1957): 5–28.

Pacther, Marc, ed. *Travelers to the New Nation 1776–1914*. Washington, D.C.: 1976.

Pope-Hennessy, Una. *Three English Women in America*. London: 1929.

Rapson, Richard L. *Britons View America: Travel Commentary, 1860–1935*. Seattle and London: 1971.

Savage, Henry Jr. *Discovering America, 1700–1875*. New York: 1979.

Thistlethwaite, Frank. *The Anglo-American Connection in the Early Nineteenth Century*. Philadelphia: 1959.

18. *Ireland*

[The following are primarily studies of Anglo-Irish authors and are introduced here for comparative purposes]

Finneran, Richard, ed. *Anglo-Irish Literature, a Review of Research*. New York: 1976.

Flanagan, Thomas. *The Irish Novelists, 1800–1850*. New York: 1959.

McCormack, W.J. *Ascendency and Tradition in Anglo-Irish Literary History from 1798 to 1939*. London: 1985.

MacDonagh, Oliver. *States of Mind: A Study of Anglo-Irish Conflict, 1780–1980*. London and Boston: 1983.

O'Brien, Conor Cruise. *Neighbours: Four Lectures*. London and Boston: 1980.

Sheeran, P.F. "Colonists and Colonized: Some Aspects of Anglo-Irish Literature from Swift to Joyce." *Yearbook of English Studies* 13 (1983): 97–115.

Sloan, Barry. *The Pioneers of Anglo-Irish Fiction, 1800–50*. London and Totowa, NJ: 1984.

A GUIDE TO AUTHORS

[The following entries list major travels and a selection of relevant secondary material.]

ARNOLD, Matthew (1822–88), as a boy traveled to Ireland and twice to the continent; visited George Sand at Nohant, France, in 1846, in the same year to Paris; Switzerland 1848, 1849 ("Stanzas in Memory of the Author of 'Obermann,'" *Switzerland* lyrics); honeymoon journey in 1851 to Paris, the Grande Chartreuse, Milan, Vienna, Venice ("Dover Beach," "Stanzas from the Grand Chartreuse"); repeated European holidays thereafter; in 1859 as school inspector to France, Switzerland, Holland ("Stanzas from Carnac"; "A Southern Night"; *England and the Italian Question*, 1859; *The Popular Education of France*, 1861; *A French Eton*, 1864); again on educational business to France, Germany, Italy and Switzerland in 1865 (*Schools and Universities on the Continent*, 1868; also *Culture and Anarchy*, 1869, and *Friendship's Garland*, 1871), and to Germany, France, and Switzerland 1885–86; visited the United States on lecture tours, 1883–84 and 1886. See Christophe Campos, *The View of France from Arnold to Bloomsbury* (London: 1965); David J. DeLaura, *Hebrew and Hellene in Victorian England: Newman, Arnold and Pater* (Austin, TX, and London: 1969); F.J.W. Harding, *Matthew Arnold, the Critic, and France* (Geneva: 1964); Park Honan, *Matthew Arnold: A Life* (New York and London: 1981); John Henry Raleigh, *Matthew Arnold and American Culture* (Berkeley and Los Angeles: 1957); Heinrich Straumann, "Matthew Arnold and the Continental Idea," *The English Mind*, ed. Hugh Sykes Davies and George Watson (Cambridge: 1964) 240–56; Iris Esther Sells, *Matthew Arnold and France: The Poet* (1935; New York: 1970); James Simpson, *Matthew Arnold and Goethe* (London: 1979).

ARNOLD, Thomas (1823–1900), the younger, emigrated to New Zealand, 1847; 1850–56, Inspector of Schools in Tasmania; taught in the Catholic University in Dublin until 1862; returned to Dublin in 1882. See *Letters of Thomas Arnold the Younger, 1850–1900*, ed. James Bertram (Auckland, NZ, and London: 1980); *New Zealand Letters of Thomas Arnold the Younger, with Further Letters from Van Diemen's Land and Letters of Arthur Hugh Clough, 1847–51*, ed. James Bertram (London and Wellington: 1966); Kenneth Allott, "Thomas Arnold the Younger, New Zealand, and the 'Old Democratic Fervour,'" *Landfall* (1961).

ARNOLD, Williams Delafield (1828–59), Indian army and later Director of Public Instruction in the Punjab, 1848–59 (*Oakfield; or, Fellowship in the East*, 1853). See Kenneth Allott, introduction to *Oakfield* (Leicester, Eng., and New York: 1973); E.M. Forster, "William Arnold," *Two Cheers for Democracy* (London: 1951); Frances J. Woodward, *The Doctor's Disciples* (London: 1954).

BORROW, George (1803–81), traveled for the Bible Society in France, Germany, Russia, and the East, 1833–35, Portugal and Spain, 1835–40 (*The Zincali*, 1841; *The Bible in Spain*, 1843). See Michael Collie, *George Borrow, Eccentric* (Cambridge and New York: 1982); A.G. Cross, "George Borrow and Russia," *Modern Language Review* 64 (1969): 363–71; Rudolph Scheville, "George Borrow, English Humorist in Spain," *University of California Chronicle* 18 (1916): 1–24.

BRONTË, Charlotte (1816–55), taught in the Pensionnat Héger in Brussels, 1842–43 (*The Professor*, completed 1846, pub. 1857; *Shirley*, 1849; *Villette*, 1853); visited Ireland on her honeymoon, 1854. See Enid L. Duthie, *The Foreign Vision of Charlotte Brontë* (London: 1975); Gayatri Chakravorty Spivak, "Three Women's Texts and a Critique of Imperialism," *Critical Inquiry* 12 (1985): 243–61

BROWNING, Elizabeth Barrett (1806–61), traveled to Paris with her parents in 1815; eloped with Robert Browning to Paris and Pisa in 1846, settling in Florence in 1847. Thereafter traveled within Italy and London via Paris. See Sandra M. Gilbert, "From *Patria* to *Matria*: Elizabeth Barrett Browning's Risorgimento," *PMLA* 99 (1984): 194–211; Roy E. Gridley, *The Brownings and France* (London: 1982); Rosalie Mander, *Mrs. Browning: The Story of Elizabeth Barrett* (London: 1980).

BROWNING, Robert (1812–89), made an early visit to Russia; traveled to Italy in 1838 (*Sordello*, 1840; *Pippa Passes*, 1841–46), again in 1844, and moved to Italy with Elizabeth Barrett Browning in 1846, residing first at Pisa, then Florence (*Men and Women*, 1855). *The Ring and the Book*, 1868–69, was written after his wife's death and his return to London in 1861. Later visited France, Switzerland, and Italy and died in Venice. See Roy E. Gridley, *The Brownings and France* (London: 1982); Louise Greer, *Browning and America* (Chapel Hill, NC: 1952); Jacob Korg, *Browning and Italy* (Athens, OH: 1983).

BULWER-LYTTON, Edward (1803–73), traveled to France in 1825, to Germany and Italy 1833–34 (*The Pilgrims of the Rhine*, 1834; *The Last Days of Pompeii*, 1834; *Rienzi*, 1835) and subsequently a number of times to Europe. As an MP (1831–41, 1852–66) he was involved in West Indian and other colonial issues; Secretary of State for the Colonies 1858–59. His interest in Australia enters into *The Caxtons*

(1849). See James L. Campbell, *Edward Bulwer-Lytton* (Boston: 1986); Allan Conrad Christensen, *Edward Bulwer-Lytton: The Fiction of New Regions* (Athens, GA: 1976); Coral Lansbury, *Arcady in Australia: The Evocation of Australia in Nineteenth-Century English Literature* (Melbourne: 1970); Richard A. Zipser, *Edward Bulwer-Lytton and Germany* (Berne and Frankfurt: 1974).

BURNES, Sir Alexander (1805–41), in 1832 explored the region around the Oxus and Caspian (*Travels into Bokhara*, 1834). Burnes was killed in an insurrection at Kabul, Afghanistan.

BURTON, Sir Richard Francis (1821–90), military service in India 1842–49, where he learned a number of Asian languages and the art of disguise (*Scinde; or the Unhappy Valley*, 1851; *Goa and the Blue Mountains*, 1851, etc). Traveled in disguise to Arabia (*Personal Narrative of a Pilgrimage to El-Medinah and Meccah*, 1855–56). With John Speke explored East Africa (*First Footsteps in East Africa*, 1856; *The Lake Regions of Central Africa*, 1860). Also traveled to and wrote about North and South America and West Africa, and translated an unexpurgated edition of *The Arabian Nights* (1885–88). See Achmed Abdullah and T. Compton Pakenham, *Dreamers of Empire* (1929; Freeport, NY: 1968); Thomas J. Assad, *Three Victorian Travellers: Burton, Blunt, Doughty* (London: 1964); Fawn Brodie, *The Devil Drives: A Life of Sir Richard Burton* (New York and London: 1967).

BUTLER, Samuel (1835–1902), sheep rancher in New Zealand 1859–64 (*A First Year in Canterbury Settlement*, 1863); the satires *Erewhon* (1872) and *Erewhon Revisited* (1901) are set there but are also influenced by Switzerland and northern Italy (*Alps and Sanctuaries*, 1881; *Ex Voto*, 1888). Traveled to Sicily and Greece 1892–95 to support his theory that the *Odyssey* was written by a woman (*The Authoress of the Odyssey*, 1897). See Joseph Jay Jones, *The Cradle of Erewhon: Samuel Butler in New Zealand* (Austin, TX: 1959).

CARLYLE, Thomas (1795–1881), interpreter of German culture and author of *The French Revolution* (1837); traveled to Paris, 1824; to the Netherlands, 1842; to Ireland, 1846 and 1849; to Germany, 1852 and 1858 (*History of Frederick the Great*, 1858–65); to France and northern Italy, 1866. An important influence on imperialist thought. See C.A. Bodelsen, *Studies in Mid-Victorian Imperialism* (New York: 1968); Charles Gavan Duffy, *Conversations with Carlyle* (London: 1892); Fred Kaplan, *Thomas Carlyle: A Biography* (Cambridge: 1983).

CLOUGH, Arthur Hugh (1819–61), lived in Charleston, SC, as a child; first important trip to Europe to Paris, 1848; to Switzerland and Rome, 1849 (*Amours de Voyage*, 1858); to Venice, 1850 (*Dipsychus*, written 1850, pub. 1865); returned to America, 1852; traveled in Europe, 1861 (*Mari Magno*), dying in Florence 1861. See R.K. Biswas, *Arthur Hugh Clough* (Oxford: 1972); Michael Timko, *Innocent Victorian: The Satiric Poetry of Arthur Hugh Clough* (Athens, OH: 1966).

COLLINS, William Wilkie (1824–89), traveled with his family to Italy in 1836 (*Antonina; or, the Fall of Rome*, 1850); in 1855 visited Dickens in Paris (*The Frozen Deep*); "The Perils of Certain English Prisoners" (1857, with Dickens) is influenced by the Indian Mutiny; *The Moonstone* (1868) brings Indian mystery to England. Visited America in 1873–74 to give public readings. *The Haunted Hotel* (1878) is set in Venice. See John R. Reed, "English Imperialism and the Unacknowledged Crime of *The Moonstone*," *Clio* 2 (1973): 281–90.

CURZON, Robert (1810–73), traveled to Egypt and the Holy Land, 1833–34; Albania and Mount Athos, 1837 (*Visits to Monasteries in the Levant*, 1849); government service in the Middle East, 1841–44. *Armenia* (1854) is the product of a year's residence there. Travels to Italy led to his *A Short Account of Some of the Most Celebrated Libraries of Italy* (1854). See Ian H.C. Fraser, *The Heir of Parham: Robert Curzon 14th Baron Zouche* (Harleston, Eng.: 1986).

DICKENS, Charles (1812–70), traveled to America in 1842 (*American Notes*, 1842; *Martin Chuzzlewit*, 1843–44) and 1867–68; to France, Switzerland, and Italy in 1844–45 (*Pictures from Italy*, 1846), thereafter repeatedly to France and Switzerland and to Italy again in 1853 (*Little Dorrit*, 1855–57). See (among others) William Burgan, "Little Dorrit in Italy," *Nineteenth-Century Fiction* 29 (1975): 393–411; Michael Cotsell, "Politics and Peeling Frescoes: Layard of Nineveh and *Little Dorrit*," *Dickens Studies Annual* 15 (1986): 181–200; Floris Delattre, *Dickens et la France* (Paris: 1927); Sidney P. Moss, *Charles Dickens' Quarrel with America* (Troy, NY: 1984); Michael Slater, ed., *Dickens on America and the Americans* (Austin, TX: 1978).

DILKE, Sir Charles Wentworth (1843–1911), traveled across America to Australia and New Zealand, returning via Ceylon, India, and Egypt (*Greater Britain: A Record of Travel in English-Speaking Countries during 1866 and 1867*, 1868), and again round the world in 1875, this time visiting China and Japan. Radical MP 1868–85 with strong connections with French Republicans. See C.A. Bodelsen, *Studies in Mid-Victorian Imperialism* (New York: 1968).

DISRAELI, Benjamin, Earl of Beaconsfield (1804–81), early travel to Belgium and the Rhine, 1824; to Switzerland and Italy, 1826; to Spain, Italy, and the Levant, 1828–31. As a leading British statesman he was to play an important part in the politics of Europe and Empire. See

Robert Blake, *Disraeli* (London: 1966); *Disraeli's Grand Tour: Benjamin Disraeli in the Holy Land, 1830–31*, ed. Robert Blake (Oxford: 1982); Thom Braun, *Disraeli the Novelist* (London and Boston: 1981); Freda Harcourt, "Disraeli's Imperialism, 1866–68: A Question of Timing," *Historical Journal* 23 (1980): 87–109; B.R. Jerman, *The Young Disraeli* (Princeton: 1960); Daniel R. Schwarz, *Disraeli's Fiction* (New York and London: 1979); Richard A. Levine, "Disraeli's *Tancred* and 'The Great Asian Mystery,'" *Nineteenth-Century Fiction* 22.1 (1967): 71–85; Stanley R. Stembridge, "Disraeli and the Millstones," *Journal of British Studies* 5.1 (1965): 122–39 (on D's colonial policy); Donald Sultana, *Benjamin Disraeli in Spain, Malta and Albania 1830–32* (London: 1976).

ELIOT, George (1819–80), traveled to Geneva 1849–50 after death of father; to Germany 1854–55 with George Henry Lewes; thereafter repeatedly with Lewes to Europe, notably to Italy in 1860 and 1861 (*Romola, 1862–63); Spain, 1866–67 (The Spanish Gypsy,* 1868); Rome in 1869 (*Middlemarch,* 1871–72); France and Germany, 1873, where she researched the Jewish portions of *Daniel Deronda* (1876). Her last visit to Europe was her wedding visit to Venice with John Cross in 1880. See (among others) Gisela Argyle, *German Elements in the Fiction of George Eliot, Gissing and Meredith* (Frankfurt: 1979); William Baker, "The Kabbalah, Mordecai, and George Eliot's Religion of Humanity," *Yearbook of English Studies* 3 (1973): 216–21; Judith Skelton Grant, "Italians with the White Mice in *Middlemarch* and *Little Dorrit,*" *English Language Notes* 16 (1979): 232–34; Irving Howe, "George Eliot and the Jews," *Partisan Review* 46 (1979): 359–75; Anthony McCabb, *George Eliot's Knowledge of German Life and Letters* (Salzburg: 1982); Lawrence Poston, "Setting and Theme in *Romola,*" *Nineteenth-Century Fiction* 20 (1966): 355–66; Brian Swann, "George Eliot's Ecumenical Jew, or, The Novel as Outdoor Temple," *Novel* 8 (1974): 39–50; Joseph Wiesenfarth, "The Greeks, the Germans, and George Eliot," *Browning Institute Studies* 10 (1982): 91–104; Hugh Witemeyer, "George Eliot, Naumann, and the Nazarenes," *Victorian Studies* 18 (1974): 145–58.

FROUDE, James Anthony (1818–94), as well as European travel, visited Ireland in 1842 and repeatedly thereafter (*The English in Ireland in the Eighteenth Century,* 1872–74, etc.); lectured in the United States in 1872; toured South Africa 1874–75 ("Leaves from a South African Journal," *Short Studies,* 3rd ser., 1877); Norway in 1881; Australia in 1884–85 (*Oceana, or England and Her Colonies,* 1886); the West Indies in 1886–87 (*English in the West Indies; or, the Bow of Ulysses,* 1888). See C.A. Bodelson, *Studies in Mid-Victorian Imperialism* (New York: 1968); Jeffrey Paul van Arx, *Progress and Pessimism: Religion, Politics, and History in Late Nineteenth-Century Britain* (Cambridge, MA: 1985).

GASKELL, Elizabeth (1810–65), visited Heidelberg in 1841, traveling via Bruges, Ghent, and Antwerp; Paris in 1853 (some influence on *North and South*, 1855) and 1854; Brussels in 1856 (*Life of Charlotte Bronte*, 1857); Rome and other Italian cities in 1857, where she met Charles Eliot Norton ("It was in those charming Roman days that my life, at any rate, culminated."); France and Italy in 1863; France (twice) in 1865. See Winifred Gerin, *Elizabeth Gaskell: A Biography* (Oxford: 1976).

KINGLAKE, Alexander William (1809–91), traveled in 1835 to the Middle East (*Eothen*, 1844); in 1845 to Russia and to Algeria; in 1854 to the Crimea (*Invasion of the Crimea*, 1863–87). See Gerald De Gaury, *Travelling Gent: The Life of Alexander Kinglake* (Boston and London: 1972); Iran B. Hassani Jewett, *Alexander W. Kinglake* (Boston: 1981); William S. Johnston, "William Kinglake's 'A Summer in Russia': A Neglected Memoir of Saint Petersburg in 1845," *Texas Studies in Literature and Language* 9 (1967): 103–15.

KINGSLEY, Charles (1819–75), toured the Rhine in 1851 and France in 1864; *Two Years Ago* (1857) shows his interest in the Crimean War (his tract, "Brave Words to Brave Soldiers," was distributed to the army) and the Australian diggings; sailed to the West Indies in 1869 (*At Last!*, 1871) and lectured in America in 1874. See William J. Baker, "Charles Kingsley and the Crimean War: A Study in Chauvinism," *Southern Humanities Review* 4 (1979): 247–56; Robert Bernard Martin, *The Dust of Combat: A Life of Charles Kingsley* (London: 1959); *Charles Kingsley's American Notes: Letters from a Lecture Tour, 1874*, ed. Robert Martin (Princeton: 1958); John O. Waller, "Charles Kingsley and the American Civil War," *Studies in Philology* 60 (1963): 554–68.

KINGSLEY, Henry (1830–76), resided in Australia 1853–58, where he began his writing career (*The Recollections of Geoffrey Hamlyn*, 1859; *The Hillyars and the Burtons*, 1865; *The Boy in Grey*, 1871, etc.); *Ravenshoe* (1862) includes scenes of the Crimean War and *Stretton* (1869) of the Indian Mutiny. Kingsley wrote in support of Governor Eyre both as an explorer and an administrator. As a war correspondent in the Franco-Prussian War, he was horrified by the slaughter. See J.S.D. Mellick, *The Passing Guest: A Life of Henry Kingsley* (New York: 1983); John Barnes, *Henry Kingsley and Colonial Fiction* (Melbourne and New York: 1971); William H. Scheuerle, *The Neglected Brother: A Study of Henry Kingsley* (Tallahassee, FL: 1971); Angela Thirkell, "Henry Kingsley, 1830–1876," *Nineteenth-Century Fiction* 5 (1950): 175–87; "The Works of Henry Kingsley," *Nineteenth-Century Fiction* 5 (1951): 273–93.

LANDOR, Walter Savage (1775–1864), joined the Spanish rising in 1808 (*Count Julian*, 1812); resided in Florence 1821–35 and after 1858. His writings include many Italian and European subjects. See Guido Fornelli, *W.S. Landor e l'Italia* (Forli, Italy: 1931); Lilian Whiting, *The Florence of Landor* (London and Cambridge, MA: 1905).

LAYARD, Austen Henry (1817–94), spent part of his childhood in France and Italy; in 1839 journeyed overland to Constantinople and Persia. Supported by Stratford Canning, British Ambassador to Turkey, began excavations in the region of Nineveh, 1845 (*Nineveh and Its Remains*, 1849); a second series of excavations followed (*Discoveries in the Ruins of Nineveh and Babylon*, 1853). Subsequently visited Italy, writing on Italian frescoes, the Crimean battlefields, and India. Lead parliamentary opposition to mismanagement of Crimean War and in 1877–78 supported Disraeli's Eastern policy, negotiating the British occupation of Cyprus. See Gordon Waterfield, *Layard of Nineveh* (London: 1963).

MACAULAY, Thomas Babington (1800–59), 1834–37 Legal Member of the Supreme Council of India ("Minute on Indian Education," 1835, etc.), where he was author of the Indian Penal Code; in 1838 first journey to Italy. See R.K. Das Gupta, "Macaulay's Writings on India," *Historians of India, Pakistan and Ceylon*, ed. C.H. Philips (Oxford: 1961) 230–40; Gerald Sirkin and Natalie Robinson, "The Battle of Indian Education: Macaulay's Opening Salvo Newly Discovered," *Victorian Studies* 14 (1971): 407–28; Eric Stokes, *The English Utilitarians and India* (Oxford: 1959).

MARRYAT, Frederick (1792–1848), naval captain who served in the Atlantic, the West Indies, and the East; 1836 resided at Brussels; 1837–38 toured Canada and the United States (*A Diary in America*, 1839). His novels draw extensively on his travels.

MARTINEAU, Harriet (1802–76), traveled in America 1834–36 (*Society in America*, 1837; *Retrospect of Western Travel*, 1838; *How to Observe*, 1838); to Italy, 1839; to Egypt, the Holy Land, and Syria, 1846–47 (*Eastern Life, Past and Present*, 1848). Many of her other works relate to abroad, among them the anti-slavery *The "Manifest Destiny" of the American Union* (1857); *British Rule in India* (1857); and *Suggestions Towards the Future Government of India* (1858). The novel *Ireland* (1832) addresses the question of Irish poverty; *The Hour and the Man* (1841) is about Toussaint L'Ouverture. See Marghanita Laski, "Harriet Martineau" in *Travels to the New Nation 1776–1914*, ed. Marc Pacther (Washington, D.C.: 1976); Una Pope-Hennessy, *Three English Women in America* (London: 1929); Gillian Thomas, *Harriet Martineau* (Boston: 1985).

MILL, John Stuart (1806–73), resided in France 1820–21, and traveled in 1830 to Paris to see the Revolution; employed by the India House between 1823–58. His wife, Harriet Taylor, died at Avignon in 1858 and for the remainder of his life Mill spent half the year there. Mill was much influenced by European thought and wrote on many of the great international issues of the day. See *John Mill's Boyhood Visit to France: Being a Journal and Notebook*, ed. Anna Jean Mill (Toronto: 1960); Iris Wessel Mueller, *John Stuart Mill and French Thought* (Urbana, IL: 1956); Eric Stokes, *The English Utilitarians and India* (Oxford: 1959).

NEWMAN, John Henry, Cardinal (1801–90), traveled to the Mediterranean, 1832–33 (poems in *Lyra Apostolica*, 1836; *Callista*, 1856, is set in North Africa); after conversion to Catholic Church to Milan and Rome (1846–47), also Naples, Monte Cassino; attempted to found the Catholic University of Ireland in Dublin, 1854–58; after being made Cardinal visited Rome in 1879. See Wilfred Ward, *The Life of John Henry Cardinal Newman*, 2 vols. (London: 1921).

PATER, Walter Horatio (1839–94), traveled in 1865 to Italy, particularly Ravenna, Pisa, Florence (*Studies in the History of the Renaissance*, 1873); to Rome, 1882 (*Marius the Epicurean*, 1885). See John J. Conlon, *Walter Pater and the French Tradition* (Lewisburg, NJ, London, and Toronto: 1982); David J. DeLaura, *Hebrew and Hellene in Victorian England: Newman, Arnold and Pater* (Austin, TX, and London: 1969); Enid Starkie, *From Gautier to Eliot: The Influence of France on British Literature, 1851–1939* (London: 1960).

READE, Charles (1814–84), wrote a play, *Gold* (1853), set in the Australian gold diggings, and his novels *It Is Never Too Late to Mend* (1856) and *Foul Play* (1868) include Australian scenes.

ROSSETTI, Dante Gabriel (1828–82), of Italian descent, though he never visited Italy. Traveled to Paris and Belgium 1849; to Paris 1855 and 1860.

RUSKIN, John (1819–1900), traveled constantly to Europe, particularly the Swiss and French Alps, northern Italy, and the cathedral towns of France. Large sections of *The Poetry of Architecture* (1838) draw on his boyhood travels; volumes 1, 4 and 5 of *Modern Painters* (1843, 1856, 1860) make extended use of his alpine studies, while volumes 2 (1846) and 5 (1860) contain sections on medieval and Renaissance Italian art; *Seven Lamps of Architecture* (1849) draws on his study of French as well as Italian cathedrals; *The Stones of Venice* (1851–53) uses notes and drawings made at Venice in 1849–50 and 1851–52; later published several guides and short histories of Italian cities, including

Mornings in Florence (1875–77) and *St. Martin's Rest* (1877–84), as well as short pieces and fragments on French and Swiss subjects. See *Ruskin in Italy: Letters to His Parents, 1845*, ed. Harold I. Shapiro (Oxford: 1972); *Ruskin's Letters from Venice, 1851–1852*, ed. John Lewis Bradley (New Haven: 1955); *Letters from the Continent, 1858*, ed. John Hayman (Toronto and Buffalo, NY: 1982); Jeanne Clegg, *Ruskin and Venice* (London: 1981); Robert Hewison, *Ruskin and Venice* (London: 1978); John Unrau, *Ruskin and St. Marks* (London: 1984); J.G. Links, *The Ruskins in Normandy* (London: 1968); Elisabeth Koenig, *John Ruskin und die Schweiz* (Bern: 1943).

SWINBURNE, Algernon Charles (1837–1909), traveled to France and Italy, 1861; to Paris, 1863; to Italy, 1864 (*Poems and Ballads*, 1866); met Mazzini in 1867 (*Songs before Sunrise*, 1871); again to France, 1868, 1882. In later life an opponent of Germany, Russia and Irish nationalism.

TENNYSON, Alfred Lord (1809–92), traveled to France and Spain, 1830; the Low Countries and the Rhine, 1832; Rotterdam and Amsterdam, 1841; France, Italy, and Switzerland, 1851; Norway, 1858; Portugal, 1859; France (Pyrenees), 1861; Brittany and Normandy, 1864; Low Countries and Rhine, 1865; Paris, 1868; Switzerland, 1869; France and Switzerland, 1872; Switzerland and Northern Italy, 1873; Denmark and Norway, 1883. See Michael C.C. Adams, "Tennyson's Crimean War Poetry: A Cross-Cultural Approach," *Journal of the History of Ideas* 40 (1979): 405–22; James R. Bennett, "The Historical Abuse of Literature: Tennyson's *"Maud: A Monodrama* and the Crimean War," *English Studies* 62 (1981): 34–45; Hallman B. Bryant, "The African Genesis of Tennyson's 'Timbuctoo,'" *Tennyson Research Bulletin* 3 (1981): 196–202; W.D. Paden, *Tennyson in Egypt: A Study of the Imagery in His Earlier Work* (1942; New York : 1971).

THACKERAY, William Makepeace (1811–63), b. Calcutta, sent to school in England, 1817; traveled to France, 1829, 1830; to Germany 1830–31; studied art in Paris, 1834–35; to Paris and Germany again 1840–41 (*The Paris Sketch Book*, 1840); to Ireland, 1842 (*Irish Sketch-Book*, 1843; *The Luck of Barry Lyndon*, 1844); to the Low Countries, 1843; to the Mediterranean and Middle East, 1844–45 (*Notes of a Journey from Cornhill to Grand Cairo*, 1846); to Italy, 1844–45, 1853–54 (*The Newcomes*, 1853–55); toured America, 1852–53, 1855–56. See John Carey, *Thackeray: Prodigal Genius* (London: 1977); J.G. Wilson, *Thackeray in the United States* (London: 1904).

TROLLOPE, Anthony (1815–82), resided in Ireland 1841–51, 1853–59; as well as extensive travel in Europe, visited the Middle East in 1858; the West Indies, 1858–59 (*The West Indies and the Spanish Main*, 1859);

North America five times (*North America*, 1862); Australia and New Zealand twice (*Australia and New Zealand*, 1873); South Africa, 1877 (*South Africa*, 1878); Iceland, 1878 (*How the 'Mastiffs' Went to Iceland*, 1878); Ireland again in 1882. See J.H. Davidson, "Anthony Trollope and the Colonies," *Victorian Studies* 12 (1969): 305–30; Janet Egleson Dunleavy, "Trollope and Ireland," *Trollope Centenary Essays*, ed. John Halperin (New York: 1982) 53–69; Stephen Gwynn, "Trollope and Ireland," *Contemporary Review* 129 (1926): 72–79; John Halperin, "Trollope, James, and the International Theme," *Yearbook of English Studies* 7 (1977): 141–47; "Trollope and the American Civil War," *Clio* 13 (1984): 149–55; E.W. Wittig, "Trollope's Irish Fiction," *Eire-Ireland* 9 (1974): 97–118.

TROLLOPE, Frances Milton (1780–1863), resided in America 1827–31 (*Domestic Manners of the Americans*, 1832; *The Refugee in America*, 1832); traveled to Belgium and Germany, 1833 (*Belgium and Western Germany in 1833*, 1834); to Paris, 1835 (*Paris and the Parisians in 1835*, 1836); to Austria, 1836–37 (*Vienna and the Austrians*, 1838; *A Romance of Vienna*, 1838); to Italy, 1842 (*A Visit to Italy*, 1842), making a permanent home at Florence. Other of her works derive from these and other journeys. See Marcus Cunliffe, "Frances Trollope 1780–1863," *Travelers to the New Nation*, ed. Mark Pacther (Washington, D.C.: 1976) 11–22; Helen Heineman, *Mrs. Trollope: The Triumphant Feminine in the Nineteenth Century* (Athens, OH: 1979), *Frances Trollope* (Boston: 1984), and other studies; Ada B. Nisbet, "Mrs. Trollope's *Domestic Manners*," *Nineteenth-Century Fiction* 4 (1950): 319–24; Una Pope-Hennessy, *Three English Women in America* (London: 1929).

TROLLOPE, Thomas Adolphus (1810–92), traveled with his father to America, 1828; in 1839 to Britanny with his mother; in 1843 settled with her at Florence, subsequently traveling widely in Europe, and writing many travel books and novels with European settings. See Lawrence Poston III, "Thomas Adolphus Trollope: A Victorian Anglo-Florentine," *Bulletin of the John Rylands Library* 49 (1966): 133–64.

WARBURTON, Eliot (1810–52), Anglo-Irish background, toured Middle East in 1843 (*The Crescent and the Cross*, 1844). Subsequently traveled in Europe and Central America, dying when the ship the *Amazon* caught fire. Collected materials for a *History of the Poor* in Ireland.

INDEX

Abbeville (France), Ruskin on, 23
aestheticism, 22, 25
Afghanistan, 6
Africa, *41*; "dark continent", 41;
exploration of, 41, 116; British cruisers
off coast of, 4; Tennyson on Timbuctoo,
116–7; Charlotte Brontë and the
Ashantee, 174. See also North Africa,
South Africa.
African Civilization Society, 4
Albany, New York, in Trollope, 248–9
Alexandria, 55
Algiers, 35
Alpine Club, the 12, 29; Ruskin on, 190
Alps, the, the Romantics and, 28; the
Victorians and, 28–9; painters of, 29;
mountaineers in, 29; in Samuel Butler,
44; in Ruskin, 29, 208f; too unchanging
for Dickens, 132; crossing them in *Little
Dorrit*, 11, 134; and in *David
Copperfield*, 134–5. See also Switzerland.
American Civil War, British attitudes to, 9;
sympathy with Confederacy, 9, 47; but
liberals support North, 9, 47; Walter
Bagehot on, 47
Anglo-Indians, 100–1
Anglo-Indian literature, 18
Anglo-Irish literature, 18, 48
Anglo-Saxon character and expansion, myth
of, 16, 124
Apennines (Italy), 134
Arabian Nights, childhood reading of
travellers, 34; translated by Burton, 37;
Dickens looks for their equivalent
abroad, 132, 133, 138, 173
Arabs, admiration for desert Arabs, 36;
Disraeli in praise of, 57
Arctic, the, 18, Franklin's expeditions to,
28; in Gaskell's *Sylvia's Lovers*, 20
Arezzo (Italy), 218
Argentine, the, wars of extermination
against Indians, 42; inhabitants of Tierra
Del Fuego, 42
Arnold, Matthew, "culture" and English

politics, 8–9; critical of English
grandiosity and provinciality, 9, 17, 19;
his "Europeanism", *142–56*; influence of
his father's European awareness, 144; his
poetry and the European "sentimental
school", 146–7; his European poems,
147–53; and his love for Mary Claude,
147; Europe in his criticism, 152–5; the
comparative method, 155–6; early visit to
France, 144; France as an influence, 143,
144–5; at Paris, 15; no revolutionary
millenium, 24; society of the Second
Empire, 25; as a spokesman for French
culture, 25; on French lubricity, 25;
"culture" and English politics, 8–9; on
Germany, 143; German intellectual life,
145; he is weak on Italy, 143, 156; on
American Philistinism, 21, 47–8, 155; on
European Jewish artists, 27–8, 146, 154;
and the east, 35, 39; his criticism of
expansion, 39; reversal of a British racial
myth, 16; use of fictive foreigners in his
writings, 17, 142; on Charlotte Brontë,
270. *Works*: 1. Poetry: "The Church of
Brou", 152; "Dover Beach", 149–50, 153;
"Empedocles on Etna", 146, 153; "To
Marguerite—Continued", 148;
"Memorial Verses", 146; "Parting", 149;
"Rugby Chapel", 22; "The Scholar
Gypsy", 149; "Sohrab and Rustum", 35;
"A Southern Night", 21, 39; "Stanzas
from Carnac", 39; "Stanzas from the
Grande Chartreuse", 147, 150–2, 153;
"Stanzas in Memory of the Author of
'Obermann'", 153; "Thyrsis", 149. 2.
Prose: *Culture and Anarchy*, 143, 146;
Essays in Criticism, 143, 152; *A French
Eton*, 143; *Friendship's Garland*, 27, 143;
"My Countrymen", 9; *On the Study of
Celtic Literature*, 16; "Preface" to *Poems*
1853, 19; *Popular Education in France*,
153; travels and writings, *281*.
Arnold, Frances (wife of W.D. Arnold),
death of, 39

291

looking, 16; Tennyson and a decline in, 22

West Indies, 40–1; in Brontë's *Jane Eyre*, 179–80; in Eliot's *Daniel Deronda*, 257, 271. See Barbados, Jamaica.

Wills, Alfred, 12; *Wanderings Among the High Alps*, 29

Women's writings and travel, and a marginal sagedom, 14; championing life abroad, 17; Trollope on the woman traveller, 244

Wordsworth, William, and pedestrianism, 12; on mountains in general, 28–9; and Switzerland, 190, 191, 192, 194

Young England, 55, 59–60
Young Ireland, 4–5; Carlyle and, 85, 89
Youghal (Ireland), 90

Zambezi River, the, 41